The Literature of the Law

For my mother

The Literature of the Law

A Thoughtful Entertainment
for Lawyers and Others

Selected and Introduced by
Brian Harris OBE QC

Foreword by
The Right Honourable Sir Edward Eveleigh ERD

Illustrations by
John Walkerdine

BLACKSTONE
PRESS LIMITED

*This book has been printed digitally and produced in a standard specification
in order to ensure its continuing availability*

OXFORD
UNIVERSITY PRESS

Great Clarendon Street, Oxford OX2 6DP

Oxford University Press is a department of the University of Oxford.
It furthers the University $\tilde{\text{o}}$ objective of excellence in research, scholarship,
and education by publishing worldwide in

Oxford New York

Auckland Bangkok Buenos Aires Cape Town Chennai
Dar es Salaam Delhi Hong Kong Istanbul Karachi Kolkata
Kuala Lumpur Madrid Melbourne Mexico City Mumbai Nairobi
S‹ o Paulo Shanghai Taipei Tokyo Toronto

Oxford is a registered trade mark of Oxford University Press
in the UK and in certain other countries

Published in the United States
by Oxford University Press Inc., New York

A Blackstone Press Book

© Brian Harris 1998

© Illustrations, John Walkerdine 1998

The moral rights of the author have been asserted

Database right Oxford University Press (maker)

Reprinted 2003

ISBN 1-85431-733-4

Printed in Great Britain by
Antony Rowe Ltd., Eastbourne

ACKNOWLEDGEMENTS

I am greatly indebted to Andrew Tabachnik, of the English and New York State Bars, and (from a layman's point of view) John Wallace for reading an early version of the text in manuscript and for their many helpful suggestions. They are not to be blamed for any remaining infelicities, legal or otherwise. My thanks are also due to those friends and colleagues who suggested material for inclusion in this book and to Michael Walsh for supplying the photograph from which the drawing at page 140 was made.

I am also grateful to the following for permission to reproduce the material indicated:

Barry Rose Publishers in respect of extracts from *Advocacy for the Advocate* by Eric Crowther OBE and from *Crime Every Day* by Stanley French;
Butterworths in respect of the extract from *Forensic Fables* by 'O' and from the *All England Law Reports* and *Family Law Reports*;
David Higham Associates Ltd in respect of the extract from *The Life of Mr Justice Swift* by E. S. Fay;
Heinemann Educational Publishers (a division of Reed Educational & Professional Publishing Ltd) in respect of the extract from *A Man for All Seasons* by Robert Bolt;
Peters Fraser Dunlop Group Ltd in respect of the extract from *The Life of Sir Edward Marshall Hall KC* by Edward Marjoribanks MP;
The Controller of Her Majesty's Stationery Office in respect of the Crown copyright in the report of the *Inquiry into the Disorders at Red Lion Square*, Cmnd 5919;
The West Group in respect of extracts from the *Supreme Court Reporter* and the *Federal Reporter*.

LAWYERS' LAW

The law the lawyers know about is property and land;
But why the leaves are on the trees,
And why the waves disturb the seas,
Why honey is the food of bees,
Why horses have such tender knees,
Why winters come when rivers freeze,
Why Faith is more than what one sees,
And Hope survives the worst disease,
And Charity is more than these,
They do not understand.

H. D. C. Pepler, *The Devil's Devices.*

FOREWORD

A busy lawyer is usually interested in cases only for the point of law which they have decided or affirmed. He goes straight to the page where the headnote tells him he will find the legal principle upon which the decision is based: he seldom has the time or the inclination to read every word of a judgment in the law reports.

In this book Brian Harris has presented us with some of the gems that the busy lawyer will pass over — passages that are uplifting, angry, wry or simply odd.

A vast amount of material must have been read to select something of interest to the layman and lawyer alike. I myself, over the years, have looked at a number of the cases referred to in this book but I have missed much that Brian Harris has selected.

I have now read most of them for the first time while sitting in the Mediterranean sun. A busman's holiday is not always such a bad thing.

Ted Eveleigh

CONTENTS

Acknowledgements   v

Lawyers' Law   vi

Foreword   vii

Introduction   xi

1. **Though the Heavens Fall**   1
   or Defending the Law
2. **Amid the Clash of Arms**   23
   or The Law in Wartime
3. **Let the Black Go Free**   43
   or The Law and the Downtrodden
4. **The Golden Thread**   75
   or The Law and the Accused
5. **The First Casualty**   115
   or The Law and Human Rights
6. **The Incoming Tide**   141
   or The Law and the Constitution
7. **Life's Dominion**   179
   or The Law of Life and Death
8. **Fearful Saints**   229
   or Reforming the Law
9. **Scandalising the Court**   245
   or The Law of Contempt
10. **Homer Nodding**   259
    or Judicial Infirmities

CONTENTS

11. **With Respect**   271
    or The Art of the Advocate
12. **The High Profession**   297
    or The Life of a Lawyer
13. **The Life of the Law**   315
    or The Law and Justice
14. **When the Wind Blows**   335
    or The Rule of Law

Epilogue: The Spirit Which Is Not Too Sure That It Is Right   339

INTRODUCTION

Litigation is seldom exciting to anyone without a direct interest in it. Even when grappling with the most profound issues lawyers, like philosophers and theologians, manage all too often to strip them of every vestige of human interest. But when a penetrating legal intellect is combined with outstanding felicity of expression the results can be electrifying, even to the non-lawyer. This book attempts to substantiate that claim with examples of the very best in judicial pronouncements over four centuries and two continents.

The problem with any anthology is knowing what order to impose on it. Alphabetical would have been pointless and chronological only slightly less so. While this is not a polemic (far from it) I was pleased to discover that the passages I had chosen fell naturally into a number of themes, some curious, some inspiring, but most of considerable topical interest. Thus, it has been possible to devote one chapter, for example, to such life-and-death decisions as when doctors are justified in discontinuing life-support measures for a brain-dead patient, another to human rights (on the eve of the partial incorporation into our laws of the European Convention), and yet another to the implications of constitutional change (now very much in the air). Law reform, the independence of the judiciary and the protection of minorities form the subjects of other chapters.

Judges are entrusted with great powers. Not only do they determine the law, they also assess unaided the justice of the causes argued before them. This awesome responsibility is discharged — in this country at any rate — by men and women who are not elected but appointed. (Indeed, the very idea of electing a judge — commonplace in America — is regarded here as risible.) Nor are appointments to even the highest courts subject to scrutiny by the legislature after the American manner. While their decisions may be subject to appeal, judges are otherwise answerable to no one. Except in the lowest ranks, a judge cannot for all practical purposes be dismissed from office. Judicial independence is held to justify this unique security of tenure, but it does leave us with an unelected and largely uncontrolled caste deciding some of the most contentious issues in society. What is extraordinary is not that judges are sometimes criticised but that they are generally held in such high esteem.

I hope the reader will share my profound respect for most of the unwitting contributors to this anthology, but it would be wrong to open it in the expectation of discovering only the words of judicial super-heroes. I have not shrunk from including the judgment of a Chief Justice of the United States Supreme Court which, had it not been for the small matter of a civil war, might have held back for a generation the emancipation of the slaves. Or the remarks of a controversial Lord Chief Justice expressing himself all too unwisely on the subject of crime and punishment. Or the tale of the Chief Justice of the Common Pleas who, after bravely defying his Sovereign, felt constrained to abase himself before that individual.

Not all the selections are serious. So, for example, we read of the prisoner who threw a 'brickbat' at the judge and of the awful consequences that befell him, of the bored clerk who attempted to inject laughing gas into the Crown Court and his lucky escape from punishment, and of the punter who sought to recover his winnings on a bet on the outcome of a civil action.

The Atlantic has never been a barrier to the common law. Lord Camden's powerful condemnation of the abuse of police powers still rings in American ears, while English judges owe much to American judgments on such issues as telephone tapping and the right to free speech. What the two countries have in common, of course, is the spirit rather than the detail of the law. That spirit is just as active in the jurisprudence of other nations and it was my own limitations rather than any disregard for Scottish, Irish and Commonwealth sources that constrained the scope of this selection.

Even so, a word of explanation is called for as to why so many extracts from American judgments should appear in a book of this nature. If the quality of the judges in the lower American courts is, by English standards, mixed, that of its higher judiciary is second to none. Furthermore, when it comes to considering the great issues of the day the interpretation of a written constitution affords unique opportunities to deal in broad principle rather than narrow precedent. As Lord Justice Hoffmann remarked, 'to argue from moral rather than purely legal principles is a somewhat unusual enterprise for [an English] judge to undertake' (though this is exactly what he proceeded to do in one of the most impressive judgments in this book — see A case for emotion in chapter 7).

It is interesting to note in how many instances the judgment selected has been that of a minority on the Bench. Consider the words of Lord Atkin angrily rejecting what he regarded as oppressive war-time regulations, the noble opinion of Mr Justice Frankfurter on the practice of American children 'saluting the flag', Lord Denning's bitter assertion that in denying a widow her day in court over a technicality 'we have marred our copybook with blots', and the brilliantly argued speech of Lord Mustill in the 'torture chamber' case. Some of these dissenters have been vindicated by later opinion, some may never be: that is not the point. The extracts have been chosen for their cogency, their courage, or — but usually and — their language.

Style is a very personal matter. Lord Scarman writes with pellucid clarity. No one can dip into an opinion of Felix Frankfurter without instantly recognising the author's fiery intellect (or that English was his second language), and who but Tom Denning could begin a judgment in an action for negligence and nuisance like this:

> In summer time village cricket is the delight of everyone. Nearly every village has its own cricket field where the young men play and the old men watch. In the village of Lintz in County Durham they have their own ground, where they have played these last 70 years. They tend it well. The wicket area is well rolled and mown. The outfield is kept short. It has a good club-house for the players and seats for the onlookers. The village team play there on Saturdays and Sundays. They belong to a league, competing with the neighbouring villages. On other evenings after work they practise while the light lasts. Yet now after these 70 years a judge of the High Court has ordered that they must not play there any more. He has issued an injunction to stop them. He has done it at the instance of a newcomer who is no lover of cricket. This newcomer has built, or has had built for him, a house on the edge of the cricket ground which four years ago was a field where cattle grazed. The animals did not mind the cricket. But now this adjoining field has been turned into a housing estate. The newcomer bought one of the houses on the edge of the cricket ground. No doubt the open space was a selling point. Now he complains that, when a batsman hits a six, the ball has been known to land in his garden or on or near his house. His wife has got so upset about it that they always go out at weekends. They do not go into the garden when cricket is being played. They say that this is intolerable. So they asked the judge to stop the cricket being played. And the judge, much against his will, has felt that he must order the cricket to be stopped with the consequences I suppose that the Lintz Cricket Club will disappear. The cricket ground will be turned to some other use. I expect for more houses or a factory. The young men will turn to other things instead of cricket. The whole village will be much the poorer. And all this because of a newcomer who has just bought a house there next to the cricket ground.[1]

It is easy to guess which way the wind is blowing.

---

[1] *Miller* v *Jackson* [1977] 3 All ER 338, 340.

INTRODUCTION

And the puckish sense of humour of Lord Hailsham shines through in the following beginning of a speech in the House of Lords:[2]

My Lords, on 25th February 1972 Mrs Voss, a Dorset housewife, entered a supermarket belonging to Tesco Stores Ltd and bought a tin of Smedleys' peas. It goes without saying that both Tesco Stores Ltd and Smedleys Ltd are firms of the highest reputation, and no one who has read this case or heard it argued could possibly conceive that what has occurred here reflects in any way on the quality of their products, still less on their commercial reputations.

Unfortunately, and without any fault or negligence on the part of the management of either company, when Mrs Voss got home, she discovered that the tin, in addition to something more than 150 peas, contained a green caterpillar, the larva of one of the species of hawk moth. This innocent insect, thus deprived of its natural destiny, was in fact entirely harmless, since, prior to its entry into the tin. it had been subjected to a cooking process of 20 minutes duration at 250°F, and, had she cared to do so, Mrs Voss could have consumed the caterpillar without injury to herself, and even, perhaps, with benefit. She was not, however, to know this, and with commendable civic zeal, she felt it her duty to report the matter to the local authority, and in consequence, grinding slow, but exceeding small, the machinery of the law was set in inexorable motion.

Thereafter, the caterpillar achieved a sort of posthumous apotheosis. From local authority to the Dorchester magistrates, from the Dorchester magistrates to a Divisional Court, presided over by the Lord Chief Justice of England, from the Lord Chief Justice to the House of Lords, the immolated insect has at length plodded its methodical way to the highest tribunal in the land. It now falls to me to deliver my opinion on its case.

(In the result the conviction of the store was affirmed).

For the curious, the judges most quoted in this book are, in descending order of frequency:

Lord Denning
Lord Scarman
Mr Justice Frankfurter
Mr Justice Learned Hand.

[2] in *Smedleys Ltd* v *Breed* [1974] 2 All ER 21, 24.

There is a famous Thurber cartoon in which two people are gazing into the penguin pen at the zoo and one asks the other, 'Why aren't they all the same height?' The unspoken answer is, of course, that they grow like that. In much the same way the length of the passages in this book varies greatly. In one, the point can be epitomised in a brief extract from the judgment, while the virtues of another may only be obtained by reading it in full. In the case of the lengthier extracts I have occasionally added sub-headings where this seemed a reasonable aid to comprehension.

It would be wearisome for the reader to be burdened with the legal minutiae of even the finest judgments and the extracts are for the most part heavily edited. (Forgive me, judges all!) The source of every passage is given in a footnote, but readers will be relieved to learn that case names have usually, and references always, been deleted from the text without acknowledgement. Where a chunk of prose has been removed this fact is indicated by an ellipsis (...). For the benefit of the non-lawyer I have set out in full the customary abbreviations of judicial status (J, LJ, LCJ, CB and so on). I have, however, retained the archaic spelling and punctuation of the eighteenth-century extracts and, in the American judgments, the spelling of that country.

A word of warning: although I have sometimes added a note explaining how the law has developed since a particular judgment, this is not a work of reference and I have nowhere attempted an exposition of present-day law.

I was tempted to call this 'The Book of Judges', but had second thoughts lest it should attract a purely devotional readership. But there was another reason. Judges do not spring fully armed from the sea: in the Anglo-American tradition they are drawn from the ranks of practising lawyers, nearly always advocates. In many ways it may be said that it is the barrister and the solicitor, more than the judge, who are at the heart of the living law. I have accordingly attempted (in chapter 12) to throw a little light on the lawyer's life and how it has changed over the years. Chapter 11 contains some fine examples of advocacy skills, from the rhetoric of the eighteenth-century impeachment of a Governor-General of India, through the theatricality of one of England's greatest criminal lawyers, to the passion of the twentieth-century 'attorney for the damned'. This is a field which the novelist has found particularly rewarding to till and where examples from life have been hard to find I have had no qualms about resorting to fiction.

To round off the book, I have gathered together some judicial observations on the nature of law and the tricky question of how it relates to justice. If any leitmotif is to be detected it is the continuing strength and adaptability of the common law.

Great claims are made for the law — usually by lawyers. They need to be taken with a pinch of salt. That is why this book begins with a poem pointing out the limits of the law and ends with the words of one of the greatest of American judges who, at a time of great peril to his country and ours, wondered:

> ... whether we do not rest our hopes too much upon constitutions, upon laws and upon courts. These are false hopes; believe me, these are false hopes. Liberty lies in the hearts of men and women. When it dies there, no constitution, no law, no court can save it. No constitution, no law, no court can even do much to help it. While it lies there, it needs no constitution, no law, no court to save it.

As it seems to me, lawyers merely fill the gap in between.

Brian Harris
March, 1998

The Royal Courts of Justice (The Law Courts in the Strand)

1. THOUGH THE HEAVENS FALL

or

Defending the Law

I will not do that which my conscience tells me is
wrong, upon this occasion, to gain the huzzas of
thousands, or the daily praise of all the papers which
come from the press: I will not avoid doing what I think
is right; though it should draw on me the whole artillery
of libels; all that falsehood and malice can invent, or
the credulity of a deluded populace can swallow.

Lord Mansfield in *R* v *John Wilkes* .[3]

A traitorous speech
Objects not worth ambition
Be you never so high
Flying in the face of common sense
The law of humanity
Having willed the end . . .
Inflexible, inexorable and deaf

---

[3] See under *Objects not worth ambition.*

A tribunal which is in thrall to any external influence can never be truly impartial. In recognition of this fact the judges have always asserted fiercely the independence of the courts.

The first passage in this chapter concerns the struggle between Edward Coke, that doughty champion of the common law, and his Sovereign, King James I of England and VI of Scotland (see under A traitorous speech*). Neither man was particularly timid or retiring and it is revealing to see how far Coke was prepared to go and where the limits of his temerity lay.*

*Hardly less fearsome than the sixteenth-century monarch was the eighteenth-century mob. We tend to think of radical disorder as a particularly twentieth-century manifestation, but the England of George III was a hotbed of social and political unrest and a judge who dared to stand up against it could legitimately fear for his life or property, as Lord Mansfield was to discover when trying one of the leading radicals of the day. His judgment in the Wilkes case remains to this day the noblest assertion of judicial independence (*Objects not worth ambition*). Many years later it found an echo in a judgment of Lord Denning when he had occasion to remind one of the principal law officers of the words of a civil war chaplain (*Be you never so high*).*

*In the mid 1990s the expiring Tory administration experienced a series of adverse judicial decisions which caused the more paranoid among them to wonder whether they were being got at by a politicised judiciary. Two of those decisions are represented here. In the first, a scheme for the compensation of victims of crimes of violence was condemned as frustrating the will of Parliament (*Flying in the face of common sense*). In the second, regulations removing financial support from asylum seekers were stigmatised by the court as 'so uncompromisingly draconian in effect that they must indeed be held* ultra vires*' (*The law of humanity*). It is unlikely that these will be the last occasions on which the impartiality of the judiciary will be questioned by an unsuccessful litigant.*

By contrast, the government successfully fought off a legal challenge when a housebound 82-year-old attempted to rely on an Act of Parliament which conferred a seemingly absolute right to *benefits. A majority of the court remedied the defect by reading into the statute a requirement that adequate resources should be available. Lord Lloyd's dissenting speech in the House of Lords courageously put the contrary point of view (* Having willed the end . . .*).*

The last extract concerns the American judge who found himself faced with extraordinary pressures on both sides of the Atlantic to reverse the finding of a jury in a murder case. (Inflexible inexorable and deaf.*) His judgment, of which only a brief extract is printed here, shows how well he acquitted himself.*

A traitorous speech

The law sometimes throws up formidable men with equally formidable frailties. Edward Coke was one such. A brilliant scholar, he became successively Solicitor-General to Elizabeth, then Speaker of the House of Commons and Attorney-General, in which latter capacity he prosecuted Essex and Raleigh with intemperate spleen. His Reports, *though controversial, were immensely influential, as were his* Institutes. *Perhaps his greatest claim to fame, however, lies in his defence of the common law against all-comers, even his king.*

Appointed Chief Justice of the Common Pleas in 1606, Coke provoked King James to anger when he claimed for the courts the right to overturn Acts of Parliament — a claim which, while ineffective here, may have influenced the framers of the American Constitution.

Anthony Mockler has written:[4]

Coke was a cantankerous man. King James could not stand it, nor could his son, King Charles, nor could Coke's great rival Francis Bacon, nor indeed could his wife, Lady Hatton. All through the memoirs, the diaries, the correspondence of the period runs that same note: Coke's cantankerousness. Yet all his enemies, all perhaps except for his wife, seem to have had a certain grudging respect for

---

[4] *Lions Under the Throne* (Frederick Muller Ltd), p. 29.

him: for his immense energy and learning, for his earnestness, for what one commentator has well called his 'grim pedantry'. It was not that he was a particularly great or even just judge, it was not that he could not be cowed, it was not that his personality was appealing. But he stood — and everybody recognised it — in a very special way for the common law of England. 'The monarch is the law, *Rex est lex loquens*, the King is the law speaking,' said Lord Chancellor Ellesmere. In a more profound sense Coke was the common law speaking: crabbed, inaccurate, often unjust, but free from flabbiness, and as embroidered by Coke's tongue, animated by Coke's emotion, passionately stirring.

'No man may be punished for his thoughts,' ruled Coke, 'for it hath been said in the Proverb, thought is free.' 'When an Act of Parliament is against common right and reason,' ruled Coke even more controversially, 'the common law will control it and adjudge such Act to be void.' 'No appeal from the King's Bench,' ruled Coke recklessly, challenging the Lord Chancellor and the Courts of Chancery, 'to any court except the High Court of Parliament.' 'The common law of England,' declared Bacon, 'is an old servant of the crown. The twelve judges of the land may be compared to the twelve lions supporting Solomon's throne.'

Coke was having none of that. 'The King is under God and the law,' he ruled. This was hardly likely to appeal to a King who had declared that: 'The state of monarchy is the supremest thing upon earth. For Kings are not only God's lieutenants upon earth and sit upon God's throne, but even by God himself they are called Gods.' 'The common law,' Coke told James in Star Chamber, 'protecteth the King.' 'A traitorous speech,' cried James, 'the King protecteth the law, and not the law the King! The King maketh judges and bishops. If the judges interpret the law themselves and suffer none else to interpret, they may easily make, of the laws, shipmen's hose.'

Coke wrote afterwards in his *Report*:

Then the King said that he thought the Law was founded upon Reason and that he and others had Reason as well as the Judges. To which it was answered by me, that true it was that God had endowed his Majesty with excellent science and great endowments of Nature. But his Majesty was not learned in the Laws of his Realm of England; and Causes ... are not to be decided by Natural Reason but by the artificial Reason and Judgement of Law which requires long study and experience before that a man can attain to cognizance of it.[5]

---

[5] The report goes on, 'that the law was the golden metwand and measure to try the causes of the subjects; and which protected His Majesty in safety and peace: with which the King was greatly offended, and said, that then he should be under the law, which was treason to affirm, as he said; to which I said, that Bracton saith, *quod Rex non debit sub homine, sed sub Deo et lege*' (For the King is not accountable to men, but to God and the law).

That was Coke's position, that was always Coke's position, and that was the position of the common lawyers, as opposed to Chancery lawyers and the 'civilians': the law of England is fixed, detailed, definite, the product of tradition and precedent, has nothing to do with the concept of an overriding 'Natural Justice' and can only be interpreted by the judges; or, in the ultimate resort, by Parliament acting as a High Court. Kings and commoners alike are subject to it. 'With which', adds the *Report*, 'the King was greatly offended, and said then he should be under the Law, which was treason to affirm (as he said).'

What Coke does not go on to report, but what a letter-writer of the time does, is how their confrontation ended: 'After which his Majesty fell in to the high indignation as the like was never known in him, looking and speaking fiercely with bended fist, offering to strike him, &c. which the Lord Coke perceiving fell flat on all fours, humbly beseeching his Majesty to take compassion on him and to pardon him if he thought zeal had gone beyond his duty and allegiance.'

In 1613 Bacon procured Coke's removal to the Court of King's Bench where it was thought he would be less troublesome. However, he soon came into conflict with the Lord Chancellor, Thomas Egerton, Baron Ellesmere, over the Court of Chancery's claim to be able to reopen a case after judgment had been given at common law. Removed from office, Coke became a Member of Parliament, where his opposition continued unabated despite serving seven months in the Tower of London for treason.

Objects not worth ambition

In eighteenth-century England the pressure sometimes came from the mob.

John Wilkes was a one-off. Extraordinarily ugly, he was nevertheless a notable ladies' man. A journalist who had entered politics, he was the editor of a paper called The North Briton, *the columns of which he filled with vituperation of his opponents. Parliamentary immunity protected him for a while, but he was eventually expelled from the House of Commons and had to face trial for seditious libel. The result of his imprisonment was widespread disorder. The fear of further disorder was advanced before the Court of King's Bench under its Chief Justice, William Murray, Lord Mansfield, as an argument for clemency. This is how Mansfield famously dealt with that argument.*[6]

The constitution does not allow reasons of State to influence our judgments: God forbid it should! We must not regard political consequences; how formidable soever they might be: if rebellion was the certain consequence, we are bound to say *'fiat justitia, ruat caelum'*.[7] The constitution trusts the King with reasons of State and policy: he may stop prosecutions; he may pardon offences; it is his, to judge whether the law or the criminal should yield. We have no election. None of us encouraged or approved the commission of either of the crimes of which the defendant is convicted: none of us had any hand in his being prosecuted. As to myself, I took no part, (in another place) in the addresses for that prosecution. We did not advise or assist the defendant to fly from justice: it was his own act; and he must take the consequences. None of us have been consulted or had any thing to do with the present prosecution. It is not in our power to stop it: it was not in our power bring it on. We cannot pardon. We are to say, what we take the law to be: if we do not speak our real opinions, we prevaricate with God and our own consciences.

I pass over many anonymous letters I have received. Those in print are public: and some of them have been brought judicially before the court. Whoever the writers are, they take the wrong way. I will do my duty, unawed. What am I to fear? That *mendax infamia* from the press, which daily coins false facts and false motives? The lies of calumny carry no terror to me. I trust, that my temper of mind, and the colour and conduct of my life, have given me a suit of armour against these arrows. If, during this King's reign, I have ever supported his government and assisted his measures; I have done it without any other reward, than the consciousness of doing what I thought right. If I have ever opposed, I have done it upon the points themselves; without mixing in party or faction, and without my collateral views. I honour the King; and respect the people: but, many things acquired by the favour of either, are, in my account, objects not worth ambition. I wish popularity: but, it is that popularity which follows; not that which is run after. It is that popularity which, sooner or later, never fails to do justice to the pursuit of noble ends, by noble means. I will not do that which my conscience tells me is wrong, upon this occasion, to gain the huzzas of thousands, or the daily praise of all the papers which come

---

[6] *R* v *Wilkes* (1770) 4 Burr 2527, 2563.
[7] Let justice be done though the heavens fall.

from the press: I will not avoid doing what I think is right; though it should draw on me the whole artillery of libels; all that falsehood and malice can invent, or the credulity of a deluded populace can swallow. I can say, with a great magistrate, upon an occasion and under circumstances not unlike, *Ego hoc animo semper fui, ut invidiam virtute partam, gloriam, non invidiam, putarem.*[8]

The threats go further than abuse: personal violence is denounced. I do not believe it: it is not the genius of the worst men of this country, in the worst of times. But I have set my mind at rest. The last end that can happen to any man, never comes too soon, if he falls in support of the law and liberty of his country: (for liberty is synonymous to law and government). Such a shock, too, might be productive of public good: it might awake the better part of the kingdom out of that lethargy which seems to have benumbed them; and bring the mad part back to their senses, as men intoxicated are sometimes stunned into sobriety.

Once for all, let it be understood, 'that no endeavours of this kind will influence any man who at present sits here'. If they had any effect, it would be contrary to their intent: leaning against their impression, might give a bias the other way. But I hope, and I know, that I have fortitude enough to resist even that weakness. No libels, no threats, nothing that has happened, nothing that can happen, will weigh a feather against allowing the defendant, upon this and every other question, not only the whole advantage he is intitled to from substantial law and justice; but every benefit from the most critical nicety of form, which any other defendant could claim under the like objection.

Lord Mansfield paid high for his principles. In 1780 his library was burned by the mob during the Gordon riots, occasioning a memorable poem by William Cowper.

Wilkes was condemned to 22 months in prison and a fine of £1,000. In accordance with the best English tradition he subsequently became Lord Mayor of London.

Be you never so high

Two hundred years later the Court of Appeal were called upon to review the discretion of the Attorney-General, the principal legal adviser to the Crown.

---

[8] I was always minded to regard unpopularity born of virtue not as a sign of envy but of glory.

As a protest against apartheid the Union of Post Office Workers had decided to call upon its members to impose a boycott on all postal communications between Britain and South Africa. Hearing of this, Mr Gouriet, the secretary of a body called the National Association for Freedom, sought an injunction against the union on the ground that the boycott would interfere with postal communications and would constitute criminal offences. For this purpose he needed the Attorney-General's consent to act as plaintiff in what is called a relator action. The Attorney-General refused his consent, but Gouriet nevertheless went ahead and issued a writ claiming an injunction. It was refused and Gouriet appealed to the Court of Appeal.

The Court of Appeal held that it had jurisdiction to grant an interim injunction, even in the absence of the Attorney-General's consent. In the course of his judgment the Master of the Rolls, Lord Denning, observed:[9]

Take warning from history. Not from a previous Attorney-General; but from a King himself. James II claimed that, by virtue of his prerogative, he could suspend or dispense with the execution of all penal laws in matters ecclesiastical. He had reasons which, to him at least, were most compelling. He desired religious toleration and civic equality. But the people of England would have none of this prerogative. The jury showed this at the trial of the Seven Bishops. And at the very first opportunity Parliament enacted the Bill of Rights of 1689. It declared:

> *... that the pretended power of suspending of laws or the execution of laws by regall authority without consent of Parlyament is illegal [and] that the pretended power of dispensing with laws or the execution of laws by regall authoritie as it hath been assumed and exercised of late is illegall.*

Mercifully our constitution has, I believe, provided a remedy.... If the Attorney-General refuses to give his consent to the enforcement of the criminal law, then any citizen in the land can come to the courts and ask that the law be enforced. This is an essential safeguard; for were it not so, the Attorney-General

---

[9] *Gouriet* v *Union of Postal Workers* [1977] 1 All ER 696, 717.

could, by his veto, saying 'I do not consent', make the criminal law of no effect. Confronted with a powerful subject whom he feared to offend, he could refuse his consent time and time again. Then that subject could disregard the law with impunity. It would indeed be above the law. This cannot be permitted. To every subject in this land, no matter how powerful, I would use Thomas Fuller's[10] words over 300 years ago: 'Be you never so high, the law is above you'.

Unfortunately for Mr Gouriet, the House of Lords is above even the Court of Appeal, whose decision it reversed later in the same year. That reversal did not in any way detract from the dictum quoted above, merely its application in this case.

Flying in the face of common sense

Throughout the 1990s act after act of the Conservative administration was struck down in the course of judicial review. In the case which follows, the House of Lords took the view that it had to protect the will of Parliament from misuse by the executive.

The Home Secretary had decided as a cost-cutting measure to replace a relatively generous scheme for the compensation of victims of crime by another that was more favourable to the Exchequer. The Fire Brigades Union, as a body representing persons likely to need to call on this service, challenged that decision. Relief was refused at first instance but granted by the Court of Appeal. The Home Secretary then appealed unsuccessfully to the House of Lords, where Lord Browne-Wilkinson began his speech as follows:[11]

Until 1964 victims who suffered personal injuries as a result of crimes of violence had no right to compensation out of public funds. On 24 June 1964 a scheme compensating such victims was announced in both Houses of Parliament. In its original form the scheme came into force on 1 August 1964.

---

[10] Fuller was a chaplain in the King's army during the Civil War and the author of *Worthies of England*.

[11] *R v Secretary of State for the Home Department, ex parte Fire Brigades Union* [1995] 2 All ER 244, 248.

It was non-statutory and was introduced under the prerogative powers, compensation being paid out of moneys voted by Parliament. The scheme (the old scheme) was modified on a number of occasions, most recently in February 1990 and January 1992. . . .

In December 1993 a White Paper was published [*which*] gave details of a proposed tariff scheme under which awards would be based upon a tariff according to the injuries received without any separate or additional payments being made for loss of earnings or other past or future expenses. The White Paper drew attention to the rise in the number of awards and cost of the old scheme and concluded that the new scheme would be more readily understood and enable claimants to receive their compensation more quickly and in a more straightforward manner. It also pointed out that the cost of administration should come down and that claimants should receive a better service.

The White Paper stated:

The present scheme is non-statutory and payments are made on an ex gratia basis. Provision was made in the Criminal Justice Act 1988 for the scheme to be placed on a statutory footing. However, at the request of the [Criminal Injuries Compensation] Board the relevant provisions were not brought into force, because this would have disrupted their efforts to deal with the heavy workload. With the impending demise of the current scheme the provisions in the 1988 Act will not now be implemented. They will accordingly be repealed when a suitable legislative opportunity occurs.

It is common ground that in some cases, particularly in relation to very serious injuries involving prolonged loss of earnings, the amount payable to the victim under the tariff scheme will be substantially less than the amount he would have received under the old scheme or the statutory scheme. . . .

It does not follow that, because the Secretary of State is not under any duty to bring the section into effect, he has an absolute and unfettered discretion whether or not to do so. So to hold would lead to the conclusion that both Houses of Parliament had passed the Bill through all its stages and the Act received the royal assent merely to confer an enabling power on the executive to decide at will whether or not to make the Parliamentary provisions a part of the law. Such a conclusion, drawn from a section to which the sidenote is 'Commencement', is not only constitutionally dangerous but flies in the face of common sense. . . .

The tariff scheme, if validly introduced under the royal prerogative, is both inconsistent with the statutory scheme contained in the 1988 Act and intended to be permanent. In practice, the tariff scheme renders it now either impossible or at least more expensive to reintroduce the old scheme or the statutory enactment of it contained in the 1988 Act. The tariff scheme involves the winding up of the old Criminal Injuries Compensation Board together with its team of those skilled in assessing compensation on the common law basis and the creation of a new body, the Criminal Injuries Compensation Authority, set up to assess compensation on the tariff basis at figures which, in some cases, will be very substantially less than under the old scheme. All this at a time when Parliament has expressed its will that there should be a scheme based on the tortious measure of damages, such will being expressed in a statute which Parliament has neither repealed nor (for reasons which have not been disclosed) been invited to repeal.

My Lords, it would be most surprising if, at the present day, prerogative powers could be validly exercised by the executive so as to frustrate the will of Parliament expressed in a statute and, to an extent, to pre-empt the decision of Parliament whether or not to continue with the statutory scheme even though the old scheme has been abandoned. It is not for the executive, as the Lord Advocate accepted, to state as it did in the White Paper that the provisions in the 1988 Act 'will accordingly be repealed when a suitable legislative opportunity occurs'. It is for Parliament, not the executive, to repeal legislation. The constitutional history of this country is the history of the prerogative powers of the Crown being made subject to the overriding powers of the democratically elected legislature as the sovereign body. The prerogative powers of the Crown remain in existence to the extent that Parliament has not expressly or by implication extinguished them. But ... if Parliament has conferred on the executive statutory powers to do a particular act, that act can only thereafter be done under the statutory powers so conferred: any pre-existing prerogative power to do the same act is *pro tanto* excluded.

The Home Secretary's appeal was dismissed.

The law of humanity

Little over a year later the courts were called upon to examine the exercise by the Home Secretary of powers concerning the financial support of persons claiming asylum in this country.

A Divisional Court of the Queen's Bench dismissed a claim for judicial review of Ministerial regulations, only for the claim to be

upheld, albeit by a majority, in the Court of Appeal. The following
extracts are from the judgment of Lord Justice Simon Brown.[12]

In recent years the number of persons seeking asylum in the United Kingdom has risen significantly, both in absolute terms and in relation to the rest of Western Europe. Of those applying, only some 25% are ultimately found to be genuine refugees: 4 to 5% as strictly defined by the Convention Relating to the Status of Refugees; some 20% being granted exceptional leave to remain as, for example, fugitives from civil war or torture for a non-1951 convention reason, the borderline between the two categories being often a very fine one. The 75% whose claims fail are regarded as economic migrants. With the numbers now applying, the time taken to resolve their claims is inevitably too long and the cost of all this to the taxpayer is enormous.

To speed up the process of decision-making and to reduce the expenditure on benefits, the respondent Secretary of State for Social Security made [*regulations*] which came into force on 5 February 1996. What in essence the 1996 regulations do is to remove all entitlement to income-related benefit from two particular categories of asylum seeker — those who submit their claims for asylum otherwise than immediately upon arrival in the United Kingdom (subject to a limited exception where the Home Secretary makes what is called an 'upheaval declaration'), and those whose claims have been rejected by the Home Secretary but who then appeal to the independent appellate authorities. The Secretary of State's intention is to discourage economic migrants from making and pursuing asylum claims. This, in turn, will speed up the system to the advantage of genuine refugees. All this is expected to save the taxpayer some £200 million p.a.

No one could dispute the desirability of these aims. There is, however, a problem. A significant number of genuine asylum seekers now find themselves faced with a bleak choice: whether to remain here destitute and homeless until their claims are finally determined, or whether instead to abandon their claims and return to face the very persecution they have fled.

The appellants' case, in essence, is that the 1996 regulations are in the result *ultra vires*. The enabling power, widely drawn though it is, cannot, they submit, have been intended to permit this degree of interference with statutory rights under the Asylum and Immigration Appeals Act 1993 and/or with fundamental human rights. . . .

---

[12] *R* v *Secretary of State for Social Security, ex parte Joint Council for the Welfare of Immigrants* [1996] 4 All ER 385, 392.

Prior to the coming into force of the 1996 regulations now impugned, all asylum seekers were entitled to urgent cases payments amounting to 90% of normal income support benefit and, in addition, to housing benefit and the other benefits 'passported' through income support. When homeless, they were in the same position ... as other homeless people, save only that they had to be content with 'any accommodation, however temporary', and 'any need they established was to be regarded as temporary only'.

After reviewing the 1996 Regulations Simon Brown went on:

It follows that from 5 February 1996 two main categories of asylum seeker are wholly excluded from benefit: (1) in-country (as opposed to on-arrival) claimants; and (2) all claimants pending appeal from an adverse determination of the Home Secretary. These I shall call 'the deprived asylum seekers'.

In the event of homelessness, the deprived asylum seekers are peculiarly disadvantaged. Not, of course, if they have a priority need for accommodation (as do roughly a third who have dependent children): then the housing authority is obliged to house them, even though they can pay no housing benefit.... But local authorities have refused to accept that asylum seekers deprived of all benefits have a priority need on the grounds of being 'vulnerable' for 'other special reason' within the meaning of section 59(1)(c) of the 1985 Act — this being a separate issue raised before us on an immediately following appeal.

If the local authorities are correct in that view, it follows that those of the deprived asylum seekers not otherwise in priority need face the following situation.

(1)   They have no access whatever either to funds or to benefits in kind.

(2)   They have no accommodation and, being ineligible for housing benefit, no prospect of securing any.

(3)   By the express terms of their leave to stay, they are invariably forbidden from seeking employment for six months and, even assuming that thereafter they apply for and obtain permission to work, their prospects of obtaining it are likely to be poor, particularly if they speak no English.

(4)   They are likely to be without family, friends or contacts and thus in a position of peculiar isolation with no network of community support.

(5)   Their claims take on average some 18 months to determine, on occasions as long as four years. An individual has no control over this and no

means of hastening a final decision. If eventually the claim succeeds there is no provision for back payment.

(6) Quite apart from the need to keep body and soul together pending the final determination of a claim, expense is likely to be incurred in pursuing it. Applicants must attend for interviews with the Home Office and with any advisers they may have. They must have an address where they can be contacted with notices of appointments or decisions. To miss an appointment or the time for appeal is to forgo their claim.

Others, it is true, face the same total loss of benefits under the various regulations: prisoners, those in holy orders and virtually all other immigrants. But prisoners and the clergy each have their own obvious support systems, respectively the State and their religious communities. And non-asylum-seeking immigrants have, since 1980, invariably been admitted subject to the condition of 'no recourse to public funds' and, more importantly, unlike asylum seekers, can in any event return to their country of origin. Truly, deprived asylum seekers are in a unique position and one which threatens total destitution. No doubt, as Mr Richards submits, voluntary organisations do what they can to help. The need, however, far exceeds their capacity. As Mr Blake puts it, charity cannot bridge the gap between the 1996 regulations and the 1993 Act....

Specific statutory rights are not to be cut down by subordinate legislation passed under the *vires* of a different Act. So much is clear....

I do not pretend to have found this by any means an easy case. Powerful arguments are advanced on both sides.... I, for my part, have no difficulty in accepting the Secretary of State's right to discourage economic migrants by restricting their benefits. That of itself indicates that the 1996 regulations are not invalid merely because of their 'chilling effect' ... upon the exercise of the deprived asylum seekers' rights under the 1993 Act.

It is, moreover, as I recognise, one thing ... to condemn direct interference with the unquestioned basic rights there identified; another to assert that the Secretary of State, here, is bound to maintain some benefits provision to asylum seekers so as to ensure that those with genuine claims will not be driven by penury to forfeit them, whether by leaving the country before their determination or through an inability to prosecute them effectively....

I have ... concluded that it is a step the court should take. Parliamentary sovereignty is not here in question: the 1996 regulations are subordinate legislation only ... Parliament, for its part, has clearly demonstrated a full commitment to the United Kingdom's 1951 convention obligations. When the regulation-making power was first conferred, there was no question of asylum seekers being deprived of all benefit and thereby rendered unable to pursue their claims. Although I reject the argument that the legislative history of this power (including, in particular, an indication to Parliament in 1986 that the government was then intending to exercise it in continuing support of asylum seekers) itself serves to limit its present scope, the fact that asylum seekers have hitherto enjoyed benefit payments appears to me not entirely irrelevant. After all, the 1993 Act confers on asylum seekers fuller rights than they had ever previously enjoyed, the right of appeal in particular. And yet these regulations for some genuine asylum seekers at least, must now be regarded as rendering these rights nugatory. Either that, or the 1996 regulations necessarily contemplate for some a life so destitute that, to my mind, no civilised nation can tolerate it. So basic are the human rights here at issue, that it cannot be necessary to resort to the Convention for the Protection of Human Rights and Fundamental Freedoms, to take note of their violation.

Nearly 200 years ago Chief Justice Lord Ellenborough said:

As to there being no obligation for maintaining poor foreigners before the statutes ascertaining the different methods of acquiring settlements, the law of humanity, which is anterior to all positive laws, obliges us to afford them relief, to save them from starving.

True, no obligation arises under article 24 of the 1951 convention until asylum seekers are recognised as refugees. But that is not to say that up to that point their fundamental needs can properly be ignored. I do not accept they can. Rather, I would hold it unlawful to alter the benefits regime so drastically as must inevitably not merely prejudice, but on occasion defeat, the statutory right of asylum seekers to claim refugee status.

If and when that status is recognised, refugees become entitled under article 24 to benefit rights equivalent to nationals. Not for one moment would I suggest that prior to that time their rights are remotely the same; only that some basic provision should be made, sufficient for genuine claimants to survive and pursue their claims.

It is not for this court to indicate how best to achieve this consistently with the Secretary of State's legitimate aim of deterring unmeritorious claims. I content myself merely with noting that many European countries, so we are told, provide benefits in kind by way of refugee hostels and meal vouchers; that urgent needs payments could be made at a significantly lower rate than the 90% rate hitherto paid; and that certain categories of claim (perhaps, as suggested, in-country claims brought more than four or six weeks post-arrival) could be processed under the 'without foundation procedure'. All that will doubtless be for consideration. For the purposes of this appeal, however, it suffices to say that I, for my part, regard the 1996 regulations now in force as so uncompromisingly draconian in effect that they must indeed be held *ultra vires*.

I would found my decision not on the narrow ground of constructive *refoulement* envisaged by the UNHCR and rejected by the Divisional Court, but rather on the wider ground that rights necessarily implicit in the 1993 Act are now inevitably being overborne. Parliament cannot have intended a significant number of genuine asylum seekers to be impaled on the horns of so intolerable a dilemma: the need either to abandon their claims to refugee status or alternatively to maintain them as best they can but in a state of utter destitution. Primary legislation alone could in my judgment achieve that sorry state of affairs.

Having willed the end . . .

Social legislation is sometimes framed in terms of a seemingly absolute duty, whereas the resources of the authorities who have to implement it are finite. This was the nub of the matter in a case which came before the House of Lords in 1997.

Michael Barry was coming up for his 82nd birthday. In the summer of 1992 he spent a short spell in hospital suffering from dizzy spells and nausea as a result of a slight stroke. He had also had several heart attacks, and could not see well. After discharge from hospital, he returned home, where he lived alone. He got around by using a Zimmer frame, having fractured his hip several years before. He had no contact with any of his family, but two friends called from time to time to do things for him. The Social Services Department assessed his needs as follows: 'Home care to call twice a week for shopping, pension, laundry cleaning. Meals-on-wheels four days a week.'

The council arranged to provide these services. In 1994 Mr Barry received a letter from the council regretting that they would no longer be able to provide him with his full needs as assessed. Cleaning and laundry services would therefore be withdrawn. The reason given was that the money allocated to the council by central government had been reduced and there was 'nowhere near enough to meet demand'.

Mr Barry commenced proceedings for judicial review. His case was that his needs were the same as they always had been. Parliament had imposed a duty on the council to do what was necessary to meet those needs, and it was no answer that they were short of money. The council's case was that in assessing Mr Barry's needs they were entitled to have regard to their overall financial resources.

By a majority the House held that needs cannot sensibly be assessed under the Act without regard to the cost of providing them. Lord Lloyd of Berwick dissented from that view with the support of Lord Steyn. In the course of his speech he said.[13]

[*The Chronically Sick and Disabled Persons Act 1970*] contemplates three separate stages. The council must first assess the individual needs of each person to whom [*the National Assistance Act 1948*] applies. Having identified those needs, the council must then decide whether it is necessary to make arrangements to meet those needs. There might be any number of reasons why, in the circumstances of a particular case, it might not be necessary for the local authority to make arrangements, for example, if the person's needs were being adequately met by a friend or relation. Or he might be wealthy enough to meet his needs out of his own pocket. But if there is no other way of meeting the individual's needs, as assessed, and the council is therefore satisfied that it is necessary for them to make arrangements to meet those needs, then the council is under a duty to make those arrangements. It is essential to a proper understanding of the Act of 1970 to keep the three stages separate. Confusion arises if the stages are telescoped....

It is not surprising, therefore, that the starting point of the whole exercise is the assessment of individual needs. The assessment is, to adopt the departmental jargon, 'needs-led'. The word 'need' like most English words has different shades of meaning. You can say to an overworked QC at the end of a busy term 'You look as though you need a holiday'. The word 'need' in section 2 is not used in that sense; which is not to say that there may not be disabled people living in very restricted circumstances who may not need a holiday in the sense which Parliament intended. To need is not the same as to want. 'Need' is the lack of what is essential for the ordinary business of living.

---

[13] *R v Gloucestershire County Council, ex parte Barry* [1997] 2 All ER 1, 5.

Who then is to decide what it is that the disabled person needs, and by what yardstick does he make his decision? I do not find the answer difficult. In the simplest case it is the individual social worker who decides. In more complicated cases there may have to be what is called a comprehensive assessment. But in every case, simple or complex, the need of the individual will be assessed against the standards of civilised society as we know them in the United Kingdom, or, in the more homely phraseology of the law, by the standards of the man on the Clapham omnibus. Those standards may vary over time. What was acceptable in Victorian England might not be acceptable today. Expectations have risen. But this does not pose any difficulty. The assessment of the needs of the disabled individual against contemporary standards is left to the professional judgment of the social worker concerned, just as the need for a bypass operation is left to the professional judgment of the heart specialist.

Who then decides what are the contemporary standards against which the social worker assesses the individual's needs? Again the answer seems straightforward. The standard is that set by the social services committee of the local authority in question. No doubt this was one of the reasons why social services committees were set up in the first place, so as to represent the views of ordinary members of the public. Standards may vary from one local authority to another. But since the United Kingdom is relatively homogeneous, the standards may be expected to approximate to each other over time.

It is said that the standards of civilised society as interpreted by the social services committee of a particular local authority is too imprecise a concept to be of any practical value. I do not agree. But even if it were so, I do not see how it becomes less imprecise by bringing into consideration the availability of resources. Resources can, of course, operate to impose a cash limit on what is provided. But how can resources help to measure the need? This, as it seems to me, is the fallacy which lies at the heart of the council's argument.

The point can be illustrated by a simple example. Suppose there are two people with identical disabilities, living in identical circumstances, but in different parts of the country. Local authority A provides for his needs by arranging for meals on wheels four days a week. Local authority B might also be expected to provide meals on wheels four days a week or its equivalent. It cannot, however, have been Parliament's intention that local authority B should be able to say 'because we do not have enough resources, we are going to reduce your needs'. His needs remain exactly the same. They cannot be affected by the local authority's inability to meet those needs. Every child needs a new pair of shoes from time to time. The need is not the less because his parents cannot afford them.

There was much discussion in the course of the hearing of the appeal about 'eligibility criteria'. This is the departmental way of describing the standard against which an individual's needs are judged. Local authorities are encouraged to publish their own eligibility criteria. The council has not fallen behind in this respect. There are elaborate tables included among our papers in which different degrees of disability are set against varying degrees of isolation from the community and other relevant factors. There are recommendations about the level of services which are appropriate for different combinations of disability and individual circumstances. Thus for a given degree of disability and a given degree of isolation (to take two of the relevant factors) the recommended home care might be for meals on wheels three times a week (or equivalent), cleaning twice a week and laundry once a fortnight. What is interesting about all this for present purposes is that nowhere in the tables is there any reference to resources. Nor is there any reason why there should be. The eligibility criteria can work perfectly well without taking resources into account. With respect to those who take a different view, I can see no necessity on grounds of logic, and no advantage on grounds of practical convenience, in bringing resources into account as a relevant factor when assessing needs.

Is it then open to a local authority to raise the threshold artificially if it does not have sufficient resources to meet the previously assessed need? This is just what Parliament did not intend when enacting the Chronically Sick and Disabled Persons Act of 1970. If a local authority could arbitrarily reduce the assessed need by raising the eligibility criteria, the duty imposed by Parliament would, in Mr Gordon's graphic phrase, be collapsed into a power. The language of section 2 admits of no halfway house.

In the course of the argument it was suggested that 'needs' in section 2 might mean 'reasonable needs'. I have no difficulty in reading 'needs' as meaning reasonable needs, in the sense that the social worker, in the exercise of his or her judgment, must act reasonably. In any event, if the needs are not reasonable it would not be necessary to make arrangements to meet the needs under the second of the three stages of the exercise. What I cannot accept is that the reasonable needs of the individual require consideration of the local authority's ability to meet those needs. . . .

Simply looking at the language of the Act of 1970, against the background of the Act of 1948, it is clear enough that Parliament did not intend that provision for the needs of the disabled should depend on the availability of resources. The intention was to treat disability as a special case. That is why the Act of 1970 has always been regarded as such an important landmark in the care of the disabled. . . .

By your lordships' decision today the council has escaped from the impossible position in which they, and other local authorities have been placed.

Nevertheless, I cannot help wondering whether they will not be regretting today's decision as much as Mr Barry. The solution lies with the government. The passing of the Chronically Sick and Disabled Persons Act 1970 was a noble aspiration. Having willed the end, Parliament must be asked to provide the means.

Inflexible, inexorable and deaf

Today the pressure is likely to come from the media.

Louise Woodward, an eighteen-year-old English au pair living with an American couple in Boston, had been charged with murder in the second degree following the death of their eight-month-old son, who had been left in her care. Under Massachusetts law Louise was entitled to reject one of the charges against her. No doubt acting upon legal advice she chose to present the jury with a choice of a conviction for second degree murder or complete acquittal — a choice apparently known in American legal circles as 'noose or loose'. The jury chose the former and Louise accordingly received the mandatory sentence of life imprisonment with no possibility of parole for 15 years.

This decision provoked uproar both New and old England. Supporters of Louise, attracted by the televised coverage of the trial and encouraged by the tabloid press, demanded that the judge exercise a rarely used power to overturn the jury's verdict, while a slightly less vocal group opposed any such course: whatever the judge did would be wrong.

Judge Hiller B. Zobel, an Associate Justice of the Massachusetts Superior Court, began his judgment as follows:

The law, John Adams told a Massachusetts jury while defending British citizens on trial for murder, is inflexible and deaf: inexorable to the cries of the defendant; 'deaf as an adder to the clamours of the populace'. His words ring true, 227 years later.

Elected officials may consider popular urging and sway to public opinion polls. Judges must follow their oaths and do their duty, heedless of editorials, letters, telegrams, picketers, threats, petitions, panellists and talk shows. In this country, we do not administer justice by plebiscite.

A judge, in short, is a public servant who must follow his conscience, whether or not he counters the manifest wishes of those he serves; whether or not his decision seems a surrender to the prevalent demands.

In a meticulously argued judgment the judge varied the jury's verdict to one of manslaughter and imposed a sentence which allowed the immediate release of Louise — a decision which seemed to at least one observer to be both wise and merciful. While this book was going to press, however, both sides had announced their intentions of appealing against verdict and sentence.

The City Arms

2. AMID THE CLASH OF ARMS

or

The Law in Wartime

In this country, amid the clash of arms, the laws are not silent.
They may be changed, but they speak the same language in war
as in peace.... In this case I have listened to arguments which
might have been addressed acceptably to the Court of King's
Bench in the time of Charles I.

Lord Atkin in *Liversidge* v *Anderson*.[14]

The defence of the realm
The laws are not silent
The keys of persuasion
All life is an experiment
In the name of security
Man being what he is

---

[14] See under *The laws are not silent*.

One test of a nation dedicated to the rule of law is the extent to which it is prepared to protect its liberties in times of war.

The exigencies of war require exceptional measures for the public safety. In Britain during two world wars these were provided by the Defence of the Realm Regulations.[15] *They did not go unchallenged. In the first passage in this chapter (See under The defence of the realm) Mr Justice Darling held that the elemental rights of the subjects of the British Crown could not easily be taken from them when the emergency had passed. And at the height of the Second World War Lord Atkin castigated the administration in deathless prose for its attitude towards the detention of persons suspected of hostile intentions (*The laws are not silent*). This plain speaking was not universally welcomed.*

Similar opprobrium attached to the distinguished Judge of the New York District Court when during the Great War he refused to convict the publishers of a magazine accused of infringing the Federal Espionage Act. He claimed that:

to assimilate agitation, legitimate as such, with direct incitement to violent resistance, is to disregard the tolerance of all methods of political agitation which in normal times is a safeguard of free government. *(The keys of persuasion)*

Quite as damning was the observation of one of the greatest of American Supreme Court Justices that:

In this case sentences of 20 years' imprisonment have been imposed for the publishing of two leaflets that I believe the defendants had as much right to publish as the government has to publish the Constitution of the United States now vainly invoked by them. *(All life is an experiment)*

State security is often advanced — sometimes justifiably — as the excuse for acts that would otherwise be repressive, but, as Mr

---

[15] Presumably similar regulations are mouldering in draft somewhere in Whitehall against the possibility of a future conflict.

Justice Jackson said in a spirited minority opinion concerning the refusal of admission to America of a US war bride, 'Security is like liberty in that many are the crimes committed in its name' *(In the name of security).*

Another great Supreme Court Justice, condemning his government for lack of due process in drawing up lists of 'disloyal' employees, reminded us that:

No better instrument has been devised for arriving at truth than to give a person in jeopardy of serious loss notice of the case against him and opportunity to meet it. Nor has a better way been found for generating the feeling, so important to a popular government, that justice has been done. *(Man being what he is)*

The defence of the realm

During the Great War of 1914–18 the ordinary laws of England were modified by what were known as the Defence of the Realm Regulations. One of these required that the consent of the Minister of Munitions be obtained before legal proceedings could be taken for the recovery of possession of a dwelling in which a munition worker was living. The reason for the rule in wartime was obvious, but what should be the position when war gives way to peace?

After the conclusion of hostilities recovery proceedings against a munition worker were successfully brought before magistrates without the Minister's consent. The worker challenged this by what is known as a case stated to the High Court.

In the course of his judgment[16] *Mr Justice Darling said:*

Counsel for the appellant has contended that this regulation violates Magna Carta, where the King declares: 'To no one will we sell, to none will we deny,

---

[16] *Chester v Bateson* [1920] 1 KB 829, 832.

to none will we delay, right or justice'. I could not hold the regulation to be bad on that ground were there sufficient authority given by a statute of the realm to those by whom the regulation was made. Magna Carta has not remained untouched; and, like every other law of England, it is not condemned to that immunity from development or improvement which was attributed to the laws of the Medes and Persians. I found my judgment rather on the passage where Lord Finlay says that Parliament may entrust great powers to His Majesty in Council, feeling certain that such powers will be reasonably exercised and further on these words of Lord Atkinson in the same case:

> It by no means follows, however, that if on the face of a regulation it enjoined or required something to be done which could not in any reasonable way aid in securing the public safety and the defence of the realm it would not be *ultra vires* and void. It is not necessary to decide this precise point on the present occasion, but I desire to hold myself free to deal with it when it arises.

Here, I think it does at last arise; and I ask myself whether it is a necessary, or even reasonable, way to aid in securing the public safety and the defence of the realm to give power to a minister to forbid any person to institute any proceedings to recover possession of a house so long as a war-worker is living in it.

The main question to be decided is whether the occupant is a workman so employed; and the regulation might have been so framed as to make this a good answer to the application for possession, still leaving that question to be decided by a court of law. But the regulation, as framed, forbids the owner of the property access to all legal tribunals in regard to this matter. This might, of course, legally be done by Act of Parliament; but I think this extreme disability can be inflicted only by direct enactment of the legislature itself, and that so grave an invasion of the rights of all subjects was not intended by the legislature to be accomplished by a departmental order, such as this one of the Minister of Munitions.

There are some instances in which Parliament has deliberately deprived certain persons of the ordinary right of citizens to resort to the King's courts for the righting of alleged wrongs. The most notorious of these is the Vexatious Actions Act 1896 which provides:

> It shall be lawful for the Attorney-General to apply to the High Court for an Order under this Act, and if he satisfies the High Court that any person has habitually and persistently instituted vexatious legal proceedings without any reasonable ground for instituting such proceedings, whether in the High Court or in any inferior court, and whether against the same person or against

different persons, the court may, after hearing such persons or giving him an opportunity of being heard, after assigning counsel in case such person is unable on account of poverty to retain counsel, order that no legal proceedings shall be instituted by that person in the High Court or any other court, unless he obtains the leave of the High Court or some judge thereof, and satisfies the court or judge that such legal proceeding is not an abuse of the process of the court, and that there is prima face ground for such proceeding. A copy of such order shall be published in the *London Gazette*.

Let it be observed how carefully, even when so high an official as the King's Attorney-General intervenes, resort to the courts of justice is preserved, and contrast this with the power of veto uncontrolled which is claimed for the Minister of Munitions.

This exceptional statute has been already enforced, as may be seen by reference to *Re Boaler*. In giving judgment in that case Lord Justice Scrutton uses these words:

One of the valuable rights of every subject of the King is to appeal to the King in his courts if he alleges that a civil wrong has been done to him, or if he alleges that a wrong punishable criminally has been done to him, or has been committed by another subject of the King. This right is sometimes abused and it is, of course, quite competent to Parliament to deprive any subject of the King of it either absolutely or in part. But the language of any such statute should be jealously watched by the courts, and should not be extended beyond its least onerous meaning unless clear words are used to justify such extension.

Darling continued:

It is to be observed that this regulation not only deprives the subject of his ordinary right to seek justice in the courts of law, but provides that merely to resort there without the permission of the Minister of Munitions first had and obtained shall of itself be a summary offence, and so render the seeker after justice liable to imprisonment and fine. I allow that in stress of war we may rightly be obliged, as we should be ready, to forgo much of our liberty, but I hold that this elemental right of the subjects of the British Crown cannot be thus easily taken from them. Should we hold that the permit of a departmental official is a necessary condition precedent for a subject of the realm who would demand justice at the seat of judgment the people would be in that unhappy condition indicated, but not anticipated, by Montesquieu, in *De l'Esprit des Lois*, where he writes: *Les Anglais pour favoriser la liberté ont ôté toutes les puissances intermediaires qui formoient leur monarchie. Ils ont bien raison de conserver cette liberté s'ils venoient à la perdre, ils seroient un des peuples les plus esclaves de la terre.*[17]

The court declared the regulation to be invalid.

The laws are not silent

This lesson had to be learned afresh during the Second World War in a decision concerning the same regulations.

Few statements in the Appellate Committee of the House of Lords have excited as much controversy as the dissenting speech of Lord Atkin in a case[18] *concerning the notorious Regulation 18B. Under this regulation the Home Secretary had authority to detain persons whom he had 'reasonable cause to believe to be of hostile origin or associations'. A Mr Liversidge was so detained in Brixton prison from where he brought an action against the Home Secretary for false imprisonment. The question was whether the words 'reasonable cause to believe' in the regulation were to be construed objectively (in which case Mr Liversidge might have had a right to particulars of the grounds upon which the Home Secretary had arrived at his belief), or subjectively (when he would not). When the case eventually got to the House of Lords the Law Lords by a majority ruled against Mr Liversidge. The notable dissenter was Lord Atkin who in the course of his speech uttered the following words:*

I view with apprehension the attitude of judges who on a mere question of construction when face to face with claims involving the liberty of the subject

---

[17] The English, in order to promote liberty, stripped the monarchy of all its inessential power. They were right to do so: if they had lost liberty they would have become one of the most oppressed peoples on earth.

[18] *Liversidge* v *Anderson* [1942] 2 AC 206, 244.

show themselves more executive minded than the executive. Their function is to give words their natural meaning, not, perhaps, in wartime leaning towards liberty, but following the dictum of Chief Baron Pollock: 'In a case in which the liberty of the subject is concerned, we cannot go beyond the natural construction of the statute'. In this country, amid the clash of arms, the laws are not silent. They may be changed, but they speak the same language in war as in peace. It has always been one of the pillars of freedom, one of the principles of liberty for which on recent authority we are now fighting, that the judges are no respecters of persons and stand between the subject and any attempted encroachments on his liberty by the executive, alert to see that any coercive action is justified in law. In this case I have listened to arguments which might have been addressed acceptably to the Court of King's Bench in the time of Charles I.

I protest, even if I do it alone, against a strained construction put on words with the effect of giving an uncontrolled power of imprisonment to the minister. To recapitulate: The words have only one meaning. They are used with that meaning in statements of the common law and in statutes. They have never been used in the sense now imputed to them. They are used in the Defence Regulations in the natural meaning, and, when it is intended to express the meaning now imputed to them, different and apt words are used in the regulations generally and in this regulation in particular. Even if it were relevant, which it is not, there is no absurdity or no such degree of public mischief as would lead to a non-natural construction. I know of only one authority which might justify the suggested method of construction: 'When I use a word,' Humpty Dumpty said in rather a scornful tone, 'it means just what I choose it to mean, neither more nor less.' 'The question is,' said Alice, 'whether you can make words mean so many different things.' 'The question is,' said Humpty Dumpty, 'which is to be master — that's all.'[19]

Admiration for Atkin's stand was far from universal. Even Lord Denning, who during the war had the task of interviewing persons detained under regulation 18B, thought Atkin's dissent to have been based on a 'technical interpretation' of the Regulations.[20] In recent years, however, legal opinion has generally been supportive of Lord Atkin, both on the narrow point of interpretation and on principle.

[19] Lewis Carroll, *Through the Looking Glass*, ch. 6.
[20] *Landmarks in the Law* (London: Butterworths, 1984), p. 231.

The keys of persuasion

In 1917 when American soldiers were engaged in lethal combat with the Kaiser's army in France the New York city postmaster refused to accept for carriage in the mail a 'revolutionary' magazine called The Masses *on the ground that its content infringed the Federal Espionage Act. The magazine carried cartoons and text suggesting that the war was for the benefit of capitalists and that the draft (conscription) was an exploitation of the working class.*

The magazine's publishers appealed successfully to the District Court for the Southern District of New York presided over by District Judge Learned Hand, as he then was. Granting the injunction Hand said:[21]

The defendant says that the cartoons and text of the magazine, constituting, as they certainly do, a virulent attack upon the war and those laws which have been enacted to assist its prosecution, may interfere with the success of the military forces of the United States. That such utterances may have the effect so ascribed to them is unhappily true; publications of this kind enervate public feeling at home which is their chief purpose, and encourage the success of the enemies of the United States abroad, to which they are generally indifferent. Dissension within a country is a high source of comfort and assistance to its enemies; the least intimation of it they seize upon with jubilation. There cannot be the slightest question of the mischievous effects of such agitation upon the success of the national project, or of the correctness of the defendant's position. . . .

The defendant's position is that to arouse discontent and disaffection among the people with the prosecution of the war and with the draft tends to promote a mutinous and insubordinate temper among the troops. This too, is true; men who become satisfied that they are engaged in an enterprise dictated by the unconscionable selfishness of the rich and effectuated by a tyrannous disregard for the will of those who must suffer and die, will be more prone to insubordination than those who have faith in the cause and acquiesce in the means. Yet to interpret the word 'cause' so broadly would ... involve

---

[21] *Masses Publishing Co.* v *Patten*, 244 F 535 (SD NY 1917).

necessarily as a consequence the suppression of all hostile criticism, and of all opinion except what encouraged and supported the existing policies, or which fell within the range of temperate argument. It would contradict the normal assumption of democratic government that the suppression of hostile criticism does not turn upon the justice of its substance or the decency and propriety of its temper. Assuming that the power to repress such opinion may rest in Congress in the throes of a struggle for the very existence of the state, its exercise is so contrary to the use and wont of our people that only the clearest expression of such a power justifies the conclusion that it was intended.

> **Billings Learned Hand (1872–1961) eventually became Chief Judge of the United States Circuit Court of Appeals for the Second Circuit. Despite having served longer than any Federal judge, he failed to attain the highest office. He has been described as the greatest American judge never to sit on the Supreme Court bench.**

The defendant's position, therefore, in so far as it involves the suppression of the free utterance of abuse and criticism of the existing law, or of the policies of the war, is not, in my judgment, supported by the language of the statute. Yet there has always been a recognized limit to such expressions, incident indeed to the existence of any compulsive power of the state itself. One may not counsel or advise others to violate the law as it stands. Words are not only the keys of persuasion, but the triggers of action, and those which have no purport but to counsel the violation of law cannot by any latitude of interpretation be a part of that public opinion which is the final source of government in a democratic state. The defendant asserts not only that the magazine indirectly through its propaganda leads to a disintegration of loyalty and a disobedience of law, but that in addition it counsels and advises resistance to existing law, especially to the draft.

To counsel or advise a man to an act is to urge upon him either that it is his interest or his duty to do it. While, of course, this may be accomplished as well by indirection as expressly, since words carry the meaning that they impart, the definition is exhaustive, I think, and I shall use it. Political agitation, by the passions it arouses or the convictions it engenders, may in fact stimulate men to the violation of law. Detestation of existing policies is easily transformed into forcible resistance of the authority which puts them in execution, and it would be folly to disregard the causal relation between the two. Yet to assimilate agitation, legitimate as such, with direct incitement to violent resistance, is to disregard the tolerance of all methods of political agitation which in normal times is a safeguard of free government. The distinction is not a scholastic subterfuge, but a hard-bought acquisition in the fight for freedom, and the purpose to disregard it must be evident when the power exists. If one stops short of urging upon others that it is their duty or their interest to resist the law, it seems to me one should not be held to have attempted to cause its violation. If that be not the test, I can see no escape from the conclusion that under this section every political agitation which can be shown to be apt to create a seditious temper is illegal. I am confident that by such language Congress had no such revolutionary purpose in view.

It seems to me, however, quite plain that none of the language and none of the cartoons in this paper can be thought directly to counsel or advise insubordination or mutiny, without a violation of their meaning quite beyond any tolerable understanding. I come, therefore, to the third phrase of the section, which forbids any one from willfully obstructing the recruiting or enlistment service of the United States. I am not prepared to assent to the plaintiff's position that this only refers to acts other than words, nor that the act thus defined must be shown to have been successful. One may obstruct without preventing, and the mere obstruction is an injury to the service; for it throws impediments in its way. Here again, however, since the question is of the expression of opinion, I construe the sentence, so far as it restrains public utterance, as I have construed the other two, and as therefore limited to the direct advocacy of resistance, to the recruiting and enlistment service. If so, the inquiry is narrowed to the question whether any of the challenged matter may be said to advocate resistance to the draft, taking the meaning of the words with the utmost latitude which they can bear....

That such comments have a tendency to arouse emulation in others is clear enough, but that they counsel others to follow these examples is not so plain. Literally at least they do not, and while, as I have said, the words are to be taken, not literally, but according to their full import, the literal meaning is the starting point for interpretation. One may admire and approve the course of a hero without feeling any duty to follow him. There is not the least implied intimation in these words that others are under a duty to follow. The most that can be said is that, if others do follow, they will get the same admiration and the same approval. Now, there is surely an appreciable distance between esteem and emulation; and unless there is here some advocacy of such emulation, I cannot see how the passages can be said to fall within the law. If they do, it would follow that, while one might express admiration and approval for the Quakers or any established sect which is excused from the draft, one could not legally express the same admiration and approval for others who entertain the same conviction, but do not happen to belong to the Society of Friends. It cannot be that the law means to curtail such expressions merely because the convictions of the class within the draft are stronger than their sense of obedience to the law. There is ample evidence in history that the Quaker is as recalcitrant to legal compulsion as any man; his obstinacy has been regarded in the act, but his disposition is as disobedient as that of any other conscientious objector. Surely, if the draft had not excepted Quakers, it would be too strong a doctrine to say that any who openly admire their fortitude or even approved their conduct was willfully obstructing the draft.

When the question is of a statute constituting a crime, it seems to me that there should be more definite evidence of the act. The question before me is quite the same as what would arise upon a motion to dismiss an indictment at the close of the proof: could any reasonable man say, not that the indirect result of the language might be to arouse a seditious disposition, for that would not be enough, but that the language directly advocated resistance to the draft? I cannot think that upon such language any verdict would stand. Of course, the language of the statute cannot have one meaning in an indictment and another when the case comes up here, because by hypothesis, if this paper is non-mailable under section 3 of title 1, its editors have committed a crime in uttering it. . . .

The defendant's action was based, as I understand it, not so much upon the narrow question whether these four passages actually advocated resistance, though that point was distinctly raised, as upon the doctrine that the general tenor and animus of the paper as a whole were subversive to authority and seditious in effect. I cannot accept this test under the law as it stands at present. The tradition of English-speaking freedom has depended in no small part upon the merely procedural requirement that the state point with exactness to just that conduct which violates the law. It is difficult and often impossible to meet the charge that one's general ethos is treasonable; such a latitude for construction implies a personal latitude in administration which contradicts the normal assumption that law shall be embodied in general propositions capable of some measure of definition. The whole crux of this case turns indeed upon this thesis. I make no question of the power of Congress to establish a personal censorship of the press under the war power; that question, as I have already said, does not arise. I am quite satisfied that it has not as yet chosen to create one and with the greatest deference it does not seem to me that anything here challenged can be illegal upon any other assumption.

This judgment was reversed on appeal. Hand's biographer [22] wrote,

> *Masses* compelled Hand to draw on his deepest personal
> resources of courage and independence and evoked the most

---

[22] Gerald Gunther, *Learned Hand: The Man and the Judge* (Harvard University Press, 1995).

important, pathbreaking opinion of his trial court tenure — an analysis that, decades later, became the law of the land.

All life is an experiment

During the same war five Russian-born anarchists were charged with conspiring to publish in New York leaflets criticising the American government for failing to condemn the German intervention in the Russian revolution and calling for a general strike. The United States Supreme Court, by a majority, upheld[23] the convictions. Of greater significance in the long run, however, was the robust dissenting opinion of Mr Justice Holmes.

In this case sentences of 20 years' imprisonment have been imposed for the publishing of two leaflets that I believe the defendants had as much right to publish as the government has to publish the Constitution of the United States now vainly invoked by them. Even if I am technically wrong, and enough can be squeezed from these poor and puny anonymities to turn the color of legal litmus paper — I will add, even if what I think the necessary intent were shown, — the most nominal punishment seems to me all that possibly could be inflicted, unless the defendants are to be made to suffer not for what the indictment alleges, but for the creed that they avow, — a creed that I believe to be the creed of ignorance and immaturity when honestly held, as I see no reason to doubt that it was held here, but which, although made the subject of examination at the trial, no one has a right even to consider in dealing with the charges before the court.

Persecution for the expression of opinions seems to me perfectly logical. If you have no doubt of your premises or your power and want a certain result with all your heart you naturally express your wishes in law and sweep away all opposition. To allow opposition by speech seems to indicate that you think the speech impotent, as when a man says that he has squared the circle, or that you do not care wholeheartedly for the result, or that you doubt either your power or your premises. But when men have realized that time has upset many fighting faiths, they may come to believe even more than they believe the very foundations of their own conduct that the ultimate good desired is better reached by free trade in ideas, — that the best test of truth is the power of the

---

[23] *Abrams* v *United States*, 250 US 616, 630 (1919).

thought to get itself accepted in the competition of the market; and that truth is the only ground upon which their wishes safely can be carried out.

That, at any rate, is the theory of our Constitution. It is an experiment, as all life is an experiment. Every year, if not every day, we have to wager our salvation upon some prophecy based upon imperfect knowledge. While that experiment is part of our system I think that we should be eternally vigilant against attempts to check the expression of opinions that we loathe and believe to be fraught with death, unless they so imminently threaten immediate interference with the lawful and pressing purposes of the law that an immediate check is required to save the country. I wholly disagree with the argument of the government that the 1st Amendment left the common law as to seditious libel in force. History seems to me against the notion. I had conceived that the United States through many years had shown its repentance for the Sedition Act of 1798, by repaying fines that it imposed. Only the emergency that makes it immediately dangerous to leave the correction of evil counsels to time warrants making any exception to the sweeping command, 'Congress shall make no law abridging the freedom of speech'. Of course, I am speaking only of expressions of opinion and exhortations, which were all that were uttered here; but I regret that I cannot put into more impressive words my belief that in their conviction upon this indictment the defendants were deprived of their rights under the Constitution of the United States.

Holmes's view of the law, though vindicated by subsequent decisions,[24] represented a volte face over his previous utterances. His biographer wrote:[25]

When one examines Holmes' free speech opinions from the perspective of doctrine and theory, one finds inconsistencies and contradictions at every turn. Those opinions, however, were the products of a writer whose principal concern was to open 'windows' on a philosophical issue, to see 'the particular in the light of the universal'. They thus appear less as doctrinal than as metaphorical statements. They aim not to achieve logical consistency but to offer 'forms of words' that convey the universal dimensions of free speech theory. Whatever the limitations of 'clear and present danger', 'the search for truth', and 'freedom for the thought that we hate' as analytical guides, they vividly encapsulate recurrent concerns and values, and they remind us that

---

[24] See *Cantwell* v *Connecticut*, 310 US 296 (1940).
[25] G. Edward White, *Justice Oliver Wendell Holmes: Law and the Inner Self* (Oxford University Press, 1993), p. 453.

Holmes the writer has glimpsed the universal in the particular. In his free speech opinions Holmes did precisely what he told Canon Sheehan he wanted to do: to put new ideas into the law, to show how particular 'solutions' to legal issues involved general theory, and to communicate with style.

In the name of security

In another case before the United States Supreme Court it took the dissenting opinions of three Justices to voice the conscience of the nation.

The petitioner, Mrs Knauff, was born in Germany in 1915. She went to Czechoslovakia during the Hitler regime. There she was married and divorced. In 1939 she went to England as a refugee. Thereafter she served with the Royal Air Force efficiently and honourably until 1946. She then secured civilian employment with the War Department of the United States in Germany. In February 1948, with the permission of the Commanding General at Frankfurt she married Kurt W. Knauff, a naturalised citizen of the United States. An honourably discharged veteran of the Second World War, he was, at the time of his marriage and subsequently, a civilian employee of the United States Army at Frankfurt.

In August 1948, Mrs Knauff sought to enter the United States to be naturalised. This application was rejected and she was detained at Ellis Island. Two months later the Assistant Commissioner of Immigration and Naturalization recommended that she be permanently excluded without a hearing on the ground that her admission would be prejudicial to the interests of the United States. The Attorney-General adopted this recommendation and entered a final order of exclusion. The District Court dismissed a writ of habeas corpus and the Court of Appeals affirmed the dismissal.

On appeal, a majority of the Supreme Court found no legal defect in the refusal of admission. 'As all other aliens, petitioner had to stand the test of security. This she failed to meet.' *Mr Justice Jackson's dissenting opinion, with which Mr Justice Black and Mr Justice Frankfurter joined, began as follows:*[26]

I do not question the constitutional power of Congress to authorize immigration authorities to turn back from our gates any alien or class of aliens. But I do not find that Congress has authorised an abrupt and brutal exclusion of the wife of an American citizen without a hearing.

Congress held out a promise of liberalized admission to alien brides, taken unto themselves by men serving in or honorably discharged from our armed services abroad, as the Act indicates. The petitioning husband is honorably discharged and remained in Germany as a civilian employee. Our military authorities abroad required their permission before marriage. The Army in Germany is not without a vigilant and security-conscious intelligence service. This woman was employed by our European Command and her record is not only without blemish, but is highly praised by her superiors. The marriage of this alien woman to this veteran was approved by the Commanding General at Frankfurt-on-Main.

Now this American citizen is told he cannot bring his wife to the United States, but he will not be told why. He must abandon his bride to live in his own country or forsake his country to live with his bride. So he went to court and sought a writ of habeas corpus, which we never tire of citing to Europe as the unanswerable evidence that our free country permits no arbitrary official detention. And the Government tells the Court that not even a court can find out why the girl is excluded. But it says we must find that Congress authorized this treatment of war brides and, even if we cannot get any reasons for it, we must say it is legal; security requires it.

Security is like liberty in that many are the crimes committed in its name. The menace to the security of this country, be it great as it may, from this girl's admission is as nothing compared to the menace to free institutions inherent in procedures of this pattern. In the name of security the police state justifies its arbitrary oppressions on evidence that is secret, because security might be prejudiced if it were brought to light in hearings. The plea that evidence of guilt must be secret is abhorrent to free men, because it provides a cloak for the malevolent, the misinformed, the meddlesome, and the corrupt to play the role of informer undetected and uncorrected. I am sure the officials here have acted from a sense of duty, with full belief in their lawful power, and no doubt upon information which, if it stood the test of trial, would justify the order of exclusion.

---

[26] *Knauff* v *Shaughnessy*, 338 US 537 (1950).

But not even they know whether it would stand this test. And anyway, as I have said before, personal confidence in the officials involved does not excuse a judge for sanctioning a procedure that is dangerously wrong in principle....

Congress will have to use more explicit language than any yet cited before I will agree that it has authorized an administrative officer to break up the family of an American citizen or force him to keep his wife by becoming an exile. Likewise, it will have to be much more explicit before I can agree that it authorized a finding of serious misconduct against the wife of an American citizen without notice of charges, evidence of guilt and a chance to meet it. I should direct the Attorney-General either to produce his evidence justifying exclusion or to admit Mrs Knauff to the country.

Man being what he is

It was not long after the Second World War that the West began to suspect their former ally, communist Russia, to be as serious a threat as Nazi Germany. Nowhere did this apprehension take firmer root than in the United States of America. While these fears were far from groundless the forms they took (in a country that likes to see itself as the defender of citizens' rights) were in some instances almost hysterical. Less irrational were the government's efforts to weed out suspected dissidents among their own staff. However, the manner in which they set about this task was open to objection.

In the late 1940s government departments in America sought to identify and dismiss disloyal government employees. Membership of a communist or otherwise subversive organisation was deemed to be a factor in determining disloyalty. Without notice or hearing and claiming authority under a Presidential Executive Order, the Attorney-General of the United States added three organisations, ostensibly of a charitable nature, to a list of groups designated by him as communist. The list was transmitted to a body called the Loyalty Review Board and disseminated by the Board to all government departments and agencies for use in the discharge of 'disloyal' employees.

The named organisations sued the Attorney-General for declaratory and injunctive relief, seeking the deletion of their names from the list because of the resulting harm to their activities. The government's motions to dismiss the complaints were granted by the lower courts, in two cases on the ground that the complaint failed to state a cause of action, and in the third on the ground that the plaintiff had no standing to sue.

On appeal, the members of the Supreme Court ruled against the government, not all for the same reasons. Mr Justice Frankfurter took his stand on the ground of due process with these words: [27]

The requirement of 'due process' is not a fair-weather or timid assurance. It must be respected in periods of calm and in times of trouble it protects aliens as well as citizens. But 'due process', unlike some legal rules, is not a technical conception with a fixed content unrelated to time, place and circumstances. Expressing as it does in its ultimate analysis respect enforced by law for that feeling of just treatment which has been evolved through centuries of Anglo-American constitutional history and civilization, 'due process' cannot be imprisoned within the treacherous limits of any formula. Representing a profound attitude of fairness between man and man, and more particularly between the individual and government, 'due process' is compounded of history, reason, the past course of decisions, and stout confidence in the strength of the democratic faith which we profess. Due process is not a mechanical instrument. It is not a yardstick. It is a process. It is a delicate process of adjustment inescapably involving the exercise of judgment by those whom the Constitution entrusted with the unfolding of the process.

Felix Frankfurter was born in 1882 in Vienna and emigrated to America with his parents in 1894. He was Professor of law at Harvard from 1914 to 1939 when he was appointed to the Supreme Court. He served as a Justice of that Court until 1962, dying some three years later.

Fully aware of the enormous powers thus given to the judiciary and especially to its Supreme Court, those who founded this nation put their trust in a judiciary truly independent — in judges not subject to the fears or allurements of a limited tenure and by the very nature of their function detached from passing and partisan influences.

[27] *Joint Anti-Fascist Refugee Committee* v *McGrath,* 341 US 123, 162 (1951).

It may fairly be said that, barring only occasional and temporary lapses, this Court has not sought unduly to confine those who have the responsibility of governing by giving the great concept of due process doctrinaire scope. The Court has responded to the infinite variety and perplexity of the tasks of government by recognizing that what is unfair in one situation may be fair in another.... Whether the *ex parte* procedure to which the petitioners were subjected duly observed 'the rudiments of fair play', ... cannot, therefore be tested by mere generalities or sentiments abstractly appealing. The precise nature of the interest that has been adversely affected, the manner in which this was done, the reasons for doing it, the available alternatives to the procedure that was followed, the protection implicit in the office of the functionary whose conduct is challenged, the balance of hurt complained of and good accomplished — these are some of the considerations that must enter into the judicial judgment....

The heart of the matter is that democracy implies respect for the elementary rights of men, however suspect or unworthy; a democratic government must therefore practice fairness; and fairness can rarely be obtained by secret, one-sided determination of facts decisive of rights. An opportunity to be heard may not seem vital when an issue relates only to technical questions susceptible of demonstrable proof on which evidence is not likely to be overlooked and argument on the meaning and worth of conflicting and cloudy data not apt to be helpful.

But in other situations an admonition of Mr Justice Holmes becomes relevant. 'One has to remember that when one's interest is keenly excited evidence gathers from all sides around the magnetic point.'

It should be particularly heeded at times of agitation and anxiety, when fear and suspicion impregnate the air we breathe. Compare Brown, *The French Revolution in English History*: 'The plea that evidence of guilt must be secret is abhorrent to free men, because it provides a cloak for the malevolent, the misinformed, the meddlesome, and the corrupt to play the role of informer undetected and uncorrected'.... Appearances in the dark are apt to look different in the light of day.

Man being what he is cannot safely be trusted with complete immunity from outward responsibility in depriving others of their rights. At least such is the conviction underlying our Bill of Rights. That a conclusion satisfies one's private conscience does not attest its reliability. The validity and moral authority of a conclusion largely depend on the mode by which it was reached. Secrecy is not congenial to truth-seeking and self-righteousness gives too slender an assurance of rightness. No better instrument has been devised for arriving at truth than to give a person in jeopardy of serious loss notice of the case against him and opportunity to meet it. Nor has a better way been found for generating the feeling, so important to a popular government, that justice has been done.

Francis Bacon in Gray's Inn

3. LET THE BLACK GO FREE

or

The Law and the Downtrodden

The air of England is too pure for any slave to breathe.
Let the black go free.

Lord Mansfield in *Sommersett's Case.*[28]

Let the black go free
The non-citizen
The compromise between candor and shame
Dangers once thought real
Free and unfettered minds
A view so much out of date
Children are like trees
Heroes not welcome
The privacy of the torture chamber

---

[28] See under *Let the black go free.*

We are so conscious of minority rights nowadays that their disregard in times past comes almost as a surprise. This chapter looks at the ways in which the courts have treated minorities and other groups whose way of life differs, for good or ill, from the norm.

It is heartening for an English lawyer to compare the vigorous rejection of slavery by an English judge (See under Let the black go free) *with the scandalous decision of the United States Supreme Court many years later that blacks were not citizens of that country and thus not entitled to the protection of its constitution (*The non-citizen).

*On the other hand, when it comes to freedom of expression we can even now read with profit the words of District Judge Learned Hand in 1913 on the subject of censorship (*The compromise between candor and shame).

*People have been persecuted for their religious beliefs (or lack of them) since the dawn of civilisation. Dismantling the unique protection accorded by law to the Christian religion (and thus discrimination against persons holding other religious beliefs or none) began in the nineteenth century. It has yet to be completed (*Dangers once thought real).

*Lord Denning figures here in two cases concerning the protection of children (*A view so much out of date *and* Children are like trees) *where, largely as a result of decisions like these, the law has been set on an entirely different path.*

*More controversially, the decriminalisation of homosexuality in the 1960s failed to resolve all questions of sexual identity. Are there special circumstances attending service in the armed forces that preclude the engagement of homosexuals? The British Army clearly thinks so and its view has been challenged in the courts more than once. The frank expression by a distinguished judge of his own opinion in this matter was a notable departure from practice that deserves our respect (*Heroes not welcome).

Sex also reared its ubiquitous head in the prosecution of a group of homosexuals for pursuing the mutual infliction of pain for sexual gratification. The majority opinion in the House of Lords upheld their convictions on the ground that their conduct was caught by an Act of Parliament over 130 years old. Lord Mustill's dissenting opinion is rewarding to read, not only for its legal scholarship, but for its common sense

---

Let the black go free

Americans are justly proud of the Thirteenth Amendment to their Constitution, which in 1865 abolished slavery throughout the United States. (It had been abolished — but only notionally — in the rebel States two years earlier by President Lincoln's emancipation proclamation.) It is easy to forget that the status of a slave was rejected by a judge in England nearly a century before.[29]

James Sommersett (the name is spelt variously in different places) had been brought as a slave from Africa to Jamaica. He had been purchased there by a Mr Stewart who took him to England intending that he should eventually return with him to Jamaica. In England the slave sought his freedom by means of a writ of habeas corpus. For Stewart it had been argued that slavery was akin to the feudal status of villeinage. Rejecting this submission, the Chief Justice of the Court of King's Bench, Lord Mansfield, has been reported[30] *as having said:*

What ground is there for saying that the status of slavery is now recognised by the law of England? That trover will lie for a slave? That a slave-market may be established in Smithfield? I care not for the supposed dicta of judges, however eminent, if they be contrary to all principle. Villeinage, when it did exist in this country, differed in many particulars from West India slavery. The lord never could have thrown the villein into chains, sent him to the West Indies, and sold him there to work in a mine or in a cane field. At any rate, villeinage has ceased in England and it cannot be revived. Every man who comes into England is entitled to the protection of English law, whatever oppression he may heretofore have suffered and whatever may be the colour of his skin.

---

[29] Though the trade in slaves was not abolished until 1807 and the status of slavery until 1833.
[30] Lives of the Chief Justices of England, 1849.

The air of England is too pure for any slave to breathe. Let the black go free.

The actual judgment is less dramatic in tone:[31]

The only question before us is, whether the cause on the return is sufficient? If it is, the negro must be remanded; if it is not, he must be discharged. Accordingly, the return states, that the slave departed and refused to serve; whereupon he was kept, to be sold abroad. So high an act of dominion must be recognized by the law of the country where it is used. The power of a master over his slave has been extremely different, in different countries. The state of slavery is of such a nature, that it is incapable of being introduced on any reasons, moral or political, but only by positive law, which preserves its force long after the reasons, occasion, and time itself from whence it was created, is erased from memory. It is so odious, that nothing can be suffered to support it, but positive law. Whatever inconveniences, therefore, may follow from the decision, I cannot say this case is allowed or approved by the law of England; and therefore the black must be discharged.

The report also makes it clear that it was in fact one of the advocates, Serjeant Davy, who in argument said:

the air of England has been gradually purifying ever since the reign of Elizabeth ... it has been asserted, and is now repeated by me, this air is too pure for a slave to breathe in.

It is estimated that there were at that time some 14,000–15,000 slaves in England whose value was about £50 each, so the commercial consequences of this judgment must have been serious.

Over half a century later another English judge, Mr Justice Best, was able to claim[32] *of the institution of slavery:*

It is a relation which has always in British courts been held inconsistent with the constitution of the country. It is matter of pride to me to recollect that, whilst economists and politicians

---

[31] 20 St Tr 1, 82, Lofft 1, 19.
[32] *Forbes* v *Cochrane* (1824) 2 B & C 448.

were recommending to the legislature the protection of this traffic, and senators were framing statutes for its promotion, and declaring it a benefit to the country, the judges of the land, above the age in which they lived, standing upon the high ground of natural right, and disdaining to bend to the lower doctrine of expediency, declared that slavery was inconsistent with the genius of the English constitution, and that human beings could not be the subject matter of property. As a lawyer I speak of that early determination, when a different doctrine was prevailing in the senate, with a considerable degree of professional pride.

The non-citizen

It is salutary to compare this robust rejection of slavery at common law with its treatment under a written constitution.

A black slave, Dredd Scott, aided by abolitionist lawyers, had sought his freedom on the ground that his master had taken him out of Missouri (where slavery had long existed) and into the American West (where slavery had been outlawed by what was known as the Missouri Compromise). The case eventually got to the Supreme Court, whose Chief Justice was the 80-year-old Roger B. Taney. Taney, who had held office so long that he had sworn in seven Presidents, was by no means inhumane: he had freed his own slaves and purchased the liberty of others. He was, however, fearful of the threat which the case presented to the Southern way of life. The majority opinion,which Taney wrote,[33] held that:

They (*i.e. slaves and their descendants*) are not included, and were not intended to be included, under the word 'citizens' in the Constitution, and can therefore claim none of the rights and privileges which that instrument provides for and secures to citizens of the United States.[34]

---

[33] *Scott v Sandford*, 60 US (19 How) 393, 404 (1857).
[34] For an excellent summary of this decision see James M. McPherson, *Battle Cry of Freedom* (Oxford University Press, 1988), pp. 170 *et seq.*

In a dissenting opinion of heroic proportions (it contained over 30,000 words) and formidable scholarship Mr Justice Curtis put the opposite point of view:

I can find nothing in the Constitution which, *proprio vigore*, deprives of their citizenship any class of persons who were citizens of the United States at the time of its adoption, or who should be native-born citizens of any State after its adoption, nor any power enabling Congress to disfranchise persons born on the soil of any State, and entitled to citizenship of such State by its Constitution and laws. And my opinion is that, under the Constitution of the United States, every free person born on the soil of a State, who is a citizen of that State by force of its Constitution or laws, is also a citizen of the United States....

It has been often asserted that the Constitution was made exclusively by and for the white race. It has already been shown that, in five of the 13 original States, colored persons then possessed the elective franchise, and were among those by whom the Constitution was ordained and established. If so, it is not true, in point of fact, that the Constitution was made exclusively by the white race. And that it was made exclusively for the white race is, in my opinion, not only an assumption not warranted by anything in the Constitution, but contradicted by its opening declaration that it was ordained and established by the people of the United States, for themselves and their posterity. And as free colored persons were then citizens of at least five States, and so in every sense part of the people of the United States, they were among those for whom and whose posterity the Constitution was ordained and established....

Slavery is sanctioned by the laws of this State, and the right to hold them under our municipal regulations is unquestionable. But we view this as a right existing by positive law of a municipal character, without foundation in the law of nature or the unwritten common law.

The following year Abraham Lincoln, upon being nominated for Senator, proclaimed: 'A house divided against itself cannot stand. I believe that this government cannot permanently endure half slave and half free.' And we all know where that led.

Mr Justice Cardozo was to comment that to read Curtis's opinion was to feel 'after the cooling time of the better half of a century the glow and fire of a faith that was content to bide its time'.[35]

---

[35] 'Law and Literature' *Yale Review of 1925.*

The compromise between candor and shame

Many people accept that there are some books which are so obscene that their publication ought not to be permitted. What they cannot agree upon is which; in other words, what should be the test of censorship?

In 1913 District Judge Learned Hand of the Southern District of New York felt constrained by binding precedent to hold that he had no power to withdraw from a jury the question of whether a novel which had been sent through the post was obscene or not. However, in the course of one of his finest judgments[36] he observed:

The question here is, therefore, whether the jury might find the book obscene under proper instructions. Lord Cockburn laid down a test in these words:

Whether the tendency of the matter charged as obscenity is to deprave and corrupt those whose minds are open to such immoral influences and into whose hands a publication of this sort may fall.

That test has been accepted by the lower Federal courts until it would be no longer proper for me to disregard it. Under this rule [*parts*] of this book might be found obscene, because they certainly might tend to corrupt the morals of those into whose hands it might come and whose minds were open to such immoral influences. Indeed, it would be just those who would be most likely to concern themselves with those parts alone, forgetting their setting and their relevancy to the book as a whole.

... I hope it is not improper for me to say that the rule as laid down, however consonant it may be with mid-Victorian morals, does not seem to me to answer to the understanding and morality of the present time, as conveyed by the words, 'obscene, lewd, or lascivious'. I question whether in the end men will regard that as obscene which is honestly relevant to the adequate expression of innocent ideas and whether they will not believe that truth and beauty are too

---

[36] *United States* v *Kennerley*, 290 F 119 (SD NY 1913).

precious to society at large to be mutilated in the interests of those most likely to pervert them to base uses. Indeed, it seems hardly likely that we are even today so lukewarm in our interest in letters or serious discussion as to be content to reduce our treatment of sex to the standard of a child's library in the supposed interest of a salacious few, or that shame will for long prevent us from adequate portrayal of some of the most serious and beautiful sides of human nature. That such latitude gives opportunity for its abuse is true enough; there will be, as there are, plenty who will misuse the privilege as a cover for lewdness and a stalking horse from which to strike at purity, but that is true today and only involves us in the same question of fact which we hope that we have the power to answer.

Yet, if the time is not yet when men think innocent all that which is honestly germane to a pure subject, however little it may mince its words, still I scarcely think that they would forbid all which might corrupt the most corruptible, or that society is prepared to accept for its own limitations those which may perhaps be necessary to the weakest of its members. If there be no abstract definition, such as I have suggested, should not the word 'obscene' be allowed to indicate the present critical point in the compromise between candor and shame at which the community may have arrived here and now? If letters must, like other kinds of conduct, be subject to the social sense of what is right, it would seem that a jury should in each case establish the standard much as they do in cases of negligence. To put thought in leash to the average conscience of the time is perhaps tolerable, but to fetter it by the necessities of the lowest and least capable seems a fatal policy.

Nor is it an objection, I think, that such an interpretation gives to the words of the statute a varying meaning from time to time. Such words as these do not embalm the precise morals of an age or place; while they presuppose that some things will always be shocking to the public taste, the vague subject matter is left to the gradual development of general notions about what is decent. A jury is especially the organ with which to feel the content comprised within such words at any given time, but to do so they must be free to follow the colloquial connotations which they have drawn up instinctively from life and common speech.

While the stand taken by Learned Hand was subsequently endorsed by the United States Supreme Court, England has not yet reconciled itself to the more liberal approach to the censorship of obscene material suggested in this judgment.

Dangers once thought real

'Christianity', said Chief Justice Raymond in the middle of the eighteenth century,[37] *'is part of the common law of England'. It was not until the early part of the twentieth century that this view was authoritatively abandoned.*[38]

The Secular Society was a company limited by guarantee which had as its first object promoting 'the principle that human conduct should be based upon natural knowledge, and not upon supernatural belief, and that human welfare in this world is the proper end of all thought and action'. In his will Charles Bowman left all his estate to the society. Upon his death the next of kin disputed the will on the ground that the objects of the society were unlawful. The Court of Appeal upheld the bequest and were supported in this by the House of Lords. In the course of his speech Lord Sumner said:

Our courts of law, in the exercise of their own jurisdiction, do not, and never did that I can find, punish irreligious words as offences against God. As to them they held that *'deorum injuriae dis curae'* [*injuries to the Gods must be dealt with by the courts of the Gods*]. They dealt with such words for their manner, their violence, or ribaldry, or, more fully stated, for their tendency to endanger the peace then and there, to deprave public morality generally, to shake the fabric of society, and to be a cause of civil strife. The words, as well as the acts, which tend to endanger society differ from time to time in proportion as society is stable or insecure in fact, or is believed by its reasonable members to be open to assault. In the present day meetings or processions are held lawful which a hundred and fifty years ago would have been deemed seditious, and this is not because the law is weaker or has changed, but because, the times having changed, society is stronger than before. In the present day reasonable men do not apprehend the dissolution or the downfall of society because religion is publicly assailed by methods not scandalous.

Whether it is possible that in the future irreligious attacks, designed to undermine fundamental institutions of our society, may come to be criminal in themselves, as constituting a public danger, is a matter that does not arise. The

---

[37] *R* v *Woolston* (1729) Fitzg 64.
[38] *Bowman* v *Secular Society Ltd* [1917] AC 406.

fact that opinion grounded on experience has moved one way does not in law preclude the possibility of its moving on fresh experience in the other; nor does it bind succeeding generations, when conditions have again changed. After all, the question whether a given opinion is a danger to society is a question of the times and is a question of fact. I desire to say nothing that would limit the right of society to protect itself by process of law from the dangers of the moment, whatever that right may be, but only to say that, experience having proved dangers once thought real to be now negligible, and dangers once very possibly imminent to have now passed away, there is nothing in the general rules as to blasphemy and irreligion, as known to the law, which prevents us from varying their application to the particular circumstances of our time in accordance with that experience.

Free and unfettered minds

The relationship of religion to individual liberty is highlighted by the offence of blasphemy. Originally an ecclesiastical offence, the modern history of this crime was recounted by Lord Justice Roskill[39] as follows:

In the disturbed history of this country during and following the Napoleonic Wars there were many prosecutions for blasphemy or for blasphemous libel, not perhaps so much for the purpose of vindicating Christian truths as for fear that their denial in such works as Paine's *Age of Reason* or some of Shelley's poems might tend to a breach of the peace, by which in those days was meant serious civil disturbance rather than violence between individuals at street corners.... between January 1821 and April 1834 (just over 13 years) there had been no less than 73 convictions for blasphemy.

As one reads the mid-nineteenth-century cases ... it becomes clear that, notwithstanding the number of prosecutions that there had been during the troubled years of the first half of that century, not only for the publication of Paine's *Age of Reason*, but even as late as 1841, the prosecution of Moxon for publishing Shelley's *Queen Mab* many years after it had been written, the view gradually if hesitatingly begins to emerge that the truth of hitherto accepted religious beliefs and indeed the historical and doctrinal foundation of Christianity itself might be challenged, and indeed attacked as wrong, provided

---

[39] *R* v *Lemon* [1978] 3 All ER 175, 182.

that the challenge or attack was carried out with proper respect and moderation so that there would be no consequent threat of a breach of the peace....

This judgment came from a decision of the Court of Appeal in what is generally known as the Gay News *case. A journal of that name had published a poem accompanied by an illustration describing in explicit detail imagined acts of sodomy and fellation with the body of Christ immediately after the moment of his death. The newspaper, its editor and publisher were all charged with blasphemous libel under an Act of 1888 and convicted by a jury at the Old Bailey before Judge King-Hamilton QC (who was, incidentally, a Jew). The editor received a suspended prison sentence and a fine and the other defendants were fined.*

The defendants appealed unsuccessfully against conviction, but the suspended sentence was quashed.

A view so much out of date

The twentieth century has also seen a welcome change in the legal status of children, brought about at first by judicial decisions, but subsequently confirmed by statute.

In 1883 the Court of Appeal declared[40] that 'the law of England ... is that the father has the control over the person, education and conduct of his children until they are 21 years of age. That is the law.' This was known as the rule in Re Agar-Ellis. *It was rejected by Lord Denning in 1969. The question he had to decide was whether a 15-year-old boy who had suffered injuries at a residential farm training centre was in the custody of his father so as to prevent him from bringing an action for damages which would otherwise be time barred.*

Denning concluded his judgment:[41]

---

[40] *Re Agar-Ellis, Agar-Ellis* v *Lascelles* (1883) 23 ChD 317.
[41] *Hewer* v *Bryant* [1969] 3 All ER 578, 582.

I utterly reject the notion that an infant is, by law, in the custody of his father until he is 21. These words 'in the custody of a parent' were first used in the Limitation Act 1939. During the next year youngsters of 18 and 19 fought the Battle of Britain. Was each of them at that time still in the custody of his father? The next use of the words was in the Law Reform (Limitation of Actions, &c.) Act 1954. Since which time pop singers of 19 have made thousands a week, and revolutionaries of 18 have broken up universities. Is each of them in the custody of his father? Of course not. Neither in law nor in fact. Counsel for the defendant realised the absurdity and sought to graft exceptions onto the rule in *Re Agar-Ellis*. But he failed to provide any satisfactory definition of his exceptions. By the time he finished, it looked to me as if the exceptions would swallow up the rule.

I would get rid of the rule in *Re Agar-Ellis* and of the suggested exceptions to it. That case was decided in the year 1883. It reflects the attitude of a Victorian parent towards his children. He expected unquestioning obedience to his commands. If a son disobeyed, his father would cut him off with 1*s*. If a daughter had an illegitimate child, he would turn her out of the house. His power only ceased when the child became 21. I decline to accept a view so much out of date. The common law can, and should, keep pace with the times. It should declare, in conformity with the recent report on *The Age of Majority*, that the legal right of a parent to the custody of a child ends at the eighteenth birthday; and even up till then, it is a dwindling right which the courts will hesitate to enforce against the wishes of the child, the older he is. It starts with a right of control and ends with little more than advice.

The law has since undergone the change Lord Denning wished to see.

Children are like trees

Similar problems have arisen with regard to children's rights to property.

There is no general rule of law preventing a person's financial affairs being arranged so as to minimise the effects of taxation. Where the arrangement conflicts with the interests of a child, however, the court may not be so tolerant. In one case the Court of

Appeal had to deal with an application to vary two trusts settled upon the plaintiff's children. When capital gains tax was introduced in 1965 the family decided to move from England to Jersey in order to minimise its effects. The settlor accordingly sought the permission of the court to vary the trusts so as to transfer them to Jersey where there was no capital gains tax. The judge refused and the plaintiff appealed to the Court of Appeal who upheld the judge's decision. In the course of his judgment[42] Lord Denning said:

Two propositions are clear: (i) in exercising its discretion, the function of the court is to protect those who cannot protect themselves. It must do what is truly for their benefit; (ii) it can give its consent to a scheme to avoid death duties or other taxes. Nearly every variation that has come before the court has tax avoidance for its principal object: and no one has ever suggested that this is undesirable or contrary to public policy.

I think it necessary, however, to add this third proposition: (iii) the court should not consider merely the financial benefit to the infants or unborn children, but also their educational and social benefit. There are many things in life more worthwhile than money. One of these things is to be brought up in this our England, which is still 'the envy of less happier lands'.[43] I do not believe it is for the benefit of children to be uprooted from England and transported to another country simply to avoid tax.... The inference is irresistible: the underlying purpose was to go [*to Jersey*] in order to avoid tax. I do not think that this will be all to the good for the children. I should imagine that, even if they had stayed in this country, they would have had a very considerable fortune at their disposal, even after paying tax. The only thing that Jersey can do for them is to give them an even greater fortune. Many a child has been ruined by being given too much. The avoidance of tax may be lawful, but it is not yet a virtue. The Court of Chancery should not encourage or support it — it should not give its approval to it — if by so doing it would imperil the true welfare of the children, already born or yet to be born.

There is one thing more. I cannot help wondering how long these young people will stay in Jersey. It may be to their financial interest at present to make their home there permanently, but will they remain there once the capital gains are safely in hand, clear of tax? They may well change their minds and come back to enjoy their untaxed gains. Is such a prospect really for the benefit of the children? Are they to be wanderers over the face of the earth, moving from this

[42] *Re Weston's Settlements* [1968] 3 All ER 338, 342.
[42] Shakespeare, *Richard II*, act 2, scene 1.

country to that, according to where they can best avoid tax? I cannot believe that to be right.

Children are like trees: they grow stronger with firm roots.

Heroes not welcome

At any time there are one or two issues of a moral nature which are on the cutting edge of controversy. Among these in the 1990s was the place of homosexuals in the armed forces.

The position of the Ministry of Defence was clear: active homosexuals were not permitted to serve. An attempt to challenge this policy by way of proceedings for judicial review proved unsuccessful,[44] but Lord Justice Simon Brown, who gave the leading judgment in the Court of Appeal, did not shrink from expressing his own view of Ministry policy. He began strikingly:

Lawrence of Arabia would not be welcome in today's armed forces: homosexual men and women are not permitted to serve. That is the policy of the Ministry of Defence. It applies to anyone of homosexual orientation — anyone sexually attracted to a member of their own sex — irrespective of whether they engage in homosexual conduct or remain celibate. It admits of no exception. The only areas of judgment or discretion involved are first, whether the homosexual orientation is genuine — sometimes doubtful amongst younger personnel and sometimes pretended to secure early discharge — and, second, whether removal should be by administrative discharge without dishonour, or pursuant to disciplinary process.

These four applicants, respectively a lesbian and three male homosexuals, were administratively discharged from the services under this policy. Each challenges the legality of such discharge, principally on the ground that the policy is irrational, but in addition on the ground that it breaches both the European Convention for the Protection of Human Rights and Fundamental Freedoms . . . and the Council Directive 'on the implementation of the principle of equal treatment for men and women as regards access to employment, vocational training and promotion, and working conditions'. All but [*one of the*

---

[44] *R* v *Ministry of Defence, ex parte Smith* [1995] 4 All ER 427.

applicants] seek reinstatement in the services; [*the other*] seeks compensation only. . . .

All four applicants had exemplary service records. Some of the reports before us are truly in the most glowing terms. In none of these cases was it suggested that the applicant's sexual orientation had in any way affected their ability to carry out their work or had any ill effect on discipline. The sexual orientation of two or three of them had been known to or suspected by their colleagues without it making the least difference to their working relationship.

After reviewing the law and the facts Simon Brown went on:

There can be no doubting the importance of the competing public interest advanced by the minister as justifying this policy: the delivery of an operationally efficient and effective fighting force. The real question becomes: is it reasonable for the minister to take the view that allowing homosexuals into the forces would imperil that interest? Is that, in short, a coherent view, right or wrong? I have already said enough to indicate my own opinion that it is a wrong view, a view that rests too firmly upon the supposition of prejudice in others and which insufficiently recognises the damage to human rights inflicted. But can it properly be stigmatised as irrational? We live in changing times. That was expressly recognised both by the select committee in its report and by the Prime Minister in July 1991. It is only recently that many of the other armed forces who do now admit homosexuals came to adopt their present policies. [*Counsel for the Crown*] submits that the full impact of these changes abroad is not yet apparent; their wisdom has still to be demonstrated. When exactly can this policy be said to have become irrational?

I do not pretend to have found this an easy case. On the contrary I recall none harder.

The protection of human rights is, [*counsel for the applicants*] submits, a matter with which the courts are particularly concerned and for which they have an undoubted responsibility. So they do. But they owe a duty too to remain within their constitutional bounds and not trespass beyond them. Only if it were plain beyond sensible argument that no conceivable damage could be done to the armed services as a fighting unit would it be appropriate for this court now to remove the issue entirely from the hands both of the military and of the government. If the Convention were part of our law and we were accordingly entitled to ask whether the policy answers a pressing social need and whether the restriction on human rights involved can be shown proportionate to its benefits, then clearly the primary judgment (subject only to a limited 'margin of appreciation') would be for us and not others: the constitutional balance would shift. But that is not the position. In exercising merely a secondary judgment, this court is bound, even though adjudicating in a human rights context, to act with some reticence. Our approach must reflect, not overlook, where responsibility ultimately lies for the defence of the realm, and recognise too that Parliament is exercising a continuing supervision over this area of prerogative power.

With all these considerations in mind, I have come finally to the conclusion that, my own view of the evidence notwithstanding, the minister's stance cannot properly be held unlawful. His suggested justification for the ban may to many seem unconvincing; to say, however, that it is outrageous in its defiance of logic is another thing. There is, I conclude, still room for two views. Similarly it is difficult to regard the policy as wholly incompatible with 'accepted moral standards'. There is no present uniformity of outlook on this issue: not everyone would condemn the ban on moral grounds, morally neutral though the ministry avow their own stance to be.

It follows from all this that I for my part would refuse these applications albeit with hesitation and regret. I conclude that the decision upon the future of this policy must still properly rest with others, notably the government and Parliament. But I make no secret of this: that my greatest concern in leaving the matter in this way is lest the policy's human rights dimension becomes depreciated once the court's doors are closed. There is little in the papers before us to instil confidence that the fundamental human rights of these applicants and others like them will be fully and faithfully recognised elsewhere....

It is not I think inappropriate in those circumstances for this court now to urge the respondent to examine the policy afresh in the light of changing attitudes and circumstances, investigating as thoroughly as may be the experience of those who have lifted their own bans. Can our forces' present discrimination really be justified in a forum alive to the human rights considerations? That I trust is a question which the Defence Council, the ministry, and the select committee will all wish to keep under close and regular review....

It follows from all this that, despite my great sympathy for these applicants, their claims must fail. There will, I know, be those who think this judgment pusillanimous. There will be others who think that in the course of it I have stepped beyond the bounds of permissible judicial comment. Naturally I disagree with both. I believe that the ministry are properly entitled to succeed on the challenge, but I believe equally that the applicants are entitled to know my personal views on the merits; after all, had we found the Directive applicable, the merits would have been determinative of the challenge.

Whether our conclusions are right or wrong, of one thing we may be sure: ours are unlikely to be the last words on this difficult subject.

The privacy of the torture chamber

To what extent should society be prepared to tolerate deviant sexual practices? Sadistic cruelty towards innocent victims must clearly be a crime, but what of violence inflicted for sexual pleasure on others with their consent?

This question reached the House of Lords in 1993.[45] Its resolution was not assisted by the fact that the law of criminal violence laboured, as it still does, under a long outdated statute.

The appellants were a group of homosexual men of a sadomaso-chistic disposition. Their activities took place at various locations where they had installed 'torture chambers' for the giving and receiving of pain by means that most people would regard as bizarre. Their activities were recorded on video and distributed only among other members of the group. They were charged with offences of assault occasioning actual bodily harm and unlawful wounding. Upon conviction at the Old Bailey sentences of up to 12 months' imprisonment were imposed on the defendants, from which they appealed unsuccessfully to the Court of Appeal. The basis of their appeals was that the offences charged did not extend to acts carried out in private with the consent of the victim.

A subsequent appeal to the House of Lords was also unsuccessful, but in a far-ranging speech of dissent Lord Mustill made the following case for acquittal which is as notable for its eloquence as its learning.[46]

My Lords, this is a case about the criminal law of violence. In my opinion it should be a case about the criminal law of private sexual relations, if about

[45] *R v Brown* [1993] 2 All ER 75.
[46] [1993] 2 All ER 75, 101.

anything at all. Right or wrong, the point is easily made. The speeches already delivered contain summaries of the conduct giving rise to the charges under the Offences against the Person Act 1861 now before the House, together with other charges in respect of which the appellants have been sentenced, and no longer appeal. Fortunately for the reader my Lords have not gone on to describe other aspects of the appellants' behaviour of a similar but more extreme kind which was not the subject of any charge on the indictment. It is sufficient to say that whatever the outsider might feel about the subject matter of the prosecutions — perhaps horror, amazement or incomprehension, perhaps sadly very few could read even a summary of the other activities without disgust. The House has been spared the video tapes, which must have been horrible. If the criminality of sexual deviation is the true ground of these proceedings, one would have expected that these above all would have been the subject of attack. Yet the picture is quite different.

The conduct of the appellants and of other co-accused was treated by the prosecuting authorities in three ways. First, there were those acts which fell squarely within the legislation governing sexual offences. These are easily overlooked, because attention has properly been concentrated on the charges which remain in dispute, but for a proper understanding of the case it is essential to keep them in view. Thus, four of the men pleaded guilty either as principals or as aiders and abettors to the charges of keeping a disorderly house. . . .

The two remaining categories of conduct comprised private acts. Some were prosecuted and are now before the House. Others, which I have mentioned, were not. If repugnance to general public sentiments of morality and propriety were the test, one would have expected proceedings in respect of the most disgusting conduct to be prosecuted with the greater vigour. Yet the opposite is the case. Why is this so? Obviously because the prosecuting authorities could find no statutory prohibition apt to cover this conduct. . . .

Conduct infringing the 1861 Act comes before the Crown Court every day. Typically it involves brutality, aggression and violence, of a kind far removed from the appellants' behaviour which, however worthy of censure, involved no animosity, no aggression, no personal rancour on the part of the person inflicting the hurt towards the recipient and no protest by the recipient. In fact, quite the reverse. Of course we must give effect to the statute if its words capture what the appellants have done, but in deciding whether this is really so it is in my opinion legitimate to assume that the choice of the 1861 Act as the basis for the relevant counts in the indictment was made only because no other statute was found which could conceivably be brought to bear upon them.

In these circumstances I find it easy to share the opinion expressed by Mr Justice Wills in a case where the accused had consensual intercourse with his wife, he knowing and she ignorant that he suffered from gonorrhoea, with the result that she was infected. The case is of general importance, since the Court for Crown Cases Reserved held that there was no offence under sections 47 and 20, since both sections required an assault, of which the wound or grievous bodily harm was the result, and that no assault was disclosed on the facts. For present purposes, however, I need only quote from the report:

> ... such considerations lead one to pause on the threshold, and inquire whether the enactment under consideration could really have been intended to apply to circumstances so completely removed from those which are usually understood when an assault is spoken of, or to deal with matters of any kind involving the sexual relation or act.

I too am led to pause on the threshold. Asking myself the same question, I cannot but give a negative answer. I therefore approach the appeal on the basis that the convictions on charges which seem to me so inapposite cannot be upheld unless the language of the statute or the logic of the decided cases positively so demand. Unfortunately, as the able arguments which we have heard so clearly demonstrate, the language of the statute is opaque, and the cases few and unhelpful. To these I now turn.

I. THE DECIDED CASES

Throughout the argument of the appeal I was attracted by an analysis on the following lines. First, one would construct a continuous spectrum of the infliction of bodily harm, with killing at one end and a trifling touch at the other. Next, with the help of reported cases one would identify the point on this spectrum at which consent ordinarily ceases to be an answer to a prosecution for inflicting harm. This could be called 'the critical level'. It would soon become plain however that this analysis is too simple and that there are certain types of special situation to which the general rule does not apply. Thus, for example, surgical treatment which requires a degree of bodily invasion well on the upper side of the critical level will nevertheless be legitimate if performed in accordance with good medical practice and with the consent of the patient. Conversely, there will be cases in which even a moderate degree of harm cannot be legitimated by consent. Accordingly, the next stage in the analysis will be to identify those situations which have been identified as special by the decided cases, and to examine them to see whether the instant case either falls within one of them or is sufficiently close for an analogy to be valid. If the answer is negative, then the court will have to decide whether simply to apply the general law simply by deciding whether the bodily harm in the case under review is above or below the critical level, or to break new ground by recognising a new special situation to which the general law does not apply.

For all the intellectual neatness of this method I must recognise that it will not do, for it imposes on the reported cases and on the diversities of human life an order which they do not possess. Thus, when one comes to map out the spectrum of ordinary consensual physical harm, to which the special situations form exceptions, it is found that the task is almost impossible, since people do not ordinarily consent to the infliction of harm. In effect, either all or almost all the instances of the consensual infliction of violence are special. They have been in the past, and will continue to be in the future, the subject of special treatment by the law.

There are other objections to a general theory of consent and violence. Thus, for example, it is too simple to speak only of consent, for it comes in various sorts. Of these, four spring immediately to mind. First, there is an express agreement to the infliction of the injury which was in the event inflicted. Next, there is express agreement to the infliction of some harm, but not to that harm which in the event was actually caused. These two categories are matched by two more, in which the recipient expressly consents not to the infliction of harm, but to engagement in an activity which creates a risk of harm; again, either the harm which actually results, or to something less. These examples do not exhaust the categories, for corresponding with each are situations of frequent occurrence in practice where the consent is not express but implied. These numerous categories are not the fruit of academic over-elaboration, but are a reflection of real life. Yet they are scarcely touched on in the cases, which just do not bear the weight of any general theory of violence and consent.

Furthermore, when one examines the situations which are said to found such a theory it is seen that the idea of consent as the foundation of a defence has in many cases been forced on to the theory, whereas in reality the reason why the perpetrator of the harm is not liable is not because of the recipient's consent, but because the perpetrator has acted in a situation where the consent of the recipient forms one, but only one, of the elements which make the act legitimate.

I have considered whether there is some common feature of those cases in which consent has been held ineffectual whose presence or absence will furnish an immediate solution when the court is faced with a new situation. The only touchstone of this kind suggested in argument was the notion of 'hostility' without which no offence of violence can be made out. This argument, which equates hostility with antagonism, is attractive because antagonism felt by the perpetrator against the recipient, and expressed in terms of violence, is present in the great majority of the offences dealt with by the courts under the 1861 Act. Nevertheless I cannot accept it as a statement of the existing law which leads automatically to a conclusion on the present appeals. It is true that [counsel] was able to cite a series of cases on indecent conduct with consenting children, in which the absence of hostility formed a ground for holding that indecent assaults were not proved. It is however clear to my mind that whatever precise meaning the word was intended to bear in the judgments there delivered it must have been different from the one for which [counsel] now contends. The facts were far removed from the present, for the accused persons did nothing to the children but merely persuaded them to do certain acts. They used no force, nor inflicted any physical harm. It is not surprising that no assault was made out, and the decisions do no more than furnish a useful reminder of the care to be taken before punishing repugnant sexual conduct under laws aimed at violence.

Furthermore this theory does not fit the situations at the upper end of the scale. The doctor who hastens the end of a patient to terminate his agony acts with the best intentions, and quite without hostility to him in any ordinary sense of the word, yet there is no doubt that notwithstanding the patient's consent he is guilty of murder. Nor has it been questioned on the argument of the present appeal that someone who inflicts serious harm, because (for example) he is inspired by a belief in the efficacy of a pseudo-medical treatment, or acts in conformity with some extreme religious tenet, is guilty of an offence notwithstanding that he is inspired only by a desire to do the best he can for the recipient. Hostility cannot, as it seems to me, be the crucial factor which in itself determines guilt or innocence, although its presence or absence may be relevant when the court has to decide as a matter of policy how to react to a new situation.

I thus see no alternative but to adopt a much narrower and more empirical approach, by looking at the situations in which the recipient consents or is deemed to consent to the infliction of violence upon him, to see whether the decided cases teach us how to react to this new challenge. I will take them in turn.

1. Death

With the exception of a few exotic specimens which have never come before the courts, euthanasia is in practice the only situation where the recipient expressly consents to being killed As the law stands today, consensual killing is murder. Why is this so? Professor Glanville Williams suggests that the arguments in support are transcendental, and I agree. Believer or atheist, the observer grants to the maintenance of human life an overriding imperative, so strong as to outweigh any consent to its termination. Some believers and some atheists now dissent from this view, but the controversy as to the position at common law does not illuminate our present task, which is to interpret a statute which is aimed at non-lethal violence.

Nor is anything gained by a study of duelling, an activity in which the recipient did not consent to being killed (quite the reverse) but did consent to running the risk. The nineteenth-century authorities were not too concerned to argue the criminality of the practice as between principals, but to stamp out this social evil by involving in the criminality those others, such as seconds and surgeons, who helped to perpetuate it. A series of nineteenth century cases ... reiterated that the dueller who inflicted the fatal wound was guilty of murder, whether he was the challenger or not, and regardless of the fact that the deceased willingly took the risk, but by then it was already very old law — certainly as old as *R* v *Taverner* where Chief Justice Coke and Mr Justice Croke expounded the heinousness of the offence with copious reference to the ancients and to Holy Scripture. Killing in cold blood was the sin of Cain, and that was that.

There is nothing to help us here.

2. *Maiming*

The act of maiming consisted of 'such a hurt of any part of a man's body whereby he is rendered less able, in fighting, either to defend himself or to annoy his adversary'. Maiming was a felony at common law. Self-maiming was also a crime, and consent was no defence to maiming by another. Maiming was also, in certain circumstances, a statutory offence under a series of Acts, now repealed, beginning with the so-called 'Coventry Act' (maiming), and continuing as part of a more general prohibition of serious offences against the person until an 1803 Act. Then it seems to have disappeared. There is no record of anyone being indicted for maim in modern times, and I doubt whether maiming would have been mentioned in the present case but for the high authority of Sir James Fitzjames Stephen, who as late as 1883 stated: 'Every one has a right to consent to the infliction upon himself of bodily harm not amounting to a maim'. No reported decision or statute was cited in support of this proposition, and the reasoning (according to a footnote) rested upon the assertion that below the level of maiming an injury was no more than an assault, to which consent was a defence.

My Lords, I cannot accept that this antique crime any longer marks a watershed for the interrelation of violence and consent. In the first place the crime is obsolete. The 1861 Act says nothing about it, as it must have done if Parliament had intended to perpetuate maiming as a special category of offence. Furthermore, the rationale of maiming as a distinct offence is now quite out of date. Apparently the permanent disablement of an adult male was criminal because it cancelled him as a fighting unit in the service of his King. I think it impossible to apply this reasoning to the present case.

Finally, the practical results of holding that maim marks the level at which consent ceases to be relevant seem to me quite unacceptable. The point cannot be better made than in terms of the only illustration given by Mr Justice Stephen: 'It is a maim to strike out a front tooth. It is not a maim to cut off a man's nose.' Evidently consent would be a defence in the latter instance, but not in the former. This is not in my view a sound basis for a modern law of violence.

3. Prize-fighting, sparring and boxing

Far removed as it is from the present appeal, I must take a little time over prize-fighting, for it furnishes in *R* v *Coney* one of the very few extended judicial analyses of the relationship between violence and consent. . . . Even at first sight it is clear that this decision involved something out of the ordinary, for the accused were charged, not with any of the serious offences of violence under the 1861 Act but with common assault; and as all concerned in the argument of the present appeal have agreed, in common with the judges in *R* v *Coney* itself, consent is usually a defence to such a charge. . . .

Sir Michael Foster distinguished beneficial recreations such as single stick fighting from:

prize-fighting and . . . other exertions of courage, strength and activity which are exhibited for lucre, and can serve no valuable purpose but on the contrary encourage a spirit of idleness and debauchery.

Thus, although consent is present in both cases the risks of serious violence and public disorder make prize-fighting something which 'the law says shall not be done', whereas the lesser risk of injury, the absence of the public disorder, the improvement of the health and skills of the participants, and the consequent benefit to the public at large combine to place sparring into a different category, which the law says 'may be done'.

That the court is in such cases making a value judgment, not dependent upon any general theory of consent is exposed by the failure of any attempt to deduce why professional boxing appears to be immune from prosecution. For money, not recreation or personal improvement, each boxer tries to hurt the opponent more than he is hurt himself, and aims to end the contest prematurely by inflicting brain injury serious enough to make the opponent unconscious, or temporarily by impairing his central nervous system through a blow to the midriff, or cutting his skin to a degree which would ordinarily be well within the scope of section 20 of the 1861 Act. The boxers display skill, strength and courage, but nobody pretends that they do good to themselves or others. The onlookers derive entertainment, but none of the physical and moral benefits which have been seen as the fruits of engagement in manly sports.... It is in my judgment best to regard this as another special situation which for the time being stands outside the ordinary law of violence because society chooses to tolerate it.

4. 'Contact' sports

Some sports, such as the various codes of football, have deliberate bodily contact as an essential element. They lie at a mid-point between fighting, where the participant knows that his opponent will try to harm him, and the milder sports where there is at most an acknowledgement that someone may be accidentally hurt. In the contact sports each player knows and by taking part agrees that an opponent may from time to time inflict upon his body (for example by a rugby tackle) what would otherwise be a painful battery. By taking part he also assumes the risk that the deliberate contact may have unintended effects, conceivably of sufficient severity to amount to grievous bodily harm. But he does not agree that this more serious kind of injury may be inflicted deliberately. This simple analysis conceals a number of difficult problems, which are discussed in a series of Canadian decisions....

The courts appear to have started with the proposition that some level of violence is lawful if the recipient agrees to it, and have dealt with the question of excessive violence by inquiring whether the recipient could really have tacitly accepted a risk of violence at the level which actually occurred. These decisions do not help us in the present appeal, where the consent of the recipients was express, and where it is known that they gladly agreed, not simply to some degree of harm, but to everything that was done. What we need to know is whether, notwithstanding the recipient's implied consent, there comes a point at which it is too severe for the law to tolerate. Whilst common sense suggests that this must be so, and that the law will not license brutality under the name of sport, one of the very few reported indications of the point at which tolerable harm becomes intolerable violence is in the direction to the jury given by Mr Justice Bramwell that the act (in this case a charge at football) would be unlawful if intended to cause 'serious hurt'. This accords with my own instinct, but I must recognise that a direction at *nisi prius*, even by a great judge, cannot be given the same weight as a judgment on appeal consequent upon full argument and reflection....

5. *Surgery*

Many of the acts done by surgeons would be very serious crimes if done by anyone else, and yet the surgeons incur no liability. Actual consent, or the substitute for consent deemed by the law to exist where an emergency creates a need for action, is an essential element in this immunity; but it cannot be a direct explanation for it, since much of the bodily invasion involved in surgery lies well above any point at which consent could even arguably be regarded as furnishing a defence. Why is this so? The answer must in my opinion be that proper medical treatment, for which actual or deemed consent is a prerequisite, is in a category of its own.

6. *Lawful correction*

It is probably still the position at common law, as distinct from statute, that a parent or someone to whom the parent has delegated authority may inflict physical hurt on his or her child, provided that it does not go too far and is for the purpose of correction and not the gratification of passion or rage.... These cases have nothing to do with consent, and are useful only as another demonstration that specially exempt situations can exist and that they can involve an upper limit of tolerable harm.

7. *Dangerous pastimes; bravado; mortification*

For the sake of completeness I should mention that the list of situations in which one person may agree to the infliction of harm, or to the risk of infliction of harm, by another includes dangerous pastimes, bravado (as where a boastful man challenges another to try to hurt him with a blow) and religious mortification. These examples have little in common with one another and even less with the present case. They do not appear to be discussed in the authorities although dangerous pastimes are briefly mentioned and I see no advantage in exploring them here.

8. *Rough horseplay*

The law recognises that community life (and particularly male community life), such as exists in the school playground, in the barrack-room and on the factory floor, may involve a mutual risk of deliberate physical contact in which a particular recipient (or even an outsider) may come off worst, and that the criminal law cannot be too tender about the susceptibilities of those involved. I think it hopeless to attempt any explanation in terms of consent.... it appears to me that as a matter of policy the courts have decided that the criminal law does not concern itself with these activities, provided that they do not go too far. It also seems plain that as the general social appreciation of what is tolerable and of the proper role of the State in regulating the lives of individuals changes with the passage of time, so we shall expect to find that the assumptions of the criminal justice system about what types of conduct are properly excluded from its scope, and about what is meant by going 'too far', will not remain constant.

9. Prostitution

Prostitution may well be the commonest occasion for the voluntary acceptance of the certainty, as distinct from the risk, of bodily harm. It is very different from the present case. There is no pretence of mutual affection. The prostitute, as beater or beaten, does it for money. The dearth of reported decisions on the application of the 1861 Act clearly shows how the prosecuting authorities have (rightly in my view) tended to deal with such cases, if at all, as offences against public order.... The law simply treats some acts as criminal per se irrespective of consent.

10. Fighting

I doubt whether it is possible to give a complete list of the situations where it is conceivable that one person will consent to the infliction of physical hurt by another, but apart from those already mentioned only one seems worth considering namely what one may call 'ordinary' fighting. Perhaps it is unduly complicated to suggest that the public interest might annul the defence of consent in certain situations and then in the shape of 'good reason' recreate it. Nevertheless I am very willing to recognise that the public interest may sometimes operate in one direction and sometimes in the other. But even if it be correct that fighting in private to settle a quarrel is so much against the public interest as to make it automatically criminal even if the fighter is charged only with assault (a proposition which I would wish to examine more closely should the occasion arise), I cannot accept that the infliction of bodily harm, and especially the private infliction of it, is invariably criminal absent some special factor which decrees otherwise. I prefer to address each individual category of consensual violence in the light of the situation as a whole. Sometimes the element of consent will make no difference and sometimes it will make all the difference. Circumstances must alter cases. For these reasons I consider that the House is free, as the Court of Appeal in the present case was not, to consider entirely afresh whether the public interest demands the interpretation of the 1861 Act in such a way as to render criminal the acts done by the appellants.

II. AN UNLAWFUL ACT

I can find nothing in [the old cases] to suggest that the consensual infliction of hurt is transmuted into an offence of violence simply because it is chargeable as another offence. Even in the prize-fighting cases, which come closest to this idea, the tendency of these events to attract a disorderly crowd was relevant not because the fighters might have been charged, if anyone had cared to do so, with the separate offence of causing a breach of the peace, but rather because this factor was a reason why the events were placed as a matter of policy in a category which the law treated as being in itself intrinsically unlawful notwithstanding the presence of consent. I am satisfied that it was in this sense that the courts made reference to the unlawfulness of the conduct under examination, and not to its criminality *aliunde*.

III.   THE EUROPEAN CONVENTION ON HUMAN RIGHTS

The appellants relied on the Convention for the Protection of Human Rights and Fundamental Freedoms for two reasons. First, because it was said to support an argument that the law as it now stood should be interpreted or developed in a sense favourable to the appellants, and, secondly, because in the event of failure before the House the appellants intend to pursue the matter before the European Court of Human Rights, and for this purpose must show that their local remedies have been exhausted....

[*Lord Mustill went on to describe the argument from the right of privacy as, altogether, more substantial.*] Not of course because the enunciation of a qualified right of privacy in article 8 leads inexorably to a conclusion in the appellants' favour, since even after all these years the United Kingdom has still failed to comply with its treaty obligation to enact the Convention. Nor because I consider that the individual provisions of the Convention will always point unequivocally to the right answer in a particular case. Far from it. Emphasis on human duties will often yield a more balanced and sharply focused protection for the individual than the contemporary preoccupation with human rights. The sonorous norms of the Convention, valuable as they unquestionably are in recalling errant States to their basic obligations of decency towards those in their power, are often at the same time too general and too particular to permit a reasoned analysis of new and difficult problems. Article 8 provides a good example.

The jurisprudence with which this article, in common with other terms of the Convention, is rapidly becoming encrusted shows that in order to condemn acts which appear worthy of censure they have had to be forced into the mould of article 8, and referred to the concept of privacy, for want of any other provision which will serve. I do not deny that the privacy of the conduct was an important element in the present case, but I cannot accept that this fact on its own can yield an answer.

Nevertheless, I believe that the general tenor of the decisions of the European Court of Human Rights does furnish valuable guidance on the approach which the English courts should adopt, if free to do so, and I take heart from the fact that the European authorities, balancing the personal considerations invoked by article 8(1) against the public interest considerations called up by article 8(2), clearly favour the right of the appellants to conduct their private lives undisturbed by the criminal law: a conclusion at which I have independently arrived for reasons which I must now state.

IV. PUBLIC POLICY

The purpose of this long discussion has been to suggest that the decks are clear for the House to tackle completely anew the question whether the public interest requires section 47 of the 1861 Act to be interpreted as penalising an infliction of harm which is at the level of actual bodily harm, but not grievous bodily harm; which is inflicted in private (by which I mean that it is exposed to the view only of those who have chosen to view it); which takes place not only with the consent of the recipient but with his willing and glad cooperation; which is inflicted for the gratification of sexual desire, and not in a spirit of animosity or rage; and which is not engaged in for profit.

My Lords, I have stated the issue in these terms to stress two considerations of cardinal importance. Lawyers will need no reminding of the first, but since this prosecution has been widely noticed it must be emphasised that the issue before the House is not whether the appellants' conduct is morally right, but whether it is properly charged under the 1861 Act. When proposing that the conduct is not rightly so charged I do not invite your Lordships' House to endorse it as morally acceptable. Nor do I pronounce in favour of a libertarian doctrine specifically related to sexual matters. Nor in the least do I suggest that ethical pronouncements are meaningless, that there is no difference between right and wrong, that sadism is praiseworthy, or that new opinions on sexual morality are necessarily superior to the old, or anything else of the same kind. What I do say is that these are questions of private morality; that the standards by which they fall to be judged are not those of the criminal law; and that if these standards are to be upheld the individual must enforce them upon himself according to his own moral standards, or have them enforced against him by moral pressures exerted by whatever religious or other community to whose ethical ideals he responds.

The point from which I invite your Lordships to depart is simply this, that the State should interfere with the rights of an individual to live his or her life as he or she may choose no more than is necessary to ensure a proper balance between the special interests of the individual and the general interests of the individuals who together comprise the populace at large. Thus, whilst acknowledging that very many people, if asked whether the appellants' conduct was wrong, would reply 'Yes, repulsively wrong', I would at the same time assert that this does not in itself mean that the prosecution of the appellants under the Offences against the Person Act 1861 is well founded.

This point leads directly to the second. As I have ventured to formulate the crucial question, it asks whether there is good reason to impress upon section 47 an interpretation which penalises the relevant level of harm irrespective of consent: to recognise sadomasochistic activities as falling into a special category of acts, such as duelling and prize-fighting, which 'the law says shall not be done'. This is very important, for if the question were differently stated it might well yield a different answer. In particular, if it were to be held that as a matter of law all infliction of bodily harm above the level of common assault is incapable of being legitimated by consent, except in special circumstances, then we would have to consider whether the public interest required the recognition of private sexual activities as being in a specially exempt category. This would be an altogether more difficult question and one which I would not be prepared to answer in favour of the appellants, not because I do not have my own opinions upon it but because I regard the task as one which the courts are not suited to perform, and which should be carried out, if at all, by Parliament after a thorough review of all the medical, social, moral and political issues, such as was performed by the Wolfenden Committee.[47] ...

Let it be assumed however that we should embark upon this question. I ask myself, not whether as a result of the decision in this appeal, activities such as those of the appellants should cease to be criminal, but rather whether the 1861 Act (a statute which I venture to repeat once again was clearly intended to penalise conduct of a quite different nature) should in this new situation be interpreted so as to make it criminal. Why should this step be taken? Leaving aside repugnance and moral objection, both of which are entirely natural but neither of which are in my opinion grounds upon which the court could properly create a new crime, I can visualise only the following reasons.

(1) Some of the practices obviously created a risk of genito-urinary infection, and others of septicaemia. These might indeed have been grave in former times, but the risk of serious harm must surely have been greatly reduced by modern medical science.

(2) The possibility that matters might get out of hand, with grave results. It has been acknowledged throughout the present proceedings that the appellants' activities were performed as a prearranged ritual, which at the same

---

[47] Report of the Committee on Homosexual Offences and Prostitution (Cmnd 247, 1957).

time enhanced their excitement and minimised the risk that the infliction of injury would go too far. Of course things might go wrong and really serious injury or death might ensue. If this happened, those responsible would be punished according to the ordinary law, in the same way as those who kill or injure in the course of more ordinary sexual activities are regularly punished. But to penalise the appellants' conduct even if the extreme consequences do not ensue, just because they might have done so, would require an assessment of the degree of risk, and the balancing of this risk against the interests of individual freedom. Such a balancing is in my opinion for Parliament, not the courts; and even if your Lordships' House were to embark upon it the attempt must in my opinion fail at the outset for there is no evidence at all of the seriousness of the hazards to which sadomasochistic conduct of this kind gives rise....

(3)   I would give the same answer to the suggestion that these activities involved a risk of accelerating the spread of acquired immune deficiency syndrome (AIDS), and that they should be brought within the 1861 Act in the interests of public health. The consequence would be strange, since what is currently the principal cause for the transmission of this scourge, namely consenting buggery between males, is now legal. Nevertheless, I would have been compelled to give this proposition the most anxious consideration if there had been any evidence to support it. But there is none, since the case for the Crown was advanced on an entirely different ground.

(4)   There remains an argument to which I have given much greater weight. As the evidence in the present case has shown, there is a risk that strangers (and especially young strangers) may be drawn into these activities at an early age and will then become established in them for life. This is indeed a disturbing prospect, but I have come to the conclusion that it is not a sufficient ground for declaring these activities to be criminal under the 1861 Act. The element of the corruption of youth is already catered for by the existing legislation; and if there is a gap in it which needs to be filled the remedy surely lies in the hands of Parliament, not in the application of a statute which is aimed at other forms of wrongdoing. As regards proselytisation for adult sadomasochism the argument appears to me circular. For if the activity is not itself so much against the public interest that it ought to be declared criminal under the 1861 Act then the risk that others will be induced to join in cannot be a ground for making it criminal.

Leaving aside the logic of this answer, which seems to me impregnable, plain humanity demands that a court addressing the criminality of conduct such as that of the present should recognise and respond to the profound dismay which all members of the community share about the apparent increase of cruel and senseless crimes against the defenceless. Whilst doing so I must repeat for the last time that in the answer which I propose I do not advocate the decriminalisation of conduct which has hitherto been a crime; nor do I rebut a submission that a new crime should be created, penalising this conduct. The only question is whether these consensual private acts are offences against the existing law of violence. To this question I return a negative response.

> *Notwithstanding this persuasive address the majority view of the House of Lords has since been confirmed by the European Court of Human Rights.*[48]

---

[48] *Laskey v United Kingdom* (1997) 24 **EHRR** 39.

The Royal Courts of Justice

4. THE GOLDEN THREAD

or

The Law and the Accused

Our Government is the potent, the omnipresent teacher. For
good or for ill, it teaches the whole people by its example. Crime
is contagious. If the Government becomes a lawbreaker, it
breeds contempt for law; it invites every man to become a law
unto himself; it invites anarchy. To declare that, in the
administration of the criminal law, the end justifies the means —
to declare that the Government may commit crimes in order to
secure the conviction of a private criminal — would bring terrible
retribution. Against that pernicious doctrine this Court should
resolutely set its face.

Mr Justice Brandeis in *Olmstead* v *United States*.[49]

The golden thread
The charge to the jury
The wisdom as well as the mercy of the law
The right to be let alone
The feel of freedom
No source of pride
The ignoble shortcut

---

[49] See under *The right to be let alone*. This dictum is often cited. Bizarrely, while this book was
being prepared it was quoted to the court by Timothy McVeigh before he was sentenced for the
Atlanta bombing.

No one stands in greater need of the protection of the law than a person accused of crime. On the one hand is the full panoply of the State — or its instrument in the form of the prosecution (which in England is called the Crown and in America the People) — and on the other the private individual, whose resources may be minuscule by comparison and whose integrity has inevitably been put in question simply by the fact of his being accused by a credible authority.

For these reasons the common law has developed a battery of safeguards against the possibility of injustice. Probably the best known of these is the rule that the burden of proof lies on the prosecutor. The classic statement of this rule was made in the House of Lords in an appeal arising from a tantalisingly ambiguous murder case (See under The golden thread *).*

As important as the burden of proof is the standard of proof, that is to say the extent to which in a criminal trial the prosecution have to prove their case. It is vital that juries should be clearly advised on this issue and in language that they understand. A fine example of such advice is that of Geoffrey Lawrence, when at the Bar, in the case of a doctor accused of murdering his patients (The charge to the jury *).*

It is only right that the guardians of the law should seek to use every means they can to obtain proof of crime, but even this activity has to be controlled lest it should be abused. In the eighteenth century a practice grew up whereby the Secretary of State would issue what became known as a general warrant, under which his officers were authorised to enter the premises of persons suspected of crime and to search for and remove papers that might incriminate them. There was no legal authority for this practice and when it came before the court Lord Camden had no hesitation in striking it down (The wisdom as well as the mercy of the law *).*

The force of this judgment was such that it is still quoted with approval on both sides of the Atlantic. As, for example, by Mr Justice Brandeis when he could not accept the decision of a majority of his colleagues on the United States Supreme Court in admitting evidence which had been obtained as a result of telephone tapping (The right to be let alone *).*

*A similar rejection of State necessity was made by Chief Judge Learned Hand in another case involving telephone tapping (*The feel of freedom*). Overruling the decision of a lower court, he held that it was wrong to deny a woman accused of conspiracy the name of her informant.*

Phone tapping is also the subject of another extract in this chapter — by far the longest. Although the lack of legislation on tapping, to which Sir Robert Megarry drew attention, has since been remedied, his judgment is still relevant for a number of reasons. As well as examining American, German and European law on this subject, Sir Robert pointed out the limitations of judges as law makers. In relation to the debate concerning the value of a written constitution it is worth noting his observation that, 'England ... is not a country where everything is forbidden except what is expressly permitted: it is a country where everything is permitted except what is expressly forbidden.' *(*No source of pride*).*

*One of the most marked contrasts between the criminal jurisprudence of this country and that of the United States lies in their different approaches to misconduct on the part of the prosecution. In America evidence obtained as a result of police wrongdoing is hidden from the jury as the 'fruit of the poisoned tree' (*The ignoble shortcut*). In this country the approach is more relaxed on the ground that there are equally effective ways of punishing police misbehaviour without excluding logically relevant evidence. (It is sometimes forgotten that the acquittal of the guilty is as much an injustice as the conviction of the innocent.)*

The golden thread

A higher burden of proof rests upon the prosecutor in a criminal trial than upon the plaintiff in civil proceedings. Exactly what that burden is was authoritatively defined in a case arising out of events in a Dorset farmhouse in 1936.

Reginald Woolmington was a farm labourer in his early twenties married to Violet, a woman of similar age. Following disagreements, his wife left him and went back to live with her mother. Reginald was upset and went to see Violet with a gun. His story was that he intended to threaten to kill himself if she did not agree to return to him but that the gun had gone off accidentally. Whatever the truth of the matter it ended with Violet dead on the mat, shot through the heart. Reginald was convicted at Bristol Assizes before Mr Justice Swift and appealed, unsuccessfully, to the Court of Appeal. He then went to the House of Lords, who allowed his appeal on the basis of a misdirection on the part of the trial judge. The Lord Chancellor, Lord Sankey, made this memorable statement of the law:[50]

Throughout the web of the English criminal law one golden thread is always to be seen, that it is the duty of the prosecution to prove the prisoner's guilt subject to what I have already said as to the defence of insanity and subject also to any statutory exception. If, at the end of and on the whole of the case, there is a reasonable doubt, created by the evidence given by either the prosecution or the prisoner, as to whether the prisoner killed the deceased with a malicious intention, the prosecution has not made out the case and the prisoner is entitled to an acquittal. No matter what the charge or where the trial, the principle that the prosecution must prove the guilt of the prisoner is part of the common law of England and no attempt to whittle it down can be entertained.

Mr Justice Swift's error had been in following Archbold, *the leading textbook on the criminal law. The passage in question had apparently been penned by Mr Justice Avory, who was one of the members of the Court of Appeal which had upheld the judge's direction.*

The charge to the jury

Guidance for the jury on the standard of proof in a criminal trial is something that has to be undertaken with great care, as the trial for murder of Dr Bodkin Adams demonstrated. In the words of Mr Eric Crowther:[51]

The Times newspaper commented that never once during that protracted case did defending counsel, Geoffrey Lawrence QC (afterwards a High Court judge)

---

[50] *Woolmington v Director of Public Prosecutions* [1935] AC 462, 481.
[51] *Advocacy for the Advocate* (Barry Rose Publishers).

raise his voice. This is how Lawrence dealt with the burden of proof in his closing address to the jury. Note the cadence in his submissions:

> Justice is of paramount consideration here, and the only way in which this can be done is for you to judge the matter on what you have heard in this court and in this court only.
>
> What you read in the papers, what you hear in the train, what you hear in the cafés and restaurants, what your friends and relations come and tell you; rumour, gossip, all the rest of it, may be so wrong.
>
> The possibility of guilt is not enough, suspicion is not enough, probability is not enough, likelihood is not. A criminal matter is not a question of balancing probabilities and deciding in favour of a probability.
>
> If the accusation is not proved beyond reasonable doubt against the man accused in the dock, then by law he is entitled to be acquitted, because that is the way our rules work. It is no concession to give him the benefit of the doubt. He is entitled by law to a verdict of not guilty.

Lawrence had taken the bold decision not to call Dr Adams to give evidence. Nevertheless, the defendant was acquitted of murder by the jury after only a short retirement. Some part of the credit for this result must be attributed to counsel's thorough and penetrating closing speech.

The wisdom as well as the mercy of the law

Before a case can get to trial the prosecution must gather evidence of the defendant's guilt and for this purpose may need powers beyond the ordinary. An eighteenth-century case taught us that these powers need to be carefully regulated.

Radical politics were rife in the eighteenth century, when people like John Wilkes published their views in pamphlet form. One such pamphlet was The Monitor, or British Freeholder. *The Secretary of State took the view that this journal contained seditious matter and issued a warrant to search a house at Westminster, the home of a Mr Entick, the publisher's clerk. Armed with this warrant Carrington, a King's Messenger, and three of his colleagues conducted a four-hour search and removed papers. Entick subsequently brought an action for trespass against the Secretary of State and was awarded £300 in damages.*[52] *The jury had returned what is called a special verdict, finding that the defendants had acted on the authority of the Secretary of State. Such warrants, they found, had frequently been granted by Secretaries of State since the Glorious Revolution of 1688 and had never been controverted.*

Lord Camden, Chief Justice of the Court of Common Pleas, thought it time that they were. In a judgment for the plaintiff which was to echo down the years he said:

The great end for which men entered into society, was to secure their property. That right is preserved sacred and incommunicable in all instances, where it has not been taken away or abridged by some public law for the good of the whole. The cases where this right of property is set aside by positive law, are various. Distresses, executions, forfeitures, taxes, &c. are all of this description; wherein every man by common consent gives up that right for the sake of justice and the general good. By the laws of England every invasion of private property, be it ever so minute, is a trespass. No man can set his foot upon my ground without my licence, but he is liable to an action, though the damage be nothing; which is proved by every declaration in trespass, where the defendant is called upon to answer for bruising the grass and even treading upon the soil. If he admits the fact, he is bound to show by way of justification that some positive law has empowered or excused him. The justification is submitted to the judges who are to look into the books; and if such a justification can be maintained by the text of the statute law, or by the principles of common law. If no such excuse can be found or produced, the silence of the books is an authority against the defendant, and the plaintiff must have judgment.

According to this reasoning, it is now incumbent upon the defendants to show the law, by which this seizure is warranted. If that cannot be done, it is a trespass.

Papers are the owner's goods and chattels: they are his dearest property; and are so far from enduring a seizure, that they will hardly bear an inspection; and though the eye cannot by the laws of England be guilty of a trespass, yet where private papers are removed and carried away, the secret nature of those goods will be an aggravation of the trespass, and demand more considerable damages in that respect. Where is the written law that gives any magistrate such a power? I can safely answer, there is none; and therefore it is too much for us without

---

[52] *Entick* v *Carrington* (1765) 19 St Tr 1029, the full text of which was said to have been preserved in the unusual circumstances described in the *State Trials* report. Another report at 2 Wils KB 275 (which some consider more authentic) omits much of the text in the earlier report.

such authority to pronounce a practice legal, which would be subversive of all the comforts of society.

After rejecting as misleading the analogy of the power to issue a warrant to search and seize stolen goods Camden went on:

What would the Parliament say, if the judges should take upon themselves to mould an unlawful power into a convenient authority, by new restrictions? That would be, not judgment, but legislation.

I come now to the practice since the Revolution [*of 1688*], which has been strongly urged, with this emphatical addition, that an usage tolerated from the era of liberty, and continued downwards to this time through the best ages of the constitution, must necessarily have a legal commencement. Now, though that pretence can have no place in the question made by this plea, because no such practice is there alleged; yet I will permit the defendant for the present to borrow a fact from the special verdict, for the sake of giving it an answer.

Past practice no justification

If the practice began then, it began too late to be law now. If it was more ancient, the Revolution is not to answer for it; and I could have wished, that upon this occasion the Revolution had not been considered as the only basis of our liberty.

The Revolution restored this constitution to its first principles. It did no more. It did not enlarge the liberty of the subject; but gave it a better security. It neither widened nor contracted the foundation, but repaired, and perhaps added a buttress or two to the fabric; and if any Minister of State has since deviated from the principles at that time recognized, all that I can say is, that, so far from being sanctified, they are condemned by the Revolution....

This is the first instance I have met with, where the ancient, immemorable law of the land, in a public matter, was attempted to be proved by the practice of a private office.

The names and rights of public magistrates, their power and forms of proceeding as they are settled by law, have been long since written, and are to be found in books and records. Private customs indeed are still to be sought from private tradition. But whoever conceived a notion, that any part of the public law could be buried in the obscurepractice of a particular person?

> Charles Pratt, Earl Camden, (1713–94) was successively Attorney-General, Chief Justice of the Common Pleas and (in 1776) Lord Chancellor, in which post he opposed his government's American policy. He was enobled in 1786.

To search, seize, and carry away all the papers of the subject upon the first warrant: that such a right should have existed from the time whereof the memory of man runneth not to the contrary, and never yet have found a place in any book of law; is incredible. But if so strange a thing could be supposed, I do not see, how we could declare the law upon such evidence.

But still it is insisted, that there has been a general submission, and no action brought to try the right.

I answer, there has been a submission of guilt and poverty to power and the terror of punishment. But it would be strange doctrine to assert that all the people of this land are bound to acknowledge that to be universal law, which a few criminal booksellers have been afraid to dispute....

It is then said, that it is necessary for the ends of government to lodge such a power with a State officer; and that it is better to prevent the publication before than to punish the offender afterwards. I answer, if the legislature be of that opinion, they will revive the Licensing Act. But if they have not done that, I conceive they are not of that opinion. And with respect to the argument of State necessity, or a distinction that has been aimed at between State offences and others, the common law does not understand that kind of reasoning, nor do our books take notice of any such distinctions.

Serjeant Ashley was committed to the Tower by the House of Lords only for asserting in argument, that there was a 'law of State' different from the common law; and the Ship Money judges were impeached for holding, first that State necessity would justify the raising money without consent of Parliament, and secondly that the King was judge of that necessity.

If the King himself has no power to declare when the law ought to be violated for reason of State, I am sure we his judges have no such prerogative.

Lastly, it is urged as an argument of utility, that such a search is a means of detecting offenders by discovering evidence. I wish some cases had been shown where the law forceth evidence out of the owner's custody by process. There is no process against papers in civil causes. It has been often tried, but never prevailed. Nay, where the adversary has by force or fraud got possession of your own proper evidence there is no way to get it back but by action.

In the criminal law such a proceeding was never heard of and yet there are some crimes, such for instance as murder, rape, robbery and house-breaking, to say nothing of forgery and perjury, that are more atrocious than libelling. But our law has provided no paper search in these cases to help forward the conviction.

Whether this proceedeth from the gentleness of the law towards criminals or from a consideration that such a power would be more pernicious to the innocent than useful to the public, I will not say.

No duty of self-incrimination

It is very certain, that the law obligeth no man to accuse himself; because the necessary means of compelling self-accusation, falling upon the innocent as well as the guilty, would be both cruel and unjust and it should seem, that search for evidence is disallowed upon the same principle. There too the innocent would be confounded with the guilty.

Observe the wisdom as well as the mercy of the law. The strongest evidence before a trial, being only *ex parte*, is but suspicion; it is not proof. Weak evidence is a ground of suspicion, though in a lower degree; and if suspicion at large should be a ground of search, especially in the case of libels whose house would be safe?

If, however, a right of search for the sake of discovering evidence ought in any case to be allowed, this crime above all others ought to be excepted, as wanting such a discovery less than any other. It is committed in open daylight, and in the face of the world; every act of publication makes new proof; and the Solicitor of the Treasury, if he pleases, may be the witness himself.

The Messenger of the Press, by the very constitution of his office, is directed to purchase every libel that comes forth, in order to be a witness.

Nay, if the vengeance of government requires a production of the author, it is hardly possible for him to escape the impeachment of the printer, who is sure to seal his own pardon by his discovery. But suppose he should happen to be obstinate, yet the publication is stopped, and the offence punished. By this means the law is satisfied and the public secured.

I have now taken notice of everything that has been urged upon the present point and upon the whole we are all of opinion that the warrant to seize and carry away the party's papers in the case of a seditious libel, is illegal and void.

Before I conclude I desire not to be understood as an advocate for libels. All civilised governments have punished calumny with severity; and with reason; for these compositions debauch the manners of the people; they excite a spirit of disobedience and enervate the authority of government. They provoke and excite the passions of the people against their rulers, and the rulers oftentimes against the people.

After this description I shall hardly be considered as a favourer of these pernicious productions. I will always set my face against them when they come before me; and shall recommend it most warmly to the jury always to convict when the proof is clear. They will do well to consider that unjust acquittals bring an odium upon the press itself, the consequence whereof may be fatal to liberty; for if kings and great men cannot obtain justice at their hands by the ordinary course of law, they may at last be provoked to restrain that press, which the juries of their country refuse to regulate. When licentiousness is tolerated liberty is in the utmost danger; because tyranny, bad as it is, is better than anarchy; and the worst of governments is more tolerable than no government at all.

Camden's outlawing of the general warrant was to be confirmed in America by the Fourth Amendment to that country's constitution.

The right to be let alone

Lord Camden's judgment in Entick *v* Carrington *was referred to many years later and in a different continent when the United States Supreme Court had to decide to what extent the agents of law enforcement should be permitted to eavesdrop on telephone conversations.*

In 1920 after years of campaigning by the anti-alcohol lobby the Volstead Act (the Eighteenth Amendment to the Constitution) came into force prohibiting the sale of alcohol throughout the nation. The Act was vigorously enforced and one notable conviction under it fell to be reviewed by the Supreme Court.

Evidence of a conspiracy to violate the Act had been obtained over a period of nearly five months by government officers secretly tapping the lines of a telephone company connected with the chief office and some of the residences of the accused, and thus clandestinely overhearing and recording their conversations. The tapping connections were made in the basement of a large office building and on public streets and did not involve trespass upon any property of the defendants.

The Supreme Court held that the act of admitting this evidence did not compel an accused to be a witness against himself in violation of the Fifth Amendment to the Constitution (prohibition of an accused being forced to give evidence against himself), nor did it violate the Fourth Amendment (protection against unreasonable search and seizure). But the Justices were not unanimous and in a formidable dissenting opinion Mr Justice Brandeis said:[53]

The defendants were convicted of conspiring to violate the National Prohibition Act. Before any of the persons now charged had been arrested or indicted,

---

[53] *Olmstead* v *United States*, 277 US 438 (1928).

the telephones by means of which they habitually communicated with one another and with others had been tapped by federal officers. To this end, a lineman of long experience in wiretapping was employed on behalf of the Government and at its expense. He tapped eight telephones, some in the homes of the persons charged, some in their offices. Acting on behalf of the Government and in their official capacity, at least six other prohibition agents listened over the tapped wires and reported the messages taken. Their operations extended over a period of nearly five months. The typewritten record of the notes of conversations overheard occupies 775 typewritten pages. By objections seasonably made and persistently renewed, the defendants objected to the admission of the evidence obtained by wiretapping on the ground that the Government's wiretapping constituted an unreasonable search and seizure in violation of the Fourth Amendment, and that the use as evidence of the conversations overheard compelled the defendants to be witnesses against themselves in violation of the Fifth Amendment. The Government makes no attempt to defend the methods employed by its officers. Indeed, it concedes that, if wiretapping can be deemed a search and seizure within the Fourth Amendment, such wiretapping as was practiced in the case at bar was an unreasonable search and seizure, and that the evidence thus obtained was inadmissible. But it relies on the language of the Amendment, and it claims that the protection given thereby cannot properly be held to include a telephone conversation. 'We must never forget', said Chief Justice Marshall 'that it is a constitution we are expounding.' Since then, this Court has repeatedly sustained the exercise of power by Congress, under various clauses of that instrument, over objects of which the Fathers could not have dreamed....

We have likewise held that general limitations on the powers of Government, like those embodied in the due process clauses of the Fifth and Fourteenth Amendments, do not forbid the United States or the States from meeting modern conditions by regulations which, 'a century ago, or even half a century ago, probably would have been rejected as arbitrary and oppressive'.... Clauses guaranteeing to the individual protection against specific abuses of power must have a similar capacity of adaptation to a changing world. It was with reference to such a clause that this Court said, ... 'Legislation, both statutory and constitutional, is enacted, it is true, from an experience of evils, but its general language should not, therefore, be necessarily confined to the form that evil had theretofore taken. Time works changes, brings into existence new conditions and purposes. Therefore, a principle, to be vital, must be capable of wider application than the mischief which gave it birth. This is peculiarly true of constitutions. They are not ephemeral enactments, designed to meet passing occasions. They are, to use the words of Chief Justice Marshall 'designed to approach immortality as nearly as human institutions can approach it'. The future is their care, and provision for events of good and bad tendencies of which no prophecy can be made. In the application of a constitution,therefore, our contemplation cannot be only of what has been, but of what may be. Under any other rule, a constitution would indeed be as easy of application as it would be deficient in efficacy and power. Its general principles would have little value, and be converted by precedent into impotent and lifeless formulas. Rights declared in words might be lost in reality'.

When the Fourth and Fifth Amendments were adopted, 'the form that evil had theretofore taken' had been necessarily simple. Force and violence were then the only means known to man by which a Government could directly effect self-incrimination. It could compel the individual to testify — a compulsion effected, if need be, by torture. It could secure possession of his papers and other articles incident to his private life — a seizure effected, if need be, by breaking and entry. Protection against such invasion of 'the sanctities of a man's home and the privacies of life' was provided in the Fourth and Fifth Amendments by specific language. . . .

Time works changes
But 'time works changes, brings into existence new conditions and purposes'. Subtler and more far-reaching means of invading privacy have become available to the Government. Discovery and invention have made it possible for the Government, by means far more effective than stretching upon the rack, to obtain disclosure in court of what is whispered in the closet. Moreover, 'in the application of a constitution, our contemplation cannot be only of what has been but of what may be'. The progress of science in furnishing the Government with means of espionage is not likely to stop with wiretapping. Ways may someday be developed by which the Government, without removing papers from secret drawers, can reproduce them in court, and by which it will be enabled to expose to a jury the most intimate occurrences of the home. Advances in the psychic and related sciences may bring means of exploring unexpressed beliefs, thoughts and emotions. 'That places the liberty of every man in the hands of every petty officer' was said by James Otis of much lesser intrusions than these. To Lord Camden, a far slighter intrusion seemed 'subversive of all the comforts of society'. Can it be that the Constitution affords no protection against such invasions of individual security? A sufficient answer is found in *Boyd* v *United States*, a case that will be remembered as long as civil liberty lives in the United States.

This Court there reviewed the history that lay behind the Fourth and Fifth Amendments. We said with reference to Lord Camden's judgment in *Entick* v *Carrington*:

... the principles laid down in this opinion affect the very essence of constitutional liberty and security. They reach farther than the concrete form of the case there before the court, with its adventitious circumstances; they apply to all invasions on the part of the government and its employees of the sanctities of a man's home and the privacies of life. It is not the breaking of his doors, and the rummaging of his drawers, that constitutes the essence of the offence; but it is the invasion of his indefeasible right of personal security, personal liberty and private property, where that right has never been forfeited by his conviction of some public offence — it is the invasion of this sacred right which underlies and constitutes the essence of Lord Camden's judgment.

Breaking into a house and opening boxes and drawers are circumstances of aggravation; but any forcible and compulsory extortion of a man's own testimony or of his private papers to be used as evidence of a crime or to forfeit his goods is within the condemnation of that judgment. In this regard, the Fourth and Fifth Amendments run almost into each other.

In *Ex parte Jackson* it was held that a sealed letter entrusted to the mail is protected by the Amendments. The mail is a public service furnished by the Government. The telephone is a public service furnished by its authority. There is, in essence, no difference between the sealed letter and the private telephone message. As Judge Rudkin said below: True, the one is visible, the other invisible; the one is tangible, the other intangible; the one is sealed, and the other unsealed, but these are distinctions without a difference. The evil incident to invasion of the privacy of the telephone is far greater than that involved in tampering with the mails. Whenever a telephone line is tapped, the privacy of the persons at both ends of the line is invaded and all conversations between them upon any subject, and, although proper, confidential and privileged, may be overheard. Moreover, the tapping of one man's telephone line involves the tapping of the telephone of every other person whom he may call or who may call him.

As a means of espionage, writs of assistance and general warrants are but puny instruments of tyranny and oppression when compared with wiretapping. Time and again, this Court in giving effect to the principle underlying the Fourth Amendment, has refused to place an unduly literal construction upon it. This was notably illustrated in the *Boyd* case itself. Taking language in its ordinary meaning, there is no 'search' or 'seizure' when a defendant is required to produce a document in the orderly process of a court's procedure. 'The right of the people to be secure in their persons, houses, papers, and effects, against unreasonable searches and seizures' would not be violated, under any ordinary construction of language, by compelling obedience to a subpoena.

But this Court holds the evidence inadmissible simply because the information leading to the issue of the subpoena has been unlawfully secured. ... Literally, there is no 'search' or 'seizure' when a friendly visitor abstracts papers from an office; yet we held, that evidence so obtained could not be used. No court which looked at the words of the Amendment, rather than at its underlying purpose, would hold, as this Court did, that its protection extended to letters in the mails. The provision against self-incrimination in the Fifth Amendment has been given an equally broad construction. The language is: 'No person shall be compelled in any criminal case to be a witness against himself'. Yet we have held not only that the protection of the Amendment extends to a witness before a grand jury, although he has not been charged with crime, but that: [i]t applies alike to civil and criminal proceedings, wherever the answer might tend to subject to criminal responsibility him who gives it.

The privilege protects a mere witness as fully as it does one who is also a party defendant. ... The narrow language of the Amendment has been consistently construed in the light of its object, to insure that a person should not be compelled, when acting as a witness in any investigation, to give testimony which might tend to show that he himself had committed a crime. The privilege is limited to criminal matters, but it is as broad as the mischief against which it seeks to guard. ... Decisions of this Court applying the principle of the *Boyd* case have settled these things. Unjustified search and seizure violates the Fourth Amendment, whatever the character of the paper; whether the paper when taken by the federal officers was in the home, in an office, or elsewhere; whether the taking was effected by force, by fraud, or in the orderly process of a court's procedure.

From these decisions, it follows necessarily that the Amendment is violated by the officer's reading the paper without a physical seizure, without his even touching it, and that use, in any criminal proceeding, of the contents of the paper so examined — as where they are testified to by a federal officer who thus saw the document, or where, through knowledge so obtained, a copy has been procured elsewhere — any such use constitutes a violation of the Fifth Amendment.

The right to be let alone

The protection guaranteed by the Amendments is much broader in scope. The makers of our Constitution undertook to secure conditions favorable to the pursuit of happiness. They recognized the significance of man's spiritual nature, of his feelings, and of his intellect. They knew that only a part of the pain, pleasure and satisfactions of life are to be found in material things. They sought to protect Americans in their beliefs, their thoughts, their emotions and their sensations. They conferred, as against the Government, the right to be let alone — the most comprehensive of rights, and the right most valued by civilized men. To protect that right, every unjustifiable intrusion by the Government upon the privacy of the individual, whatever the means employed, must be deemed a violation of the Fourth Amendment. And the use, as evidence in a criminal proceeding, of facts ascertained by such intrusion must be deemed a violation of the Fifth.

Applying to the Fourth and Fifth Amendments the established rule of construction, the defendants' objections to the evidence obtained by wiretapping must, in my opinion, be sustained. It is, of course, immaterial where the physical connection with the telephone wires leading into the defendants' premises was made. And it is also immaterial that the intrusion was in aid of law enforcement. Experience should teach us to be most on our guard to protect liberty when the Government's purposes are beneficent. Men born to freedom are naturally alert to repel invasion of their liberty by evil-minded rulers. The greatest dangers to liberty lurk in insidious encroachment by men of zeal, well meaning but without understanding. Independently of the constitutional question, I am of opinion that the judgment should be reversed....

Here, the evidence obtained by crime was obtained at the Government's expense, by its officers, while acting on its behalf; the officers who committed these crimes are the same officers who were charged with the enforcement of the Prohibition Act; the crimes of these officers were committed for the purpose of securing evidence with which to obtain an indictment and to secure a conviction. The evidence so obtained constitutes the warp and woof of the Government's case. The aggregate of the Government evidence occupies 306 pages of the printed record. More than 210 of them are filled by recitals of the details of the wiretapping and of facts ascertained thereby. There is literally no other evidence of guilt on the part of some of the defendants except that illegally obtained by these officers.

As to nearly all the defendants (except those who admitted guilt), the evidence relied upon to secure a conviction consisted mainly of that which these officers had so obtained by violating the state law. As Judge Rudkin said below: 'Here we are concerned with neither eavesdroppers nor thieves. Nor are we concerned with the acts of private individuals.... We are concerned only with the acts of federal agents whose powers are limited and controlled by the Constitution of the United States.' The Eighteenth Amendment has not, in terms, empowered Congress to authorize anyone to violate the criminal laws of a State. And Congress has never purported to do so....

The terms of appointment of federal prohibition agents do not purport to confer upon them authority to violate any criminal law. Their superior officer, the Secretary of the Treasury, has not instructed them to commit crime on behalf of the United States. It may be assumed that the Attorney-General of the United

States did not give any such instruction. When these unlawful acts were committed, they were crimes only of the officers individually. The Government was innocent, in legal contemplation, for no federal official is authorized to commit a crime on its behalf. When the Government, having full knowledge, sought, through the Department of Justice, to avail itself of the fruits of these acts in order to accomplish its own ends, it assumed moral responsibility for the officers' crimes.... And if this Court should permit the Government, by means of its officers' crimes, to effect its purpose of punishing the defendants, there would seem to be present all the elements of a ratification. If so, the Government itself would become a lawbreaker.

Will this Court, by sustaining the judgment below, sanction such conduct on the part of the Executive? The governing principle has long been settled. It is that a court will not redress a wrong when he who invokes its aid has unclean hands. The maxim of unclean hands comes from courts of equity. But the principle prevails also in courts of law. Its common application is in civil actions between private parties. Where the Government is the actor, the reasons for applying it are even more persuasive. Where the remedies invoked are those of the criminal law, the reasons are compelling. The door of a court is not barred because the plaintiff has committed a crime. The confirmed criminal is as much entitled to redress as his most virtuous fellow citizen; no record of crime, however long, makes one an outlaw. The court's aid is denied only when he who seeks it has violated the law in connection with the very transaction as to which he seeks legal redress. Then aid is denied despite the defendant's wrong. It is denied in order to maintain respect for law; in order to promote confidence in the administration of justice; in order to preserve the judicial process from contamination. The rule is one, not of action, but of inaction. It is sometimes spoken of as a rule of substantive law. But it extends to matters of procedure, as well.

The potent, the omnipresent teacher
A defense may be waived. It is waived when not pleaded. But the objection that the plaintiff comes with unclean hands will be taken by the court itself. It will be taken despite the wish to the contrary of all the parties to the litigation. The court protects itself. Decency, security and liberty alike demand that government officials shall be subjected to the same rules of conduct that are commands to the citizen. In a government of laws, existence of the government will be imperiled if it fails to observe the law scrupulously. Our Government is the potent, the omnipresent teacher. For good or for ill, it teaches the whole people by its example. Crime is contagious. If the Government becomes a lawbreaker, it breeds contempt for law; it invites every man to become a law unto himself;

it invites anarchy. To declare that, in the administration of the criminal law, the end justifies the means — to declare that the Government may commit crimes in order to secure the conviction of a private criminal — would bring terrible retribution. Against that pernicious doctrine this Court should resolutely set its face.

The demonstrable failure of prohibition led to its repeal in 1920 by the Twenty First Amendment to the Constitution.

The feel of freedom

One of the most controversial issues in criminal jurisprudence is the extent of the defendant's right to obtain access to documents in the hands of the prosecutor. There is general agreement that the prosecutor's duty to disclose in criminal proceedings is greater than that which rests on a plaintiff in civil proceedings, but how far does it extend? Should the defendant be entitled to know, for example, the name of the person who informed against him? The American answer, as always, is based on constitutional principle.

A few years after the Second World War Judith Coplon was a political analyst in the United States Department of Justice. When temporarily working in the security section she was suspected of having passed sensitive information to a Russian spy. Federal agents had been set on her trail by a confidential informant. Prosecuted for conspiring to defraud the United States and for attempting to deliver defence information to a citizen of a foreign nation, Miss Coplon sought to learn whether the information which originally led to the tapping of her telephone was itself the result of 'wiretapping'.

The US Circuit Court of Appeals for the Second Circuit held that the trial judge was in error in refusing, on the ground of 'national security', to allow the defence to question government agents about who the informant was. Giving the judgment of the court, Chief Judge Learned Hand said:[54]

---

[54] *United States* v *Coplon* 185 F 2d 629, 638 (2d Cir 1950).

... we cannot dispense with constitutional privileges because in a specific instance they may not in fact serve to protect any valid interest of their possessor. Back of this particular privilege lies a long chapter in the history of Anglo-American institutions. Few weapons in the arsenal of freedom are more useful than the power to compel a government to disclose the evidence on which it seeks to forfeit the liberty of its citizens. All governments, democracies as well as autocracies, believe that those they seek to punish are guilty; the impediments of constitutional barriers are galling to all governments when they prevent the consummation of that just purpose. But those barriers were devised and are precious because they prevent that purpose and its pursuit from passing unchallenged by the accused, and unpurged by the alembic of public scrutiny and public criticism. A society which has come to wince at such exposure of the methods by which it seeks to impose its will upon its members, has already lost the feel of freedom and is on the path towards absolutism.

No such general rule applies in England where the informant's name is protected on grounds of public policy.

No source of pride

The issue of telephone tapping was comprehensively examined in this country by the Vice-Chancellor, Sir Robert Megarry, in 1979.

During the trial of five defendants charged with handling stolen property, the prosecutor admitted that there had been interception of the telephone conversations of one of them on the authority of the Home Secretary's warrant. The plaintiff claimed that the police action had been unlawful and sought an injunction restraining future intercepts. In a judgment that ranged over two continents and three centuries the Vice-Chancellor said:[55]

For brevity and without prejudice to the greater elaboration of the various declarations claimed, the question may be expressed in the simple form 'Is telephone tapping in aid of the police in their functions relating to crime illegal?' However, I think that I should make it clear that the only form of

---

[55] *Malone v Metropolitan Police Commissioner (No. 2)* [1979] 2 All ER 620, 629.

telephone tapping that has been debated is tapping which consists of the making of recordings by Post Office officials in some part of the existing telephone · system, and the making of those recordings available to police officers for the purposes of transcription and use. I am not concerned with any form of tapping that involved electronic devices which make wireless transmissions, nor with any process whereby anyone trespasses on to the premises of the subscriber or anyone else to affix tapping devices or the like. All that I am concerned with is the legality of tapping effected by means of recording telephone conversations from wires which, though connected to the premises of the subscriber, are not on them.

It was common ground that there was no English authority that in any way directly bore on the point.... The absence of any authority on the point is something that has to be borne in mind; but it certainly does not establish that no such right exists. This is the centenary of the telephone system in England; for the first telephone exchange was established in 1879, with a mere seven or eight subscribers. It is perhaps surprising that the question now raised has taken a hundred years to come before the courts; but there may be many explanations of that, and I certainly do not infer that a necessary or even probable explanation is that there is no right to immunity from telephone tapping. If the true view is that such a right exists, then the court must say so, despite the absence of any prior authority.

This year, in addition to being the centenary of the telephone system in England, is also the centenary of a celebrated dictum of Chief Justice Doe of New Hampshire which I mentioned during the argument. As slightly varied, it is: 'As there was a time when there were no precedents, anything that could be done with them can be done without them'. If authority on a point is lacking, neither equity nor common law is incapable of filling the gap in a proper case. Such an approach may be traced back at least to the 16th century. In *Anon.* (1588), it was said in argument that there were no cases in the books on the point in issue. But Chief Justice Anderson said:

What of that? Shall not we give judgment because it is not adjudged in the bookes before? Wee will give judgment according to reason, and if there bee no reason in the bookes, I will not regard them.

Before I examine Mr Ross-Munro's contentions, I should indicate the basic thesis of the contentions of Mr Rattee and the Solicitor-General to the contrary. This was that apart from certain limited statutory provisions, there was nothing to make governmental telephone tapping illegal; and the statutory provisions of themselves assume that such tapping is not in other respects illegal. That being so, there is no general right to immunity from such tapping. England, it may be said, is not a country where everything is forbidden except what is expressly permitted: it is a country where everything is permitted except what · is expressly forbidden.

The right to property

As the plaintiff's contentions overlap to some extent, I shall set them all out first, and in most cases postpone my consideration of their force and effect until after I have deployed them all. Mr Ross-Munro's first proposition rested in the first place on a right of property. To tap a person's telephone conversation without his consent, he said, was unlawful because that person had rights of property in his words as transmitted by the electrical impulses of the telephone system, and so the tapping constituted an interference with his property rights. An analogy that he suggested was that the important part of a letter was the words that it contained rather than the paper that it was written on. I regret to say that Mr Ross-Munro found it difficult to persuade me that there was any reality in this contention, and he did not struggle long. I do not see how words transmitted by electrical impulses could themselves (as distinct from any copyright in them) fairly be said to be the subject matter of property. At all events, no argument which even began to support such a proposition was put before me.

The right of privacy: first visited

The second ground on which Mr Ross-Munro sought to support his first proposition was that of the right of privacy. He accepted that the books assert that in English law there is no general right of privacy, and he referred me to a passage in *Halsbury's Laws of England* to this effect. But he contended that there was a particular right of privacy which the books did not mention, namely, the right to hold a telephone conversation in the privacy of one's home without molestation. In support of his contention, Mr Ross-Munro relied to a large extent on the common law offence of eavesdropping, the celebrated article on 'The right to privacy' by Samuel D. Warren and the future Mr Justice Brandeis in (1890) *Harvard Law Review*, the Fourth Amendment to the Constitution of the United States of America, *Katz* v *United States* and *Rhodes* v *Graham*. I shall mention these in turn.

The offence of eavesdropping is described in Blackstone's *Commentaries* (1809), as being committed by those who listen under walls or windows or the eaves of a house, and frame slanderous and mischievous tales. The offence constituted a common nuisance, punishable by fine and finding sureties for good behaviour. This offence fell under the same broad head, dealt with on the same page of Blackstone, as being a common scold, which was punishable by immersion in the trebucket or ducking stool. The Criminal Law Act 1967 abolished these and a number of other offences, so that eavesdropping can now speak in support of Mr. Ross-Munro with only a muted voice. . . .

The Fourth Amendment to the Constitution of the United States, which dates from the eighteenth century, runs:

> The right of the people to be secure in their persons, houses, papers, and effects, against unreasonable searches and seizures, shall not be violated, and no warrants shall issue but upon probable cause, supported by oath or affirmation, and particularly describing the place to be searched, and the persons or things to be seized.

This, it is said in *Halsbury's Laws of England*, was 'mainly based on the English cases on general warrants, especially *Entick* v *Carrington*'. Mr Ross-Munro read me extensive passages from this case, and contended that this supported the contention that, unless authorised by statute, the Secretary of State had no power to issue a warrant authorising any telephone tapping, whether general or specific. Although the language of the Fourth Amendment, chosen before telephones were known, does not seem very apt for telephone tapping, various decisions of the Supreme Court of the United States have applied it to telephone tapping effected without a proper warrant from a magistrate. In *Katz* v *United States*, the majority of the Supreme Court held that a tapping effected by attaching a device to the exterior of a public telephone booth was contrary to the Fourth Amendment, and that a conviction obtained by means of the evidence of what the accused had said in telephone conversations recorded by these means must be reversed, even though the circumstances of the tapping were such that a magistrate could properly have authorised it. The court rejected previous authority which held that the Fourth Amendment was not violated by telephone tapping which was effected without any act of trespass or any seizure of any material object. In his dissent, Mr Justice Black said that 'wiretapping is nothing more than eavesdropping by telephone'.

No general right to privacy
This decision, of course, is merely a decision reversing a conviction for wrongful admission of evidence. It was no decision that the Fourth Amendment conferred any general right to privacy. It protects individuals against various kinds of governmental intrusions, and many other acts which have nothing to do with privacy. Any protection of a general right to privacy (or a man's right to be let alone by others) is largely left to the law of the various States. . . .

[*After examining a number of American authorities, he went on*] In 1972 the Committee on Privacy, under the chairmanship of the Right Honourable Kenneth Younger, produced a valuable report on the whole subject. I shall call this the 'Younger Report'. Among many other things, the report contains a convenient summary of the development of the right of privacy in the United States of America, with many variations between the different States, and with statutes covering part of the ground. The Younger Report as a whole demonstrates the great complexity of the subject, and the difficulty of framing legislation to regulate it in a satisfactory manner. I should also mention another report, specifically concerned with telephone tapping under the authority of the Home Secretary. This is commonly called the 'Birkett Report', since Sir Norman Birkett headed the three Privy Councillors who constituted the committee. Much of this was read to me, and although the report is not authority in any technical sense, it is plainly of much value. In particular, it sets out much material on the process of telephone tapping and its authorisation. In view of the paucity of any such evidence in the case before me, this is particularly useful.

The right of confidentiality: first visited
I now turn to the third ground on which Mr Ross-Munro supports his first proposition, the right of confidentiality. This is an equitable right which is still in course of development, and is usually protected by the grant of an injunction to prevent disclosure of the confidence. Under Lord Cairns's Act 1858 damages may be granted in substitution for an injunction; yet if there is no case for the grant of an injunction, as when the disclosure has already been made, the unsatisfactory result seems to be that no damages can be awarded under this head. In such a case, where there is no breach of contract or other orthodox foundation for damages at common law, it seems doubtful whether there is any right to damages, as distinct from an account of profits. It may be, however, that a new tort is emerging, though this has been doubted. Certainly the subject raises many questions that are so far unresolved, some of which are discussed in the Younger Report.

The application of the doctrine of confidentiality to the tapping of private telephone lines is that in using a telephone a person is likely to do it in the belief that it is probable (though by no means certain) that his words will be heard only by the person he is speaking to. I do not think that it can be put higher than that. As the Younger Report points out, those who use the telephone are:

aware that there are several well-understood possibilities of being overheard. A realistic person would not therefore rely on the telephone system to protect the confidence of what he says because, by using the telephone, he would have discarded a large measure of security for his private speech.

Extension lines, private switchboards and so-called 'crossed lines', for example, all offer possibilities of being overheard. The report then pointed out that what would not be taken into account would be an unauthorised tap by induction coil or infinity transmitter. The report, which was dealing only with incursions into privacy by individuals and companies, and not the public sector, said nothing about tapping authorised by the Home Secretary. However, the substantial publicity attending the Birkett Report, and the general interest in films, television and affairs of notoriety in other countries, must mean that few telephone users can be ignorant of the real possibility that telephones are subject to the risk (which most people will probably regard as being very small in their own cases) of being tapped by some governmental body with access to the telephone system.

It is against that background that I must consider Mr Ross-Munro's submissions. He contended that the categories of confidentiality were not closed, and that they should be extended.... If A makes a confidential communication to B then A may not only restrain B from divulging or using the confidence, but also may restrain C from divulging or using it if C has acquired it from B, even if he acquired it without notice of any impropriety. In such cases it seems plain that however innocent the acquisition of the knowledge, what will be restrained is the use or disclosure of it after notice of the impropriety. In the case of a telephone conversation, said Mr Ross-Munro, any conversation that was 'reasonably intended to be private' should be treated as a confidential communication. Even if the using of the telephone must be taken as implying some sort of consent to some risk of being overheard, that could not be taken to be any kind of consent to any publication to any third party.

Mr Ross-Munro agreed that there were limits to the doctrine of confidentiality. He accepted the dictum that 'there is no confidence as to the disclosure of iniquity'.... The Master of the Rolls, Lord Denning, held that it extended 'to any misconduct of such a nature that it ought in the public interest to be disclosed to others', and was not confined to cases of crime or fraud. Mr Ross-Munro agreed that if through what are often called 'crossed lines' a person overhears what is plainly a confidential conversation, and this discloses plans to commit a crime, that person should inform the police, and he could not be said to have committed any breach of the obligation of confidentiality. But that, he contended, was very different from tapping a telephone in the hope of obtaining information about some crime, whether already committed or being planned.

Lord Denning said:

There are some things which may be required to be disclosed in the public interest, in which event no confidence can be prayed in aid to keep them secret.

In a judgment a mere four sentences long, Lord Justice Davies agreed with Lord Denning on one ground of his decision, but expressly refrained from saying anything about two other points, of which the exegesis of iniquity was one. The judgment of the third member of the court, Lord Justice Widgery, consisted of a single sentence. He said, 'I entirely agree' and went on to state that he would not take time 'in an endeavour to repeat the reasons given by my lord'. This might be read as being a complete agreement with what Lord Justice Davies had said, or with what the other two members of the court were agreed upon (which comes to the same thing), or it might be read as an agreement with all that Lord Denning had said, including that part of it on which Lord Justice Davies had refrained from expressing any view.

I do not think that I need explore the problem, which often arises, of the significance and effect of the simple words 'I agree', when uttered in the Court of Appeal. I readily accept and adopt what Lord Denning said, whether or not it expresses a majority view. I also accept the other formulation by Lord Denning that I have mentioned based on whether disclosure is in the public interest. Lord Denning extended this to all crimes, frauds and misdeeds, whether actually committed or in contemplation, but limited it to cases where the disclosure was to someone who had a proper interest to receive the information, as where the disclosure is to the police in relation to a crime. As in the case before me this is the only kind of disclosure in question, I need say no more on this limitation. Lord Justice Winn expressly concurred in Lord Denning's judgment, and I do not think Lord Justice Salmon disagreed. As between the two formulations, I think I would prefer [the formulation] that is not confined to misconduct or misdeeds. There may be cases where there is no misconduct or misdeed but yet there is a just cause or excuse for breaking confidence. The confidential information may relate to some apprehension of an impending chemical or other disaster, arising without misconduct, of which the authorities are not aware, but which ought in the public interest to be disclosed to them. However, I need not pursue this, since in the circumstances of the present case the two formulations produce no significant difference.

The European Convention: first visited
With that, I turn to Mr Ross-Munro's second main contention, based on the [*European Convention on Human Rights*]. . . . I take note of the Convention and

I shall give it due consideration in discussing English law on the point. As for the direct right which the Convention confers, it seems to me to be plain that this is a direct right in relation to the European Commission of Human Rights and the European Court of Human Rights, the bodies established by the Convention, but not in relation to the courts of this country. The Convention is plainly not of itself law in this country, however much it may fall to be considered as indicating what the law of this country should be, or should be construed as being.

Finally, there is the contention that, as no power to tap telephones has been given by either statute or common law, the tapping is necessarily unlawful. The underlying assumption of this contention, of course, is that nothing is lawful that is not positively authorised by law. As I have indicated, England is not a country where everything is forbidden except what is expressly permitted. One possible illustration is smoking. I inquired what positive authority was given by the law to permit people to smoke. Mr Ross-Munro accepted that there was none; but tapping, he said, was different. It was in general disfavour, and it offended against usual and proper standards of behaviour, in that it was an invasion of privacy and an interference with the liberty of the individual and his right to be let alone when lawfully engaged on his own affairs.

I did not find this argument convincing. A stalwart non-smoker, whether lifelong or redeemed, might consider that most or all of what Mr Ross-Munro said applied with equal force to the not inconsiderable numbers of non-smokers. In leading an ordinary life they often find themselves unable to avoid inhaling in an enclosed space the products of a combustion deliberately caused by a smoker who knows that the fumes that he is creating will spread, and will affect other people. But in any case the answer destroys the underlying assumption and mutilates the proposition. The notion that some express authorisation of law is required for acts which meet with 'general disfavour,' and 'offend against proper standards of behaviour', and so on, would make the state of the law dependent on subjective views on indefinite concepts, and would be likely to produce some remarkable and contentious results. Neither in principle nor in authority can I see any justification for this view, and I reject it. If the tapping of telephones by the Post Office at the request of the police can be carried out without any breach of the law, it does not require any statutory or common law power to justify it: it can lawfully be done simply because there is nothing to make it unlawful. The question, of course, is whether tapping can be carried out without infringing the law.

Telephone tapping
Those, then, are Mr Ross-Munro's three main contentions. Before I consider them further I must say something about the process of tapping in question. The

plaintiff has understandably produced no evidence on this, for he is in the dark. All that he has been able to do is put forward reasons for thinking that his telephone has been tapped, in addition, of course, to the admission by leading counsel for the Crown at his trial. Thus he speaks of clicking noises on his telephone, and of various events which he thinks would not have happened if his telephone had not been tapped at the time. All the evidence of the process of tapping comes from the defendant in an affidavit by the head of the Criminal Investigation Department of the Metropolitan Police. His affidavit refers to the Birkett Report, and certain conclusions in that report. He speaks of the value of tapping in the detection of major crimes, including the receiving of stolen property, and he then turns to the safeguards, which he says are still rigorously observed by the Metropolitan Police.

They are as follows. (1) No warrant to tap a telephone is sought unless 'strict conditions' laid down by the Home Office are satisfied. What those conditions are is not stated. (2) All applications are considered carefully by the Home Office and by the Secretary of State personally. (3) No tapping is authorised save by a warrant under the Secretary of State's own hand. (4) Every warrant is limited to a defined period not exceeding two months, though in a proper case this may be extended from time to time. The affidavit however, says nothing about the recommendation in the Birkett Report that every warrant should be reviewed at least once a month by the police and the Home Office. (5) Tapping is discontinued when it is no longer needed. (6) The only material transcribed from the recording is the part that the police consider to be relevant to the inquiry in hand. The record of the rest is destroyed.

As appears from the Birkett Report, the process of tapping is that the Home Secretary's warrant is sent directly to the Post Office which alone can put it into effect. The recording is a purely mechanical process: the Post Office officials do not listen to the conversations save occasionally and briefly to see whether the machines are working properly. The police merely receive the recordings which the Post Office makes available to them in obedience to the warrant. A small number of selected police officers then listen to the recordings and transcribe the passages considered to be relevant to the inquiry. The rest are destroyed. The police thus seek the tap and receive its fruits but do not do any tapping themselves: that is done by the Post Office on the authority of the Home Secretary. Furthermore, the information obtained by tapping is not put in evidence (unless it gets in by some form of inadvertence, as may have occurred in the criminal trial in this case), though it is used in the process of detection, and is valuable for this purpose....

First, I do not think that any assistance is obtained from the general warrant cases, or other authorities dealing with warrants. At common law, the only power to search premises under a search warrant issued by a justice of the peace is to search for stolen goods: see *Entick* v *Carrington*. However, many statutes authorise searches under search warrants for many different purposes; and there is admittedly no statute which in terms authorises the tapping of telephones, with or without a warrant. Nevertheless, any conclusion that the tapping of telephones is therefore illegal would plainly be superficial in the extreme. The reason why a search of premises which is not authorised by law is illegal is that it involves the tort of trespass to those premises: and any trespass, whether to land or goods or the person, that is made without legal authority is prima facie illegal. Telephone tapping by the Post Office, on the other hand, involves no act of trespass. The subscriber speaks into his telephone, and the process of tapping appears to be carried out by Post Office officials making recordings, with Post Office apparatus on Post Office premises, of the electrical impulses on Post Office wires provided by Post Office electricity. There is no question of there being any trespass on the plaintiff's premises for the purpose of attaching anything either to the premises themselves or to anything on them: all that is done is done within the Post Office's own domain. As Chief Justice Lord Camden said, 'the eye cannot by the laws of England be guilty of a trespass'; and, I would add, nor can the ear.

The history of tapping

Second, I turn to the warrant of the Home Secretary. This contrasts with search warrants in that it is issued by one of the great officers of State as such, and not by a justice of the peace acting as such. Furthermore, it does not purport to be issued under the authority of any statute or of the common law. From the Birkett Report it appears that the power to tap telephones has been exercised from time to time since the introduction of the telephone, but that not until 1937 were any warrants issued. Until then, the Post Office took the view that any operator of telephones had a power to tap conversations without infringing any rule of law. The police authorities accordingly made arrangements directly with the Director-General of the Post Office for any tapping of telephones that might be required. In 1937, however, the Home Secretary and Postmaster-General decided, as a matter of policy, that thenceforward records of telephone conversations should be made by the Post Office and disclosed to the police only on the authority of the Home Secretary. The view was taken that certain statutes which permitted the interception of letters and telegrams on the authority of a Secretary of State were wide enough to cover telephone tapping. The decision seems to have been based partly on what was desirable as a matter of policy, and partly on an application of the statutory power of interception, or some analogy to it. At all events, the decision seems plainly to have been an administrative decision not dictated or required by statute.

At that stage, the Home Secretary and the Postmaster-General were both officers of State under the Crown, and the Post Office was a department of state.

The Post Office Act 1969 changed that.... The Home Secretary's warrant, which had previously been given under administrative arrangements, now had a statutory function as being a 'requirement' under section 80, and, what is more, as a requirement that statute authorised to be 'laid' on the Post Office. Although the previous arrangements had been merely administrative, they had been set out in the Birkett Report a dozen years earlier, and the section plainly referred to these arrangements; if not, it was difficult to see what the section had in view, and certainly nothing intelligible has been suggested. A warrant was not needed to make the tapping lawful: it was lawful without any warrant. But where the tapping was done under warrant (and that is the only matter before me) the section afforded statutory recognition of the lawfulness of the tapping. In their essentials, these contentions seem to me to be sound.

[*After reviewing the legislation the Vice-Chancellor held that Parliament had provided in the Post Office Act 1969*] a clear recognition of the warrant of the Home Secretary as having an effective function in law, both as providing a defence to certain criminal charges, and also as amounting to an effective requirement for the Post Office to do certain acts.

The right of privacy

Third, there is the right of privacy. Here the contention is that, although at present no general right of privacy has been recognised by English law, there is a particular right of privacy, namely, the right to hold a telephone conversation in the privacy of one's home without molestation. This, it was said, ought to be recognised and declared to be part of English law, despite the absence of any English authority to this effect. As I have indicated, I am not unduly troubled by the absence of English authority: there has to be a first time for everything, and if the principles of English law, and not least analogies from the existing rules, together with the requirements of justice and common sense, pointed firmly to such a right existing, then I think the court should not be deterred from recognising the right.

On the other hand, it is no function of the courts to legislate in a new field. The extension of the existing laws and principles is one thing, the creation of an altogether new right is another. At times judges must, and do, legislate; but as Mr Justice Holmes once said, they do so only interstitially, and with molecular rather than molar motions. Anything beyond that must be left for legislation. No new right in the law, fully fledged with all the appropriate safeguards, can spring from the head of a judge deciding a particular case: only Parliament can create such a right.... Where there is some major gap in the law, no doubt a judge would be capable of framing what he considered to be a proper code to fill it; and sometimes he may be tempted. But he has to remember that his function is judicial, not legislative, and that he ought not to use his office to legislate in the guise of exercising his judicial powers.

One of the factors that must be relevant in such a case is the degree of particularity in the right that is claimed. The wider and more indefinite the right claimed the greater the undesirability of holding that such a right exists. Wide and indefinite rights, while conferring an advantage on those who have them, may well gravely impair the position of those who are subject to the rights. To create a right for one person, you have to impose a corresponding duty on another. In the present case, the alleged right to hold a telephone conversation in the privacy of one's own home without molestation is wide and indefinite in its scope, and in any case does not seem to be very apt for covering the plaintiff's grievance He was not 'molested' in holding his telephone conversations: he held them without 'molestation', but without their retaining the privacy that he desired. If a man telephones from his own home, but an open window makes it possible for a near neighbour to overhear what is said and the neighbour, remaining throughout on his own property, listens to the conversation, is he to be a tortfeasor? Is a person who overhears a telephone conversation by reason of a so-called 'crossed line' to be liable in damages? What of an operator of a private switchboard who listens in? Why is the right that is claimed confined to a man's own home so that it would not apply to private telephone conversations from offices, call boxes or the houses of others? If they were to be included what of the greater opportunities for deliberate overhearing that they offer? In any case, why is the telephone to be subject to this special right of privacy when there is no general right?

That is not all. Suppose that there is what for brevity I may call a right to telephonic privacy sounding in tort. What exceptions to it, if any, would there be? Would it be a breach of the right if anyone listened to a telephone conversation in which some act of criminal violence or dishonesty was being planned? Should a listener be restrained by injunction from disclosing to the authorities a conversation that would lead to the release of someone kidnapped? There are many, many questions that can and should, be asked.

Without attempting to answer these questions let me turn to the authorities on which Mr Ross-Munro relied. I do not think that the common law offence of eavesdropping, abolished over 10 years ago, gives him much help today. The gist of the offence was listening just outside a house with the object of spreading slanderous and mischievous tales; and this hardly seems apt if the listener tells nobody save the police. Telephone tapping for police purposes, too, does not involve any listening in proximity to any house, nor, of course, is it done with any object of spreading any tales, whether slanderous and mischievous or otherwise: indeed, a close confidence within official circles surrounds information obtained by tapping. I cannot see how such telephone tapping could possibly be said to be within the mischief of eavesdropping, even if eavesdropping were tortious.

As for the Warren and Brandeis article in the *Harvard Law Review*, this argues for the existence of a general right to privacy, which Mr Ross-Munro accepts does not exist in England, and does nothing to support the specialised right to telephonic privacy for which he does contend. The Fourth Amendment to the Constitution of the United States is different, of course. It has the especial force of being a part of the Constitution of that country; but there is no statute in this country which in any way corresponds to it. If there were such a statute here, it might indeed be that it would be construed in something like the same way: but there is not. Though mainly based on the English cases on general warrants, the Fourth Amendment goes far beyond anything to be found in those cases....

In the result, therefore, I can find nothing in the authorities or contentions that have been put before me to support the plaintiff's claim based on the right of privacy. I therefore hold that the claim, so far as thus based, must fail.

The right of confidentiality revisted

Fourth, there is the right of confidentiality. Let me at the outset dispose of one point. If telephone services were provided under a contract between the telephone subscriber and the Post Office, then it might be contended that there was some implied term in that contract that telephone conversations should remain confidential and be free from tapping....

The right of confidentiality accordingly falls to be considered apart from any contractual right. In such a case, it has been said that three elements are normally required if a case of breach of confidence is to succeed:

First, the information itself, in the words of the Master of the Rolls, Lord Greene, 'must have the necessary quality of confidence about it'. Secondly, that information must have been imparted in circumstances importing an obligation of confidence. Thirdly, there must be an unauthorised use of that information to the detriment of the party communicating it.

Of the second requirement, it was said:

However secret and confidential the information, there can be no binding obligation of confidence if that information is blurted out in public or is communicated in other circumstances which negative any duty of holding it confidential.

What was in issue in [the case in which that was said] was a communication by an inventor or designer to a manufacturer, and the alleged misuse of that information by the manufacturer. In the present case, the alleged misuse is not by the person to whom the information was intended to be communicated, but by someone to whom the plaintiff had no intention of communicating anything: and that, of course, introduces a somewhat different element, that of the unknown overhearer.

It seems to me that a person who utters confidential information must accept the risk of any unknown overhearing that is inherent in the circumstances of communication. Those who exchange confidences on a bus or a train run the risk of a nearby passenger with acute hearing or a more distant passenger who is adept at lip-reading. Those who speak over garden walls run the risk of the unseen neighbour in a toolshed nearby. Office cleaners who discuss secrets in the office when they think everyone else has gone run the risk of speaking within earshot of an unseen member of the staff who is working late. Those who give confidential information over an office intercommunication system run the risk of some third party being connected to the conversation. I do not see why someone who has overheard some secret in such a way should be exposed to legal proceedings if he uses or divulges what he has heard. No doubt an honourable man would give some warning when he realises that what he is hearing is not intended for his ears; but I have to concern myself with the law, and not with moral standards. There are, of course, many moral precepts which are not legally enforceable.

When this is applied to telephone conversations, it appears to me that the speaker is taking such risks of being overheard as are inherent in the system. As I have mentioned, the Younger Report referred to users of the telephone being aware that there were several well-understood possibilities of being overheard, and stated that a realistic person would not rely on the telephone system to protect the confidence of what he says. That comment seems unanswerable. In addition, so much publicity in recent years has been given to instances (real or fictional) of the deliberate tapping of telephones that it is difficult to envisage telephone users who are genuinely unaware of this possibility. No doubt a person who uses a telephone to give confidential information to another may do so in such a way as to impose an obligation of confidence on that other: but I do not see how it could be said that any such obligation is imposed on those who overhear the conversation, whether by means of tapping or otherwise.

Even if any duty of confidentiality were, contrary to my judgment, to be held to bind those who overhear a telephone conversation, there remains the question of the limits to that duty. I have already discussed and accepted the formulation of Lord Denning, that of 'just cause or excuse for breaking confidence', as well as his formulation based on whether the disclosure is in the public interest. I shall not repeat these alternative formulations; I treat the former as including the latter. If what is overheard, though confidential, is itself iniquity, it is plain that it is subject to no duty of confidence. But if there is merely a suspicion of iniquity, does that justify a deliberate overhearing by means of a tap? Even if from time to time the tap provides information about iniquity, does that justify a process of recording entire conversations, and listening to those recordings, when much of the conversations may be highly confidential and untainted by any iniquity? Further, if there is a reasonable suspicion of iniquity, can that suspicion justify tapping in order to find out whether the suspicion is well-founded, if in fact the conversations are wholly innocent?

I think that one has to approach these matters with some measure of balance and common sense. The rights and liberties of a telephone subscriber are indeed important; but so also are the desires of the great bulk of the population not to be the victims of assault, theft or other crimes. The detection and prosecution of criminals, and the discovery of projected crimes, are important weapons in protecting the public. In the nature of things it will be virtually impossible to know beforehand whether any particular telephone conversation will be criminal in nature. The question is not whether there is a certainty that the conversation tapped will be iniquitous, but whether there is just cause or excuse for the tapping and for the use made of the material obtained by the tapping.

If certain requirements are satisfied, then I think that there will plainly be just cause or excuse for what is done by or on behalf of the police. These requirements are, first, that there should be grounds for suspecting that the tapping of the particular telephone will be of material assistance in detecting or preventing crime, or discovering the criminals, or otherwise assisting in the discharge of the functions of the police in relation to crime. Second, no use should be made of any material obtained except for these purposes. Third, any knowledge of information which is not relevant to those purposes should be confined to the minimum number of persons reasonably required to carry out the process of tapping. If those requirements are satisfied, then it seems to me that there will be just cause or excuse for carrying out the tapping, and using information obtained for those limited purposes. I am not, of course, saying that nothing else can constitute a just cause or excuse: what I am saying is that if these requirements are satisfied, then in my judgment there will be a just cause or excuse. I am not, for instance, saying anything about matters of national security: I speak only of what is before me in the present case, concerning tapping for police purposes in relation to crime.

So far as the evidence goes, it seems to me that the process of tapping, as carried out on behalf of the police in relation to crime, fully conforms with these requirements: indeed, there are restrictions on tapping, and safeguards, which go beyond these requirements. The only possible difficulty is in relation to the 'strict conditions' laid down by the Home Office which have to be satisfied before the warrant of the Home Office is sought; for I do not know what these conditions are. However, [*the police*] affidavit states in relation to the plaintiff that if a warrant had been sought by the Metropolitan Police (and he says nothing as to whether in fact it was) 'the sole purpose in seeking such a warrant would have been to obtain information of value in the detection and prevention of serious crime'. This, coupled with the other evidence, makes it clear enough, I think, that the first of the three requirements that I have stated would be satisfied. Accordingly, in my judgment, if, contrary to my opinion, telephone tapping on behalf of the police is a breach of any duty of confidentiality, there is just cause or excuse for that tapping in the circumstances of this case.

I would add one comment. I have already mentioned section 5(b) of the Wireless Telegraphy Act 1949. Under this, there is no offence if the information is obtained by a Crown servant in the course of his duty or under the authority of the Postmaster-General (now the Home Secretary). This, said Mr Rattee, made it improbable that there was any general law against telephone tapping; for Parliament would hardly empower the Postmaster-General to authorise such tapping as regards the criminal law if all the time it was tortious. This contention seems to me to have some force.

The direct applicability of the European Convention
Fifth, there is Mr Ross-Munro's second main head, based on the European Convention for the Protection of Human Rights and Fundamental Freedoms and the *Klass* case. The first limb of this relates to the direct rights conferred by the Convention. Any such right is, as I have said, a direct right in relation to the European Commission of Human Rights and the European Court of Human Rights, and not in relation to the courts of this country; for the Convention is not law here.

The persuasive effect of the Convention
Sixth, there is the second limb of Mr Ross-Munro's contentions, based on the Convention and the *Klass* case as assisting the court to determine what English law is on a point on which authority is lacking or uncertain. Can it be said that in this case two courses are reasonably open to the court, one of which is inconsistent with the Convention and the other consonant with it? I readily accept that if the question before me were one of construing a statute enacted with the purpose of giving effect to obligations imposed by the Convention, the court would readily seek to construe the legislation in a way that would effectuate the Convention rather than frustrate it. However, no relevant

legislation of that sort is in existence. It seems to me that where Parliament has abstained from legislating on a point that is plainly suitable for legislation, it is indeed difficult for the court to lay down new rules of common law or equity that will carry out the Crown's treaty obligations, or to discover for the first time that such rules have always existed.

Now the West German system that came under scrutiny in the *Klass* case was laid down by statute, and it contained a number of statutory safeguards. There must be imminent danger: other methods of surveillance must be at least considerably more difficult; both the person making the request for surveillance and the method of making it are limited; the period of surveillance is limited in time, and in any case must cease when the need has passed; the person subjected to surveillance must be notified as soon as this will not jeopardise the purpose of surveillance; no information is made available to the police unless an official qualified for judicial office is satisfied that it is within the safeguards; all other information obtained must be destroyed; the process is supervised by a parliamentary board on which the opposition is represented; and there is also a supervising commission which may order that surveillance is to cease, or that notification of it is to be given to the person who has been subjected to it. Not a single one of these safeguards is to be found as a matter of established law in England, and only a few corresponding provisions exist as a matter of administrative procedure.

It does not, of course, follow that a system with fewer or different safeguards will fail to satisfy article 8 in the eyes of the European Court of Human Rights. At the same time, it is impossible to read the judgment in the *Klass* case without its becoming abundantly clear that a system which has no legal safeguards whatever has small chance of satisfying the requirements of that court, whatever administrative provisions there may be. Broadly, the court was concerned to see whether the German legislation provided 'adequate and effective safeguards against abuse'. Though in principle it was desirable that there should be judicial control of tapping, the court was satisfied that the German system provided an adequate substitute in the independence of the board and Commission from the authorities carrying out the surveillance. Further, the provisions for the subsequent notification of the surveillance when this would not frustrate its purpose were also considered to be adequate. In England, on the other hand, the system in operation provides no such independence, and contains no provision whatever for subsequent notification. Even if the system were to be considered adequate in its conditions, it is laid down merely as a matter of administrative procedure, so that it is unenforceable in law, and as a matter of law could at any time be altered without warning or subsequent notification. Certainly in law any 'adequate and effective safeguards against abuse' are wanting. In this respect English law compares most unfavourably with West German law: this is not a subject on which it is possible to feel any pride in English law.

English law fails to satisfy the Convention
I therefore find it impossible to see how English law could be said to satisfy the requirements of the Convention, as interpreted in the *Klass* case, unless that law not only prohibited all telephone tapping save in suitably limited classes of case, but also laid down detailed restrictions on the exercise of the power in those limited classes. It may perhaps be that the common law is sufficiently fertile to achieve what is required by the first limb of this; possible ways of expressing such a rule may be seen in what I have already said. But I see the greatest difficulty in the common law framing the safeguards required by the second limb. Various institutions or offices would have to be brought into being to exercise various defined functions. The more complex and indefinite the subject matter, the greater the difficulty in the court doing what it is really appropriate, and only appropriate, for the legislature to do. Furthermore, I find it hard to see what there is in the present case to require the English courts to struggle with such a problem. Give full rein to the Convention, and it is clear that when the object of the surveillance is the detection of crime, the question is not whether there ought to be a general prohibition of all surveillance, but in what circumstances, and subject to what conditions and restrictions, it ought to be permitted. It is those circumstances, conditions and restrictions which are at the centre of this case; and yet it is they which are the least suitable for determination by judicial decision.

It appears to me that to decide this case in the way that Mr Ross-Munro seeks would carry me far beyond any possible function of the Convention as influencing English law that has ever been suggested; and it would be most undesirable. Any regulation of so complex a matter as telephone tapping is essentially a matter for Parliament, not the courts; and neither the Convention nor the *Klass* case can, I think, play any proper part in deciding the issue before me. Accordingly, the second limb of Mr Ross-Munro's second main contention also fails.

I would only add that, even if it was not clear before, this case seems to me to make it plain that telephone tapping is a subject which cries out for legislation. Privacy and confidentiality are, of course, subjects of considerable complexity. Yet however desirable it may be that they should at least to some extent be defined and regulated by statute, rather than being left for slow and expensive evolution in individual cases brought at the expense of litigants and the legal aid fund, the difficulty of the subject matter is liable to discourage legislative zeal. Telephone tapping lies in a much narrower compass; the difficulties in legislating on the subject ought not to prove insuperable; and the requirements of the Convention should provide a spur to action, even if belated. This, however, is not for me to decide. I can do no more than express a hope, and offer a proleptic welcome to any statute on the subject. However much the protection of the public against crime demands that in proper cases the police should have the assistance of telephone tapping, I would have thought that in any civilised system of law the claims of liberty and justice would require that telephone users should have effective and independent safeguards against possible abuses. The fact that a telephone user is suspected of crime increases rather than diminishes this requirement: suspicions, however reasonably held, may sometimes prove to be wholly unfounded. If there were effective and independent safeguards these would not only exclude some cases of excessive zeal but also by their mere existence, provide some degree of reassurance for those who are resentful of the police or believe themselves to be persecuted. I may perhaps add that it would be wrong to allow my decision in this case to be influenced by the consideration that if the courts were to hold that all telephone tapping was illegal, this might well offer a strong and prompt inducement to the government to persuade Parliament to legislate on the subject.

The absence of a power
Seventh, there is Mr Ross-Munro's third main contention, based on the absence of any grant of powers to the executive to tap telephones. I have already held that if such tapping can be carried out without committing any breach of the law, it requires no authorisation by statute or common law; it can lawfully be done simply because there is nothing to make it unlawful. Now that I have held that such tapping can indeed be carried out without committing any breach of the law, the contention necessarily fails. I may also say that the statutory recognition given to the Home Secretary's warrant seems to me to point clearly to the same conclusion. . . .

In the result the plaintiff's claim fails in its entirety.

> *Since this judgment was given comprehensive legislation[56] of the sort Sir Robert advocated has been enacted to deal with telephone tapping. It does not detract from his many insightful comments on the issues arising in this case.*

The ignoble shortcut

> *How should the law deal with evidence which, though logically probative, has been obtained illegally? One view is that the*

---

[56] The Interception of Communications Act 1985.

evidence should be excluded as a lesson to the prosecutor to ensure the proper conduct of investigations in future. Another is that the evidence should be admitted in order to secure a just result and that the prosecutor's breach of the rules should be dealt with separately by disciplinary or even criminal proceedings. The two viewpoints were ventilated in the United States Supreme Court in 1961.[57]

Acting on information that a person wanted in connection with a recent bombing was hiding at a certain address and that there was 'a large amount of policy paraphernalia being hidden in the home' three police officers went to the apartment of a Miss Mapp without a search warrant. Miss Mapp, after telephoning her attorney, refused them entry. Three hours later and fortified by four or more other officers the police returned and forced entry. When Miss Mapp demanded to see their warrant one of the officers held up a document which he claimed was the warrant. Miss Mapp grabbed the paper. After a struggle she was handcuffed and her apartment searched. Various documents were taken, including obscene material found in the basement.

Miss Mapp was prosecuted for possession of the obscene material. No warrant was produced, nor was its non-production explained. It seems likely that no warrant in fact existed. Despite this fact Miss Mapp was convicted at the Ohio Court of Common Pleas on the ground that the evidence had not been taken from her 'by the use of brutal force'. On appeal to the Supreme Court of Ohio a majority were for quashing the conviction as unconstitutional, but under State law that majority was insufficient for such a decision. The US Supreme Court had no such constraints.

Delivering the opinion of the Court Mr Justice Clark said:

There are those who say, as did Justice (then Judge) Cardozo, that under our constitutional exclusionary doctrine '[t]he criminal is to go free because the constable has blundered.' ... In some cases this will undoubtedly be the result. But, as was said in *Elkins*, 'there is another consideration — the imperative of judicial integrity'. The criminal goes free, if he must, but it is the law that sets him free. Nothing can destroy a government more quickly than its failure to observe its own laws, or worse, its disregard of the charter of its own existence.

---

[57] *Mapp v Ohio* 367 US 643 (1961).

As Mr Justice Brandeis . . . said: 'Our government is the potent, the omnipresent teacher. For good or for ill, it teaches the whole people by its example. . . . If the government becomes a lawbreaker, it breeds contempt for law; it invites every man to become a law unto himself; it invites anarchy.' Nor can it lightly be assumed that, as a practical matter, adoption of the exclusionary rule fetters law enforcement. Only last year this Court expressly considered that contention and found that 'pragmatic evidence of a sort' to the contrary was not wanting. The Court noted that:

> The federal courts themselves have operated under the exclusionary rule for almost half a century; yet it has not been suggested either that the Federal Bureau of Investigation has thereby been rendered ineffective, or that the administration of criminal justice in the federal courts has thereby been disrupted. Moreover, the experience of the States is impressive. . . . The movement towards the rule of exclusion has been halting but seemingly inexorable.

The ignoble shortcut to conviction left open to the State tends to destroy the entire system of constitutional restraints on which the liberties of the people rest. Having once recognized that the right to privacy embodied in the Fourth Amendment is enforceable against the State, and that the right to be secure against rude invasions of privacy by State officers is, therefore, constitutional in origin, we can no longer permit that right to remain an empty promise. Because it is enforceable in the same manner and to like effect as other basic rights secured by the Due Process Clause, we can no longer permit it to be revocable at the whim of a police officer who, in the name of law enforcement itself, chooses to suspend its enjoyment. Our decision, founded on reason and truth, gives to the individual no more than that which the Constitution guarantees him, to the police officer no less than that to which honest law enforcement is entitled, and, to the courts, that judicial integrity so necessary in the true administration of justice.

The decision of the lower court was reversed and the conviction quashed.

In Britain the courts have long claimed the power (now enacted in statute)[58] to exclude evidence obtained by unlawful or improper means. But this is a discretion, not an obligation.

---

[58] The Police and Criminal Evidence Act 1984, section 78(1).

Many of the rules of the criminal law were developed when hanging was the punishment for even a minor felony. In an age when the accused enjoyed no substantive right of appeal such a sentence was incapable of rectification if events subsequently cast doubt on the correctness of the conviction. With the abolition of capital punishment, the establishment of a fully developed appeal system and, most recently, of the Criminal Cases Review Commission it could be said that the need to tip the balance in favour of the defendant has been removed altogether. At a time when our crime rate rivals that of America should we not reflect on whether the rules of evidence favour the accused unduly?

Law Society Hall

5. THE FIRST CASUALTY

or

The Law and Human Rights

Freedom of speech is always the first casualty under a
totalitarian regime.

Lord Bridge of Harwich
in *Attorney-General* v *Guardian Newspapers Ltd.*[59]

Freedom of speech established
The first casualty
Believing in the power of reason
Freedom of speech exists only under law
A balance has to be struck
A man may speak the thing he will

---

[59] See under *The first casualty.*

Nowadays everyone, from the infant to the political activist, is accustomed to expressing his desires in terms of a claim of right. Most are prepared to acknowledge a distinction between those rights which the law will enforce and those which it will not, but this does little to dampen their enthusiasm since claimants then assert for their desires a moral (or human or fundamental) right, the unenforceability of which is simply a defect of current law.

Entrenched rights have typically been secured by force, whether from a colonial power, as in America, the ancien régime, *as in France, or, as happened in this country, from an over-mighty sovereign.*

THE GREAT CHARTER

On 15 June 1215, on an island between Staines and Windsor King John met his barons with a view to endorsing his total submission to the claims which they had successfully prosecuted by force of arms. As one misty eyed historian wrote:[60]

It is impossible to gaze without reverence on the earliest monument of English freedom which we can see with our own eyes and touch with our own hands, the great Charter to which from age to age patriots have looked back as the basis of English liberty.

In fact, most of the 63 clauses of the Great Charter benefited no one but the barons, but tucked away among them were two which were to have lasting influence:

39. No freeman shall be taken, imprisoned, disseised, outlawed, banished, or in any way destroyed, nor will we proceed against or prosecute him, except by the lawful judgment of his peers and by the law of the land.

40. To no one will we sell, to no one will we deny or delay right or justice.[61]

---

[60] J. R. Green, *A Short History of the English People* (1874).
[61] For the record, the Great Charter did not establish trial by jury and did not create the writ of habeas corpus, as falsely claimed in the Petition of Right.

Four hundred years later in the strained polity of the seventeenth century Parliament enjoyed a minor victory over another unpopular monarch. Passed by both Houses of Parliament in 1628 and eventually accepted by King Charles, the Petition of Right was directed mainly against arbitrary imprisonment and taxation without Parliamentary authority. Significant though it was, this concession was not enough to keep the King's head on his shoulders.

The next English declaration of rights was not wrested from an unpopular monarch, but conceded by an ambitious claimant to the throne. Based on the Declaration of Right of the previous year the Bill of Rights of 1689 was accepted by William of Orange as part of the settlement of the Glorious Revolution. It proscribed the royal power to suspend laws and prohibited excessive bail and fines, as well as cruel and unusual punishments (a somewhat curious phrase that was later to be appropriated by the framers of the American Constitution). The Bill of Rights also provided for free elections, freedom of speech in Parliament and for the redress of grievances. Apart from a few notable exceptions these measures had little effect on an Englishman's liberties and it was not until a century later and in other lands that the banner was picked up, and with greater effect.

England's diffuse and, it must be said, vestigial roll of human rights pales into insignificance beside those of the nation States created in the Age of Enlightenment, notably France and America.

HUMAN RIGHTS IN AMERICA AND FRANCE

The Massachusetts Bodie of Liberties (1641) has been described as 'Western history's — and probably history's — first comprehensive bill of rights'.[62] *Massachusetts' example was copied by other American colonies, notably in Pennsylvania's Charter of Privileges (1701).*

When the Constitution of the newly formed United States of America was being considered by the Continental Congress four States, Virginia, Massachussets, New York and Pennsylvania,

---

[62] Alfred H. Wright, *The Life of the Law* (Crown Publishers Inc., 1996).

refused to sign without explicit protection of civil liberties. As a result, 10 amendments were approved which form the centrepiece of American civil rights. Modelled by James Maddison on the Virginia Declaration of Rights, they are known in that country as the Bill of Rights (1789, ratified 1791). To this day these rights play a large part in defining the relationship between the American citizen and his or her government. An English lawyer coming for the first time to an American Bill of Rights suit may be flabbergasted at the literalness with which these rights are taken: nothing save the claim of another right may gainsay them, sometimes, it seems, not even common sense.

The French Declaration of the Rights of Man and of the Citizen (1789)[63] proclaimed general principles rather than practically enforceable rights. If the purpose of the Declaration was to guard against what Mr Justice Brandeis described as 'the occasional tyrannies of governing majorities' it was a signal failure, as the victims of the Terror would have affirmed had they lived to do so.

HUMAN RIGHTS GO INTERNATIONAL

But the halcyon days of human rights were yet to come. After the Second World War the victorious nations sought to spread the benefits of human rights throughout the planet. The United Nations Universal Declaration of Human Rights (1948) was the disappointing outcome. Despite pious words in the Charter of the United Nations and the setting up of a Commission of Human Rights the Declaration proved to be unenforceable. As a result, the States comprising the Council of Europe decided to go it alone with a more specific and more readily enforceable measure, the Convention for the Protection of Human Rights and Fundamental Freedoms (1953).

The interpretation of the Convention by the European Court of Human Rights has sometimes led to consequences not readily foreseeable from its bare words, some of them involving costly demands on the public purse. Countries like England that pride themselves on their concern for liberty have been the subject of

---

[63] We should not forget the *Declaration of the Rights of Women and Citizenesses* of Olympia de Gouges, 1791. For the text of this extraordinarily prescient document see Norman Davies, *Europe: A History* (Oxford University Press, 1996), p. 716.

constant attack, while less scrupulous nations have escaped attention. Most recently, the Blair government has announced its intention to incorporate the 'principles' of the Convention into English law. Whatever form the legislation takes it is likely to have incalculably profound effects on the ways we live and are governed.

THE RIGHT OF FREE SPEECH

The complete spectrum of human rights is too broad to embrace in a work of this nature, so the rest of this chapter concentrates on the right to free speech, one of the most prized in the politically active West.

It is easy to forget that the right of free speech originated, almost by accident, in seventeenth-century England, as the extract from Lord Scarman's speech set out below recounts (see under Freedom of speech established*). Doubts about the efficacy of the common law to assure this right led a member of the House of Lords to ponder whether statutory safeguards were not necessary. The contrary view is put by another judge in the same case (* The first casualty *).*

THE PROBLEM OF CONFLICTING RIGHTS

In the 1960s the 'me generation' took to the idea of human rights like a vexatious litigant to the legal aid fund. Inevitably, they lost sight of the fact that every right is accompanied by a duty.[64] Perhaps the greatest problem to which the notion of human rights can give rise is how one person's right should be balanced against another's. The Constitution of the United States of America, like the Universal Declaration of Human Rights, gives no assistance in this respect and it has been left to the judges to work out an accommodation (Believing in the power of reason *).*

That no single formula is likely to suffice for the reconciliation of conflicting rights is demonstrated by the opinion of an American

---

[64] It is probably too late now to take up Lord Mustill's percipient remark that 'Emphasis on human duties will often yield a more balanced and sharply focused protection for the individual than the contemporary preoccupation with human rights (see under *The privacy of the torture chamber*).

judge in a case where the constitutional right of free speech came into conflict with the constitutional right of free assembly. Rejecting the 'dogma of absolute freedom for irresponsible and provocative utterance' he observed that:

> The choice is not between order and liberty. It is between liberty with order and anarchy without either. (*Freedom of speech exists only under law.*)

English judges have long been accustomed to the pragmatic resolution of conflicting rights, as witness the report of Lord Scarman on the Red Lion Square disorders (A balance has to be struck) or the judgment of Lord Denning in a case involving the National Front (A man may speak the thing he will).

The European Convention offers an intermediate approach by incorporating in each clause a clear statement of the circumstances in which the particular right may be subordinated to another. With the imminent incorporation into English law of the principles of the European Convention we live on the cusp of great changes.

Freedom of speech established

The right of free speech is not so old as the right to liberty of the person, but it is still older than some realise. As Lord Scarman noted:[65]

Milton, in his famous address to Lords and Commons, urged that freedom to print and publish should not be shackled or restricted, and said in his peroration: 'give me the liberty to know, to utter, and to argue freely, according to conscience, above all liberties'.[66] The fetters on such liberties did not disappear until Parliament in 1694 refused to renew the Licensing Act.[67] By this refusal, as Dicey has pointed out, Parliament 'established freedom of the press without any knowledge of the importance of what they were doing', and achieved 'what Milton's *Areopagitica* had failed to do'. Thenceforward

---

[65] *Home Office* v *Harman* [1982] 1 All ER 532, 543.

[66] *Areopagitica* (1666).

[67] An Act of 1685 forbidding the printing of any book without a licence. Legislation of this nature had been in force in one form or another since the time of Henry VIII.

freedom of communication became part of the English common law. Everyone thereafter had that right, except in so far as the communication offended against some clear provision of the law (such as defamation or, later, copyright). When the Americans made into fundamental constitutional law what they saw as the basic rights vouchsafed to them by their heritage of the common law, the very first amendment to the Constitution, inscribed in the Bill of Rights 1791, contained the following provisions: 'Congress shall make no law ... abridging the freedom of speech, or of the press.'

He added tellingly

These large rights, basic to human dignity and therefore of great weight in any balance, cannot, however, be absolute.

The case concerned the right of a solicitor to reveal to a journalist documents which she had received under an implied undertaking of confidence. The solicitor, Miss Harriet Harman, was at the time legal officer for the National Council for Civil Liberties (now Liberty). She subsequently became a Member of Parliament and, in 1997, Secretary of State for Social Security.

The first casualty

The lack of a statutory right of free speech has caused unease to at least one English judge.

Peter Wright was a disaffected former officer of the Secret Intelligence Service. While living in Australia he wrote his memoirs under the title, Spycatcher. *Two English newspapers, the* Guardian *and the* Observer, *published allegations contained in these memoirs. Fearing a breach of national security, the Attorney-General sought and obtained in Australia interlocutory injunctions restraining further disclosures. He subsequently obtained similar injunctions in this country except in respect of material already revealed in open court in Australia.*

Three more newspapers thereupon published material from the manuscript, which resulted in the Attorney-General bringing proceedings for criminal contempt.

Wright's memoirs were subsequently published in America. It was not possible under United States law for the Attorney-General to prevent this and the work soon became freely available in this country. The Sunday Times *published substantial extracts from the book and from the extracts which had appeared in other papers. The* Guardian *and the* Observer *then applied to have the interlocutory injunctions lifted. Meanwhile, the Attorney-General applied to commit the* Sunday Times *for contempt.*

The Vice-Chancellor[68] dismissed the interlocutory injunctions, but was reversed on appeal. The House of Lords dismissed the newspapers' appeals and allowed cross-appeals. In a notable dissenting speech[69] Lord Bridge of Harwich examined the arguments in favour the injunctions and observed trenchantly:

Having no written constitution, we have no equivalent in our law to the First Amendment to the Constitution of the United States of America. Some think that puts freedom of speech on too lofty a pedestal. Perhaps they are right. We have not adopted as part of our law the European Convention on Human Rights to which this country is a signatory. Many think that we should. I have hitherto not been of that persuasion, in large part because I have had confidence in the capacity of the common law to safeguard the fundamental freedoms essential to a free society including the right to freedom of speech which is specifically safeguarded by article 10 of the Convention. My confidence is seriously undermined by your Lordships' decision. All the judges in the courts below in this case have been concerned not to impose any unnecessary fetter on freedom of speech. I suspect that what the Court of Appeal would have liked to achieve, and perhaps set out to achieve by its compromise solution, was to inhibit the *Sunday Times* from continuing the serialisation of *Spycatcher*, but to leave the press at large at liberty to discuss and comment on the *Spycatcher* allegations. If there were a method of achieving these results which could be sustained in law, I can see much to be said for it on the merits. But I can see nothing whatever, either in law or on the merits, to be said for the maintenance of a total ban on discussion in the press of this country of matters of undoubted public interest and concern which the rest of the world now knows all about and can discuss freely. Still less can I approve your Lordships' decision to throw in for good measure a restriction on reporting court proceedings in Australia which the Attorney-General had never even asked for.

---

[68] That is, the head of the Chancery Division of the High Court.
[69] *Attorney-General* v *Guardian Newspapers Ltd* [1987] 3 All ER 316, 343.

Freedom of speech is always the first casualty under a totalitarian regime. Such a regime cannot afford to allow the free circulation of information and ideas among its citizens. Censorship is the indispensable tool to regulate what the public may and what they may not know. The present attempt to insulate the public in this country from information which is freely available elsewhere is a significant step down that very dangerous road. The maintenance of the ban, as more and more copies of the book *Spycatcher* enter this country and circulate here, will seem more and more ridiculous. If the government are determined to fight to maintain the ban to the end, they will face inevitable condemnation and humiliation by the European Court of Human Rights in Strasbourg. Long before that they will have been condemned at the bar of public opinion in the free world.

But there is another alternative. The government will surely want to reappraise the whole *Spycatcher* situation in the light of the views expressed in the courts below and in this House. I dare to hope that they will bring to that reappraisal qualities of vision and of statesmanship sufficient to recognise that their wafer-thin victory in this litigation has been gained at a price which no government committed to upholding the values of a free society can afford to pay.

In a later case involving the same parties, Lord Goff of Chievely advanced a contrary point of view in these words:[70]

I can see no inconsistency between English law on this subject and article 10 of the Convention for the Protection of Human Rights and Fundamental Freedoms. This is scarcely surprising, since we may pride ourselves on the fact that freedom of speech has existed in this country perhaps as long as, if not longer than, it has existed in any other country in the world. The only difference is that, whereas article 10 of the Convention, in accordance with its avowed purpose, proceeds to state a fundamental right and then to qualify it, we in this country (where everybody is free to do anything, subject only to the provisions of the law) proceed rather on an assumption of freedom of speech, and turn to our law to discover the established exceptions to it.

In this case the House of Lords[71] *decided that the government was not in a position to win the assistance of the court in restricting the publication of information imparted in confidence by it or its*

---

[70] *Attorney-General* v *Guardian Newspapers Ltd (No. 2)* [1988] 3 All ER 545, 660.
[71] *Attorney-General* v *Guardian Newspapers Ltd (No. 2)* [1988] 3 All ER 545.

predecessors unless it could show that publication would be harmful to the public interest. Since Spycatcher *was widely available outside the United Kingdom it was held that its further publication here could not damage the public interest.*

These proceedings illustrate the dangers of courts attempting to emulate King Canute.

Believing in the power of reason

The American Constitution is silent on the question of how one Constitutional right should be balanced against another and the judges have been left to sort out this problem.

In the course of an otherwise unremarkable opinion in the United States Supreme Court Mr Justice Brandeis essayed the following exposition of the balance which sometimes has to be struck between conflicting rights.

The petitioner, Charlotte Whitney, was convicted of assisting in organising the Communist Labor Party of California, of being a member of it and of assembling with it. These acts were said to constitute a crime because the party was formed to teach criminal syndicalism (or the advocacy of change in the owner- ship of industry *). Miss Whitney appealed successfully against conviction on the basis of the liberty guaranteed by the Fourteenth Amendment.*

Brandeis said:[72]

Those who won our independence believed that the final end of the State was to make men free to develop their faculties, and that, in its government, the deliberative forces should prevail over the arbitrary. They valued liberty both as an end, and as a means. They believed liberty to be the secret of happiness,

---

[72] *Whitney* v *California*, 274 US 357 (1927).

and courage to be the secret of liberty. They believed that freedom to think as you will and to speak as you think are means indispensable to the discovery and spread of political truth; that, without free speech and assembly, discussion would be futile; that, with them, discussion affords ordinarily adequate protection against the dissemination of noxious doctrine; that the greatest menace to freedom is an inert people; that public discussion is a political duty, and that this should be a fundamental principle of the American government.

They recognised the risks to which all human institutions are subject. But they knew that order cannot be secured merely through fear of punishment for its infraction; that it is hazardous to discourage thought, hope and imagination; that fear breeds repression; that repression breeds hate; that hate menaces stable government; that the path of safety lies in the opportunity to discuss freely supposed grievances and proposed remedies, and that the fitting remedy for evil counsels is good ones. Believing in the power of reason as applied through public discussion, they eschewed silence coerced by law — the argument of force in its worst form. Recognising the occasional tyrannies of governing majorities, they amended the Constitution so that free speech and assembly should be guaranteed.

Fear of serious injury cannot alone justify suppression of free speech and assembly. Men feared witches and burnt women. It is the function of speech to free men from the bondage of irrational fears. To justify suppression of free speech, there must be reasonable ground to fear that serious evil will result if free speech is practiced. There must be reasonable ground to believe that the danger apprehended is imminent. There must be reasonable ground to believe that the evil to be prevented is a serious one. Every denunciation of existing law tends in some measure to increase the probability that there will be violation of it. Condonation of a breach enhances the probability. Expressions of approval add to the probability. Propagation of the criminal state of mind by teaching syndicalism increases it. Advocacy of law-breaking heightens it still further.

But even advocacy of violation, however reprehensible morally, is not a justification for denying free speech where the advocacy falls short of incitement and there is nothing to indicate that the advocacy would ·be immediately acted on. The wide difference between advocacy and incitement, between preparation and attempt, between assembling and conspiracy, must be borne in mind. In order to support a finding of clear and present danger, it must be shown either that immediate serious violence was to be expected or was advocated, or that the past conduct furnished reason to believe that such advocacy was then contemplated.

Those who won our independence by revolution were not cowards. They did not fear political change. They did not exalt order at the cost of liberty. To courageous, self-reliant men, with confidence in the power of free and fearless reasoning applied through the processes of popular government, no danger flowing from speech can be deemed clear and present unless the incidence of the evil apprehended is so imminent that it may befall before there is opportunity for full discussion. If there be time to expose through discussion the falsehood and fallacies, to avert the evil by the processes of education, the remedy to be applied is more speech, not enforced silence. Only an emergency can justify repression. Such must be the rule if authority is to be reconciled with freedom. Such, in my opinion, is the command of the Constitution.

It is therefore always open to Americans to challenge a law abridging free speech and assembly by showing that there was no emergency justifying it. Moreover, even imminent danger cannot justify resort to prohibition of these functions essential to effective democracy unless the evil apprehended is relatively serious. Prohibition of free speech and assembly is a measure so stringent that it would be inappropriate as the means for averting a relatively trivial harm to society. A police measure may be unconstitutional merely because the remedy, although effective as means of protection, is unduly harsh or oppressive. Thus, a State might, in the exercise of its police power, make any trespass upon the land of another a crime, regardless of the results or of the intent or purpose of the trespasser. It might, also, punish an attempt, a conspiracy, or an incitement to commit the trespass. But it is hardly conceivable that this Court would hold constitutional a statute which punished as a felony the mere voluntary assembly with a society formed to teach that pedestrians had the moral right to cross unenclosed, unposted, wastelands and to advocate their doing so, even if there was imminent danger that advocacy would lead to a trespass. The fact that speech is likely to result in some violence or in destruction of property is not enough to justify its suppression. There must be the probability of serious injury to the State. Among free men, the deterrents ordinarily to be applied to prevent crime are education and punishment for violations of the law, not abridgment of the rights of free speech and assembly.

> **Louis D. Brandeis was nominated to the Supreme Court by Woodrow Wilson in 1916 and served until 1939, dying two years later. His name is still associated with the Brandeis brief, the notion he advanced many years before as an advocate[73] that the court, when considering the mischief that a statute is intended to rectify, should have regard to social study investigations.**

---

[73] See *Muller v Oregon*, 208 US 412 (1907).

Freedom of speech exists only under law

No single test is likely to be able to resolve satisfactorily all the problems inherent in conflicting rights, as was demonstrated by the dissenting opinion of a member of the United States Supreme Court in 1948.

Father Terminiello, described as a Catholic priest, but in fact under suspension by his Bishop, had been brought to Chicago from Birmingham, Alabama, to speak at a public meeting of the Christian Veterans of America. When he arrived there was a crowd of some three or four hundred outside the building shouting threats and throwing stones. They tried to break down the door. Terminiello then made an inflammatory speech abusing the Communists in Russia and outside the hall. He was accordingly charged with and found guilty of an offence under a local ordinance.

The judge in instructing the jury had placed a construction upon the ordinance which permitted conviction should the jury find that the defendant's speech had stirred people to anger, invited public dispute or brought about a condition of unrest. No objection had been taken on this point, either in the trial court or in the State appellate court. Nevertheless, when the case reached the Supreme Court the justices, by a majority, held that this construction rendered the ordinance an infringement of the constitutional right of free speech.

Four justices dissented. One of them was Mr Justice Jackson, who said:[74]

The Court reverses this conviction by reiterating generalized approbations of freedom of speech with which, in the abstract, no one will disagree. Doubts as to their applicability are lulled by avoidance of more than passing reference to the circumstances of Terminiello's speech and judging it as if he had spoken to persons as dispassionate as empty benches, or like a modern Demosthenes practicing his Philippics on a lonely seashore.

---

[74] *Terminiello* v *City of Chicago*, 337 US 1 (1949).

But the local court that tried Terminiello was not indulging in theory. It was dealing with a riot and with a speech that provoked a hostile mob and incited a friendly one, and threatened violence between the two. When the trial judge instructed the jury that it might find Terminiello guilty of inducing a breach of the peace if his behavior stirred the public to anger, invited dispute, brought about unrest, created a disturbance or molested peace and quiet by arousing alarm, he was not speaking of these as harmless or abstract conditions. He was addressing his words to the concrete behavior and specific consequences disclosed by the evidence. He was saying to the jury, in effect, that if this particular speech added fuel to the situation already so inflamed as to threaten to get beyond police control, it could be punished as inducing a breach of peace. When the light of the evidence not recited by the Court is thrown upon the Court's opinion, it discloses that underneath a little issue of Terminiello and his hundred-dollar fine lurk some of the most far-reaching constitutional questions that can confront a people who value both liberty and order. This Court seems to regard these as enemies of each other and to be of the view that we must forgo order to achieve liberty. So it fixes its eyes on a conception of freedom of speech so rigid as to tolerate no concession to society's need for public order.

An old proverb warns us to take heed lest we 'walk into a well from looking at the stars'.

After reviewing the facts of the case Jackson went on:

Terminiello, of course, disclaims being a fascist. Doubtless many of the indoor audience were not consciously such. His speech, however, followed, with fidelity that is more than coincidental, the pattern of European fascist leaders. The street mob, on the other hand, included some who deny being communists, but Terminiello testified and offered to prove that the demonstration was communist-organized and communist-led. He offered literature of left-wing organizations calling members to meet and 'mobilize' for instruction as pickets and exhorting followers: 'All out to fight Fascist Smith'.

As this case declares a nationwide rule that disables local and state authorities from punishing conduct which produces conflicts of this kind, it is unrealistic not to take account of the nature, methods and objectives of the forces involved. This was not an isolated, spontaneous and unintended collision of political, racial or ideological adversaries. It was a local manifestation of a worldwide and standing conflict between two organized groups of revolutionary fanatics, each of which has imported to this country the strong-arm technique developed in the struggle by which their kind has devastated Europe. Increasingly, American cities have to cope with it. One faction organizes a mass meeting, the other organizes pickets to harass it; each organizes squads to counteract the other's pickets; parade is met with counterparade. Each of these mass demonstrations has the potentiality, and more than a few the purpose, of disorder and violence. This technique appeals not to reason but to fears and mob spirit; each is a show of force designed to bully adversaries and to overawe the indifferent. We need not resort to speculation as to the purposes for which these tactics are calculated nor as to their consequences. Recent European history demonstrates both. Hitler summed up the strategy of the mass demonstration as used by both fascism and communism: 'We should not work in secret conventicles but in mighty mass demonstrations, and it is not by dagger and poison or pistol that the road can be cleared for the movement but by the conquest of the streets. We must teach the Marxists that the future master of the streets is National Socialism, just as it will some day be the master of the state.' (*Mein Kampf.*) First laughed at as an extravagant figure of speech, the battle for the streets became a tragic reality when an organised *Sturmabteilung* began to give practical effect to its slogan that 'possession of the streets is the key to power in the State'.

The present obstacle to mastery of the streets by either radical or reactionary mob movements is not the opposing minority. It is the authority of local governments which represent the free choice of democratic and law-abiding elements, of all shades of opinion but who, whatever their differences, submit them to free elections which register the results of their free discussion. The fascist and communist groups, on the contrary, resort to these terror tactics to confuse, bully and discredit those freely chosen governments. Violent and noisy shows of strength discourage participation of moderates in discussions so fraught with violence and real discussion dries up and disappears. And people lose faith in the democratic process when they see public authority flouted and impotent and begin to think the time has come when they must choose sides in a false and terrible dilemma such as was posed as being at hand by the call for the Terminiello meeting: 'Christian Nationalism or World Communism — Which?'

This drive by totalitarian groups to undermine the prestige and effectiveness of local democratic governments is advanced whenever either of them can win from this Court a ruling which paralyzes the power of these officials. This is such a case. The group of which Terminiello is a part claims that his behavior, because it involved a speech, is above the reach of local authorities. If the mild action those authorities have taken is forbidden, it is plain that hereafter there is nothing effective left that they can do. If they can do nothing as to him, they are equally powerless as to rival totalitarian groups. Terminiello's victory today certainly fulfils the most extravagant hopes of both right and left totalitarian groups, who want nothing so much as to paralyze and discredit the only democratic authority and can curb them in their battle for the streets.

I am unable to see that the local authorities have transgressed the Federal Constitution. Illinois imposed no prior censorship or suppression upon Terminiello. On the contrary, its sufferance and protection was all that enabled him to speak. It does not appear that the motive in punishing him is to silence the ideology he expressed as offensive to the State's policy or as untrue, or has any purpose of controlling his thought or its peaceful communication to others. There is no claim that the proceedings against Terminiello are designed to discriminate against him or the faction he represents or the ideas that he bespeaks. There is no indication that the charge against him is a mere pretext to give the semblance of legality to a covert effort to silence him or to prevent his followers or the public from hearing any truth that is in him.

A trial court and jury has found only that in the context of violence and disorder in which it was made, this speech was a provocation to immediate breach of the peace and therefore cannot claim Constitutional immunity from punishment. Under the Constitution as it has been understood and applied, at least until most recently, the State was within its powers in taking this action.

A substantive evil

Rioting is a substantive evil, which I take it no one will deny that the State and the City have the right and the duty to prevent and punish. Where an offense is induced by speech, the Court has laid down and often reiterated a test of the power of the authorities to deal with the speaking as also an offense. 'The question in every case is whether the words used are used in such circumstances and are of such a nature as to create a clear and present danger that they will bring about the substantive evils that Congress [or the State or City] has a right to prevent' (Mr Justice Holmes). No one ventures to contend that the State on the basis of this test, for whatever it may be worth, was not justified in punishing Terminiello. In this case the evidence proves beyond dispute that danger of rioting and violence in response to the speech was clear, present and immediate. If this Court has not silently abandoned this long-standing test and substituted for the purposes of this case an unexpressed but more stringent test, the action of the State would have to be sustained.

After reviewing earlier decisions of the court he said:

However, these wholesome principles are abandoned today and in their place is substituted a dogma of absolute freedom for irresponsible and provocative utterance which almost completely sterilizes the power of local authorities to keep the peace as against these kind of tactics.

Before giving the First and Fourteenth Amendments to the Constitution this effect, we should recall that our application of the First Amendment to Illinois rests entirely on authority which this Court has voted to itself. The relevant parts of the First Amendment, with emphasis supplied, reads: '*Congress* shall make *no* law ... abridging the freedom of speech'. This restrains no authority except Congress. Read as literally as some would do, it restrains Congress in terms so absolute that no legislation would be valid if it touched free speech, no matter how obscene, treasonable, defamatory, inciting or provoking. If it seems strange that no express qualifications were inserted in the Amendment, the answer may be that limitations were thought to be implicit in the definition of 'freedom of speech' as then understood. Or it may have been thought unnecessary to delegate to Congress any power over abuses of free speech. The Federal Government was then a new and experimental authority, remote from the people, and it was supposed to deal with a limited class of national problems. Inasmuch as any breaches of peace from abuse of free speech traditionally were punishable by state governments, it was needless to reserve that power in a provision drafted to exclude only Congress from such a field of law-making.

The Fourteenth Amendment forbade states to deny the citizen 'due process of law'. But its terms gave no notice to the people that its adoption would strip their local governments of power to deal with such problems of local peace and order as we have here. Nor was it hinted by this Court for over half a century that the Amendment might have any such effect. In 1922, with concurrence of the most liberty-alert Justices of all times — Holmes and Brandeis — this Court declared flatly that the Constitution does not limit the power of the state over free speech. In later years the Court shifted this dogma and decreed that the Constitution does this very thing and that state power is bound by the same limitation as Congress. I have no quarrel with this history. I recite the method by which the right to limit the state has been derived only from this Court's own assumption of the power, with never a submission of legislation or amendment into which the people could write any qualification to prevent abuse of this liberty, as bearing upon the restraint I consider as becoming an exercise of self-given and unappealable power.

It is significant that provisions adopted by the people with awareness that they applied to their own states have universally contained qualifying terms. The Constitution of Illinois is representative of the provisions put in nearly all state constitutions and reads: 'Every person may freely speak, write and publish on all subjects, being responsible for the abuse of that liberty.' That is what I think is meant by the cryptic phrase 'freedom of speech', as used in the Federal Compact, and that is the rule I think we should apply to the states.

This absence from the Constitution of any expressed power to deal with abuse of freedom of speech has enabled the Court to soar aloof from any consideration of the abuses which create problems for the states and to indulge in denials of local authority, some of which seem to me improvident in the light of functions which local governments must be relied on to perform for our free society. Quite apart from any other merits or defects, recent decisions have almost completely immunized this battle for the streets from any form of control....

I do not think we should carry this handicap further, as we do today, but should adhere to the principles heretofore announced to safeguard our liberties against abuse as well as against invasion. It should not be necessary to recall these elementary principles, but it has been a long time since some of them were even mentioned in this Court's writing on the subject and results indicate they may have been overlooked....

I begin with the oft-forgotten principle which this case demonstrates, that freedom of speech exists only under law and not independently of it. What would Terminiello's theoretical freedom of speech have amounted to had he not been given active aid by the officers of the law? He could reach the hall only with their help, could talk only because they restrained the mob, and could make his getaway only under their protection. We would do well to recall the words of Chief Justice Hughes: 'Civil liberties, as guaranteed by the Constitution, imply the existence of an organized society maintaining public order without which liberty itself would be lost in the excesses of unrestrained abuses.'

This case demonstrates also that this Court's service to free speech is essentially negative and can consist only of reviewing actions by local magistrates. But if free speech is to be a practical reality, affirmative and immediate protection is required; and it can come only from nonjudicial sources. It depends on local police, maintained by law-abiding taxpayers, and who, regardless of their own feelings, risk themselves to maintain supremacy of law. Terminiello's theoretical right to speak free from interference would have no reality if Chicago should withdraw its officers to some other section of the city, or if the men assigned to the task should look the other way when the crowd threatens Terminiello. Can society be expected to keep these men at Terminiello's service if it has nothing to say of his behavior which may force them into dangerous action?

No one will disagree that the fundamental, permanent and overriding policy of police and courts should be to permit and encourage utmost freedom of utterance. It is the legal right of any American citizen to advocate peaceful adoption of fascism or communism, socialism or capitalism. He may go far in expressing sentiments whether pro-semitic or anti-semitic, pro-negro or anti-negro, pro-Catholic or anti-Catholic. He is legally free to argue for some anti-American system of government to supersede by constitutional methods the one we have. It is our philosophy that the course of government should be controlled by a consensus of the governed. This process of reaching intelligent popular decisions requires free discussion. Hence we should tolerate no law or custom of censorship or suppression.

But we must bear in mind also that no serious outbreak of mob violence, race rioting, lynching or public disorder is likely to get going without help of some speech-making to some mass of people. A street may be filled with men and women and the crowd still not be a mob. Unity of purpose, passion and hatred, which merges the many minds of a crowd into the mindlessness of a mob, almost invariably is supplied by speeches. It is naive, or worse, to teach that oratory with this object or effect is a service to liberty. No mob has ever protected any liberty, even its own, but if not put down it always winds up in an orgy of lawlessness which respects no liberties.

Law indifferent to talk
In considering abuse of freedom by provocative utterances it is necessary to observe that the law is more tolerant of discussion than are most individuals or communities. Law is so indifferent to subjects of talk that I think of none that it should close to discussion. Religious, social and political topics that in other times or countries have not been open to lawful debate may be freely discussed here.

Because a subject is legally arguable, however, does not mean that public sentiment will be patient of its advocacy at all times and in all manners. So it happens that, while peaceful advocacy of communism or fascism is tolerated by the law, both of these doctrines arouse passionate reactions. A great number of people do not agree that introduction to America of communism or fascism is even debatable. Hence many speeches, such as that of Terminiello, may be legally permissible but may nevertheless in some surroundings, be a menace to peace and order. When conditions show the speaker that this is the case, as it did here, there certainly comes a point beyond which he cannot indulge in provocations to violence without being answerable to society.

Determination of such an issue involves a heavy responsibility. Courts must beware lest they become mere organs of popular intolerance. Not every show of opposition can justify treating a speech as a breach of peace. Neither speakers nor courts are obliged always and in all circumstances to yield to prevailing opinion and feeling.

As a people grow in capacity for civilization and liberty their tolerance will grow, and they will endure, if not welcome discussion even on topics as to which they are committed. They regard convictions as tentative and know that time and events will make their own terms with theories by whomever and by whatever majorities they are held and many will be proved wrong. But on our way to this idealistic state of tolerance the police have to deal with men as they are. The crowd mind is never tolerant of any idea which does not conform to its herd opinion. It does not want a tolerant effort at meeting of minds. It does not know the futility of trying to mob an idea.

Domestic tranquillity
Released from the sense of personal responsibility that would restrain even the worst individuals in it if alone and brave with the courage of numbers, both radical and reactionary mobs endanger liberty as well as order. The authorities must control them and they are entitled to place some checks upon those whose behavior or speech calls such mobs into being. When the right of society to freedom from probable violence should prevail over the right of an individual to defy opposing opinion, presents a problem that always tests wisdom and often calls for immediate and vigorous action to preserve public order and safety. I do not think that the Constitution of the United States denies to the states and the municipalities power to solve that problem in the light of local conditions at least so long as danger to public order is not invoked in bad faith, as a cover for censorship or suppression. The preamble declares domestic tranquility as well as liberty to be an object in founding a Federal Government and I do not think the Forefathers were naive in believing both can be fostered by the law.

Certain practical reasons reinforce the legal view that cities and states should be sustained in the power to keep their streets from becoming the battleground for these hostile ideologies to the destruction and detriment of public order. There is no other power that can do it. Theirs are the only police that are on the spot. The Federal Government has no police force. The Federal Bureau of Investigation is, and should remain, not a police but an investigative service. To date the only federal agency for preserving and restoring order when local authority fails has been the Army. And when the military steps in, the court takes a less liberal view of the rights of the individual and sustains most arbitrary exercises of military power.... Every failure of local authority to deal with riot problems results in a demand for the establishment of a federal police or intervention by federal authority. In my opinion, locally established and controlled police can never develop into the menace to general civil liberties that is inherent in a federal police.

The ways in which mob violence may be worked up are subtle and various. Rarely will a speaker directly urge a crowd to lay hands on a victim or class of victims. An effective and safer way is to incite mob action while pretending to deplore it, after the classic example of Antony, and this was not lost on Terminiello. And whether one may be the cause of mob violence by his own personification or advocacy of ideas which a crowd already fears and hates, is not solved merely by going through a transcript of the speech to pick out 'fighting words'. The most insulting words can be neutralized if the speaker will smile when he says them, but a belligerent personality and an aggressive manner may kindle a fight without use of words that in cold type shock us. True judgment will be aided by observation of the individual defendant, as was possible for this jury and trial court but impossible for us.

There are many appeals these days to liberty, often by those who are working for an opportunity to taunt democracy with its stupidity in furnishing them the weapons to destroy it as did Goebbels when he said:

Invocation of constitutional liberties as part of the strategy for overthrowing them presents a dilemma to a free people which may not be soluble by constitutional logic alone.

But I would not be understood as suggesting that the United States can or should meet this dilemma by suppression of free, open and public speaking on the part of any group or ideology. Suppression has never been a successful permanent policy; any surface serenity that it creates is a false security, while conspiratorial forces go underground. My confidence in American institutions and in the sound sense of the American people is such that if with a stroke of the pen I could silence every fascist and communist speaker, I would not do it. For I agree with Woodrow Wilson, who said:

I have always been among those who believed that the greatest freedom of speech was the greatest safety, because if a man is a fool, the best thing to do is to encourage him to advertise the fact by speaking. It cannot be so easily discovered if you allow him to remain silent and look wise, but if you let him speak, the secret is out and the world knows that he is a fool. So it is by the exposure of folly that it is defeated; not by the seclusion of folly, and in this free air of free speech men get into that sort of communication with one another which constitutes the basis of all common achievement.

But if we maintain a general policy of free speaking, we must recognize that its inevitable consequence will be sporadic local outbreaks of violence, for it is the nature of men to be intolerant of attacks upon institutions, personalities and ideas for which they really care. In the long run, maintenance of free speech will be more endangered if the population can have no protection from the abuses which lead to violence. No liberty is made more secure by holding that its abuses are inseparable from its enjoyment. We must not forget that it is the free democratic communities that ask us to trust them to maintain peace with liberty and that the factions engaged in this battle are not interested permanently in either. What would it matter to Terminiello if the police batter up some communists or, on the other hand, if the communists batter up some policemen? Either result makes grist for his mill; either would help promote hysteria and the demand for strong-arm methods in dealing with his adversaries. And what, on the other hand, have the communist agitators to lose from a battle with the police?

This Court has gone far toward accepting the doctrine that civil liberty means the removal of all restraints from these crowds and that all local attempts to maintain order are impairments of the liberty of the citizen. The choice is not between order and liberty. It is between liberty with order and anarchy without either. There is danger that, if the Court does not temper its doctrinaire logic with a little practical wisdom, it will convert the constitutional Bill of Rights into a suicide pact.

I would affirm the conviction.

A balance has to be struck

It is interesting to compare this opinion with the extra-judicial observations of a distinguished liberal judge this side of the Atlantic concerning a similar situation.

Following a serious disturbance in Red Lion Square, London, on 30 April 1974, Lord Scarman, a member of the Appellate Committee of the House of Lords, was appointed to review the events and actions which led to the disorder and to consider whether any lessons might be learned. His report contained the following passages:

Amongst our fundamental human rights there are, without doubt, the rights of peaceful assembly and public protest and the right to public order and tranquillity. Civilised living collapses — it is obvious — if public protest becomes violent protest or public order degenerates into the quietism imposed by successful oppression. But the problem is more complex than a choice between two extremes — one, a right to protest whenever and wherever you will and the other, a right to continuous calm upon our streets unruffled by the noise and obstructive pressure of the protesting procession. A balance has to be struck, a compromise found that will accommodate the exercise of the right to protest within a framework of public order which enables ordinary citizens, who are not protesting, to go about their business and pleasure without obstruction or inconvenience. The fact that those who at any one time are concerned to secure the tranquillity of the streets are likely to be the majority must not lead us to deny the protesters their opportunity to march: the fact that the protesters are desperately sincere and are exercising a fundamental human right must not lead us to overlook the rights of the majority.[75]

The report concluded:

The common law has successfully enshrined the principle of the matter. It concentrates attention on public order. There must be disorder, or the threat of disorder, before police powers may be used: but, when they are needed, the powers exist, and are strong. Moreover it is a policeman's duty to use them. But all of us, not only policemen, are by law under a duty to preserve the Queen's Peace. We must exercise restraint in our own behaviour — even in the face of provocation. The law assumes the existence of a tolerant and self-disciplined society. The law requires of the citizen as the necessary condition for the exercise of his rights that he respects the rights of others, even though he may fundamentally disagree with them and totally disapprove of their policies. On 15 June, failure to respect the rights of others, which some carried to the lengths of an aggressive determination to frustrate the rights of others, was the reason for the violence in Red Lion Square.[76]

A man may speak the thing he will

A few years later Lord Denning had to consider the rights of a deeply offensive organisation.

The National Front, a belligerently nationalistic party opposed to racial integration, had entered into a contract with the Great Yarmouth borough council to hold its 1979 annual conference in the council's Wellington pavilion. Following local elections there was a change of control of the council and the new council resolved to withdraw the conference facility.

Unable to find an alternative location the National Front brought legal proceedings claiming specific performance of the contract

---

[75] *Inquiry into the Disorders at Red Lion Square* (Cmnd 5919), para. 5.
[76] Ibid., para. 117.

(that is an order of the court requiring the council to honour its undertaking).

The judge of first instance, Mr Justice Tasker Watkins VC, granted the relief sought and the council appealed to the Court of Appeal. The Master of the Rolls, Lord Denning, dismissing the appeal,[77] said, after rejecting a number of technical objections:

We come to the real point in the case: whether or not, as a matter of discretion, we should order specific performance of this contract.

Mr Justice Tasker Watkins ordered the new council to perform the contract. He did so because of the importance of freedom of speech and freedom of assembly. These are among our most precious freedoms. Freedom of speech means freedom, not only for the views of which you approve, but also freedom for the views of which you most heartily disapprove. This is a land, in the words of the poet,[78] where:

A man may speak the thing he will.
A land of settled government.
A land of just and old renown,
Where Freedom slowly broadens down
From precedent to precedent.

But, mark you, freedom of speech can be abused. It can be used so as to promote violence; to propagate racial hatred and class warfare; and to undermine the structure of society itself. History provides examples. Such as when Hitler led the Germans to believe that they were the master race, and inflamed them so that they expelled and massacred the Jews. Or when the communists have used their freedom to destroy the freedom of others. If there were any evidence that the National Front were abusing this freedom, it might turn the scale. But there is no evidence of it here.

Freedom of assembly is another of our precious freedoms. Everyone is entitled to meet and assemble with his fellows to discuss their affairs and to promote their views; so long as it is not done to propagate violence or do anything unlawful.

Lord Denning concluded that, since the meeting was a private meeting essential to the constitution of the party and since there

---

[77] *Verrall* v *Great Yarmouth Borough Council* [1980] 1 All ER 839, 842.
[78] Tennyson, 'You ask me why'.

had been no history of trouble at such meetings, the newly constituted council must honour the commitments of the old.

The European Convention on Human Rights offers a model different both from English and American constitutionality pragmatism by laying down for every right a list of circumstances in which it may be overriden. For example, the rights to freedom of peaceful assembly and freedom of association are qualified in article 11 of the Convention as follows:

No restrictions shall be placed on the exercise of these rights other than such as are prescribed by law and are necessary in a democratic society in the interests of national security or public safety, for the prevention of disorder or crime, for the protection of health or morals or for the protection of the rights and freedoms of others.

The United States Supreme Court

6. THE INCOMING TIDE

or

The Law and the Constitution

The tendency of focusing attention on constitutionality is to
make constitutionality synonymous with wisdom, to regard a
law as all right if it is constitutional. Such an attitude is a great
enemy of liberalism.

Mr Justice Frankfurter
in *West Virginia State Board of Education* v *Barnette*[79]

Liberty perverted
Our heritage and our hopes
The wellspring of our civilization
Choose between freedom and fear

---

[79] See under *Our heritage and our hopes.*

Britain, almost uniquely among developed nations, is without a written constitution.[80] *This does not mean that it does not have a constitution; it does, and much of it is in written form. It does mean that there is at the heart of the State a void that can be filled by Royal Prerogative or judicial construction required by the needs of the day. But that void is rapidly getting smaller.*

As a result of an Act of 1972 English law has become subordinate to European law in many important respects, with correspondingly profound consequences for our jurisprudence. These effects were memorably described by Lord Denning as follows:[81]

The first and fundamental point is that the Treaty of Rome concerns only those matters which have a European element, that is to say, matters which affect people or property in the nine countries of the Common Market besides ourselves. The treaty does not touch any of the matters which concern solely the mainland of England and the people in it. These are still governed by English law. They are not affected by the treaty. But when we come to matters with a European element, the treaty is like an incoming tide. It flows into the estuaries and up the rivers. It cannot be held back. Parliament has decreed that the treaty is henceforward to be part of our law. It is equal in force to any statute. . . .

The statute is expressed in forthright terms which are absolute and all-embracing. Any rights or obligations created by the treaty are to be given legal effect in England without more ado. Any remedies or procedures provided by the treaty are to be made available here without being open to question. In future in transactions which cross the frontiers we must no longer speak or think of English law as something on its own. We must speak and think of Community rights and obligations and we must give effect to them. This means a great effort for the lawyers. We have to learn a new system. The treaty with the regulations and directives, covers many volumes. The case law is contained in hundreds of reported cases both in the European Court of Justice

---

[80] This was not always the case, as witness the Instrument of Government of 1653 and the Humble Petition and Advice of 1657.

[81] *H. P. Bulmer Ltd* v *J. Bollinger SA* [1974] 2 All ER 1226, 1231.

and in the national courts of the nine. Many must be studied before the right result can be reached. We must get down to it.

The Treaty of Rome, however influential, is not a written constitution, but developments are now taking place in this country that may lead to one.

First, there is the forthcoming incorporation into our laws of the principles of the European Convention on Human Rights (see chapter 5). Secondly, there is the movement towards devolution proposed by the Labour government and adopted enthusiastically by Scotland and indifferently by Wales. Reform of the House of Lords is proposed. Nor is it impossible to exclude the possibility of a reconsideration of the role of the head of State. With all these changes in the air the next step is likely to be their incorporation into a new Constitutional settlement. In this chapter we examine by reference to American experience one of the aspects of a written constitution which can give rise to unexpected difficulties.

It is impossible not to admire the style and content of the American Constitution. The British in particular should be proud of the way in which the Founding Fathers so liberally appropriated concepts and even language from the former colonial power. The fact that the Constitution has stood the test of time for so long is powerful testimony to the abilities and imagination of those who drafted it. But we should not be blind to its problems.

The United States Supreme Court is empowered under the American Constitution to strike down acts of the legislature that it deems to be unconstitutional. This means that the Court, instead of deciding the case before it on a pragmatic assessment of present-day needs, has to rely on its construction of a document composed (however brilliantly) some two centuries ago. It is arguable that such an approach is superior to the case-by-case method of the common law. Many of the issues referred to the Court, however, are not solely, or even mainly, issues of law, but issues which in any other circumstances would fall to be decided by the democratically elected Congress. It is true that in arriving at its decisions the Court does not confine itself to a narrow legalistic approach to construction but accepts social work studies and other relevant evidence, but it may be questioned whether lawyers are the best judges of such non-legal issues. In practice, it must be said, the US Supreme Court enjoys a large measure of popular support, but on some occasions its members have been distinctly uneasy at their role as legislators.

As well as the lack of democratic accountability for what are very often social policy decisions there is the additional problem that a court normally decides only the precise point before it. Because the Supreme Court has this semi-legislative function it has perforce to attempt to lay down comprehensive rules whenever it changes direction. In general, courts are not well equipped to do this. Certainly, they are less fitted to the task than a deliberative assembly which can look at social issues in a wider context and attempt to assess all the consequences of its decisions. These difficulties too have been noted with concern by some distinguished members of the Court.

At the turn of the century Mr Justice Holmes declined to go along with his colleagues on the Supreme Court in striking down as unreasonable worker protection legislation of the State of New York. The constitutional protection of liberty, he said, was not intended to prevent the majority from enacting laws which a reasonable person could uphold (See under Liberty perverted*).*

In much the same way thirty five years later Mr Justice Frankfurter attempted unsuccessfully to uphold the constitutionality of a State law underpinning the daily ceremony which takes place in American schools of saluting the flag and pledging allegiance (Our heritage and our hope *).*

In a later case Frankfurter took the argument further: 'The too easy transition from disapproval of what is undesirable to condemnation as unconstitutional, has led some of the wisest judges to question the wisdom of our scheme in lodging such authority in courts.' (The wellspring of our civilization). *In that case he had occasion to affirm, in an opinion that explored the limits of tolerance, the constitutionality of seemingly repressive legislation.*

The opposite point of view is represented here by an opinion of Mr Justice Douglas (Choose between freedom and fear *). He took his* *stand on a fairly secure redoubt. Lawyers have long been suspicious of laws which punish ideas rather than actions and when an official of the Communist Party was prosecuted simply for being a member of it Douglas would have rejected the legislation as unconstitutional:* 'We legalize today guilt by association, sending a man to prison when he committed no unlawful act.' *His colleagues did not agree.*

The closer we move to a written constitution, the greater will be the responsibility of the courts. We would do well to ponder the implications for this country of American experience in this respect.

Liberty perverted

In a sense it may be said that the history of the United States of America is, for good or ill, the history of the tension between the federal republic and its constituent States. The American Constitution was designed to clarify this relationship, but problems still come regularly before the Supreme Court. The issue of States' rights was considered at the beginning of the twentieth century in a dissenting opinion of one of the most respected members of that Court.

The labour laws of the State of New York prohibited a bakery employer from requiring or permitting an employee to work more than 10 hours a day or 60 hours a week. The law was challenged on the basis of the Fourteenth Amendment to the Constitution, which bars any State from depriving 'any person of life, liberty or property without due process of law'.

By a majority of five to four the Court held that the State law was an unreasonable, unnecessary and arbitrary interference with the right of the individual to his personal liberty.

Mr Justice Holmes expressed his dissent from the majority in the following words:[82]

---

[82] *Lochner* v *New York*, 198 US 45 (1905).

This case is decided upon an economic theory which a large part of the country does not entertain. If it were a question whether I agreed with that theory, I should desire to study it further and long before making up my mind. But I do not conceive that to be my duty, because I strongly believe that my agreement or disagreement has nothing to do with the right of a majority to embody their opinions in law.

Oliver Wendell Holmes was the son of the similarly named author of *The Autocrat of the Breakfast Table*. Born in 1841, he was as a child dandled on the knees of John Quincy Adams, sixth President of the United States. As a brevet colonel during the Civil War he famously rebuked President Lincoln for peering over the wall of Fort Stevens when under fire, while towards the end of his distinguished tenure as a Supreme Court Justice one of his law clerks was Alger Hiss, the suspected Russian spy later convicted of perjury. Holmes was one of the most original minds that America has produced. He died in 1935 surrounded by the honours of his country and admired by lawyers everywhere. He is buried near another Massachusetts man, John F. Kennedy.

It is settled by various decisions of this Court that State constitutions and State laws may regulate life in many ways which we, as legislators, might think as injudicious, or, if you like, as tyrannical, as this, and which, equally with this, interfere with the liberty to contract. Sunday laws and usury laws are ancient examples. A more modern one is the prohibition of lotteries. The liberty of the citizen to do as he likes so long as he does not interfere with the liberty of others to do the same, which has been a shibboleth for some well-known writers, is interfered with by school laws, by the Post Office, by every State or municipal institution which takes his money for purposes thought desirable, whether he likes it or not. The Fourteenth Amendment does not enact Mr Herbert Spencer's Social Statics. The other day we sustained the Massachusett's vaccination law and State statutes and decisions cutting down the liberty to contract by way of combination are familiar to this court. Two years ago, we upheld the prohibition of sales of stock on margins or for future delivery in the Constitution of California. The decision sustaining an eight-hour law for miners is still recent. Some of these laws embody convictions or prejudices which judges are likely to share. Some may not. But a constitution is not intended to embody a particular economic theory, whether of paternalism and the organic relation of the citizen to the State or of laissez-faire. It is made for people of fundamentally differing views, and the accident of our finding certain opinions natural and familiar or novel and even shocking ought not to conclude our judgment upon the question whether statutes embodying them conflict with the Constitution of the United States.

General propositions do not decide concrete cases. The decision will depend on a judgment or intuition more subtle than any articulate major premise. But I think that the proposition just stated, if it is accepted, will carry us far toward the end. Every opinion tends to become a law. I think that the word liberty in the Fourteenth Amendment is perverted when it is held to prevent the natural outcome of a dominant opinion, unless it can be said that a rational and fair man necessarily would admit that the statute proposed would infringe fundamental principles as they have been understood by the traditions of our people and our law. It does not need research to show that no such sweeping condemnation can be passed upon the statute before us. A reasonable man might think it a proper measure on the score of health. Men whom I certainly could not pronounce unreasonable would uphold it as a first instalment of a general regulation of the hours of work. Whether in the latter aspect it would be open to the charge of inequality I think it unnecessary to discuss.

Our heritage and our hopes

A similar issue came before another great American judge in a case concerning the daily practice of American children to 'salute the flag' and pledge allegiance. They do this by extending the right arm, palm upward, declaring, 'I pledge allegiance to the flag of the United States of America and to the Republic for which it stands; one Nation, indivisible, with liberty and justice for all'.

When the State Board of Education of West Virginia made saluting the flag compulsory some Jehovah's Witnesses refused to allow their children to observe the requirement on religious grounds and expulsions followed. A District Court of three judges enjoined the enforcement of the regulation, but on appeal the United States Supreme Court held,[83] by a majority, that the State law violated the First and Fourteenth Amendments to the Constitution.

---

[83] *West Virginia State Board of Education* v *Barnette*, 319 US 624 (1943).

*Mr Justice Frankfurter dissented from the majority in one of his
most widely admired opinions, which is reproduced here almost in
its entirety.*

One who belongs to the most vilified and persecuted minority in history is not
likely to be insensible to the freedoms guaranteed by our Constitution.

Were my purely personal attitude relevant, I should wholeheartedly associate
myself with the general libertarian views in the Court's opinion, representing,
as they do, the thought and action of a lifetime. But, as judges, we are neither
Jew nor gentile, neither Catholic nor agnostic. We owe equal attachment to the
Constitution, and are equally bound by our judicial obligations whether we
derive our citizenship from the earliest or the latest immigrants to these shores.
As a member of this Court, I am not justified in writing my private notions of
policy into the Constitution, no matter how deeply I may cherish them or how
mischievous I may deem their disregard. The duty of a judge who must decide
which of two claims before the Court shall prevail, that of a State to enact and
enforce laws within its general competence or that of an individual to refuse
obedience because of the demands of his conscience, is not that of the ordinary
person.

It can never be emphasized too much that one's own opinion about the
wisdom or evil of a law should be excluded altogether when one is doing one's
duty on the bench. The only opinion of our own even looking in that direction
that is material is our opinion whether legislators could, in reason, have enacted
such a law. In the light of all the circumstances, including the history of this
question in this Court, it would require more daring than I possess to deny that
reasonable legislators could have taken the action which is before us for review.
Most unwillingly, therefore, I must differ from my brethren with regard to
legislation like this.

Judicial self-restraint

I cannot bring my mind to believe that the 'liberty' secured by the Due Process
Clause gives this Court authority to deny to the State of West Virginia the
attainment of that which we all recognize as a legitimate legislative end,
namely, the promotion of good citizenship, by employment of the means here
chosen. Not so long ago, we were admonished that the only check upon our
own exercise of power is our own sense of self-restraint. For the removal of
unwise laws from the statute books, appeal lies not to the courts, but to the ballot
and to the processes of democratic government.... We have been told that
generalities do not decide concrete cases. But the intensity with which a general
principle is held may determine a particular issue, and whether we put first

things first may decide a specific controversy. The admonition that judicial self-restraint alone limits arbitrary exercise of our authority is relevant every time we are asked to nullify legislation. The Constitution does not give us greater veto power when dealing with one phase of 'liberty' than with another, or when dealing with grade school regulations than with college regulations that offend conscience. In neither situation is our function comparable to that of a legislature, or are we free to act as though we were a super-legislature.

Judicial self-restraint is equally necessary whenever an exercise of political or legislative power is challenged. There is no warrant in the constitutional basis of this Court's authority for attributing different roles to it depending upon the nature of the challenge to the legislation. Our power does not vary according to the particular provision of the Bill of Rights which is invoked. The right not to have property taken without just compensation has, so far as the scope of judicial power is concerned, the same constitutional dignity as the right to be protected against unreasonable searches and seizures, and the latter has no less claim than freedom of the press or freedom of speech or religious freedom. In no instance is this Court the primary protector of the particular liberty that is invoked. This Court has recognized what hardly could be denied, that all the provisions of the first 10 Amendments are 'specific' prohibitions. But each specific Amendment, insofar as embraced within the Fourteenth Amendment, must be equally respected, and the function of this Court does not differ in passing on the constitutionality of legislation challenged under different Amendments.

When Mr Justice Holmes, speaking for this Court, wrote that it must be remembered that legislatures are ultimate guardians of the liberties and welfare of the people in quite as great a degree as the courts ... he went to the very essence of our constitutional system and the democratic conception of our society. He did not mean that for only some phases of civil government this Court was not to supplant legislatures and sit in judgment upon the right or wrong of a challenged measure. He was stating the comprehensive judicial duty and role of this Court in our constitutional scheme whenever legislation is sought to be nullified on any ground, namely, that responsibility for legislation lies with legislatures, answerable as they are directly to the people, and this Court's only and very narrow function is to determine whether, within the broad grant of authority vested in legislatures, they have exercised a judgment for which reasonable justification can be offered. ...

Judges exercised [*the*] legislative function in New York for nearly 50 years. ... But the framers of the Constitution denied such legislative powers to the federal judiciary. They chose instead to insulate the judiciary from the legislative function. They did not grant to this Court supervision over legislation. The reason why, from the beginning, even the narrow judicial authority to nullify legislation has been viewed with a jealous eye is that it serves to prevent the full play of the democratic process. The fact that it may be an undemocratic aspect of our scheme of government does not call for its rejection or its disuse. But it is the best of reasons, as this Court has frequently recognized, for the greatest caution in its use....

The role of the legislature
Under our constitutional system, the legislature is charged solely with civil concerns of society. If the avowed or intrinsic legislative purpose is either to promote or to discourage some religious community or creed, it is clearly within the constitutional restrictions imposed on legislatures, and cannot stand. But it by no means follows that legislative power is wanting whenever a general nondiscriminatory civil regulation, in fact, touches conscientious scruples or religious beliefs of an individual or a group. Regard for such scruples or beliefs undoubtedly presents one of the most reasonable claims for the exertion of legislative accommodation. It is, of course, beyond our power to rewrite the State's requirement by providing exemptions for those who do not wish to participate in the flag salute or by making some other accommodations to meet their scruples. That wisdom might suggest the making of such accommodations, and that school administration would not find it too difficult to make them, and yet maintain the ceremony for those not refusing to conform, is outside our province to suggest. Tact, respect, and generosity toward variant views will always commend themselves to those charged with the duties of legislation so as to achieve a maximum of good will and to require a minimum of unwilling submission to a general law. But the real question is, who is to make such accommodations, the courts or the legislature?

This is no dry, technical matter. It cuts deep into one's conception of the democratic process — it concerns no less the practical differences between the means for making these accommodations that are open to courts and to legislatures. A court can only strike down. It can only say 'This or that law is void'. It cannot modify or qualify, it cannot make exceptions to a general requirement. And it strikes down not merely for a day. At least the finding of unconstitutionality ought not to have ephemeral significance unless the Constitution is to be reduced to the fugitive importance of mere legislation.

When we are dealing with the Constitution of the United States, and, more particularly, with the great safeguards of the Bill of Rights, we are dealing with principles of liberty and justice 'so rooted in the traditions and conscience of our people as to be ranked as fundamental' — something without which 'a fair and enlightened system of justice would be impossible'.... If the function of this Court is to be essentially no different from that of a legislature, if the considerations governing constitutional construction are to be substantially those that underlie legislation, then indeed judges should not have life tenure, and they should be made directly responsible to the electorate. There have been many, but unsuccessful, proposals in the last 60 years to amend the Constitution to that end....

Conscientious scruples, all would admit, cannot stand against every legislative compulsion to do positive acts in conflict with such scruples. We have been told that such compulsions override religious scruples only as to major concerns of the state. But the determination of what is major and what is minor itself raises questions of policy. For the way in which men equally guided by reason appraise importance goes to the very heart of policy. Judges should be very diffident in setting their judgment against that of a state in determining what is, and what is not, a major concern, what means are appropriate to proper ends, and what is the total social cost in striking the balance of imponderables.

What one can say with assurance is that the history out of which grew constitutional provisions for religious equality and the writings of the great exponents of religious freedom — Jefferson, Madison, John Adams, Benjamin Franklin — are totally wanting in justification for a claim by dissidents of exceptional immunity from civic measures of general applicability, measures not, in fact, disguised assaults upon such dissident views. The great leaders of the American Revolution were determined to remove political support from every religious establishment. They put on an equality the different religious sects — Episcopalians, Presbyterians, Catholics, Baptists, Methodists, Quakers, Huguenots — which, as dissenters, had been under the heel of the various orthodoxies that prevailed in different colonies. So far as the state was concerned, there was to be neither orthodoxy nor heterodoxy. And so Jefferson and those who followed him wrote guaranties of religious freedom into our constitutions. Religious minorities, as well as religious majorities, were to be equal in the eyes of the political state. But Jefferson and the others also knew that minorities may disrupt society. It never would have occurred to them to write into the Constitution the subordination of the general civil authority of the state to sectarian scruples. The constitutional protection of religious freedom terminated disabilities, it did not create new privileges. It gave religious equality, not civil immunity. Its essence is freedom from conformity to religious dogma, not freedom from conformity to law because of religious dogma.

Religious loyalties may be exercised without hindrance from the state, but the state may not exercise that which, except by leave of religious loyalties, is within the domain of temporal power. Otherwise, each individual could set up his own censor against obedience to laws conscientiously deemed for the public good by those whose business it is to make laws. The prohibition against any religious establishment by the government placed denominations on an equal footing — it assured freedom from support by the government to any mode of worship and the freedom of individuals to support any mode of worship. Any person may therefore believe or disbelieve what he pleases. He may practice what he will in his own house of worship or publicly within the limits of public order. But the lawmaking authority is not circumscribed by the variety of religious beliefs — otherwise, the constitutional guaranty would be not a protection of the free exercise of religion, but a denial of the exercise of legislation. The essence of the religious freedom guaranteed by our Constitution is therefore this: no religion shall either receive the state's support or incur its hostility. Religion is outside the sphere of political government.

Secular and religious laws
This does not mean that all matters on which religious organizations or beliefs may pronounce are outside the sphere of government. Were this so, instead of the separation of church and state, there would be the subordination of the state on any matter deemed within the sovereignty of the religious conscience. Much that is the concern of temporal authority affects the spiritual interests of men. But it is not enough to strike down a non-discriminatory law that it may hurt or offend some dissident view. It would be too easy to cite numerous prohibitions and injunctions to which laws run counter if the variant interpretations of the Bible were made the tests of obedience to law. The validity of secular laws cannot be measured by their conformity to religious doctrines. It is only in a theocratic state that ecclesiastical doctrines measure legal right or wrong.

An act compelling profession of allegiance to a religion, no matter how subtly or tenuously promoted, is bad. But an act promoting good citizenship and national allegiance is within the domain of governmental authority, and is therefore to be judged by the same considerations of power and of constitutionality as those involved in the many claims of immunity from civil obedience because of religious scruples. That claims are pressed on behalf of sincere religious convictions does not, of itself, establish their constitutional validity. Nor does waving the banner of religious freedom relieve us from examining into the power we are asked to deny the states. Otherwise, the doctrine of separation of church and state, so cardinal in the history of this nation and for the liberty of our people, would mean not the disestablishment of a state church, but the establishment of all churches, and of all religious groups. The subjection of dissidents to the general requirement of saluting the flag, as a measure conducive to the training of children in good citizenship, is very far from being the first instance of exacting obedience to general laws that have offended deep religious scruples. Compulsory vaccination, food inspection regulations, the obligation to bear arms, testimonial duties, compulsory medical treatment, — these are but illustrations of conduct that has often been compelled in the enforcement of legislation of general applicability even though the religious consciences of particular individuals rebelled at the exaction.

Law is concerned with external behaviour
Law is concerned with external behavior, and not with the inner life of man. It rests in large measure upon compulsion. Socrates lives in history partly because he gave his life for the conviction that the duty of obedience to secular law does not presuppose consent to its enactment or belief in its virtue. The consent upon which free government rests is the consent that comes from sharing in the process of making and unmaking laws. The state is not shut out from a domain because the individual conscience may deny the state's claim. The individual conscience may profess what faith it chooses. It may affirm and promote that faith — in the language of the Constitution, it may 'exercise' it freely — but it cannot thereby restrict community action through political organs in matters of community concern, so long as the action is not asserted in a discriminatory way, either openly or by stealth. One may have the right to practice one's religion and at the same time owe the duty of formal obedience to laws that run counter to one's belief.

Compelling belief implies denial of opportunity to combat it and to assert dissident views. Such compulsion is one thing. Quite another matter is submission to conformity of action while denying its wisdom or virtue, and with ample opportunity for seeking its change or abrogation. . . .

Parents have the privilege of choosing which schools they wish their children to attend. And the question here is whether the state may make certain requirements that seem to it desirable or important for the proper education of those future citizens who go to schools maintained by the states, or whether the pupils in those schools may be relieved from those requirements if they run counter to the consciences of their parents. Not only have parents the right to send children to schools of their own choosing, but the state has no right to bring such schools 'under a strict governmental control' or give affirmative direction concerning the intimate and essential details of such schools, entrust their control to public officers, and deny both owners and patrons reasonable choice and discretion in respect of teachers, curriculum, and textbooks. . . . Why should not the state likewise have constitutional power to make reasonable provisions for the proper instruction of children in schools maintained by it?

When dealing with religious scruples, we are dealing with an almost numberless variety of doctrines and beliefs entertained with equal sincerity by the particular groups for which they satisfy man's needs in his relation to the mysteries of the universe. There are, in the United States, more than 250 distinctive established religious denominations. In the State of Pennsylvania, there are 120 of these, and, in West Virginia, as many as 65. But if religious scruples afford immunity from civic obedience to laws, they may be invoked by the religious beliefs of any individual even though he holds no membership in any sect or organized denomination. Certainly this Court cannot be called upon to determine what claims of conscience should be recognized, and what should be rejected as satisfying the 'religion' which the Constitution protects. That would, indeed, resurrect the very discriminatory treatment of religion which the Constitution sought forever to forbid.

And so, when confronted with the task of considering the claims of immunity from obedience to a law dealing with civil affairs because of religious scruples, we cannot conceive religion more narrowly than in the terms in which Judge Augustus N. Hand recently characterized it:

> It is unnecessary to attempt a definition of religion; the content of the term is found in the history of the human race, and is incapable of compression into a few words. Religious belief arises from a sense of the inadequacy of reason as a means of relating the individual to his fellow men and to his universe.... [It] may justly be regarded as a response of the individual to an inward mentor, call it conscience or God, that is, for many persons at the present time, the equivalent of what has always been thought a religious impulse.

The Bible in school

Consider the controversial issue of compulsory Bible reading in public schools. The educational policies of the states are in great conflict over this, and the state courts are divided in their decisions on the issue whether the requirement of Bible reading offends constitutional provisions dealing with religious freedom. The requirement of Bible reading has been justified by various state courts as an appropriate means of inculcating ethical precepts and familiarizing pupils with the most lasting expression of great English literature. Is this Court to overthrow such variant state educational policies by denying states the right to entertain such convictions in regard to their school systems because of a belief that the King James version is, in fact, a sectarian text to which parents of the Catholic and Jewish faiths and of some Protestant persuasions may rightly object to having their children exposed?

On the other hand, the religious consciences of some parents may rebel at the absence of any Bible reading in the schools.... Or is this Court to enter the old controversy between science and religion by unduly defining the limits within which a state may experiment with its school curricula? The religious consciences of some parents may be offended by subjecting their children to the Biblical account of creation, while another state may offend parents by prohibiting a teaching of biology that contradicts such Biblical account....

What of conscientious objections to what is devoutly felt by parents to be the poisoning of impressionable minds of children by chauvinistic teaching of history? This is very far from a fanciful suggestion, for, in the belief of many thoughtful people, nationalism is the seedbed of war. There are other issues in the offing which admonish us of the difficulties and complexities that confront states in the duty of administering their local school systems. All citizens are taxed for the support of public schools, although this Court has denied the right of a state to compel all children to go to such schools, and has recognized the right of parents to send children to privately maintained schools. Parents who are dissatisfied with the public schools thus carry a double educational burden.

Children who go to public school enjoy in many states derivative advantages, such as free textbooks, free lunch, and free transportation in going to and from school. What of the claims for equality of treatment of those parents who, because of religious scruples, cannot send their children to public schools? What of the claim that, if the right to send children to privately maintained schools is partly an exercise of religious conviction, to render effective this right, it should be accompanied by equality of treatment by the state in supplying free textbooks, free lunch, and free transportation to children who go to private schools? What of the claim that such grants are offensive to the cardinal constitutional doctrine of separation of church and state? These questions assume increasing importance in view of the steady growth of parochial schools, both in number and in population.

I am not borrowing trouble by adumbrating these issues, nor am I parading horrible examples of the consequences of today's decision. I am aware that we must decide the case before us, and not some other case. But that does not mean that a case is dissociated from the past, and unrelated to the future. We must decide this case with due regard for what went before and no less regard for what may come after. Is it really a fair construction of such a fundamental concept as the right freely to exercise one's religion that a state cannot choose to require all children who attend public school to make the same gesture of allegiance to the symbol of our national life because it may offend the conscience of some children, but that it may compel all children to attend public school to listen to the King James version although it may offend the consciences of their parents? And what of the larger issue of claiming immunity from obedience to a general civil regulation that has a reasonable relation to a public purpose within the general competence of the state? ... Another member of the sect now before us insisted that, in forbidding her two little girls, aged nine and 12, to distribute pamphlets, Oregon infringed her and their freedom of religion in that the children were engaged in 'preaching the gospel of God's Kingdom'. A procedural technicality led to the dismissal of the case, but the problem remains. ...

These questions are not lightly stirred. They touch the most delicate issues, and their solution challenges the best wisdom of political and religious statesmen. But it presents awful possibilities to try to encase the solution of these problems within the rigid prohibitions of unconstitutionality. We are told that a flag salute is a doubtful substitute for adequate understanding of our institutions. The states that require such a school exercise do not have to justify it as the only means for promoting good citizenship in children, but merely as one of diverse means for accomplishing a worthy end. We may deem it a foolish measure, but the point is that this Court is not the organ of government to resolve doubts as to whether it will fulfil its purpose. Only if there be no doubt that any reasonable mind could entertain can we deny to the states the right to resolve doubts their way, and not ours.

That which to the majority may seem essential for the welfare of the state may offend the consciences of a minority. But, so long as no inroads are made upon the actual exercise of religion by the minority, to deny the political power of the majority to enact laws concerned with civil matters, simply because they may offend the consciences of a minority, really means that the consciences of a minority are more sacred and more enshrined in the Constitution than the consciences of a majority. We are told that symbolism is a dramatic but primitive way of communicating ideas. Symbolism is inescapable. Even the most sophisticated live by symbols. But it is not for this Court to make psychological judgments as to the effectiveness of a particular symbol in inculcating concededly indispensable feelings, particularly if the state happens to see fit to utilize the symbol that represents our heritage and our hopes.

To reject the swastika

And surely only flippancy could be responsible for the suggestion that constitutional validity of a requirement to salute our flag implies equal validity of a requirement to salute a dictator. The significance of a symbol lies in what it represents. To reject the swastika does not imply rejection of the Cross. And so it bears repetition to say that it mocks reason and denies our whole history to find in the allowance of a requirement to salute our flag on fitting occasions the seeds of sanction for obeisance to a leader. To deny the power to employ educational symbols is to say that the state's educational system may not stimulate the imagination because this may lead to unwise stimulation.

The right of West Virginia to utilize the flag salute as part of its educational process is denied because, so it is argued, it cannot be justified as a means of meeting a 'clear and present danger' to national unity. In passing, it deserves to be noted that the four cases which unanimously sustained the power of states to utilize such an educational measure arose and were all decided before the present World War. But to measure the state's power to make such regulations as are here resisted by the imminence of national danger is wholly to misconceive the origin and purpose of the concept of 'clear and present danger'.

To apply such a test is for the Court to assume, however unwittingly, a legislative responsibility that does not belong to it. To talk about 'clear and present danger' as the touchstone of allowable educational policy by the states whenever school curricula may impinge upon the boundaries of individual conscience is to take a felicitous phrase out of the context of the particular situation where it arose and for which it was adapted. Mr Justice Holmes used the phrase 'clear and present danger' in a case involving mere speech as a means by which alone to accomplish sedition in time of war. By that phrase, he meant merely to indicate that, in view of the protection given to utterance by the First Amendment, in order that mere utterance may not be proscribed, the words used are used in such circumstances, and are of such a nature, as to create a clear and present danger that they will bring about the substantive evils that Congress has a right to prevent. The 'substantive evils' about which he was speaking were inducement of insubordination in the military and naval forces of the United States and obstruction of enlistment while the country was at war. He was not enunciating a formal rule that there can be no restriction upon speech, and, still less, no compulsion where conscience balks, unless imminent danger would thereby be wrought 'to our institutions or our government'.

The flag salute exercise has no kinship whatever to the oath tests so odious in history. For the oath test was one of the instruments for suppressing heretical beliefs. Saluting the flag suppresses no belief, nor curbs it. Children and their parents may believe what they please, avow their belief and practice it. It is not even remotely suggested that the requirement for saluting the flag involves the slightest restriction against the fullest opportunity on the part both of the children and of their parents to disavow, as publicly as they choose to do so, the meaning that others attach to the gesture of salute. All channels of affirmative free expression are open to both children and parents. Had we before us any act of the state putting the slightest curbs upon such free expression, I should not lag behind any member of this Court in striking down such an invasion of the right to freedom of thought and freedom of speech protected by the Constitution. . . .

The changing views of the Court

The Court has no reason for existence if it merely reflects the pressures of the day. Our system is built on the faith that men set apart for this special function, freed from the influences of immediacy and from the deflections of worldly ambition, will become able to take a view of longer range than the period of responsibility entrusted to Congress and legislatures. We are dealing with matters as to which legislators and voters have conflicting views. Are we as judges to impose our strong convictions on where wisdom lies? That which three years ago had seemed to five successive Courts to lie within permissible areas of legislation is now outlawed by the deciding shift of opinion of two Justices. What reason is there to believe that they or their successors may not have another view a few years hence? Is that which was deemed to be of so fundamental a nature as to be written into the Constitution to endure for all times to be the sport of shifting winds of doctrine?

Of course, judicial opinions, even as to questions of constitutionality, are not immutable. As has been true in the past, the Court will from time to time reverse its position. But I believe that never before these Jehovah's Witnesses cases (except for minor deviations subsequently retraced) has this Court overruled decisions so as to restrict the powers of democratic government. Always heretofore it has withdrawn narrow views of legislative authority so as to authorize what formerly it had denied.

In view of this history, it must be plain that what 13 Justices found to be within the constitutional authority of a state, legislators cannot be deemed unreasonable in enacting. Therefore, in denying to the states what heretofore has received such impressive judicial sanction, some other tests of unconstitutionality must surely be guiding the Court than the absence of a rational justification for the legislation. But I know of no other test which this Court is authorized to apply in nullifying legislation. In the past, this Court has from time to time set its views of policy against that embodied in legislation by finding laws in conflict with what was called the 'spirit of the Constitution'. Such undefined destructive power was not conferred on this Court by the Constitution. Before a duly enacted law can be judicially nullified, it must be forbidden by some explicit restriction upon political authority in the Constitution.

Equally inadmissible is the claim to strike down legislation because, to us as individuals, it seems opposed to the 'plan and purpose' of the Constitution. That is too tempting a basis for finding in one's personal views the purposes of the

Founders. The uncontrollable power wielded by this Court brings it very close to the most sensitive areas of public affairs. As appeal from legislation to adjudication becomes more frequent, and its consequences more far-reaching, judicial self-restraint becomes more, and not less, important, lest we unwarrantably enter social and political domains wholly outside our concern.

I think I appreciate fully the objections to the law before us. But to deny that it presents a question upon which men might reasonably differ appears to me to be intolerance. And since men may so reasonably differ, I deem it beyond my constitutional power to assert my view of the wisdom of this law against the view of the State of West Virginia.

Jefferson's opposition to judicial review has not been accepted by history, but it still serves as an admonition against confusion between judicial and political functions. As a rule of judicial self-restraint, it is still as valid as Lincoln's admonition. For those who pass laws not only are under duty to pass laws. They are also under duty to observe the Constitution. And even though legislation relates to civil liberties, our duty of deference to those who have the responsibility for making the laws is no less relevant or less exacting. And this is so especially when we consider the accidental contingencies by which one man may determine constitutionality and thereby confine the political power of the Congress of the United States and the legislatures of 48 states. The attitude of judicial humility which these considerations enjoin is not an abdication of the judicial function. It is a due observance of its limits.

Moreover, it is to be borne in mind that, in a question like this, we are not passing on the proper distribution of political power as between the states and the central government. We are not discharging the basic function of this Court as the mediator of powers within the federal system. To strike down a law like this is to deny a power to all government. The whole Court is conscious that this case reaches ultimate questions of judicial power and its relation to our scheme of government. It is appropriate, therefore, to recall an utterance as wise as any that I know in analyzing what is really involved when the theory of this Court's function is put to the test of practice.

The analysis is that of James Bradley Thayer:[84]

> ... there has developed a vast and growing increase of judicial interference with legislation. This is a very different state of things from what our fathers contemplated, a century and more ago, in framing the new system. Seldom, indeed, as they imagined, under our system, would this great, novel, tremendous power of the courts be exerted — would this sacred ark of the covenant be taken from within the veil.

---

[84] An academic authority on constitutional law.

Marshall himself expressed truly one aspect of the matter, when he said in one of the later years of his life: No questions can be brought before a judicial tribunal of greater delicacy than those which involve the constitutionality of legislative acts. If they become indispensably necessary to the case, the court must meet and decide them; but if the case may be determined on other grounds, a just respect for the legislature requires that the obligation of its laws should not be unnecessarily and wantonly assailed.

And again, a little earlier than this, he laid down the one true rule of duty for the courts. When he went to Philadelphia at the end of September, in 1831, on that painful errand of which I have spoken, in answering a cordial tribute from the Bar of that city, he remarked that, if he might be permitted to claim for himself and his associates any part of the kind things they had said, it would be this, that they had 'never sought to enlarge the judicial power beyond its proper bounds, nor feared to carry it to the fullest extent that duty required'. That is the safe twofold rule; nor is the first part of it any whit less important than the second; nay, more; today, it is the part which most requires to be emphasized. For just here comes in a consideration of very great weight.

Great and, indeed, inestimable as are the advantages in a popular government of this conservative influence — the power of the judiciary to disregard unconstitutional legislation — it should be remembered that the exercise of it, even when unavoidable, is always attended with a serious evil, namely that the correction of legislative mistakes comes from the outside, and the people thus lose the political experience, and the moral education and stimulus that come from fighting the question out in the ordinary way, and correcting their own errors. . . .

It is the courts that can do most to cure the evil, and the opportunity is a very great one. Let them resolutely adhere to first principles. Let them consider how narrow is the function which the constitutions have conferred on them — the office merely of deciding litigated cases; how large, therefore, is the duty intrusted to others, and above all to the legislature. It is that body which is charged, primarily, with the duty of judging of the constitutionality of its work. The constitutions generally give them no authority to call upon a court for advice; they must decide for themselves, and the courts may never be able to say a word. Such a body, charged, in every state, with almost all the legislative power of the people, is entitled to the most entire and real respect; is entitled, as among all rationally permissible opinions as to what the constitution allows, to its own choice.

Courts, as has often been said, are not to think of the legislators, but of the legislature — the great, continuous body itself, abstracted from all the transitory individuals who may happen to hold its power. It is this majestic representative of the people whose action is in question, a coordinate department of the government, charged with the greatest functions, and invested, in contemplation of law, with whatsoever wisdom, virtue, and knowledge the exercise of such functions requires.

To set aside the acts of such a body, representing in its own field, which is the very highest of all, the ultimate sovereign, should be a solemn, unusual, and painful act. Something is wrong when it can ever be other than that. And if it be true that the holders of legislative power are careless or evil, yet the constitutional duty of the court remains untouched; it cannot rightly attempt to protect the people by undertaking a function not its own. On the other hand, by adhering rigidly to its own duty, the court will help, as nothing else can, to fix the spot where responsibility lies, and to bring down on that precise locality the thunderbolt of popular condemnation.

The judiciary, today, in dealing with the acts of their coordinate legislators, owe to the country no greater or clearer duty than that of keeping their hands off these acts wherever it is possible to do it. For that course — the true course of judicial duty always — will powerfully help to bring the people and their representatives to a sense of their own responsibility. There will still remain to the judiciary an ample field for the determinations of this remarkable jurisdiction, of which our American law has so much reason to be proud; a jurisdiction which has had some of its chief illustrations and its greatest triumphs, as in Marshall's time, so in ours, while the courts were refusing to exercise it. . . .

Of course, patriotism cannot be enforced by the flag salute. But neither can the liberal spirit be enforced by judicial invalidation of illiberal legislation. Our constant preoccupation with the constitutionality of legislation, rather than with its wisdom, tends to preoccupation of the American mind with a false value. The tendency of focusing attention on constitutionality is to make constitutionality synonymous with wisdom, to regard a law as all right if it is constitutional. Such an attitude is a great enemy of liberalism. Particularly in legislation affecting freedom of thought and freedom of speech, much which should offend a free-spirited society is constitutional. Reliance for the most precious interests of civilization, therefore, must be found outside of their vindication in courts of law. Only a persistent positive translation of the faith of a free society into the convictions and habits and action of a community is the ultimate reliance against unabated temptations to fetter the human spirit.

In this decision Frankfurter was criticised by some for failing the liberal cause. In fact, he was simply attempting to apply the law as he saw it.

The wellspring of our civilization

Ultimately, as Mr Justice Frankfurter observed in the following case, 'The right of a government to maintain its existence — self-preservation — is the most pervasive aspect of sovereignty'.

The Smith Act of 1940 made it an offence for anyone knowingly or wilfully to advocate the overthrow or destruction of the Government of the United States by force or violence. The eleven petitioners had been accused of a breach of the Act by agreeing to set up the Communist Party of the United States, which was alleged to have exactly that aim. All had been found guilty and sentenced to five years' imprisonment and a fine of $10,000. The constitutionality of the Smith Act was challenged before the Supreme Court.[85]

Rejecting the appeals against conviction Frankfurter said:

In enacting a statute which makes it a crime for the defendants to conspire to do what they have been found to have conspired to do, did Congress exceed its constitutional power?

Few questions of comparable import have come before this Court in recent years. The appellants maintain that they have a right to advocate a political theory, so long, at least, as their advocacy does not create an immediate danger of obvious magnitude to the very existence of our present scheme of society. On the other hand, the Government asserts the right to safeguard the security of the Nation by such a measure as the Smith Act. Our judgment is thus solicited on a conflict of interests of the utmost concern to the well-being of the country. This conflict of interests cannot be resolved by a dogmatic preference for one or the other, nor by a sonorous formula which is in fact only a euphemistic disguise for an unresolved conflict. If adjudication is to be a rational process, we cannot escape a candid examination of the conflicting claims with full recognition that both are supported by weighty title deeds.

There come occasions in law, as elsewhere, when the familiar needs to be recalled. Our whole history proves even more decisively than the course of decisions in this Court that the United States has the powers inseparable from a sovereign nation; 'America has chosen to be, in many respects, and to many

---

[85] *Dennis* v *United States*, 341 US 494 (1951).

purposes, a nation; and for all these purposes, her government is complete; to all these objects, it is competent'. The right of a government to maintain its existence — self-preservation — is the most pervasive aspect of sovereignty. 'Security against foreign danger', wrote Madison, 'is one of the primitive objects of civil society.' The constitutional power to act upon this basic principle has been recognized by this Court at different periods and under diverse circumstances. 'To preserve its independence, and give security against foreign aggression and encroachment, is the highest duty of every nation, and to attain these ends nearly all other considerations are to be subordinated. It matters not in what form such aggression and encroachment come.... The government, possessing the powers which are to be exercised for protection and security, is clothed with authority to determine the occasion on which the powers shall be called forth.' The most tragic experience in our history is a poignant reminder that the Nation's continued existence may be threatened from within. To protect itself from such threats, the Federal Government 'is invested with all those inherent and implied powers which, at the time of adopting the Constitution, were generally considered to belong to every government as such, and as being essential to the exercise of its functions'.

But even the all-embracing power and duty of self-preservation are not absolute. Like the war power, which is indeed an aspect of the power of self-preservation, it is subject to applicable constitutional limitations. Our Constitution has no provision lifting restrictions upon governmental authority during periods of emergency, although the scope of a restriction may depend on the circumstances in which it is invoked.

The First Amendment
The First Amendment is such a restriction. It exacts obedience even during periods of war; it is applicable when war clouds are not figments of the imagination no less than when they are. The First Amendment categorically demands that 'Congress shall make no law respecting an establishment of religion, or prohibiting the free exercise thereof; or abridging the freedom of speech, or of the press; or the right of the people peaceably to assemble, and to petition the Government for a redress of grievances'. The right of a man to think what he pleases, to write what he thinks, and to have his thoughts made available for others to hear or read has an engaging ring of universality. The Smith Act and this conviction under it no doubt restrict the exercise of free speech and assembly. Does that, without more, dispose of the matter?

Just as there are those who regard as invulnerable every measure for which the claim of national survival is invoked, there are those who find in the Constitution a wholly unfettered right of expression. Such literalness treats the words of the Constitution as though they were found on a piece of outworn parchment instead of being words that have called into being a nation with a past to be preserved for the future. The soil in which the Bill of Rights grew was not a soil of arid pedantry. The historic antecedents of the First Amendment preclude the notion that its purpose was to give unqualified immunity to every expression that touched on matters within the range of political interest.…

The language of the First Amendment is to be read not as barren words found in a dictionary but as symbols of historic experience illumined by the presuppositions of those who employed them. Not what words did Madison and Hamilton use, but what was it in their minds which they conveyed? Free speech is subject to prohibition of those abuses of expression which a civilized society may forbid. As in the case of every other provision of the Constitution that is not crystallized by the nature of its technical concepts, the fact that the First Amendment is not self-defining and self-enforcing neither impairs its usefulness nor compels its paralysis as a living instrument.

The English inheritance
'The law is perfectly well settled', this Court said over 50 years ago, 'that the first 10 amendments to the Constitution, commonly known as the Bill of Rights, were not intended to lay down any novel principles of government, but simply to embody certain guaranties and immunities which we had inherited from our English ancestors, and which had from time immemorial been subject to certain well-recognized exceptions arising from the necessities of the case. In incorporating these principles into the fundamental law there was no intention of disregarding the exceptions, which continued to be recognized as if they had been formally expressed.' That this represents the authentic view of the Bill of Rights and the spirit in which it must be construed has been recognized again and again in cases that have come here within the last 50 years. Absolute rules would inevitably lead to absolute exceptions, and such exceptions would eventually corrode the rules. The demands of free speech in a democratic society as well as the interest in national security are better served by candid and informed weighing of the competing interests, within the confines of the judicial process, than by announcing dogmas too inflexible for the non-Euclidean problems to be solved.

But how are competing interests to be assessed? Since they are not subject to quantitative ascertainment, the issue necessarily resolves itself into asking, who is to make the adjustment? — who is to balance the relevant factors and ascertain which interest is in the circumstances to prevail? Full responsibility for the choice cannot be given to the courts. Courts are not representative bodies. They are not designed to be a good reflex of a democratic society. Their judgment is best informed, and therefore most dependable, within narrow limits. Their essential quality is detachment, founded on independence. History teaches that the independence of the judiciary is jeopardized when courts become embroiled in the passions of the day and assume primary responsibility in choosing between competing political, economic and social pressures.

Primary responsibility for adjusting the interests which compete in the situation before us of necessity belongs to the Congress. The nature of the power to be exercised by this Court has been delineated in decisions not charged with the emotional appeal of situations such as that now before us. We are to set aside the judgment of those whose duty it is to legislate only if there is no reasonable basis for it.

After reviewing six types of case in which the Court had resolved conflicts between freedom of speech and competing interests Frankfurter went on:

We have enjoyed so much freedom for so long that we are perhaps in danger of forgetting how much blood it cost to establish the Bill of Rights.

Of course no government can recognize a 'right' of revolution, or a 'right' to incite revolution if the incitement has no other purpose or effect. But speech is seldom restricted to a single purpose, and its effects may be manifold. A public interest is not wanting in granting freedom to speak their minds even to those who advocate the overthrow of the Government by force. For, as the evidence in this case abundantly illustrates, coupled with such advocacy is criticism of defects in our society. Criticism is the spur to reform; and Burke's admonition that a healthy society must reform in order to conserve has not lost its force. Astute observers have remarked that one of the characteristics of the American Republic is indifference to fundamental criticism. It is a commonplace that there may be a grain of truth in the most uncouth doctrine, however false and repellent the balance may be. Suppressing advocates of overthrow inevitably will also silence critics who do not advocate overthrow but fear that their criticism may be so construed. No matter how clear we may be that the defendants now before us are preparing to overthrow our Government at the propitious moment, it is self-delusion to think that we can punish them for their advocacy without adding to the risks run by loyal citizens who honestly believe in some of the reforms these defendants advance. It is a sobering fact that in sustaining the convictions before us we can hardly escape restriction on the interchange of ideas.

We must not overlook the value of that interchange. Freedom of expression is the wellspring of our civilization — the civilization we seek to maintain and further by recognizing the right of Congress to put some limitation upon expression. Such are the paradoxes of life. For social development of trial and error, the fullest possible opportunity for the free play of the human mind is an indispensable prerequisite. The history of civilization is in considerable measure the displacement of error which once held sway as official truth by beliefs which in turn have yielded to other truths. Therefore the liberty of man to search for truth ought not to be fettered, no matter what orthodoxies he may challenge. Liberty of thought soon shrivels without freedom of expression. Nor can truth be pursued in an atmosphere hostile to the endeavor or under dangers which are hazarded only by heroes.

After pointing out that to this day historians have conflicting views on the origins and conduct of the French Revolution, or, for that matter, varying interpretations of the Glorious Revolution of 1688, Frankfurter said:

In the light of their experience, the Framers of the Constitution chose to keep the judiciary dissociated from direct participation in the legislative process. In asserting the power to pass on the constitutionality of legislation, Marshall and his Court expressed the purposes of the Founders. But the extent to which the exercise of this power would interpenetrate matters of policy could hardly have been foreseen by the most prescient. The distinction which the Founders drew between the Court's duty to pass on the power of Congress and its complementary duty not to enter directly the domain of policy is fundamental. But in its actual operation it is rather subtle, certainly to the common understanding. Our duty to abstain from confounding policy with constitutionality demands perceptive humility as well as self-restraint in not declaring unconstitutional what in a judge's private judgment is deemed unwise and even dangerous.

Even when moving strictly within the limits of constitutional adjudication, judges are concerned with issues that may be said to involve vital finalities. The too easy transition from disapproval of what is undesirable to condemnation as unconstitutional, has led some of the wisest judges to question the wisdom of our scheme in lodging such authority in courts. But it is relevant to remind that in sustaining the power of Congress in a case like this nothing irrevocable is done. The democratic process at all events is not impaired or restricted. Power and responsibility remain with the people and immediately with their representatives. All the Court says is that Congress was not forbidden by the Constitution to pass this enactment and that a prosecution under it may be brought against a conspiracy such as the one before us.

The wisdom of the assumptions underlying the legislation and prosecution is another matter. In finding that Congress has acted within its power, a judge does not remotely imply that he favors the implications that lie beneath the legal issues. Considerations there enter which go beyond the criteria that are binding upon judges within the narrow confines of their legitimate authority. The legislation we are here considering is but a truncated aspect of a deeper issue. For me it has been most illuminatingly expressed by one in whom responsibility and experience have fructified native insight, the Director-General of the British Broadcasting Corporation:

> We have to face up to the fact that there are powerful forces in the world today misusing the privileges of liberty in order to destroy her. The question must be asked, however, whether suppression of information or opinion is the true defense. We may have come a long way from Mill's famous dictum that: 'If all mankind minus one were of one opinion, and only one person were of the contrary opinion, mankind would be no more justified in silencing that one person, than he, if he had the power, would be justified in silencing mankind', but Mill's reminders from history as to what has happened when suppression was most virulently exercised ought to warn us that no debate is ever permanently won by shutting one's ears or by even the most Draconian policy of silencing opponents. The debate must be won. And it must be won with full information. Where there are lies, they must be shown for what they are. Where there are errors, they must be refuted. It would be a major defeat if the enemies of democracy forced us to abandon our faith in the power of informed discussion and so brought us down to their own level. Mankind is so constituted, moreover, that if, where expression and discussion are concerned, the enemies of liberty are met with a denial of liberty, many men of goodwill will come to suspect there is something in the proscribed doctrine after all. Erroneous doctrines thrive on being expunged. They die if exposed.[86]

The internal danger

In the context of this deeper struggle, another voice has indicated the limitations of what we decide today. No one is better equipped than George F. Kennan to speak on the meaning of the menace of Communism and the spirit in which we should meet it.

> If our handling of the problem of Communist influence in our midst is not carefully moderated — if we permit it, that is, to become an emotional preoccupation and to blind us to the more important positive tasks before us — we can do a damage to our national purpose beyond comparison greater than anything that threatens us today from the Communist side. The

---

[86] Sir William Haley, 'What standards for broadcasting?', *Measure*, vol. 1, No. 3 (Summer 1950), at pp. 211–12.

American Communist party is today, by and large, an external danger. It represents a tiny minority in our country; it has no real contact with the feelings of the mass of our people; and its position as the agency of a hostile foreign power is clearly recognized by the overwhelming mass of our citizens.

But the subjective emotional stresses and temptations to which we are exposed in our attempt to deal with this domestic problem are not an external danger: they represent a danger within ourselves — a danger that something may occur in our own minds and souls which will make us no longer like the persons by whose efforts this republic was founded and held together, but rather like the representatives of that very power we are trying to combat: intolerant, secretive, suspicious, cruel, and terrified of internal dissension because we have lost our own belief in ourselves and in the power of our ideals. The worst thing that our Communists could do to us, and the thing we have most to fear from their activities, is that we should become like them.

That our country is beset with external dangers I readily concede. But these dangers, at their worst, are ones of physical destruction, of the disruption of our world security, of expenses and inconvenience and sacrifice. These are serious, and sometimes terrible things, but they are all things that we can take and still remain Americans.

The internal danger is of a different order. America is not just territory and people. There is lots of territory elsewhere, and there are lots of people; but it does not add up to America. America is something in our minds and our habits of outlook which causes us to believe in certain things and to behave in certain ways, and by which, in its totality, we hold ourselves distinguished from others. If that once goes there will be no America to defend. And that can go too easily if we yield to the primitive human instinct to escape from our frustrations into the realms of mass emotion and hatred and to find scapegoats for our difficulties in individual fellow-citizens who are, or have at one time been, disoriented or confused.[87]

Civil liberties draw at best only limited strength from legal guaranties. Preoccupation by our peoples with the constitutionality, instead of with the wisdom, of legislation or of executive action is preoccupation with a false value. Even those who would most freely use the judicial brake on the democratic process by invalidating legislation that goes deeply against their grain, acknowledge, at least by paying lip service, that constitutionality does not exact a sense of proportion or the sanity of humor or an absence of fear.

---

[87] George F. Kennan, 'Where do you stand on Communism?', *New York Times Magazine*, 27 May 1951, pp. 7, 53, 55.

Focusing attention on constitutionality tends to make constitutionality synony-mous with wisdom. When legislation touches freedom of thought and freedom of speech, such a tendency is a formidable enemy of the free spirit. Much that should be rejected as illiberal, because repressive and envenoming, may well be not unconstitutional. The ultimate reliance for the deepest needs of civilization must be found outside their vindication in courts of law; apart from all else, judges, howsoever they may conscientiously seek to discipline themselves against it, unconsciously are too apt to be moved by the deep undercurrents of public feeling. A persistent, positive translation of the liberating faith into the feelings and thoughts and actions of men and women is the real protection against attempts to straitjacket the human mind. Such temptations will have their way, if fear and hatred are not exorcised. The mark of a truly civilized man is confidence in the strength and security derived from the inquiring mind. We may be grateful for such honest comforts as it supports, but we must be unafraid of its incertitudes. Without open minds there can be no open society. And if society be not open the spirit of man is mutilated and becomes enslaved.

This decision of the Court was condemned, somewhat extravagant-ly, by one of the dissentients on the bench, William Douglas, as 'marking' (along with the decision in Scales *below) 'the greatest decline in free speech in the history of the nation'.*[88]

Choose between freedom and fear

Mr Justice Douglas had another opportunity to advance his point of view in a case which came before the Supreme Court a decade or so later.[89]

Junius Irving Scales was chairman of the North and South Carolina Districts of the Communist Party. He recruited new members and promoted the education of young party members at secret schools. He criticised the 'aggression' of America in Korea and described the 'atrocities' committed on Korean citizens. He had stated that the party was setting up underground means of communication and

---

[88] *The Court Years 1939–1975: The Autobiography of William O. Douglas* (New York: Random House, 1980).
[89] *Scales* v *United States*, 367 US 203 (1961).

that he himself had 'gone underground'. On one occasion students
were shown how to kill a person with a pencil. Scales had suggested
that the Negroes in the South should foment a violent revolution
and had claimed that the goals of Communism could only be
achieved by violent revolution started by the working classes.

Convicted of violating the membership clause of the Smith Act,
Scales appealed to the Supreme Court (which might be described
as ironic in light of his views on the corruption of American
society). The Court held by a majority that the terms of the Act were
not impermissibly vague. Nor did it infringe the First Amendment
concerning freedom of speech.

Douglas dissociated himself from the majority in an opinion that
boldly affirmed the libertarian tradition of the Court.

When we allow petitioner to be sentenced to prison for six years for being a 'member' of the Communist Party, we make a sharp break with traditional concepts of First Amendment rights and make serious Mark Twain's lighthearted comment that 'It is by the goodness of God that in our country we have those three unspeakably precious things: freedom of speech, freedom of conscience, and the prudence never to practice either of them'.

Even the Alien and Sedition Laws — shameful reminders of an early chapter in intolerance — never went so far as we go today. They were aimed at conspiracy and advocacy of insurrection and at the publication of 'false, scandalous and malicious' writing against the Government. . . . The Government then sought control over the press 'in order to strike at one of the chief sources of disaffection and sedition'. There is here no charge of conspiracy, no charge of any overt act to overthrow the Government by force and violence, no charge of any other criminal act. The charge is being a 'member' of the Communist Party, 'well knowing' that it advocated the overthrow of the Government by force and violence, 'said defendant intending to bring about such overthrow by force and violence as speedily as circumstances would permit'. That falls far short of a charge of conspiracy. Conspiracy rests not in intention alone but in an agreement with one or more others to promote an unlawful project. No charge of any kind or sort of agreement hitherto embraced in the concept of a conspiracy is made here.

Guilt by association
We legalize today guilt by association, sending a man to prison when he committed no unlawful act. Today's break with tradition is a serious one. It borrows from the totalitarian philosophy. As stated by O'Brian:

The Smith Act of 1940 made it unlawful for any person to be or to become a member of or affiliate with any society, group, or assembly which teaches, advocates, or encourages the overthrow or destruction of any government in the United States by force or violence. These statutes, therefore, imported into our law the alien doctrine of guilt by association, which up to this time had been regarded as abhorrent and which had never been recognized either by the courts or by the Department of Justice, even during the perils and excitements of the First World War.

The case is not saved by showing that petitioner was an active member.

After reviewing the facts in the case Douglas went on:

Not one single illegal act is charged to petitioner. That is why the essence of the crime covered by the indictment is merely belief — belief in the proletarian revolution, belief in Communist creed.

Spinoza summed up in a sentence much of the history of the struggle of man to think and speak what he believes:

Laws which decree what every one must believe, and forbid utterance against this or that opinion, have too often been enacted to confirm or enlarge the power of those who dared not suffer free inquiry to be made, and have by a perversion of authority turned the superstition of the mob into violence against opponents.

'The thought of man shall not be tried, for the devil himself knoweth not the thought of man', said Chief Justice Brian. The crime of belief — presently prosecuted — is a carryback to the old law of treason where men were punished for compassing the death of the King. That law, which had been employed for 'suppression of political opposition or the expression of ideas or beliefs distasteful to those in power', was rejected here, and the treason clause of our Constitution was 'most praised for the reason that it prevented the use of treason trials as an instrument of political faction'. Sedition or treason in the realm of politics and heresy in the ecclesiastical field had long centered on beliefs as the abhorrent criminal act. The struggle on this side of the Atlantic was to get rid of that concept and to punish men not for what they thought but for overt acts against the peace of the Nation. Montesquieu, who was a force in the thinking of those times, proclaimed against punishing thoughts or words:

There was a law passed in England under Henry VIII, by which whoever predicted the king's death was declared guilty of high treason. This law was extremely vague; the terror of despotic power is so great that it recoils upon those who exercise it. In the king's last illness, the physicians would not venture to say he was in danger; and surely they acted very right. . . . Marsyas dreamed that he had cut Dionysius's throat. Dionysius put him to death, pretending that he would never have dreamed of such a thing by night if he had not thought of it by day. This was a most tyrannical action: for though it had been the subject of his thoughts; yet he had made no attempt towards it. The laws do not take upon them to punish any other than overt acts.

Words do not constitute an overt act; they remain only in idea.

These were the notions that led to the restrictive definition of treason, presently contained in Article III, paragraph 3, of the Constitution, which requires overt acts. Our long and painful experience with the law of treason, wholly apart from the First Amendment, should be enough warning that we as a free people should not venture again into the field of prosecuting beliefs.

That was the philosophy behind *Board of Education* v *Barnette*:

We can have intellectual individualism and the rich cultural diversities that we owe to exceptional minds only at the price of occasional eccentricity and abnormal attitudes. When they are so harmless to others or to the State as those we deal with here, the price is not too great. But freedom to differ is not limited to things that do not matter much. That would be a mere shadow of freedom. The test of its substance is the right to differ as to things that touch the heart of the existing order.

If there is any fixed star in our constitutional constellation, it is that no official, high or petty, can prescribe what shall be orthodox in politics, nationalism, religion, or other matters of opinion or force citizens to confess by word or act their faith therein. If there are any circumstances which permit an exception, they do not now occur to us.

Beliefs on trial

Nothing but beliefs is on trial in this case. They are unpopular and to most of us revolting. But they are nonetheless ideas or dogmas or faiths within the broad framework of the First Amendment. The creed truer to our faith was stated by the Bar Committee which in 1920 protested the refusal of the New York Assembly to seat five members of the Socialist Party:

. . . it is of the essence of the institutions of liberty that it be recognized that guilt is personal and cannot be attributed to the holding of opinion or to mere intent in the absence of overt acts.

Belief in the principle of revolution is deep in our traditions. The Declaration of Independence proclaims it:

> ... whenever any Form of Government becomes destructive of these Ends, it is the Right of the People to alter or to abolish it, and to institute new Government, laying its Foundation on such Principles, and organizing its Powers in such Form, as to them shall seem most likely to effect their Safety and Happiness.

This right of revolution has been and is a part of the fabric of our institutions. Last century when Russia invaded Hungary and subdued her, Louis Kossuth came here to enlist American support. On January 8, 1852, Lincoln spoke in sympathy of the Hungarian cause and was a member of a committee which on January 9, 1852, submitted Resolutions in Behalf of Hungarian Freedom. Among these resolutions was one that read:

> That it is the right of any people, sufficiently numerous for national independence, to throw off, to revolutionize, their existing form of government, and to establish such other in its stead as they may choose.

On January 12, 1848, Lincoln in an address before the United States House of Representatives stated: 'Any people anywhere, being inclined and having the power, have the right to rise up, and shake off the existing government, and form a new one that suits them better. This is a most valuable, — a most sacred right, which we hope and believe, is to liberate the world'.[90]

British colonial philosophy

Of course, government can move against those who take up arms against it. Of course, the constituted authority has the right of self-preservation. But we deal in this prosecution of Scales only with the legality of ideas and beliefs, not with overt acts. The Court speaks of the prevention of 'dangerous behavior' by punishing those 'who work to bring about that behavior'. That formula returns man to the dark days when government determined what behavior was 'dangerous' and then policed the dissidents for tell-tale signs of advocacy. What is 'dangerous behavior' that must be suppressed in its talk-stage has had a vivid history even on this continent. The British colonial philosophy was summed up by Sir William Berkeley, who served from 1641 to 1677 as Virginia's Governor:

---

[90] One wonders what Lincoln thought of his own words 13 years later at the outbreak of the War between the States. (Ed.)

... I thank God, there are no free schools nor printing, and I hope we shall not have these hundred years; for learning has brought disobedience, and heresy, and sects into the world, and printing has divulged them, and libels against the best government. God keep us from both!

The history is familiar; much of it is reviewed in Chafee.[91] He states in one paragraph what I think is the Jeffersonian conception of the First Amendment rights involved in the present case:

We must choose between freedom and fear — we cannot have both. If the citizens of the United States persist in being afraid, the real rulers of this country will be fanatics fired with a zeal to save grown men from objectionable ideas by putting them under the care of official nursemaids.

In recent years we have been departing, I think, from the theory of government expressed in the First Amendment. We have too often been 'balancing' the right of speech and association against other values in society to see if we, the judges, feel that a particular need is more important than those guaranteed by the Bill of Rights....

It also runs counter to Madison's views of the First Amendment as we are advised by his eminent biographer, Irving Brant:

When Madison wrote, 'Congress shall make no law' infringing these rights, he did not expect the Supreme Court to decide, on balance, whether Congress could or could not make a law infringing them. It was true, he observed in presenting his proposals, that state legislative bodies had violated many of the most valuable articles in bills of rights. But that furnished no basis for judging the effectiveness of the proposed amendments:

If they are incorporated into the Constitution, independent tribunals of justice will consider themselves in a peculiar manner the guardians of those rights; they will be an impenetrable bulwark against every assumption of power in the Legislative or Executive; they will be naturally led to resist every encroachment upon rights expressly stipulated for in the Constitution by the declaration of rights.

This statement by Madison, along with all the rest of his speech, is so devastating to the 'balance theory' that efforts have been and are being made

---

[91] *The Blessings of Liberty* (1956).

to discredit its authenticity. The *Annals of Congress*, it is said, is not an official document, but a compilation of stenographic reports (by a shorthand reporter admitted to the floor for that purpose) published in the press and containing numerous errors. That is true, although the chief complaint was that partially caught sentences were meaningless. In general, that which was clearly reported was truly reported. In the case of this all-important speech, Madison spoke from notes, and the notes in his handwriting are in the Library of Congress. They parallel the speech from end to end, scantily, but leaving no doubt of the fundamental faithfulness of the report.

Brant goes on to relate how Madison opposed a resolution of censure against societies creating the political turmoil that was behind the Whiskey Rebellion. He expressed in the House the view that opinions are not objects of legislation. 'If we advert to the nature of Republican Government, we shall find that the censorial power is in the people over the Government, and not in the Government over the people.'

The trend of history, as Jefferson noted, has been against the rights of man. He wrote that 'The natural progress of things is for liberty to yield and government to gain ground'. The formula he prepared for a society where ideas flourished was not punishment of the unorthodox but education and enlightenment of the masses. Jefferson wrote to Madison on December 20, 1787:

I own, I am not a friend to a very energetic government. It is always oppressive. It places the governors indeed more at their ease, at the expense of the people. The late rebellion in Massachusetts has given more alarm, than I think it should have done. Calculate that one rebellion in thirteen States in the course of eleven years, is but one for each State in a century and a half. No country should be so long without one. Nor will any degree of power in the hands of government, prevent insurrections. In England, where the hand of power is heavier than with us, there are seldom half a dozen years without an insurrection. In France, where it is still heavier, but less despotic, as Montesquieu supposes, than in some other countries, and where there are always two or three hundred thousand men ready to crush insurrections, there have been three in the course of the three years I have been here, in every one of which greater numbers were engaged than in Massachusetts, and a great deal more blood was spilt. In Turkey, where the sole nod of the despot is death, insurrections are the events of every day. Compare again the ferocious depredations of their insurgents, with the order, the moderation and the almost self-extinguishment of ours. And say, finally, whether peace is best preserved by giving energy to the government, or information to the people. This last is the most certain, and the most legitimate engine of government. Educate and inform the whole mass of the people. Enable them to see that it is their interest to preserve peace and order, and they will preserve them. And it requires no very high degree of education to convince them of this. They are the only sure reliance for the preservation of our liberty.

This is the only philosophy consistent with the First Amendment. When belief in an idea is punished as it is today, we sacrifice those ideals and substitute an alien, totalitarian philosophy in their stead.

'The most indifferent arguments', Bismarck said, 'are good when one has a majority of bayonets'.

That is also true when one has the votes.

What we lose by majority vote today may be reclaimed at a future time when the fear of advocacy, dissent, and nonconformity no longer cast a shadow over us.

In considering the (undoubted) advantages of a written constitution we should not forget the words of Thomas Jefferson, when writing to his friend, Samuel Kercheval, on 12 July 1816:

Some men look at constitutions with sanctimonious reverence, and deem them like the ark of the covenant, too sacred to be touched. They ascribe to the men of the preceding age a wisdom more than human, and suppose what they did to be beyond amendment. I knew that age well; I belonged to it, and labored with it. It deserved well of its country. It was very like the present, but without the experience of the present; and forty years of experience in government is worth a century of book-reading; and this they would say themselves, were they to rise from the dead. I am certainly not an advocate for frequent and untried changes in laws and constitutions. I think moderate imperfections had better be borne with; because, when once known, we accommodate ourselves to them, and find practical means of correcting their ill effects. But I know also, that laws and institutions must go hand in hand with the progress of the human mind. As that becomes more developed, more enlightened, as new discoveries are made, new truths disclosed, and manners and opinions change with the change of circumstances, institutions must advance also, and keep pace with the times. We might as well require a man to wear still the coat which fitted him as a boy, as civilized society to remain ever under the regimen of their barbarous ancestors.

Memorial Tablet, Temple

7. LIFE'S DOMINION

or

The Law of Life and Death

In my view the choice which the law makes must reassure
people that the courts do have full respect for life, but that they
do not pursue the principle to the point at which it has become
almost empty of any real content and when it involves the
sacrifice of other important values such as human dignity and
freedom of choice.

Lord Justice Hoffmann in *Airedale NHS Trust* v *Bland.*[92]

**A view so much out of date
One theory of life
A case for emotion
What price a child's life?
Earnest and profound debate**

---

[92] See under *A case for emotion.*

The great end for which men entered into society, said Lord Camden, was to secure their property. That may be, but nowadays, few issues, however personal, are outside the scope of litigation. Some question whether it is appropriate for lawyers to decide unaided questions of personal and medical ethics, but until a better machinery is devised that is what must happen. So far, the record of the judges is impressive, as the following extracts demonstrate.

A good example was the challenge by the redoubtable Victoria Gillick to government advice permitting the provision of contraceptive advice to minors. Upholding the advice, Lord Scarman accepted that:

It can be said by way of criticism of this view of the law that it will result in uncertainty and leave the law in the hands of the doctors. The uncertainty is the price which has to be paid to keep the law in line with social experience. (See under *A view so much out of date*)

A few years earlier it fell to Mr Justice Blackmun, sitting in the United States Supreme Court, to define a woman's right to an abortion. Like Lord Scarman in the Gillick *case he found it helpful to consult the views of an eighteenth-century Vinerian professor of law at Oxford. However, Blackmun's researches went even further back in time — as far as Hippocrates, by way of Galen (* One theory of life *). It is worth noting that in laying down the law on this most difficult of issues the American courts had no alternative but to construe the language of their 200-year-old constitution, while England's legislators were free to eschew principle in preference for what science and contemporary morality would allow.*

Another dilemma posed by the advances of modern medicine concerned the fate of an 18-year-old football supporter caught in the panic at Hillsborough Stadium in 1989. His chest was badly crushed but, with medical intervention, his body was kept alive. Eventually the health authority applied to the court for permission to discontinue their efforts. The case went to the House of Lords, but the passage quoted here is from the judgment of Lord Justice Hoffmann in the Court of Appeal (A case for emotion *).*

*It is one thing to discontinue supporting a life that is already gone and quite another to deny to a patient medical treatment that might prevent her death. A young girl was seriously ill and the only course that might have saved her life was medical treatment of a largely untested nature. After no doubt agonising consideration the health authority decided they were not justified in providing that treatment. Her father sought the assistance of the courts. This was granted at first instance by Mr Justice Laws, whose fine judgment is printed below. He concluded that there was a small but significant prospect of overall success for the child if the treatment were to be carried out and ordered the Health Authority to reconsider its decision (*What price a child's life?*). His decision was overturned by the House of Lords, but the final outcome turned out not to depend on the courts at all.*

While this case did not call for the scholarship and far-ranging reviews that appear in other judgments in this chapter it is nevertheless of interest for its painstakingly detailed examination of the facts of a distressing dilemma. And it is on examinations of this nature that experience suggests such cases are best decided.

*The chapter ends with a recent American judgment concerning physician-assisted suicide (*Earnest and profound debate*) which could be studied with profit by all concerned with this difficult issue.*

A view so much out of date

Few developments have wrought more dramatic changes in the sexual, and thus social, life of ordinary people than the discovery this century of effective measures of contraception. Most people regard this development as benign, but there are obvious problems in providing contraceptive advice to young people.

A memorandum of guidance issued by the Department of Health and Social Security encouraged, and in certain circumstances recommended, health authorities, doctors and others concerned in family planning services to provide contraceptive advice and treatment to girls without the consent or knowledge of a parent.

Victoria Gillick, then a mother of five daughters under the age of 16, challenged the advice in the courts. The judge of first instance dismissed her application and she appealed successfully to the Court of Appeal. The House of Lords took a different view.

The following extracts are taken from the speech of Lord Scarman[93] who agreed with the majority in dismissing Mrs Gillick's application.

The law has ... to be found by a search in the judge-made law for the true principle. The legal difficulty is that in our search we find ourselves in a field of medical practice where parental right and a doctor's duty may point us in different directions. This is not surprising. Three features have emerged in today's society which were not known to our predecessors: (1) contraception as a subject for medical advice and treatment; (2) the increasing independence of young people; and (3) the changed status of women. In times past contraception was rarely a matter for the doctor; but with the development of the contraceptive pill for women it has become part and parcel of everyday medical practice, as is made clear by the department's *Handbook of Contraceptive Practice*. Family planning services are now available under statutory powers to all without any express limitation as to age or marital status. Young people, once they have attained the age of 16, are capable of consenting to contraceptive treatment, since it is medical treatment; and, however extensive the parental right in the care and upbringing of children, it cannot prevail so as to nullify the 16-year-old's capacity to consent which is now conferred by statute. Furthermore, women have obtained by the availability of the pill a choice of lifestyle with a degree of independence and of opportunity undreamed of until this generation and greater, I would add, than any law of equal opportunity could by itself effect.

The law ignores these developments at its peril. The House's task, therefore, as the supreme court in a legal system largely based on rules of law evolved over the years by the judicial process is to search the overfull and cluttered shelves of the law reports for a principle or set of principles recognised by the judges over the years but stripped of the details which, however appropriate in their day, would, if applied today, lay the judges open to a justified criticism for failing to keep the law abreast of the society in which they live and work.

It is, of course, a judicial commonplace to proclaim the adaptability and flexibility of the judge-made common law. But this is more frequently

---

[93] *Gillick v West Norfolk and Wisbech Area Health Authority* [1985] 3 All ER 402, 419.

proclaimed than acted on. The mark of the great judge from Coke through Mansfield to our day has been the capacity and the will to search out principle, to discard the detail appropriate (perhaps) to earlier times and to apply principle in such a way as to satisfy the needs of his own time. If judge-made law is to survive as a living and relevant body of law, we must make the effort, however inadequately, to follow the lead of the great masters of the judicial art.

In this appeal, therefore, there is much in the earlier case law which the House must discard; almost everything I would say but its principle. For example, the horrendous decisions of the late nineteenth century asserting the power of the father over his child were rightly remaindered to the history books by the Court of Appeal, an important case to which I shall return later.

Yet the decisions of earlier generations may well afford clues to the true principle of the law. . . . It is the duty of this House to look at, through and past the decisions of earlier generations so that it may identify the principle which lies behind them. Even Lord Eldon (no legal revolutionary) once remarked, when invited to study precedent (the strength of which he never underrated):

> . . . all law ought to stand upon principle, and unless decision has removed out of the way all argument and all principle, so as to make it impossible to apply them to the case before you, you must find out what is the principle upon which it must be decided.

Approaching the earlier law in this way, one finds plenty of indications as to the principles governing the law's approach to parental right and the child's right to make his or her own decision. Parental rights clearly do exist, and they do not wholly disappear until the age of majority. Parental rights relate to both the person and the property of the child: custody, care and control of the person and guardianship of the property of the child. But the common law has never treated such rights as sovereign or beyond review and control. Nor has our law ever treated the child as other than a person with capacities and rights recognised by law. The principle of the law, as I shall endeavour to show, is that parental rights are derived from parental duty and exist only so long as they are needed for the protection of the person and property of the child. The principle has been subjected to certain age limits set by statute for certain purposes; and in some cases the courts have declared an age of discretion at which a child acquires before the age of majority the right to make his (or her) own decision. But these limitations in no way undermine the principle of the law, and should not be allowed to obscure it.

Let me make good, quite shortly, the proposition of principle. . . . It is abundantly plain that the law recognises that there is a right and a duty of parents to determine whether or not to seek medical advice in respect of their child, and, having received advice, to give or withhold consent to medical treatment. The question in the appeal is as to the extent and duration of the right and the circumstances in which outside the two admitted exceptions to which I have earlier referred it can be overridden by the exercise of medical judgment.

[T]he modern statute law recognises the existence of parental right.... It is derived from parental duty. A most illuminating discussion of parental right is to be found in Blackstone's *Commentaries*. He analyses the duty of the parent as the 'maintenance ... protection, and ... education' of the child. He declares that the power of parents over their children is derived from their duty and exists 'to enable the parent more effectually to perform his duty, and partly as a recompense for his care and trouble in the faithful discharge of it'. In ch. 17 he discusses the relation of guardian and ward. It is, he points out, a relation 'derived out of [the relation of parent and child]: the guardian being only a temporary parent, that is, for so long a time as the ward is an infant, or under age'. A little later in the same chapter he again emphasises that the power and reciprocal duty of a guardian and ward are the same, *pro tempore*, as that of a father and child and adds that the guardian, when the ward comes of age (as also the father who becomes guardian 'at common law' if an estate be left to his child), must account to the child for all that he has transacted on his behalf. He then embarks on a discussion of the different ages at which for different purposes a child comes of sufficient age to make his own decision; and he cites examples, viz. a boy might at 12 years old take the oath of allegiance; at 14 he might consent to marriage or choose his guardian 'and, if his discretion be actually proved, may make his testament of his personal estate'; at 18 he could be an executor: all these rights and responsibilities being capable of his acquiring before reaching the age of majority at 21.

The two chapters provide a valuable insight into the principle and flexibility of the common law. The principle is that parental right or power of control of the person and property of his child exists primarily to enable the parent to discharge his duty of maintenance, protection and education until he reaches such an age as to be able to look after himself and make his own decisions. Blackstone does suggest that there was a further justification for parental right, viz. as a recompense for the faithful discharge of parental duty; but the right of the father to the exclusion of the mother and the reward element as one of the reasons for the existence of the right have been swept away by the guardianship of minors legislation. ... He also accepts that by statute and by case law varying ages of discretion have been fixed for various purposes. But it is clear that this was done to achieve certainty where it was considered necessary and in no way limits the principle that parental right endures only so long as it is needed for the protection of the child.

The duration of parental rights
Although statute has intervened in respect of a child's capacity to consent to medical treatment from the age of 16 onwards, neither statute nor the case law has ruled on the extent and duration of parental right in respect of children under the age of 16. More specifically, there is no rule yet applied to contraceptive treatment, which has special problems of its own and is a latecomer in medical practice. It is open, therefore, to the House to formulate a rule. The Court of Appeal favoured a fixed age limit of 16 basing itself on a view of the statute law which I do not share and on its view of the effect of the older case law which for the reasons already given I cannot accept. It sought to justify the limit by the public interest in the law being certain. Certainty is always an advantage in the law, and in some branches of the law it is a necessity. But it brings with it an inflexibility and a rigidity which in some branches of the law can obstruct justice, impede the law's development and stamp on the law the mark of obsolescence where what is needed is the capacity for development.

The law relating to parent and child is concerned with the problems of the growth and maturity of the human personality. If the law should impose on the process of 'growing up' fixed limits where nature knows only a continuous process, the price would be artificiality and a lack of realism in an area where the law must be sensitive to human development and social change. If certainty be thought desirable, it is better that the rigid demarcations necessary to achieve it should be laid down by legislation after a full consideration of all the relevant factors than by the courts, confined as they are by the forensic process to the evidence adduced by the parties and to whatever may properly fall within the judicial notice of judges. Unless and until Parliament should think fit to intervene, the courts should establish a principle flexible enough to enable justice to be achieved by its application to the particular circumstances proved by the evidence placed before them.

The underlying principle of the law was exposed by Blackstone and can be seen to have been acknowledged in the case law. It is that parental right yields to the child's right to make his own decisions when he reaches a sufficient understanding and intelligence to be capable of making up his own mind on the matter requiring decision. Lord Denning MR captured the spirit and principle of the law when he said:

I would get rid of the rule in *Re Agar-Ellis* and of the suggested exceptions to it. That case was decided in the year 1883. It reflects the attitude of a Victorian parent towards his children. He expected unquestioning obedience to his commands. If a son disobeyed, his father would cut him off with 1s. If a daughter had an illegitimate child, he would turn her out of the house. His power only ceased when the child became 21 — I decline to accept a view so much out of date. The common law can, and should, keep pace with the times. It should declare, in conformity with the recent report on the *Age of Majority* under the chairmanship of Mr Justice Latey, that the legal right of a parent to the custody of a child ends at the eighteenth birthday; and even up till then, it is a dwindling right which the courts will hesitate to enforce against the wishes of the child, the older he is. It starts with a right of control and ends with little more than advice.

But his is by no means a solitary voice.

For the reasons which I have endeavoured to develop, the case law of the nineteenth and earlier centuries is no guide to the application of the law in the conditions of today. The *Agar-Ellis* cases (the power of the father) cannot live with the modern statute law. The habeas corpus 'age of discretion' cases are also no guide as to the limits which should be accepted today in marking out the bounds of parental right, of a child's capacity to make his or her own decision and of a doctor's duty to his patient. Nevertheless the 'age of discretion' cases are helpful in that they do reveal the judges as accepting that a minor can in law achieve an age of discretion before coming of full age. The 'age of discretion' cases are cases in which a parent or guardian (usually the father) has applied for habeas corpus to secure the return of his child who has left home without his consent. The courts would refuse an order if the child had attained the age of discretion, which came to be regarded as 14 for boys and 16 for girls, and did not wish to return. The principle underlying them was plainly that an order would be refused if the child had sufficient intelligence and understanding to make up his own mind. . . .

The principle is clear; and a fixed age of discretion was accepted by the courts by analogy from the Abduction Acts. . . . While it is unrealistic today to treat a sixteenth-century Act as a safe guide in the matter of a girl's discretion, and while no modern judge would dismiss the intelligence of a teenage girl as intellectual precocity, we can agree with Chief Justice Cockburn as to the principle of the law: the attainment by a child of an age of sufficient discretion to enable him or her to exercise a wise choice in his or her own interests.

After reviewing an earlier decision of the House Scarman went on:

In the light of the foregoing I would hold that as a matter of law the parental right to determine whether or not their minor child below the age of 16 will have medical treatment terminates if and when the child achieves a sufficient understanding and intelligence to enable him or her to understand fully what is proposed. It will be a question of fact whether a child seeking advice has sufficient understanding of what is involved to give a consent valid in law. Until the child achieves the capacity to consent, the parental right to make the decision continues save only in exceptional circumstances. Emergency, parental neglect, abandonment of the child or inability to find the parent are examples of exceptional situations justifying the doctor proceeding to treat the child without parental knowledge and consent; but there will arise, no doubt, other exceptional situations in which it will be reasonable for the doctor to proceed without the parent's consent.

When applying these conclusions to contraceptive advice and treatment it has to be borne in mind that there is much that has to be understood by a girl under the age of 16 if she is to have legal capacity to consent to such treatment. It is not enough that she should understand the nature of the advice which is being given: she must also have a sufficient maturity to understand what is involved. There are moral and family questions, especially her relationship with her parents; long-term problems associated with the notional impact of pregnancy and its termination; and there are the risks to health of sexual intercourse at her age, risks which contraception may diminish but cannot eliminate. It follows that a doctor will have to satisfy himself that she is able to appraise these factors before he can safely proceed on the basis that she has at law capacity to consent to contraceptive treatment. And it further follows that ordinarily the proper course will be for him, as the guidance lays down, first to seek to persuade the girl to:

bring her parents into consultation, and, if she refuses, not to prescribe contraceptive treatment unless he is satisfied that her circumstances are such that he ought to proceed without parental knowledge and consent.

I am, therefore, satisfied that the department's guidance can be followed without involving the doctor in any infringement of parental right. Unless, therefore, to prescribe contraceptive treatment for a girl under the age of 16 is either a criminal offence or so close to one that to prescribe such treatment is contrary to public policy, the department's appeal must succeed.

THE CRIMINAL LAW CASE

If this case should be made good, the discussion of parental right is, of course, an irrelevance if it be criminal or contrary to public policy to prescribe contraception for a girl under the age of 16 on the ground that sexual intercourse with her is unlawful and a crime on the part of her male partner, the fact that her parent knew and consented cannot make it any less so. I confess that I find the submission based on criminality or public policy surprising.... Clearly a doctor who gives a girl contraceptive advice or treatment not because in his clinical judgment the treatment is medically indicated for the maintenance or restoration of her health but with the intention of facilitating her having unlawful sexual intercourse may well be guilty of a criminal offence. It would depend, as my noble and learned friend Lord Fraser observes, on the doctor's intention, a conclusion hardly to be wondered at in the field of the criminal law. The department's guidance avoids the trap of declaring that the decision to prescribe the treatment is wholly a matter of the doctor's discretion. He may prescribe only if she has the capacity to consent or if exceptional circumstances exist which justify him in exercising his clinical judgment without parental consent. The adjective 'clinical' emphasises that it must be a medical judgment based on what he honestly believes to be necessary for the physical, mental and emotional health of his patient. The bona fide exercise by a doctor of his clinical judgment must be a complete negation of the guilty mind which is an essential ingredient of the criminal offence of aiding and abetting the commission of unlawful sexual intercourse.

PUBLIC POLICY

The public policy point fails for the same reason. It cannot be said that there is anything necessarily contrary to public policy in medical contraceptive treatment if it be medically indicated as in the interest of the patient's health; for the provision of such treatment is recognised as legitimate by Parliament. If it should be prescribed for a girl under 16 the fact that it may eliminate a health risk in the event of the girl having unlawful sexual intercourse is an irrelevance unless the doctor intends to encourage her to have that intercourse. If the prescription is the bona fide exercise of his clinical judgment as to what is best for his patient's health, he has nothing to fear from the criminal law or from any public policy based on the criminality of a man having sexual intercourse with her.

It can be said by way of criticism of this view of the law that it will result in uncertainty and leave the law in the hands of the doctors. The uncertainty is the price which has to be paid to keep the law in line with social experience, which is that many girls are fully able to make sensible decisions about many matters before they reach the age of 16. I accept that great responsibilities will lie on the medical profession. It is, however, a learned and highly trained profession regulated by statute and governed by a strict ethical code which is vigorously enforced. Abuse of the power to prescribe contraceptive treatment for girls under the age of 16 would render a doctor liable to severe professional penalty.

The truth may well be that the rights of parents and children in this sensitive area are better protected by the professional standards of the medical profession than by a priori legal lines of division between capacity and lack of capacity to consent since any such general dividing line is sure to produce in some cases injustice, hardship and injury to health.

One theory of life

The right of a woman to terminate her pregnancy has been the source of much debate in recent years, both in and out of the courts, occasioned partly by a dawning recognition of women's rights over their own bodies and partly by advances in medical science. The issue came before the United States Supreme Court in 1973.

Jane Roe, an unmarried, pregnant woman, wanted an abortion but was unable to obtain one legally in her home State of Texas because her life did not appear to be threatened by the continuation of the pregnancy. Nor could she afford to evade the law by travelling out of the State. Wishing to terminate her pregnancy by an abortion 'performed by a competent, licensed physician, under safe, clinical conditions', she claimed that the Texas statutes on abortion were unconstitutionally vague and that they abridged her constitutional right of personal privacy. Miss Roe purported to sue 'on behalf of herself and all other women' similarly situated.

Apart from its intrinsic interest the opinion of Mr Justice Blackmun[94] is notable for its meticulous examination of the history of the subject, from the Hippocratic oath, through the English common law and statutes, to the views of the American Medical Association (omitted in this extract). It demonstrates vividly the interaction of law, ethics and medical science. The English lawyer, however, will be surprised at the way in which the mother's rights had to be subsumed under the constitutional doctrine of privacy.

We forthwith acknowledge our awareness of the sensitive and emotional nature of the abortion controversy, of the vigorous opposing views, even among

---

[94] *Roe* v *Wade*, 410 US 113 (1973).

physicians, and of the deep and seemingly absolute convictions that the subject inspires. One's philosophy, one's experiences, one's exposure to the raw edges of human existence, one's religious training, one's attitudes toward life and family and their values, and the moral standards one establishes and seeks to observe, are all likely to influence and to color one's thinking and conclusions about abortion. In addition, population growth, pollution, poverty, and racial overtones tend to complicate and not to simplify the problem. Our task, of course, is to resolve the issue by constitutional measurement, free of emotion and of predilection. We seek earnestly to do this, and, because we do, we have inquired into, and in this opinion place some emphasis upon, medical and medical-legal history and what that history reveals about man's attitudes toward the abortion procedure over the centuries. We bear in mind, too, Mr Justice Holmes' admonition in his now-vindicated dissent in *Lochner* v *New York*:[95]

[The Constitution] is made for people of fundamentally differing views, and the accident of our finding certain opinions natural and familiar or novel and even shocking ought not to conclude our judgment upon the question whether statutes embodying them conflict with the Constitution of the United States.

... It perhaps is not generally appreciated that the restrictive criminal abortion laws in effect in a majority of States today are of relatively recent vintage. Those laws, generally proscribing abortion or its attempt at any time during pregnancy except when necessary to preserve the pregnant woman's life, are not of ancient or even of common law origin. Instead, they derive from statutory changes effected, for the most part, in the latter half of the nineteenth century.

ANCIENT ATTITUDES

These are not capable of precise determination. We are told that, at the time of the Persian Empire, abortifacients were known, and that criminal abortions were severely punished. We are also told, however, that abortion was practiced in Greek times as well as in the Roman Era, and that 'it was resorted to without scruple'. The Ephesian, Soranos, often described as the greatest of the ancient gynecologists, appears to have been generally opposed to Rome's prevailing free-abortion practices. He found it necessary to think first of the life of the

---

[95] 198 US 45, 76 (1905). See *Liberty perverted* in chapter 6.

mother, and he resorted to abortion when, upon this standard, he felt the procedure advisable. Greek and Roman law afforded little protection to the unborn. If abortion was prosecuted in some places, it seems to have been based on a concept of a violation of the father's right to his offspring. Ancient religion did not bar abortion.

THE HIPPOCRATIC OATH

What then of the famous Oath that has stood so long as the ethical guide of the medical profession and that bears the name of the great Greek (460?–377? BC), who has been described as the Father of Medicine, the 'wisest and the greatest practitioner of his art', and the 'most important and most complete medical personality of antiquity', who dominated the medical schools of his time, and who typified the sum of the medical knowledge of the past? The Oath varies somewhat according to the particular translation, but in any translation the content is clear:

> I will give no deadly medicine to anyone if asked, nor suggest any such counsel; and in like manner, I will not give to a woman a pessary to produce abortion.

Or:

> I will neither give a deadly drug to anybody if asked for it, nor will I make a suggestion to this effect. Similarly, I will not give to a woman an abortive remedy.

Although the Oath is not mentioned in any of the principal briefs in this case … it represents the apex of the development of strict ethical concepts in medicine, and its influence endures to this day. Why did not the authority of Hippocrates dissuade abortion practice in his time and that of Rome? The late Dr Edelstein provides us with a theory. The Oath was not uncontested even in Hippocrates' day; only the Pythagorean school of philosophers frowned upon the related act of suicide. Most Greek thinkers, on the other hand, commended abortion, at least prior to viability. For the Pythagoreans, however, it was a matter of dogma. For them, the embryo was animate from the moment of conception, and abortion meant destruction of a living being. The abortion clause of the Oath, therefore, 'echoes Pythagorean doctrines', and '[i]n no other stratum of Greek opinion were such views held or proposed in the same spirit of uncompromising austerity'. Dr Edelstein then concludes that the Oath originated in a group representing only a small segment of Greek opinion, and that it certainly was not accepted by all ancient physicians. He points out that medical writings down to Galen (AD 130–200) 'give evidence of the violation of almost every one of its injunctions'.

But with the end of antiquity, a decided change took place. Resistance against suicide and against abortion became common. The Oath came to be popular. The emerging teachings of Christianity were in agreement with the Pythagorean ethic. The Oath 'became the nucleus of all medical ethics', and 'was applauded as the embodiment of truth'. Thus, suggests Dr Edelstein, it is 'a Pythagorean manifesto, and not the expression of an absolute standard of medical conduct'. This, it seems to us, is a satisfactory and acceptable explanation of the Hippocratic Oath's apparent rigidity. It enables us to understand, in historical context, a long-accepted and revered statement of medical ethics.

THE COMMON LAW

It is undisputed that, at common law, abortion performed before 'quickening' — the first recognizable movement of the fetus *in utero*, appearing usually from the 16th to the 18th week of pregnancy — was not an indictable offense. The absence of a common law crime for pre-quickening abortion appears to have developed from a confluence of earlier philosophical, theological, and civil and canon law concepts of when life begins. These disciplines variously approached the question in terms of the point at which the embryo or fetus became 'formed' or recognizably human, or in terms of when a 'person' came into being, that is, infused with a 'soul' or 'animated'. A loose consensus evolved in early English law that these events occurred at some point between conception and live birth. This was 'mediate animation'. Although Christian theology and the canon law came to fix the point of animation at 40 days for a male and 80 days for a female, a view that persisted until the 19th century, there was otherwise little agreement about the precise time of formation or animation. There was agreement, however, that, prior to this point, the fetus was to be regarded as part of the mother, and its destruction, therefore, was not homicide. Due to continued uncertainty about the precise time when animation occurred, to the lack of any empirical basis for the 40–80-day view, and perhaps to Aquinas' definition of movement as one of the two first principles of life, Bracton focused upon quickening as the critical point. The significance of quickening was echoed by later common law scholars, and found its way into the received common law in this country. Whether abortion of a quick fetus was a felony at common law, or even a lesser crime, is still disputed. Bracton, writing early in the 13th century, thought it homicide. But the later and predominant view, following the great common law scholars, has been that it was, at most, a lesser offense.

In a frequently cited passage, Coke took the position that abortion of a woman 'quick with childe' is 'a great misprision, and no murder'. Blackstone followed, saying that, while abortion after quickening had once been considered manslaughter (though not murder), 'modern law' took a less severe view. A recent review of the common law precedents argues, however, that those precedents contradict Coke, and that even post-quickening abortion was never established as a common law crime. This is of some importance, because, while most American courts ruled, in holding or dictum, that abortion of an unquickened fetus was not criminal under their received common law, others followed Coke in stating that abortion of a quick fetus was a 'misprision', a term they translated to mean 'misdemeanor'. That their reliance on Coke on this aspect of the law was uncritical and, apparently in all the reported cases, dictum (due probably to the paucity of common law prosecutions for post-quickening abortion), makes it now appear doubtful that abortion was ever firmly established as a common law crime even with respect to the destruction of a quick fetus.

THE ENGLISH STATUTORY LAW

England's first criminal abortion statute, Lord Ellenborough's Act, came in 1803. It made abortion of a quick fetus a capital crime, but it provided lesser penalties for the felony of abortion before quickening, and thus preserved the 'quickening' distinction. This contrast was continued in the general revision of 1828. It disappeared, however, together with the death penalty, in 1837 and did not reappear in the Offences against the Person Act of 1861 that formed the core of English anti-abortion law until the liberalizing reforms of 1967.

In 1929, the Infant Life (Preservation) Act came into being. Its emphasis was upon the destruction of 'the life of a child capable of being born alive'. It made a willful act performed with the necessary intent a felony. It contained a proviso that one was not to be found guilty of the offense unless it is proved that the act which caused the death of the child was not done in good faith for the purpose only of preserving the life of the mother. A seemingly notable development in the English law was the case of *R* v *Bourne* (1939). This case apparently answered in the affirmative the question whether an abortion necessary to preserve the life of the pregnant woman was excepted from the criminal penalties of the 1861 Act. In his instructions to the jury, [Mr Justice] Macnaghten referred to the 1929 Act, and observed that that Act related to 'the case where a child is killed by a willful act at the time when it is being delivered in the ordinary course of nature'. He concluded that the 1861 Act's use of the word, 'unlawfully', imported the same meaning expressed by the specific proviso in the 1929 Act, even though there was no mention of preserving the mother's life in the 1861 Act. He then construed the phrase 'preserving the life of the mother' broadly, that is, 'in a reasonable sense', to include a serious and permanent threat to the mother's health, and instructed the jury to acquit Dr Bourne if it found he had acted in a good faith belief that the abortion was necessary for this purpose. The jury did acquit.

Recently, Parliament enacted a new abortion law. This is the Abortion Act of 1967. The Act permits a licensed physician to perform an abortion where two other licensed physicians agree (a) that the continuance of the pregnancy would involve risk to the life of the pregnant woman, or of injury to the physical or mental health of the pregnant woman or any existing children of her family, greater than if the pregnancy were terminated, or (b) that there is a substantial risk that, if the child were born it would suffer from such physical or mental abnormalities as to be seriously handicapped. The Act also provides that, in making this determination, 'account may be taken of the pregnant woman's actual or reasonably foreseeable environment'. It also permits a physician, without the concurrence of others, to terminate a pregnancy where he is of the good faith opinion that the abortion 'is immediately necessary to save the life or to prevent grave permanent injury to the physical or mental health of the pregnant woman'.

THE AMERICAN LAW

In this country, the law in effect in all but a few States until mid-19th century was the pre-existing English common law. Connecticut, the first State to enact abortion legislation, adopted in 1821 that part of Lord Ellenborough's Act that related to a woman 'quick with child'. The death penalty was not imposed. Abortion before quickening was made a crime in that State only in 1860. In 1828, New York enacted legislation that, in two respects, was to serve as a model for early anti-abortion statutes. First, while barring destruction of an unquickened fetus as well as a quick fetus, it made the former only a misdemeanor, but the latter second-degree manslaughter. Second, it incorporated a concept of therapeutic abortion by providing that an abortion was excused if it shall have been necessary to preserve the life of such mother, or shall have been advised by two physicians to be necessary for such purpose. . . .

It is thus apparent that, at common law, at the time of the adoption of our Constitution, and throughout the major portion of the nineteenth century, abortion was viewed with less disfavor than under most American statutes currently in effect. Phrasing it another way, a woman enjoyed a substantially broader right to terminate a pregnancy than she does in most States today. At least with respect to the early stage of pregnancy, and very possibly without such a limitation, the opportunity to make this choice was present in this country well into the nineteenth century. Even later, the law continued for some time to treat less punitively an abortion procured in early pregnancy....

It has been argued occasionally that these laws were the product of a Victorian social concern to discourage illicit sexual conduct. Texas, however, does not advance this justification in the present case, and it appears that no court or commentator has taken the argument seriously. The appellants and amici contend, moreover, that this is not a proper State purpose at all and suggest that, if it were, the Texas statutes are overbroad in protecting it, since the law fails to distinguish between married and unwed mothers.

A second reason is concerned with abortion as a medical procedure. When most criminal abortion laws were first enacted, the procedure was a hazardous one for the woman. This was particularly true prior to the development of antisepsis. Antiseptic techniques, of course, were based on discoveries by Lister, Pasteur, and others first announced in 1867, but were not generally accepted and employed until about the turn of the century. Abortion mortality was high. Even after 1900, and perhaps until as late as the development of antibiotics in the 1940s, standard modern techniques such as dilatation and curettage were not nearly so safe as they are today. Thus, it has been argued that a State's real concern in enacting a criminal abortion law was to protect the pregnant woman, that is, to restrain her from submitting to a procedure that placed her life in serious jeopardy. Modern medical techniques have altered this situation. Appellants and various amici refer to medical data indicating that abortion in early pregnancy, that is, prior to the end of the first trimester, although not without its risk, is now relatively safe. Mortality rates for women undergoing early abortions, where the procedure is legal, appear to be as low as or lower than the rates for normal childbirth. Consequently, any interest of the State in protecting the woman from an inherently hazardous procedure, except when it would be equally dangerous for her to forgo it, has largely disappeared.

Of course, important State interests in the areas of health and medical standards do remain. The State has a legitimate interest in seeing to it that abortion, like any other medical procedure, is performed under circumstances that insure maximum safety for the patient. This interest obviously extends at least to the performing physician and his staff, to the facilities involved, to the availability of aftercare, and to adequate provision for any complication or emergency that might arise. The prevalence of high mortality rates at illegal 'abortion mills' strengthens, rather than weakens, the State's interest in regulating the conditions under which abortions are performed. Moreover, the risk to the woman increases as her pregnancy continues. Thus, the State retains a definite interest in protecting the woman's own health and safety when an abortion is proposed at a late stage of pregnancy.

The third reason is the State's interest — some phrase it in terms of duty — in protecting prenatal life. Some of the argument for this justification rests on the theory that a new human life is present from the moment of conception. The State's interest and general obligation to protect life then extends, it is argued, to prenatal life. Only when the life of the pregnant mother herself is at stake, balanced against the life she carries within her, should the interest of the embryo or fetus not prevail. Logically, of course, a legitimate State interest in this area need not stand or fall on acceptance of the belief that life begins at conception or at some other point prior to live birth.

In assessing the State's interest, recognition may be given to the less rigid claim that as long as at least potential life is involved, the State may assert interests beyond the protection of the pregnant woman alone. Parties challenging State abortion laws have sharply disputed in some courts the contention that a purpose of these laws, when enacted, was to protect prenatal life. Pointing to the absence of legislative history to support the contention, they claim that most State laws were designed solely to protect the woman. Because medical advances have lessened this concern, at least with respect to abortion in early pregnancy, they argue that with respect to such abortions the laws can no longer be justified by any State interest.

There is some scholarly support for this view of original purpose. The few State courts called upon to interpret their laws in the late nineteenth and early twentieth centuries did focus on the State's interest in protecting the woman's health, rather than in preserving the embryo and fetus. Proponents of this view point out that in many States, including Texas, by statute or judicial interpretation, the pregnant woman herself could not be prosecuted for self-abortion or for cooperating in an abortion performed upon her by another. They claim that adoption of the 'quickening' distinction through received common law and State statutes tacitly recognizes the greater health hazards inherent in late abortion and impliedly repudiates the theory that life begins at conception. It is with these interests, and the weight to be attached to them, that this case is concerned. . . .

This right of privacy, whether it be founded in the Fourteenth Amendment's concept of personal liberty and restrictions upon State action, as we feel it is, or, as the District Court determined, in the Ninth Amendment's reservation of rights to the people, is broad enough to encompass a woman's decision whether or not to terminate her pregnancy. The detriment that the State would impose upon the pregnant woman by denying this choice altogether is apparent. Specific and direct harm medically diagnosable even in early pregnancy may be involved. Maternity, or additional offspring, may force upon the woman a distressful life and future. Psychological harm may be imminent. Mental and physical health may be taxed by child care. There is also the distress, for all concerned, associated with the unwanted child, and there is the problem of bringing a child into a family already unable, psychologically and otherwise, to care for it. In other cases, as in this one, the additional difficulties and continuing stigma of unwed motherhood may be involved.

All these are factors the woman and her responsible physician necessarily will consider in consultation. On the basis of elements such as these, appellant and some amici argue that the woman's right is absolute and that she is entitled to terminate her pregnancy at whatever time, in whatever way, and for whatever reason she alone chooses. With this we do not agree. Appellant's arguments that Texas either has no valid interest at all in regulating the abortion decision, or no interest strong enough to support any limitation upon the woman's sole determination, are unpersuasive. The Court's decisions recognizing a right of privacy also acknowledge that some State regulation in areas protected by that right is appropriate. As noted above, a State may properly assert important interests in safeguarding health, in maintaining medical standards, and in protecting potential life. At some point in pregnancy, these respective interests become sufficiently compelling to sustain regulation of the factors that govern the abortion decision. The privacy right involved, therefore, cannot be said to be absolute. In fact, it is not clear to us that the claim asserted by some amici that one has an unlimited right to do with one's body as one pleases bears a close relationship to the right of privacy previously articulated in the Court's decisions. The Court has refused to recognize an unlimited right of this kind in the past. We, therefore, conclude that the right of personal privacy includes the abortion decision, but that this right is not unqualified, and must be considered against important state interests in regulation. . . .

The pregnant woman cannot be isolated in her privacy. She carries an embryo and, later, a fetus, if one accepts the medical definitions of the developing young in the human uterus. . . . The situation therefore is inherently different from marital intimacy, or bedroom possession of obscene material, or marriage, or procreation, or education. . . . As we have intimated above, it is reasonable and appropriate for a State to decide that, at some point in time another interest, that of health of the mother or that of potential human life, becomes significantly involved. The woman's privacy is no longer sole and any right of privacy she possesses must be measured accordingly.

Texas urges that, apart from the Fourteenth Amendment, life begins at conception and is present throughout pregnancy, and that, therefore, the State has a compelling interest in protecting that life from and after conception. We need not resolve the difficult question of when life begins. When those trained in the respective disciplines of medicine, philosophy, and theology are unable to arrive at any consensus, the judiciary, at this point in the development of man's knowledge, is not in a position to speculate as to the answer. It should be sufficient to note briefly the wide divergence of thinking on this most sensitive and difficult question. There has always been strong support for the view that life does not begin until live birth. This was the belief of the Stoics. It appears to be the predominant, though not the unanimous, attitude of the Jewish faith. It may be taken to represent also the position of a large segment of the Protestant community, insofar as that can be ascertained; organized groups that have taken a formal position on the abortion issue have generally regarded abortion as a matter for the conscience of the individual and her family.

As we have noted, the common law found greater significance in quickening. Physicians and their scientific colleagues have regarded that event with less interest and have tended to focus either upon conception, upon live birth, or upon the interim point at which the fetus becomes 'viable', that is, potentially viable to live outside the mother's womb, albeit with artificial aid. Viability is usually placed at about seven months (28 weeks) but may occur earlier, even at 24 weeks. The Aristotelian theory of 'mediate animation', that held sway throughout the Middle Ages and the Renaissance in Europe, continued to be official Roman Catholic dogma until the nineteenth century, despite opposition to this 'ensoulment' theory from those in the Church who would recognize the existence of life from the moment of conception. The latter is now, of course, the official belief of the Catholic Church. As one brief amicus discloses, this is a view strongly held by many non-Catholics as well, and by many physicians. Substantial problems for precise definition of this view are posed, however, by new embryological data that purport to indicate that conception is a 'process' over time, rather than an event, and by new medical techniques such as menstrual extraction, the 'morning-after' pill, implantation of embryos, artificial insemination, and even artificial wombs.

In areas other than criminal abortion, the law has been reluctant to endorse any theory that life, as we recognize it, begins before live birth, or to accord legal rights to the unborn except in narrowly defined situations and except when the rights are contingent upon live birth. For example, the traditional rule of tort law denied recovery for prenatal injuries even though the child was born alive. That rule has been changed in almost every jurisdiction. In most States, recovery is said to be permitted only if the fetus was viable, or at least quick, when the injuries were sustained, though few courts have squarely so held. In a recent development, generally opposed by the commentators, some States permit the parents of a stillborn child to maintain an action for wrongful death because of prenatal injuries. Such an action, however, would appear to be one to vindicate the parents' interest and is thus consistent with the view that the fetus, at most, represents only the potentiality of life. Similarly, unborn children have been recognized as acquiring rights or interests by way of inheritance or other devolution of property, and have been represented by guardians *ad litem*. Perfection of the interests involved, again, has generally been contingent upon live birth. In short, the unborn have never been recognized in the law as persons in the whole sense.

In view of all this, we do not agree that, by adopting one theory of life, Texas may override the rights of the pregnant woman that are at stake. We repeat, however, that the State does have an important and legitimate interest in preserving and protecting the health of the pregnant woman, whether she be a resident of the State or a nonresident who seeks medical consultation and treatment there, and that it has still another important and legitimate interest in protecting the potentiality of human life. These interests are separate and distinct. Each grows in substantiality as the woman approaches term and, at a point during pregnancy, each becomes 'compelling'. With respect to the State's important and legitimate interest in the health of the mother, the 'compelling' point, in the light of present medical knowledge, is at approximately the end of the first trimester. This is so because of the now-established medical fact, referred to above ..., that, until the end of the first trimester mortality in abortion may be less than mortality in normal childbirth. It follows that, from and after this point, a State may regulate the abortion procedure to the extent that the regulation reasonably relates to the preservation and protection of maternal health.

Examples of permissible State regulation in this area are requirements as to the qualifications of the person who is to perform the abortion; as to the licensure of that person; as to the facility in which the procedure is to be performed, that is, whether it must be a hospital or may be a clinic or some other place of less-than-hospital status; as to the licensing of the facility; and the like. This means, on the other hand, that, for the period of pregnancy prior to this 'compelling' point, the attending physician, in consultation with his patient, is free to determine, without regulation by the State, that, in his medical judgment, the patient's pregnancy should be terminated. If that decision is reached, the judgment may be effectuated by an abortion free of interference by the State.

With respect to the State's important and legitimate interest in potential life, the 'compelling' point is at viability. This is so because the fetus then presumably has the capability of meaningful life outside the mother's womb. State regulation protective of fetal life after viability thus has both logical and biological justifications. If the State is interested in protecting fetal life after viability, it may go so far as to proscribe abortion during that period, except when it is necessary to preserve the life or health of the mother. Measured against these standards, Article 1196 of the Texas Penal Code, in restricting legal abortions to those 'procured or attempted by medical advice for the purpose of saving the life of the mother', sweeps too broadly. The statute makes no distinction between abortions performed early in pregnancy and those performed later, and it limits to a single reason, 'saving' the mother's life, the legal justification for the procedure. The statute, therefore, cannot survive the constitutional attack made upon it here.

Readers will not be surprised to learn that Harry Blackman had once acted as legal counsel to the renowned Mayo Clinic.

A case for emotion

Arthur Hugh Clough wrote,[96]

Thou shalt not kill; but needst not strive
Officiously to keep alive.

In law however the position is less clear.

The worst football disaster in British history occurred in 1989 at the Hillsborough Stadium in Sheffield where Liverpool were playing away. Among the injured was an 18-year-old man, Anthony Bland, whose chest was badly crushed but whose life the doctors managed to preserve.

Some three years later the Health Authority responsible for Bland's care applied to the court for declarations that it and the responsible physician could lawfully discontinue life-sustaining treatment and medical support measures designed to keep him alive. Their action was supported by the parents and family of the young man. The declarations were granted by the judge, whereupon the Official Solicitor appealed unsuccessfully to the Court of Appeal and the House of Lords. All the judgments and speeches in this case were exceptionally thoughtful, but that of Lord Justice Hoffmann in the Court of Appeal stands out.[97]

---

[96] *The Latest Decalogues.*
[97] *Airedale NHS Trust* v *Bland* [1993] 1 All ER 821, 849.

Non-lawyers will need to know that the Official Solicitor is a public official whose duty it is to intervene in proceedings such as the following where the subject of the litigation cannot by reason of age, mental incapacity or otherwise speak for himself.

Anthony Bland was a cheerful teenager from Keighley in Yorkshire. He enjoyed pop music, football and drinking with his friends. In the spectators' pen at Hillsborough football stadium on 15 April 1989 his lungs were crushed by the pressure of the crowd around him. He ceased breathing until resuscitated by first aid. While he could not breathe his brain was deprived of oxygen.

The human brain consists of the cerebral hemispheres and the lower centre of the brain, which is called the brain stem. The cerebral hemispheres, or more precisely their outer layers, which are called the cerebral cortex, contain the function of consciousness. Without them, we cannot see, hear, feel pain or pleasure, or make any voluntary movements. The brain stem controls the body's semi-autonomous movements, like breathing, reflex actions and the beating of the heart.

The cerebral cortex requires a constant supply of oxygen, glucose and blood. An interruption of oxygen for a few minutes can cause extensive damage to the cells of the cortex, which never regenerate. But the brain stem is relatively resistant to being deprived of oxygen. It may therefore continue to function, and enable the heart to beat, the lungs to breathe and the stomach to digest, after the cortex has been irretrievably destroyed. This condition has been called 'persistent vegetative state'.

Since 15 April 1989 Anthony Bland has been in a persistent vegetative state. He lies in Airedale General Hospital in Keighley, fed liquid food by a pump through a tube passing through his nose and down the back of his throat into the stomach. His bladder is emptied through a catheter inserted through his penis, which from time to time has caused infections requiring dressing and antibiotic treatment. His stiffened joints have caused his limbs to be rigidly contracted so that his arms are tightly flexed across his chest and his legs unnaturally contorted. Reflex movements in the throat cause him to vomit and dribble. Of all this, and the presence of members of his family who take turns to visit him, Anthony Bland has no consciousness at all. The parts of his brain which provided him with consciousness have turned to fluid. The darkness and oblivion which descended at Hillsborough will never depart. His body is alive, but he has no life in the sense that even the most pitifully handicapped but conscious human being has a life. But the advances of modern medicine permit him to be kept in this state for years, even perhaps for decades.

The question in this appeal is whether the court should in these circumstances declare that those in charge of caring for Anthony Bland may lawfully stop providing the artificial means of keeping him alive. This is a terrible decision because the consequence is that he will die. It is a question which until relatively recently would never have arisen. A person who had irreversibly lost consciousness would quickly have died: from lack of nutrition or from one of the many complications which have afflicted Anthony Bland's body over the past three years and which medical technology has been able to hold at bay. Modern medicine therefore faces us with fundamental and painful decisions about life and death which cannot be answered on the basis of normal everyday assumptions.

For reasons which I will eventually state quite briefly, I agree with the Master of the Rolls, Sir Thomas Bingham and Lord Justice Butler-Sloss that in English law it would be lawful for the Airedale Hospital to stop keeping Anthony Bland alive. But this case has caused a great deal of public concern. People are worried, perhaps not so much about this particular case, but about where it may lead. Is the court to assume the role of God and decide who should live and who should die? Is Anthony Bland to die because the quality of his life is so miserable? Does this mean that the court would approve the euthanasia of seriously handicapped people? And what about the manner of his death? Can it ever be right to cause the death of a human being by deliberately depriving him of food? This is not an area in which any difference can be allowed to exist between what is legal and what is morally right. The decision of the court should be able to carry conviction with the ordinary person as being based not merely on legal precedent but also upon acceptable ethical values. For this reason I shall start by trying to explain why I think it would be not only lawful but right to let Anthony Bland die. In the course of doing so I shall also try to explain why the principles upon which this judgment rests do not make it a precedent for morally unacceptable decisions in the future.

To argue from moral rather than purely legal principles is a somewhat unusual enterprise for a judge to undertake. It is not the function of judges to lay down systems of morals and nothing which I say is intended to do so. But it seemed to me that in such an unusual case as this, it would clarify my own thought and perhaps help others, if I tried to examine the underlying moral principles which have led me to the conclusion at which I have arrived. In doing so, I must acknowledge the assistance I have received from reading the manuscript of Professor Ronald Dworkin's forthcoming book, *Life's Dominion*, and from conversations with him and Professor Bernard Williams.

The sanctity of life

I start with the concept of the sanctity of life. Why do we think it would be a tragedy to allow Anthony Bland to die? It could be said that the entire tragedy took place at Hillsborough and that the curtain was brought down when

Anthony Bland passed into a persistent vegetative state. Until then his life was precious to him and his family. But since then he has had no consciousness of his life and it could be said to be a matter of indifference to him whether he lives or dies. But the fact is that Anthony Bland is still alive. The mere fact that he is still a living organism means that there remains an epilogue of the tragedy which is being played out. This is because we have a strong feeling that there is an intrinsic value in human life, irrespective of whether it is valuable to the person concerned or indeed to anyone else. Those who adhere to religious faiths which believe in the sanctity of all God's creation and in particular that human life was created in the image of God himself will have no difficulty with the concept of the intrinsic value of human life. But even those without any religious belief think in the same way. In a case like this we should not try to analyse the rationality of such feelings. What matters is that, in one form or another, they form part of almost everyone's intuitive values. No law which ignores them can possibly hope to be acceptable.

Our belief in the sanctity of life explains why we think it is almost always wrong to cause the death of another human being, even one who is terminally ill or so disabled that we think that if we were in his position we would rather be dead. Still less do we tolerate laws such as existed in Nazi Germany, by which handicapped people or inferior races could be put to death because someone else thought that their lives were useless.

But the sanctity of life is only one of a cluster of ethical principles which we apply to decisions about how we should live. Another is respect for the individual human being and in particular for his right to choose how he should live his own life. We call this individual autonomy or the right of self-determination. And another principle, closely connected, is respect for the dignity of the individual human being: our belief that quite irrespective of what the person concerned may think about it, it is wrong for someone to be humiliated or treated without respect for his value as a person. The fact that the dignity of an individual is an intrinsic value is shown by the fact that we feel embarrassed and think it wrong when someone behaves in a way which we think demeaning to himself, which does not show sufficient respect for himself as a person.

No one, I think, would quarrel with these deeply rooted ethical principles. But what is not always realised, and what is critical in this case, is that they are not always compatible with each other. Take, for example, the sanctity of life and the right of self-determination. We all believe in them and yet we cannot always have them both. The patient who refuses medical treatment which is necessary to save his life is exercising his right to self-determination. But allowing him, in effect, to choose to die, is something which many people will believe offends the principle of the sanctity of life. Suicide is no longer a crime, but its decriminalisation was a recognition that the principle of self-determination should in that case prevail over the sanctity of life.

I accept that the sanctity of life is a complex notion, often linked to religion, on which differing views may be held. The Jehovah's Witness who refuses a blood transfusion even though he knows this may result in his death, would probably not consider that he was sacrificing the principle of the sanctity of life to his own right of self-determination. He would probably say that a life which involved receiving a transfusion was so defiled as no longer to be an object of sanctity at all. But someone else might think that his death was a tragic waste and did offend against the sanctity of life. I do not think it would be a satisfactory answer to such a person to say that if he could only see it from the point of view of the Jehovah's Witness, he would realise that the principle of the sanctity of life had not been sacrificed but triumphantly upheld. Similarly it is possible to qualify the meaning of the sanctity of life by including, as some cultures do, concepts of dignity and fulfilment as part of the essence of life. In this way one could argue that, properly understood, Anthony Bland's death would not offend against the sanctity of life. But I do not think that this would satisfy the many people who feel strongly that it does. I think it is better to accept this and confront it.

The right of self-determination
A conflict between the principles of the sanctity of life and the individual's right of self-determination may therefore require a painful compromise to be made. In the case of the person who refuses an operation without which he will certainly die, one or other principle must be sacrificed. We may adopt a paternalist view, deny that his autonomy can be allowed to prevail in so extreme a case, and uphold the sanctity of life. Sometimes this looks an attractive solution, but it can have disturbing implications. Do we insist upon patients accepting life-saving treatment which is contrary to their strongly held religious beliefs? Should one force-feed prisoners on hunger strike? English law is, as one would expect, paternalist towards minors. But it upholds the autonomy of adults. A person of full age may refuse treatment for any reason or no reason at all, even if it appears certain that the result will be his death.

I do not suggest that the position which English law has taken is the only morally correct solution. Some might think that in cases of life and death, the law should be more paternalist even to adults. The point to be emphasised is that there is no morally correct solution which can be deduced from a single ethical principle like the sanctity of life or the right of self-determination. There must be an accommodation between principles, both of which seem rational and good, but which have come into conflict with each other.

It would therefore be in accordance with the English approach to resolving the conflict between the right to self-determination and the sanctity of life that, if Anthony Bland were to be momentarily restored to consciousness with full knowledge that he would shortly revert to his persistent vegetative state, and if he were to instruct those caring for him that he no longer wanted artificially to be kept alive, the doctors and nurses would be obliged to respect his wishes. If he were to give such an instruction, I think that many would feel that his wishes be obeyed, not only because they were his wishes, but because (unlike the case of a person who for religious reasons refuses treatment which could restore him to vigorous health) his wishes were entirely understandable. The horror of his situation is such that few would not think it perfectly reasonable for him to decide that, as he had already lost all sense and consciousness, he would prefer to die.

In this case, however, Anthony Bland has not made such a decision and never will. Some people make it clear in advance that, if they should fall into a state which seems to them in anticipation to be intolerable, they do not want life-sustaining treatment to be continued. The right of self-determination entails that such wishes should be respected. Different jurisdictions have varying requirements about how clearly such wishes should be expressed. But Anthony Bland expressed none at all. There is nothing to show that in the course of his short life he gave the matter any thought. All that his family can say is that from their knowledge of him and his general attitude to life, the things that interested him and gave him pleasure, he would not have wanted to survive in his present state.

Does this mean that people who have not expressed their wishes in advance and are now incapable of expression must lose all right to have treatment discontinued and that those caring for them are in every case under a corresponding duty to keep them alive as long as medical science will allow? Counsel for the Official Solicitor said that this was so. If they have not chosen, the court has no right to choose on their behalf. I think that the fallacy in this argument is that choice cannot be avoided. To continue treatment is as much a choice as to discontinue it. Why is it not an act of choice to decide to continue to invade the privacy of Anthony Bland's body with tubes, catheters, probes and injections? If on account of his unconsciousness he is obliged to submit to such treatment, one cannot say that it is because the court is refusing to choose on his behalf. One way or the other, a choice is being made. It is only if one thinks it natural and normal to want treatment that continuing to provide it seems not so much a choice as a given state of affairs. And of course in most cases this would be true. In a case in which it was being said that a person should not be given treatment which would avoid death and restore him to full health, one would want to know that this was his personal choice and that it had been expressed very clearly indeed.

But Anthony Bland's is not a normal case. The continuation of artificial sustenance and medical treatment will keep him alive but will not restore him to having a life in any sense at all. It is necessary to emphasise the awful certainty of his fate. We all know of cases in which doctors have been mistaken and where people have recovered to live meaningful lives after being given over for dead. But no one has ever recovered any vestige of consciousness after being in a persistent vegetative state for more than a year. Anthony Bland has been in this state for more than three years. He has been examined by a number of the most eminent doctors and they are unanimous that there is no hope whatever of any consciousness being regained. They say that this is the worst case of irreversible cortex damage that they have seen. Nor is this a case in which one has to make an assessment of the quality of life which Anthony Bland has. We all know and admire people who suffer pain and disability, of whom many would think that in their position they would rather be dead, and yet who endure their lives and derive meaning and satisfaction from living. But the very concept of having a life has no meaning in relation to Anthony Bland. He is alive but has no life at all.

Counsel for the Official Solicitor argued that however vestigial Anthony Bland's life might be, one could not assume that he would choose to die. Being unconscious, he felt no pain or humiliation and therefore had no interests which suffered from his being kept alive. Anthony Bland was in fact indifferent to whether he lived or died and there was nothing to put in the balance against the intrinsic value of his life.

I think that the fallacy in this argument is that it assumes that we have no interests except in those things of which we have conscious experience. But this does not accord with most people's intuitive feelings about their lives and deaths. At least a part of the reason why we honour the wishes of the dead about the distribution of their property is that we think it would wrong them not to do so, despite the fact that we believe that they will never know that their will has been ignored. Most people would like an honourable and dignified death and we think it wrong to dishonour their deaths, even when they are unconscious that this is happening. We pay respect to their dead bodies and to their memory because we think it an offence against the dead themselves if we do not. Once again I am not concerned to analyse the rationality of these feelings. It is enough that they are deeply rooted in our ways of thinking and that the law cannot possibly ignore them. Thus I think that counsel for the Official Solicitor offers a seriously incomplete picture of Anthony Bland's interests when he confines them to animal feelings of pain or pleasure. It is demeaning to the human spirit to say that, being unconscious, he can have no interest in his personal privacy and dignity, in how he lives or dies.

Anthony Bland therefore has a recognisable interest in the manner of his life and death which helps the court to apply the principles of self-determination and the value of the individual. We can say from what we have learned of Anthony Bland from those closest to him that, forced as we are to choose, we think it is more likely that in his present state he would choose to die than to live. There is no suggestion that he was, for example, motivated by any religious principles which would have made him want his life in its present state prolonged. We can also say that in allowing him to die, we would be showing more respect to him as an individual than by keeping him alive.

Conflicting principles

Thus it seems to me that we are faced with conflicting ethical principles. On the one hand, Anthony Bland is alive and the principle of the sanctity of life says that we should not deliberately allow him to die. On the other hand, Anthony Bland is an individual human being and the principle of self-determination says he should be allowed to choose for himself and that, if he is unable to express his choice, we should try our honest best to do what we think he would have chosen. We cannot disclaim this choice because to go on is as much a choice as to stop. Normally we would unquestioningly assume that anyone would wish to live rather than die. But in the extraordinary case of Anthony Bland, we think it more likely that he would choose to put an end to the humiliation of his being and the distress of his family. Finally, Anthony Bland is a person to whom respect is owed and we think that it would show greater respect to allow him to die and be mourned by his family than to keep him grotesquely alive.

There is no formula for reconciling this conflict of principles and no easy answer. It does no good to seize hold of one of them, such as the sanctity of life, and say that because it is valid and right, as it undoubtedly is, it must always prevail over other principles which are also valid and right. Nor do I think it helps to say that these principles are all really different ways of looking at the same thing. Counsel for the Attorney-General said that there was:

> ... no conflict between having regard to the quality of life and respecting the sanctity of life; on the contrary they are complementary; the principle of the sanctity of life embraces the need for full respect to be accorded to the dignity and memory of the individual.

To my mind, this is rhetoric intended to dull the pain of having to choose. For many people, the sanctity of life is not at all the same thing as the dignity of the individual. We cannot smooth away the differences by interpretation. Instead, we are faced with a situation which has been best expressed by Sir Isaiah Berlin:[98]

---

[98] 'Two Concepts of Liberty' in *Four Essays on Liberty* (1969), p. 168, 170.

The world that we encounter in ordinary experience is one in which we are faced with choices between ends equally ultimate, and claims equally absolute, the realisation of some of which must inevitably involve the sacrifice of others. . . . The knowledge that it is not merely in practice but in principle impossible to reach clear-cut and certain answers, even in an ideal world of wholly good and rational men and wholly clear ideas — may madden those who seek for final solutions and single, all-embracing systems, guaranteed to be eternal. Nevertheless it is a conclusion that cannot be escaped by those who, with Kant, have learnt the truth that out of the crooked timber of humanity no straight thing was ever made.

In my view the choice which the law makes must reassure people that the courts do have full respect for life, but that they do not pursue the principle to the point at which it has become almost empty of any real content and when it involves the sacrifice of other important values such as human dignity and freedom of choice. I think that such reassurance can be provided by a decision, properly explained, to allow Anthony Bland to die. It does not involve, as counsel for the Official Solicitor suggested, a decision that he may die because the court thinks that his 'life is not worth living'. There is no question of his life being worth living or not worth living because the stark reality is that Anthony Bland is not living a life at all. None of the things that one says about the way people live their lives — well or ill, with courage or fortitude, happily or sadly — have any meaning in relation to him. This in my view represents a difference in kind from the case of the conscious but severely handicapped person. It is absurd to conjure up the spectre of eugenics as a reason against the decision in this case.

Thus in principle I think it would be right to allow Anthony Bland to die. Is this answer affected by the proposed manner of his death? Some might say that as he is going to die, it does not matter how. Why wait for him to expire for lack of food or be carried off by an untreated infection? Would it not be more humane simply to give him a lethal injection? No one in this case is suggesting that Anthony Bland should be given a lethal injection. But there is concern about ceasing to supply food as against, for example, ceasing to treat an infection with antibiotics. Is there any real distinction? In order to come to terms with our intuitive feelings about whether there is a distinction, I must start by considering why most of us would be appalled if he was given a lethal injection. It is, I think, connected with our view that the sanctity of life entails its inviolability by an outsider. Subject to exceptions like self-defence, human life is inviolate even if the person in question has consented to its violation. That is why although suicide is not a crime, assisting someone to commit suicide is. It follows that, even if we think Anthony Bland would have consented, we would not be entitled to end his life by a lethal injection.

Life must come to an end

On the other hand, we recognise that, one way or another, life must come to an end. We do not impose on outsiders an unqualified duty to do everything possible to prolong life as long as possible. I think that the principle of inviolability explains why, although we accept that in certain cases it is right to allow a person to die (and the debate so far has been over whether this is such a case) we hold without qualification that no one may introduce an external agency with the intention of causing death. I do not think that the distinction turns upon whether what is done is an act or omission. This leads to barren arguments over whether the withdrawal of equipment from the body is a positive act or an omission to keep it in place. The distinction is between an act or omission which allows an existing cause to operate and the introduction of an external agency of death.

What complicates this distinction, however, is another ethical principle which demands that we should show kindness and humanity to our fellow human beings. At the most basic level, this principle insists that we should, if we are able to do so, provide food and shelter to a human being in our care who is unable to provide them for himself. If someone allows a small child or invalid in his care to starve to death, we do not say that he allowed nature to take its course. We think he has committed a particularly wicked crime. We treat him as if he had introduced an external agency of death. It is the same ethical principle which requires doctors and hospitals to provide the patients in their care with such medical attention and nursing as they are reasonably able to give.

In the normal case there is no moral difference between violations of these two principles — the prohibition on violating the person and the positive duty to act with humanity towards the helpless. Starving a child to death is no different from giving him poison. But there are two distinctions between the prohibition on external violation and the duty to provide humane care and assistance. One distinction is that the duty to provide care — for example to provide medical treatment — ceases when such treatment can serve no humane purpose. In cases when further treatment can prolong the life of the patient only for a short period and at the cost of great pain and suffering, the doctor is under no obligation to continue. Indeed, the duty to act with kindness and humanity points in the opposite direction. But the prohibition on violating the person is absolute. Whatever the patient's sufferings, no one is entitled to introduce an external agency of death. . . .

The debate over euthanasia centres on the agonising conflict which can arise when, as in that case, the duty to act with kindness and humanity comes into conflict with the absolute prohibition on the violation of the person. At the moment English law unequivocally resolves this conflict by giving priority to the latter principle. This is not the place to debate whether this is the only morally or socially acceptable position. In the present case, no such issue arises. This is not a case about euthanasia because it does not involve any external agency of death. It is about whether, and how, the patient should be allowed to die.

The denial of food

It is, I think, the duty to act with kindness and humanity which leads people to say that, whatever may be the position about artificial medical treatment, it cannot be right to deny the patient food. The giving of food to a helpless person is so much the quintessential example of kindness and humanity that it is hard to imagine a case in which it would be morally right to withhold it. If it is right that Anthony Bland should be allowed to die, then refrain from giving antibiotics and let him be carried off by an infection. But do not allow him to starve.

American writers have referred to these qualms about denial of food as the 'sloganism' and 'emotional symbolism' of food. I do not think that one should make light of these deeply intuitive feelings, which derive, as I have said, from a principle of kindness which is a badge of our humanity. But like the principle of the sanctity of life, they cease to provide true guidance in the extreme case. It is of course hard to imagine a case in which it could be humane to deny food to a patient. But this case stretches the imagination. To deny someone food is wrong because it causes suffering and death. But Anthony Bland cannot suffer and his condition is such that it is right that he should be allowed to die. His interest in the manner of his death — and it is a very important one — is that it should not be distressing or humiliating. If, therefore, withdrawal of nourishment would produce distressing symptoms of which Anthony Bland was unconscious but which were visible to the nursing staff and family, this would be a good reason for allowing him to die in some other way. But the medical evidence is that suitable sedation can prevent any untoward symptoms and that withdrawal of nourishment is the most gentle and controlled way in which to allow him to die.

Counsel for the Official Solicitor opened this appeal by saying that the President of the Family Division, Sir Stephen Brown, 'had held that it was lawful for a doctor to starve his patient to death'. This is emotive language and by that I do not mean that this is not a proper case for emotion. It certainly is. By emotive language I mean language which evokes emotional images which are false, which have no application to the present case. The use of the language is intended to evoke images of cruelty, suffering and unwelcome death. Such images have no part to play in arriving at an answer to the problem, already difficult enough, which this case presents to the court.

I said that there were two distinctions between the prohibition on violating the person and the duty to provide care and assistance. So far I have mentioned only one. The second is that while the prohibition on violation is absolute, the duty to provide care is restricted to what one can reasonably provide. No one is under a moral duty to do more than he can, or to assist one patient at the cost of neglecting another. The resources of the National Health Service are not limitless and choices have to be made. This qualification on the moral duty to provide care did not enter into the argument in this case at all. The Airedale NHS Trust invited us to decide the case on the assumption that its resources were unlimited and we have done so. But one is bound to observe that the cost of keeping a patient like Anthony Bland alive is very considerable and that in another case the health authority might conclude that its resources were better devoted to other patients. We do not have to consider such a case, but in principle the allocation of resources between patients is a matter for the health authority and not for the courts.

After dealing with the legal authorities Hoffman concluded:

I should emphasise that this is not a case in which some past act on the part of a doctor is being called into question. If the issue was whether such an act had given rise to civil or criminal liability, the fact that the doctor has acted in accordance with responsible professional opinion would usually be determinative. But in this case the plaintiff hospital trust is seeking the opinion of the court as to whether future conduct will be lawful. It has invited the court to decide whether, on medical facts which are not in dispute, the termination of life-support would be justified as being in the best interests of the patient. This is a purely legal (or moral) decision which does not require any medical expertise and is therefore appropriately made by the court.

I would dismiss the appeal.

What price a child's life?

When health resources are short (when are they not?) what priority should be given to costly experimental treatment that stands only a small chance of prolonging the life of a child and what role, if any, should the courts have in the decision making? These questions came before Mr Justice Laws in 1995.[99]

---

[99] *R v Cambridge Health Authority, ex parte B* [1995] 1 FLR 1055.

A 10-year-old child, known in the proceedings only as B, had suffered a relapse of acute myeloid leukaemia. Since first becoming ill five years before she had been treated with two courses of chemotherapy, total body irradiation and a bone marrow transplant. Her doctors and other experts were of opinion that the child had a very short time to live and that no further treatment could usefully be administered. The father obtained further medical opinion from a Dr Gravett to the effect that another course of chemotherapy might be undertaken, with a chance of success estimated at 10 to 20%, at a cost of £15,000, followed, if that were successful, by a second transplant with a similar chance of success, at a cost of £60,000.

The health authority was unwilling to fund further treatment on the grounds: (1) that it would cause considerable suffering and not be in the child's best interests; (2) that the substantial expenditure on a procedure with such a small prospect of success and of an experimental nature would not be an effective use of limited resources, bearing in mind the present and future needs of other patients. The child applied to the court to quash that decision.

The judgment began:

Of all human rights, most people would accord the most precious place to the right of life itself. Sometimes public authorities, who are subject to the jurisdiction of this court, have the power of life and death — or at least to decide, as I find is the case here, whether a person otherwise facing certain death should, by means of resources at the public body's disposal, be given the chance of life. . . .

It is, of course, no part of my function to make medical judgments: not only because I have not the competence, but because the judicial review court does not generally re-decide the merits of administrative decisions, since to do so would be to usurp the role of the decision-maker which has been confided to him by or under Act of Parliament. What I must do, however, is to make such findings of fact as are necessary to enable me to determine whether there has been an error of law in the decision-making process under review. In my judgment, looking at the whole of the evidence, there is a small but significant prospect of overall success for B if Dr Gravett carries out the proposed treatment. But even if after achieving remission Dr Gravett were to proceed to a second transplant and that too does its work, there is of course no guarantee that B would never suffer a subsequent relapse. However, if the necessary funds are made available for Dr Gravett to embark on B's treatment, she would enjoy what I will call a worthwhile chance of life. It may be very modest. It may be less than 10%. But to anyone confronting the prospect of extinction in a few weeks such a chance of longer, perhaps much longer, survival must be unimaginably precious. In fact B has not been told, I understand, of her critical condition. Her father speaks for her. She is only 10. Why do the respondents say that their discretion is properly exercised by denying the necessary funds for her treatment?

After reviewing the arguments of the health authority Laws went on:

However agonising the circumstances, if this decision was taken within the legal limits of the respondents' statutory functions, this court would have no place to interfere. What then are those limits? It is not, I think, necessary to set out the terms of the relevant legislation, since there has been no dispute before me turning on the words in which it is couched.... It is, however, beyond contest that the respondents owe to the applicant the statutory duty to provide medical services and services required for the diagnosis and treatment of illness. It is also common ground that there is a discretion as to how that duty is to be fulfilled, and it may be assumed for present purposes that the discretion extends to cases of 'extra-contractual referrals', as they are called.

From the outset ... I entertained the greatest doubt whether the decisive touchstone was the crude *Wednesbury*[100] bludgeon. It seemed to me that the fundamental right, the right to life, was engaged in the case....

After reviewing the legal authorities he referred to:

... a developing feature of our domestic jurisprudence relating to fundamental rights which should now I think be regarded as having a secure home in the common law.... The principle is that certain rights, broadly those occupying a central place in the European Convention on Human Rights and obviously including the right to life, are not to be perceived merely as moral or political aspirations nor as enjoying a legal status only upon the international plane of this country's Convention obligations. They are to be vindicated as sharing with other principles the substance of the English common law. Concretely, the law requires that where a public body enjoys a discretion whose exercise may

---

[100] *Wednesbury* is the name of the case which laid down one of the tests for judicial review.

infringe such a right, it is not to be permitted to perpetrate any such infringement unless it can show a substantial objective justification on public interest grounds. The public body itself is the first judge of the question whether such a justification exists. The court's role is secondary.... Such a distribution of authority is required by the nature of the judicial review jurisdiction, and the respect which the courts are certainly obliged to pay to the powers conferred by Parliament upon bodies other than themselves. But the decision-maker has to recognise that he can only infringe such a fundamental right by virtue of an objection of substance put forward in the public interest.

I should emphasise that this reasoning does not at all promote the incorporation into our law of the European Convention on Human Rights, which is solely a matter for Parliament. The courts have no power to incorporate it, for the elementary reason that they are not the legislature. However, the European Convention on Human Rights may be deployed by the judges, not as a statutory text (a status which manifestly it does not possess), but as persuasive legal authority to resolve outstanding uncertainties in the common law....

Even if the common law is certain the courts will still, when appropriate, consider whether the UK is in breach of article 10 [*of the European Convention*].

In the light of these materials the first two questions I must decide, it seems to me, are whether the respondents in the present case have (a) taken a decision which interferes with the applicant's right to life; and (b) if they have, whether they have offered a substantial public interest justification for doing so.

[*Counsel for the health authority*] much pressed the submission that his clients had done no positive act to threaten anyone's life; they had done nothing whatever to violate the applicant's right to life; all they had done was to arrive at a decision about the use of public funds. But the fact is that without funding for Dr Gravett's treatment, the applicant will soon certainly die. If the funding is made available, she might not. As things stand at present, the respondents are the only apparent source of the necessary funds. I do not consider that in relation to the putative infringement of a fundamental right there is as regards the obligation of a public body a difference of principle between act and omission. In other areas of law, notably the criminal law, such a distinction may possess a high importance. But in a public law case like the present the question is whether a distinct administrative decision is lawful. The decision-maker is answerable to the court whether the decision is in negative or affirmative form. The decision in this case has, to the knowledge of the decision-maker, materially affected for the worse the applicant's chances of life. I hold that the applicant's right to life is assaulted by it, and accordingly the decision can only be justified on substantial public interest grounds.

It follows that the next question for my determination is whether the reasons for the decision put forward by the respondents, which I have described, may reasonably constitute such justification.

The first reason, namely that the proposed treatment would not be in B's best interests, requires some little analysis. I entirely accept these submissions put forward by [*counsel*]:

(a)   there are no perceptible circumstances in which a doctor might properly be ordered to administer treatment contrary to his own clinical judgment or his professional conscience: ... But there is no question of such an order being made in this case. The doctor who would treat B, Dr Gravett, is entirely willing to do so;

(b)   it is reasonable and proper for the respondents, in making a decision whether to fund a particular course of treatment, to give determinative weight to the views of the specialist doctors whom they consult ... upon the *medical* issues arising in the case; and there is no whisper of a suggestion that the high competence of the doctors on whose opinions Dr Zimmern[101] relied should be called in question. The difficulty, however, is as to the nature of the issue upon which their opinion was given and in due course acted upon.

The expertise of (*two further doctors*) was rightly deployed by the respondents, as it seems to me, in relation to two questions:

(1)   What chances of success, in terms first of a remission after chemotherapy, and secondly as to the results of a further transplant, might be expected from Dr Gravett's proposed treatment? As to that, there is no significant difference between them and Dr Gravett.

(2)   What are the objective disadvantages of the treatment, in terms of the suffering the patient would be likely to endure, and the risks to life which the treatment itself would involve, when set against the quality of life which the applicant might enjoy in the short time left to her if she were treated palliatively?

Those are objective questions which in essence only the medical experts can answer. But there is a third question: given authoritative advice as to these first two issues, is it in the best interests of the patient to undergo the treatment or decline it?

In the present case, [*the doctors*] have put forward their own views in answer to this third question. Their advice has not been limited to the first two. But in

---

[101] A doctor whose affidavit evidence was put in by the respondent.

my judgment the third question is not one upon which the doctors possess an authoritative voice. At least in a case like the present it is not, in the end, a medical question at all. Test it by supposing that the patient was not a little girl, but a grown adult of sound understanding. The options would surely be put to him. The pros and cons would be explained. Upon the question what course of action was in his best interests, his views would be respected. I apprehend they would be treated as determinative. If he decided not to undergo the treatment, that would be the end of the matter. If he decided that he wished to take his chance with it, neither the doctors nor the health authority would turn round and say, it is against his best interests, and of those interests they are the sole judges. The treatment might perhaps still be refused as an unjustifiable use of scarce resources; but that engages the respondents' second reason for their decision, with which I am not presently dealing.

[*Counsel for the child*] was at pains to submit that I am not here concerned with a case of an adult, so that such an analogy is of no assistance. I disagree. Of course it may readily be assumed that a 10-year-old child, in circumstances like those of this case, cannot make for herself an informed decision upon the question which course of action is in her best interests. That being so, someone else must take the decision for her. But it should not be the doctors; it should be her family, here — her father. He has duties and responsibilities to her shared by no one else. The doctors' obligation is to ascertain and explain all the medical facts, and in the light of them articulate the choice that must be faced. Their expert views on the medical issues, however, do not constitute the premises of a syllogism from which an inevitable conclusion as to what is in the best interests of the patient may be deduced. It is not at all a matter of deduction from the medical facts. It is a personal question which the patient, if he is of full age and capacity, will decide in the light of medical advice. In the case of a little child, others must decide it — not the experts, but those having, legally and morally, overall care of the patient....

The difficulty in this case does not merely consist in the fact that the doctors, on whose opinion Dr Zimmern relied, purported to decide what was in B's best interests. It is also clear that Dr Zimmern did not regard the father's wish that the treatment be carried out as a relevant circumstance for the purpose of his decision whether to authorise funding....

In these circumstances the first reason put forward for the respondents' decision cannot amount to a substantial justification for their depriving B of such chance of life as Dr Gravett's proposed treatment would offer. But in my judgment this conclusion does not depend only on the jurisprudence which I have sought to outline concerning fundamental rights. The ordinary *Wednesbury* principle produces the result, on the facts here, that the respondents have at the least failed to have regard to a relevant consideration, namely B's

216

family's views — which are the legitimate surrogate for her own — as to whether the proposed treatment would be in her best interests . . .

'Experimental' treatment

The presumptively 'experimental' nature of the proposed treatment also engages the second justification for their action put forward by the respondents, namely that funding the treatment would be an ineffective use of resources. Dr Zimmern says that he has been influenced by Department of Health advice and directions 'with regard to the funding of treatments which have not been proven to be of benefit'. The first difficulty is that no material from the Department of Health has been put before the court. I acknowledge at once that the timescale in which the respondents have been required to prepare for the hearing of this judicial review has as a result of directions made by myself been extremely short. But if there were anything of critical importance emanating from the Department of Health, it must be to hand and one might reasonably have expected to have seen it. Dr Zimmern's reference to Department of Health material does not, in my judgment, assist the respondents.

. . . it is no doubt self-evident that funds available for health care are indeed not limitless. And of course it is the respondents, not I, who must decide how they are to be distributed. But merely to point to the fact that resources are finite tells one nothing about the wisdom or, what is relevant for my purposes, the legality of a decision to withhold funding in a particular case, . . . I have no idea where in the order of things the respondents place a modest chance of saving the life of a 10-year-old girl. I have no evidence about the respondents' budget either generally or in relation to the 'extra-contractual referrals'. Dr Zimmern's evidence about money consists only in grave and well-rounded generalities. I quite accept . . . that the court should not make orders with consequences for the use of Health Service funds in ignorance of the knock-on effect on other patients. But where the question is whether the life of a 10-year-old child might be saved, by however slim a chance, the responsible authority must in my judgment do more than toll the bell of tight resources. They must explain the priorities that have led them to decline to fund the treatment. They have not adequately done so here.

I have already said that upon the conventional *Wednesbury* principle the respondents have in my judgment failed to have regard to a material factor, namely the family's perception of B's best interests, entertained on her behalf. I also incline to accept [*counsel for the health authority's*] submission that Dr Zimmern's decision fails to pay any attention to an important feature of the case from the funding point of view, namely by the very definition of B's problem the respondents could only be asked in the first place to provide the £15,000 required for the proposed chemotherapy. Given the melancholy probability of that treatment's modest chances, the likelihood is that the more expensive transplant measure would not arise. It seems to me that the respondents as a reasonable authority should have considered the case distinctly on the basis that the first call was for £15,000 only. On the evidence they do not appear to have done so.

For the reasons I have set out in the narrative of this judgment, the respondents' decision not to advance funds for B's treatment must be quashed.

[*Counsel for the health authority*] submits that I should also order mandamus to go to require the authority to fund the first stage of Dr Gravett's treatment, the chemotherapy. Such relief would only be appropriate if it was demonstrated to my satisfaction that the respondents' only lawful course of action was to fund the treatment. I am not persuaded that is so. I have accepted that at present no sufficient justification has been shown to refuse this chance of life to B. I have in the course of this judgment held that if it is to be refused, it must be on substantial objective grounds. The possible saving of a 10-year-old life, otherwise to be quickly snuffed out, must be high indeed as a priority on any health authority's agenda, assuming in the particular case (as is the fact here) that the family approve the measures to be taken. But I cannot say that the respondents' refusal to fund the treatment is inevitably unlawful. Certainly, they should have given their minds to the two essential propositions which in the event I have set out in this judgment, viz. (1) that the decision adversely affected the applicant's life, which should have been accorded an overriding priority unless the decision enjoyed substantial objective justification, and (2) that B's best interests did not fall to be determined as a purely medical question, and that accordingly the father's views were of great importance. But if they now carry out this task properly, which they must do immediately, I cannot say that they are bound to fund the treatment. It is possible for all I know that the financial constraints, and other deserving cases, are more pressing than at present appears. However hard it is to imagine a proper basis upon which this treatment — at least its initial part — could justifiably be withheld, I cannot determine that no such basis might exist.

The right course therefore is to issue an order of certiorari to quash the respondents' decision to decline to provide the further funding. The decision must be retaken in the light of this judgment.

Appeal to the Court of Appeal against this judgment was swift and successful, the Master of the Rolls, Sir Thomas Bingham, saying:[102]

---

[102] *R* v *Cambridge Health Authority, ex parte B* [1995] 2 All ER 136, 137.

I have no doubt that in a perfect world any treatment which a patient, or a patient's family, sought would be provided if doctors were willing to give it, no matter how much it cost, particularly when a life was potentially at stake. It would, however, in my view, be shutting one's eyes to the real world if the court were to proceed on the basis that we do live in such a world. It is common knowledge that health authorities of all kinds are constantly pressed to make ends meet. They cannot pay their nurses as much as they would like; they cannot provide all the treatments they would like; they cannot purchase all the extremely expensive medical equipment they would like; they cannot carry out all the research they would like; they cannot build all the hospitals and specialist units they would like. Difficult and agonising judgments have to be made as to how a limited budget is best allocated to the maximum advantage of the maximum number of patients. That is not a judgment which the court can make. In my judgment, it is not something that a health authority such as this authority can be fairly criticised for not advancing before the court.

Despite the fact that the treatment was subsequently paid for by a private benefactor, Jaymee Bowen (the child's real name) died some 14 months after the court case. Her bravery in the face of adversity commanded universal admiration.

After Jaymee's death Stephen Thornton, chief executive of Cambridge and Huntingdon Health Commission, said: 'Medical science moves on and the decision we took 12 months ago might have been different had we faced it today'.[103]

Earnest and profound debate

In America, as in this country, there is widespread and concerned interest in the question of whether doctors should be permitted to end the suffering of terminally ill patients. This issue came before the United States Supreme Court only recently as a result of a challenge to a Washington State law which forbade assisted suicide.

The respondents were physicians who practised in Washington, occasionally treating the terminally ill. But for Washington's

[103] *The Times*, 23 May 1996.

assisted suicide law, they would have assisted these patients in ending their lives. Along with three gravely ill, pseudonymous plaintiffs (who had since died) and Compassion in Dying, a non-profit organisation that counsels people considering physician-assisted suicide, they sought a declaration that the Washington law was, on its face, unconstitutional.

Chief Justice Rehnquist, delivering the opinion of the Court,[104] *said:*

The question presented in this case is whether Washington's prohibition against 'caus[ing]' or 'aid[ing]' a suicide offends the Fourteenth Amendment to the United States Constitution. We hold that it does not.

We begin, as we do in all due process cases, by examining our Nation's history, legal traditions and practices.... In almost every State — indeed, in almost every Western democracy — it is a crime to assist a suicide. The States' assisted suicide bans are not innovations. Rather, they are long-standing expressions of the States' commitment to the protection and preservation of all human life.... Indeed, opposition to and condemnation of suicide — and, therefore, of assisting suicide — are consistent and enduring themes of our philosophical, legal, and cultural heritages....

The common law tradition
More specifically, for over 700 years, the Anglo-American common law tradition has punished or otherwise disapproved of both suicide and assisting suicide. In the 13th century, Henry de Bracton, one of the first legal treatise writers, observed that '[j]ust as a man may commit felony by slaying another so may he do so by slaying himself'. The real and personal property of one who killed himself to avoid conviction and punishment for a crime were forfeit to the king; however, thought Bracton, 'if a man slays himself in weariness of life or because he is unwilling to endure further bodily pain ... [only] his movable goods [were] confiscated'. Thus, '[t]he principle that suicide of a sane person, for whatever reason, was a punishable felony was ... introduced into English common law'. Centuries later, Sir William Blackstone, whose *Commentaries on the Laws of England* not only provided a definitive summary of the common law but was also a primary legal authority for eighteenth and nineteenth-century American lawyers, referred to suicide as 'self-murder' and 'the pretended heroism, but real cowardice, of the Stoic philosophers, who

---

[104] *Washington v Glucksberg*, 138 L Ed 2d 772 (1997).

destroyed themselves to avoid those ills which they had not the fortitude to endure'. Blackstone emphasized that 'the law has ... ranked [suicide] among the highest crimes', although, anticipating later developments, he conceded that the harsh and shameful punishments imposed for suicide 'borde[r] a little upon severity'.

For the most part, the early American colonies adopted the common law approach.... Over time, however, the American colonies abolished these harsh common law penalties. William Penn abandoned the criminal forfeiture sanction in Pennsylvania in 1701, and the other colonies (and later, the other States) eventually followed this example. Zephaniah Swift, who would later become Chief Justice of Connecticut, wrote in 1796 that '[t]here can be no act more contemptible, than to attempt to punish an offender for a crime, by exercising a mean act of revenge upon lifeless clay, that is insensible of the punishment. There can be no greater cruelty, than the inflicting [of] a punishment, as the forfeiture of goods, which must fall solely on the innocent offspring of the offender ... [Suicide] is so abhorrent to the feelings of mankind, and that strong love of life which is implanted in the human heart, that it cannot be so frequently committed, as to become dangerous to society. There can of course be no necessity of any punishment.' This statement makes it clear, however, that the movement away from the common law's harsh sanctions did not represent an acceptance of suicide; rather, as Chief Justice Swift observed, this change reflected the growing consensus that it was unfair to punish the suicide's family for his wrongdoing. Nonetheless, although States moved away from Blackstone's treatment of suicide, courts continued to condemn it as a grave public wrong. That suicide remained a grievous, though non-felonious, wrong is confirmed by the fact that colonial and early State legislatures and courts did not retreat from prohibiting assisting suicide.

Between 1857 and 1865, a New York commission led by Dudley Field drafted a criminal code that prohibited 'aiding' a suicide and, specifically, 'furnish[ing] another person with any deadly weapon or poisonous drug, knowing that such person intends to use such weapon or drug in taking his own life'. By the time the Fourteenth Amendment was ratified, it was a crime in most States to assist a suicide. In this century, the Model Penal Code also prohibited 'aiding' suicide, prompting many States to enact or revise their assisted suicide bans. The Code's drafters observed that 'the interests in the sanctity of life that are represented by the criminal homicide laws are threatened by one who expresses a willingness to participate in taking the life of another, even though the act may be accomplished with the consent, or at the request, of the suicide victim'. Though deeply rooted, the States' assisted suicide bans have in recent years been reexamined and, generally, reaffirmed.

221

Living wills
Because of advances in medicine and technology, Americans today are increasingly likely to die in institutions, from chronic illnesses. Public concern and democratic action are therefore sharply focused on how best to protect dignity and independence at the end of life, with the result that there have been many significant changes in State laws and in the attitudes these laws reflect. Many States, for example, now permit 'living wills', surrogate health care decision-making, and the withdrawal or refusal of life-sustaining medical treatment. At the same time, however, voters and legislators continue for the most part to reaffirm their States' prohibitions on assisting suicide. The Washington statute at issue in this case was enacted in 1975 as part of a revision of that State's criminal code. Four years later, Washington passed its Natural Death Act, which specifically stated that the 'withholding or withdrawal of life-sustaining treatment . . . shall not, for any purpose, constitute a suicide' and that '[n]othing in this chapter shall be construed to condone, authorize, or approve mercy killing'. Washington voters rejected a ballot initiative which, had it passed, would have permitted a form of physician-assisted suicide. Washington then added a provision to the Natural Death Act expressly excluding physician-assisted suicide.

After reviewing recent developments Rehnquist went on:

. . . the States are currently engaged in serious, thoughtful examinations of physician-assisted suicide and other similar issues. For example, New York State's Task Force on Life and the Law — an ongoing, blue-ribbon commission composed of doctors, ethicists, lawyers, religious leaders, and interested laymen — was convened in 1984 and commissioned with 'a broad mandate to recommend public policy on issues raised by medical advances'. After studying physician-assisted suicide, however, the Task Force unanimously concluded that '[l]egalizing assisted suicide and euthanasia would pose profound risks to many individuals who are ill and vulnerable. . . . [T]he potential dangers of this dramatic change in public policy would outweigh any benefit that might be achieved.'

Attitudes toward suicide itself have changed since Bracton, but our laws have consistently condemned, and continue to prohibit, assisting suicide. Despite changes in medical technology and notwithstanding an increased emphasis on the importance of end-of-life decision-making, we have not retreated from this prohibition. Against this backdrop of history, tradition, and practice, we now turn to respondents' constitutional claim.

The Due Process Clause guarantees more than fair process, and the 'liberty' it protects includes more than the absence of physical restraint. The Clause also provides heightened protection against government interference with certain fundamental rights and liberty interests. In a long line of cases, we have held that, in addition to the specific freedoms protected by the Bill of Rights, the 'liberty' specially protected by the Due Process Clause includes the rights to marry, to have children, to direct the education and upbringing of one's children, to marital privacy, to use contraception, to bodily integrity, and to abortion. We have also assumed, and strongly suggested, that the Due Process Clause protects the traditional right to refuse unwanted lifesaving medical treatment. But we 'ha[ve] always been reluctant to expand the concept of substantive due process because guideposts for responsible decision making in this uncharted area are scarce and open-ended'. By extending constitutional protection to an asserted right or liberty interest, we, to a great extent, place the matter outside the arena of public debate and legislative action. We must therefore 'exercise the utmost care whenever we are asked to break new ground in this field', lest the liberty protected by the Due Process Clause be subtly transformed into the policy preferences of the members of this Court. . . .

Is there a right to die?
In addition, by establishing a threshold requirement — that a challenged State action implicate a fundamental right — before requiring more than a reasonable relation to a legitimate State interest to justify the action, it avoids the need for complex balancing of competing interests in every case.

Turning to the claim at issue here, the Court of Appeals stated that '[p]roperly analyzed, the first issue to be resolved is whether there is a liberty interest in determining the time and manner of one's death', or, in other words, '[i]s there a right to die?' Similarly, respondents assert a 'liberty to choose how to die' and a right to 'control of one's final days', and describe the asserted liberty as 'the right to choose a humane, dignified death', and 'the liberty to shape death'. As noted above, we have a tradition of carefully formulating the interest at stake in substantive due process cases. . . . We now inquire whether this asserted right has any place in our Nation's traditions.

Here, as discussed above, we are confronted with a consistent and almost universal tradition that has long rejected the asserted right, and continues explicitly to reject it today, even for terminally ill, mentally competent adults. To hold for respondents, we would have to reverse centuries of legal doctrine and practice, and strike down the considered policy choice of almost every State. Respondents contend, however, that the liberty interest they assert is consistent with this Court's substantive due process line of cases, if not with this Nation's history and practice. According to respondents, our liberty jurisprudence, and the broad, individualistic principles it reflects, protects the 'liberty of competent, terminally ill adults to make end-of-life decisions free of undue government interference'. The question presented in this case, however, is whether the protections of the Due Process Clause include a right to commit suicide with another's assistance.

After examining two leading cases he continued:

The history of the law's treatment of assisted suicide in this country has been and continues to be one of the rejection of nearly all efforts to permit it. That being the case, our decisions lead us to conclude that the asserted 'right' to assistance in committing suicide is not a fundamental liberty interest protected by the Due Process Clause.

The Constitution also requires, however, that Washington's assisted suicide ban be rationally related to legitimate government interests. This requirement is unquestionably met here. As the court below recognized, Washington's assisted suicide ban implicates a number of State interests. First, Washington has an 'unqualified interest in the preservation of human life'. The State's prohibition on assisted suicide, like all homicide laws, both reflects and advances its commitment to this interest. This interest is symbolic and aspirational as well as practical: 'While suicide is no longer prohibited or penalized, the ban against assisted suicide and euthanasia shores up the notion of limits in human relationships. It reflects the gravity with which we view the decision to take one's own life or the life of another, and our reluctance to encourage or promote these decisions.'

Respondents admit that '[t]he State has a real interest in preserving the lives of those who can still contribute to society and enjoy life'. The Court of Appeals also recognized Washington's interest in protecting life, but held that the 'weight' of this interest depends on the 'medical condition and the wishes of the person whose life is at stake'. Washington, however, has rejected this sliding scale approach and, through its assisted suicide ban, insists that all persons' lives, from beginning to end, regardless of physical or mental condition, are under the full protection of the law. This remains true ... even for those who are near death.

Relatedly, all admit that suicide is a serious public health problem, especially among persons in otherwise vulnerable groups. The State has an interest in preventing suicide, and in studying, identifying, and treating its causes.

Those who attempt suicide — terminally ill or not — often suffer from depression or other mental disorders.... The New York Task Force, however, expressed its concern that, because depression is difficult to diagnose, physicians and medical professionals often fail to respond adequately to seriously ill patients' needs. Thus, legal physician-assisted suicide could make it more difficult for the State to protect depressed or mentally ill persons, or those who are suffering from untreated pain, from suicidal impulses. The State also has an interest in protecting the integrity and ethics of the medical profession. In contrast to the Court of Appeals' conclusion that 'the integrity of the medical profession would [not] be threatened in any way by [physician-assisted suicide]', the American Medical Association, like many other medical and physicians' groups, has concluded that '[p]hysician-assisted suicide is fundamentally incompatible with the physician's role as healer'. And physician-assisted suicide could, it is argued, undermine the trust that is essential to the doctor–patient relationship by blurring the time-honored line between healing and harming.

Vulnerable groups
Next, the State has an interest in protecting vulnerable groups — including the poor, the elderly, and disabled persons — from abuse, neglect, and mistakes. The Court of Appeals dismissed the State's concern that disadvantaged persons might be pressured into physician-assisted suicide as 'ludicrous on its face'. We have recognized, however, the real risk of subtle coercion and undue influence in end-of-life situations.

Similarly, the New York Task Force warned that '[l]egalizing physician-assisted suicide would pose profound risks to many individuals who are ill and vulnerable.... The risk of harm is greatest for the many individuals in our society whose autonomy and well being are already compromised by poverty, lack of access to good medical care, advanced age, or membership in a stigmatized social group.' If physician-assisted suicide were permitted, many might resort to it to spare their families the substantial financial burden of end-of-life health-care costs. The State's interest here goes beyond protecting the vulnerable from coercion; it extends to protecting disabled and terminally ill people from prejudice, negative and inaccurate stereotypes, and 'societal indifference'.

The State's assisted suicide ban reflects and reinforces its policy that the lives of terminally ill, disabled, and elderly people must be no less valued than the lives of the young and healthy, and that a seriously disabled person's suicidal impulses should be interpreted and treated the same way as anyone else's.

Finally, the State may fear that permitting assisted suicide will start it down the path to voluntary and perhaps even involuntary euthanasia. The Court of Appeals struck down Washington's assisted suicide ban only 'as applied to competent, terminally ill adults who wish to hasten their deaths by obtaining medication prescribed by their doctors'. Washington insists, however, that the impact of the court's decision will not and cannot be so limited. If suicide is protected as a matter of constitutional right, it is argued, 'every man and woman in the United States must enjoy it'.

The Court of Appeals' decision, and its expansive reasoning, provide ample support for the State's concerns. The court noted, for example, that the 'decision of a duly appointed surrogate decision-maker is for all legal purposes the decision of the patient himself', that 'in some instances, the patient may be unable to self-administer the drugs and ... administration by the physician ... may be the only way the patient may be able to receive them', and that not only physicians, but also family members and loved ones, will inevitably participate in assisting suicide.

Thus, it turns out that what is couched as a limited right to 'physician-assisted suicide' is likely, in effect, a much broader license, which could prove extremely difficult to police and contain. Washington's ban on assisting suicide prevents such erosion. This concern is further supported by evidence about the practice of euthanasia in the Netherlands. The Dutch government's own study revealed that in 1990, there were 2,300 cases of voluntary euthanasia (defined as 'the deliberate termination of another's life at his request'), 400 cases of assisted suicide, and more than 1,000 cases of euthanasia without an explicit request. In addition to these latter 1,000 cases, the study found an additional 4,941 cases where physicians administered lethal morphine overdoses without the patients' explicit consent. This study suggests that, despite the existence of various reporting procedures, euthanasia in the Netherlands has not been limited to competent, terminally ill adults who are enduring physical suffering, and that regulation of the practice may not have prevented abuses in cases involving vulnerable persons, including severely disabled neonates and elderly persons suffering from dementia.

The New York Task Force, citing the Dutch experience, observed that 'assisted suicide and euthanasia are closely linked', and concluded that the 'risk of ... abuse is neither speculative nor distant'. Washington, like most other States, reasonably ensures against this risk by banning, rather than regulating, assisting suicide.

We need not weigh exactingly the relative strengths of these various interests. They are unquestionably important and legitimate, and Washington's ban on assisted suicide is at least reasonably related to their promotion and protection. We therefore hold that [*the Washington law*] does not violate the Fourteenth Amendment, either on its face or 'as applied to competent, terminally ill adults who wish to hasten their deaths by obtaining medication prescribed by their doctors'. Throughout the Nation, Americans are engaged in an earnest and profound debate about the morality, legality, and practicality of physician-assisted suicide. Our holding permits this debate to continue, as it should in a democratic society.

Profound human issues such as those dealt with in this chapter cannot be resolved simply by reference to legal precedent. Although the pre-existing law has been considered in every case it has figured more as part of the historical background than in its usual role as precedent. It is encouraging to see how widely the judges have cast their net, weighing the merits of solutions adopted in other jurisdictions as well as their own, of medical research and of social work scholarship.

While the English judges have sometimes looked to social studies to assist them in arriving at a decision their researches have not usually been anywhere as extensive as those of their American cousins. The heavily edited judgment of Chief Justice Rehnquist in the last case, for example, does not do justice to the extent to which the Court had reference to social studies (which have been omitted here only because of their number and difficulty of access). Perhaps such studies will figure more prominently as sources of law when, in future, the English judges have to grapple with the problems which will undoubtedly be thrown up by the incorporation into our laws of the principles of the European Convention on Human Rights.

The Temple Church

8.   FEARFUL SAINTS

or

Reforming the Law

We have not followed the handwriting of our predecessors. We have marred our copybook with blots, and the more's the pity of it.

Lord Denning in *Re Pritchard.*[105]

Heresy dignified by the name of reform
Reform by mockery
Reform by passion
Reform by non-enforcement
The copybook marred
Instead of 'saints', read 'judges'
The length of the Chancellor's foot
The delicate balance

---

[105] See under *The copybook marred.*

A fiction was once maintained by the judges that the common law is all comprehending and that if a situation arose not covered by precedent the law was nevertheless there, as it were above the judge's head, waiting to be found by some process of forensic ratiocination. Of course, this was nonsense, a device designed to distract attention from the fact that in such circumstances the judges had no alternative but to make new law. But even laws made by Parliament can be defective or can become outdated.

What is a judge to do, then, when he believes the law he is required to administer does not allow him to do justice in the case before him? Judges fall into three categories when responding to this problem, the conservative, the bold and the cunning. The conservative judge, like Viscount Simonds (see under Heresy dignified by the name of reform*) believes that he should steer clear of anything which smacks of law reform. The bold judge, like Lord Denning in his more ambitious moments, does whatever he thinks necessary, while the cunning judge pokes fun at outdated laws or enforces them in such a way as to indicate their inadequacy.*

Although it comes down to us in various forms the address of Mr Justice Maule to a convicted bigamist mocked mercilessly the archaic divorce laws of his day (Reform by mockery *). A few years later the plight of a young girl caused Mr Justice Swift passionately to condemn the same laws (* Reform by passion *). While change followed in both cases it was slow and inadequate, a characteristic of divorce law reform over the ages.*

Judges do not usually take kindly to magistrates declining to punish offenders. A notable exception is reproduced below (Reform by non-enforcement *). It is all the more astonishing in that it is a judgment of the formidable Lord Goddard.*

No one in recent times has enjoyed a wider reputation as a reforming judge than Lord Denning, but even his efforts were not always successful, as the following extracts demonstrate. His regret at being unable, by reason of what he regarded as a mere technicality, to do justice to a widow chide us to this day (The copybook marred *). When he later attempted to rectify a similar anomaly he was overruled, indeed rebuked, by the House of Lords (* Instead of 'saints' read 'judges' *). He came into conflict with their*

Lordships once again when he sought to ignore a precedent of that House. Even the great Lord Scarman was against him on the point:

> ... if people and Parliament come to think that the judicial power is to be confined by nothing other than the judge's sense of what is right (or, as Selden put it, by the length of the Chancellor's foot), confidence in the judicial system will be replaced by fear of it becoming uncertain and arbitrary in its application. Society will then be ready for Parliament to cut the power of the judges. (*The length of the Chancellor's foot.*)

But there is another, more potent, constraint upon law reform by the judiciary, namely the pre-eminence of Parliament. As Lord Mustill put it when rejecting a liberal interpretation of legislation on the part of the Court of Appeal:

> ... some of the arguments addressed would have the court push to the very boundaries of the distinction between court and Parliament established in, and recognised ever since, the Bill of Rights 1688. Three hundred years have passed since then, and the political and social landscape has changed beyond recognition. But the boundaries remain; they are of crucial significance to our private and public lives; and the courts should, I believe, make sure that they are not overstepped. (*The delicate balance.*)

Heresy dignified by the name of reform

The orthodox approach to legal interpretation was characteristically expressed in 1962 by the then Lord Chancellor, Viscount Simonds, when he observed:[106]

Learned counsel for the respondents claimed that [*a particular argument*] was the orthodox view and asked your Lordships to reject any proposition that impinged on it. To that invitation I readily respond. For to me heterodoxy, or, as some might say, heresy, is not the more attractive because it is dignified by the name of reform. Nor will I easily be led by an undiscerning zeal for some abstract kind of justice to ignore our first duty, which is to administer justice

---

[106] *Scruttons Ltd* v *Midland Silicones Ltd* [1962] 1 All ER 1, 7.

according to law, the law which is established for us by Act of Parliament or the binding authority of precedent. The law is developed by the application of old principles to new circumstances. Therein lies its genius. Its reform by the abrogation of those principles is the task not of the courts of law but of Parliament.

By Viscount Simonds' lights the proper course for a judge faced with a bad rule was to administer the law as he found it and draw the attention of the authorities to the problem. This can work, but not always swiftly.

Which is why some judges have been moved to resort to other means.

Reform by mockery

Achieving divorce laws which are at the same time rational, workable and fair has proved to be as elusive as the quest for the Holy Grail. From time to time judges have been constrained to point out anomalies in this branch of the law. Perhaps the most deeply biting in their sarcasm were the following words of Mr Justice Maule at the Warwick assizes in 1844[107] when passing sentence on a hawker convicted of bigamy:

Prisoner at the bar, you have been convicted of the offence of bigamy, that is to say, of marrying a woman while you have a wife still alive, though it is true she has deserted you, and is still living in adultery with another man. You have, therefore, committed a crime against the laws of your country, and you have also acted under a very serious misapprehension of the course which you ought to have pursued.

You should have gone to the ecclesiastical court and there obtained against your wife a decree *a mensa et thoro*.[108]

You should then have brought an action in the courts of common law and recovered, as no doubt you would have recovered, damages against your wife's paramour.

---

[107] Holdsworth, *History of English Law*, vol. 1, p. 623, 7th ed. (Methuen & Co., 1956). Different versions appear elsewhere, for example in Richard O'Sullivan's *The Spirit of the Common Law*.
[108] An early form of judicial separation. Literally, from bed and board.

Armed with these decrees you should have approached the legislature, and obtained an Act of Parliament, which would have rendered you free, and legally competent to marry the person whom you have taken on yourself to marry with no such sanction.

It is quite true that these proceedings would have cost you many hundreds of pounds, whereas you probably have not as many pence. But the law knows no distinction between rich and poor. The sentence of the court upon you therefore is that you be imprisoned for one day, which period has already been exceeded, as you have been in custody since the commencement of the assizes.

It took 13 years for this situation to be even partly remedied.

Maule was described by Mr Justice Hawkins as having been a man of great wit, good sense, a curious humour and a keen apprehension with little love of mediocrities. One story of Maule, the advocate, is that before the hearing of an appeal in the House of Lords he had a heavy lunch of stout and steak; Follett, his leader, who had lunched off sherry and biscuits, asked why he was lunching so plentifully. 'To reduce myself to the intellectual level of the Judges', said Maule.[109]

Reform by passion

Years later the divorce laws remained a disgrace.

Mr Justice Swift is perhaps best remembered for his North Country witticisms from the bench, but he was also a religious and deeply compassionate man. One day a young girl was called to give evidence that both her father and her mother were living in adultery. In the words of Swift's biographer:[110]

When he looked at that girl and heard the miserable story that was being put to her, Swift saw in this case the quintessence of all that he had abhorred and detested in the divorce laws of England since the days 12 years before when he had startled the public by his plea for a cleaner and a better way. He felt rising again within him the indignation that he had voiced so soberly in that earlier day, an indignation tinged now by a bitterness brought by the passing years.

---

[109] Richard O'Sullivan, Op. cit.
[110] E. S. Fay, *The Life of Mr Justice Swift* (Methuen & Co., 1939), at p. 150.

The tide of protest rose within his breast till it would not be denied. He granted the decree, and he spoke on, speaking those things that had for so long accumulated within him clamouring for the relief of utterance. He said:

It is most terrible that these unhappy people, who have long since made up their minds that they cannot live together — in this particular case they have been separated for 16 or 17 years, and have both made fresh alliances — it is dreadful that, having been separated all that time, so that one side or other may regularise their position it is necessary that a daughter should have to be called to prove her mother's adultery.

Those who talk about the sanctity of marriage, those who talk about 'whom God hath joined together', those who lay the greatest emphasis upon 'let no man put asunder', do not see, or do not realise, the pain and suffering which come into the witness-box.

What dreadful stories I have heard today! ... And now this petitioner comes here and tells me they want to be separated. Why should they not be? They have — in fact, in truth — been separated for 16 years. They want to be separated in law. But in order that they might be separated in law, the wretched daughter has got to be brought here to tell me on oath that she knows that for 14 years her mother has been living with a man who is not her father, and that her father has been living with a woman who is not her mother.

Do not let it be said that I do not approve of divorces at assizes. I disapprove of the whole system, wherever it may have to be carried out. To my mind the divorce laws of this country are wicked and cruel.

These people ought not to be subjected to the dreadful indignities to which they are subjected, and I wish some of those learned ecclesiastics who have so much concern for the wellbeing of society would come and sit here [*the judge pointed to the well of the court*] where they would be mere spectators, or come and sit here [*indicating the Bench*] where they would have to deal with these matters.

Those words were spoken in March 1937. In July of that year the House of Commons passed a Bill giving effect to some of the recommendations of the Royal Commission of 1912 upon divorce reform. How far Maule's remarks, coming as they did from the senior judge of the King's Bench Division, contributed to the change in the law it is impossible to assess.

Swift died three months after the passing of the Act and three months before it came into force.

Reform by non-enforcement

There can be no more effective way of expressing disapproval of a bad law than to refuse to enforce it. Juries have from time to time brought in 'perverse' verdicts which, however, have commanded widespread respect. To do likewise is not within the power of a judge, still less a magistrate. Nevertheless, he can make his views known just as effectively by imposing no or no substantive penalty for an offence, and that is exactly what the Hornsey magistrates did in one notable case.

Those who lived through the Second World War will remember carrying an identity card and thinking nothing of it. In times of peace the case for the obligatory carrying of identification is more controversial. Only a few years after the end of the War it was still the practice of at least some English police forces to require motorists to produce their identity cards under authority of the National Registration Act 1939. One motorist refused to produce his, either to the police officer or to a police station. (In fact, he threw the form requiring production on to the pavement.) The motorist was prosecuted and convicted by the Hornsey magistrates who imposed an absolute discharge, that is to say, no punishment.

A Divisional Court of the King's Bench held by a majority that the Act was still in force. However, the Lord Chief Justice, Lord Goddard, went on to observe:[111]

[T]he court wishes to express its emphatic approval of the way the justices dealt with this case by granting an absolute discharge for, although the police may have powers, it does not follow that they ought to exercise them on all occasions or as a matter of routine. From what we have been told by counsel for the respondent it is obvious that the police now, as a matter of routine, demand the production of national registration identity cards whenever they stop or interrogate a motorist for whatever cause. Of course, if they are looking for a stolen car or have reason to believe that a particular motorist is engaged in committing a crime, that is one thing, but to demand a national registration identity card from all and sundry, for instance, from a lady who may leave her car outside a shop longer than she should or some trivial matter of that sort is

---

[111] *Willcock v Muckle* [1951] 3 All ER 367.

235

wholly unreasonable. This Act was passed for security purposes, and not for the purposes for which, apparently, it is now sought to be used. To use Acts of Parliament, passed for particular purposes during war, in times when the war is past, except that technically a state of war exists, tends to turn law-abiding subjects into law-breakers, which is a most undesirable state of affairs.

Further, in this country we have always prided ourselves on the good feeling that exists between the police and the public and such action tends to make the people resentful of the acts of the police and inclines them to obstruct the police instead of to assist them. For those reasons I hope that, if a similar case comes before any other bench of justices, they will deal with the case as did the Hornsey bench and grant an absolute discharge. In the Road Traffic Acts 1930 and 1934, Parliament dealt with the matter of endorsements on licences and so forth and, if the police do not think that those Acts give them sufficient powers or think that the administration of those Acts is difficult, they can go to Parliament and ask for further powers. They ought not to use a security Act, which was passed for a particular purpose, as they have done in this case.

The need to carry identity documents was abolished shortly after.

The copybook marred

Few judges in recent times have been as willing as Lord Denning to take a view of a disputed point of law that accords with what he perceived to be the justice of the case, as the following examples demonstrate.

In the first instance,[112] where a widow's claim looked likely to be defeated by a mere technicality, Denning would have allowed the appeal, but, as he said:

My brethren take a different view. They think the defect is fatal and that the plaintiff must be driven from the judgment seat without a hearing. I greatly regret that this should be so: quite recently Lord Justice Holroyd Pearce recalled the proud boast of Lord Justice Bowen:

It may be asserted without fear of contradiction that it is not possible in the year 1887 for an honest litigant in Her Majesty's Supreme Court to be

---

[112] *Re Pritchard* [1963] 1 All ER 872, 879.

defeated by any mere technicality, any slip, any mistaken step in his litigation.

The present case, and some others which I have quoted, show that in this year, 1963, the assertion can no longer be made. We have not followed the handwriting of our predecessors. We have marred our copybook with blots, and the more's the pity of it.

Instead of 'saints', read 'judges'

In the second instance Denning felt that his power to do justice was constrained by a procedural rule which he accordingly declined to observe.

In the mid 1970s the courts rediscovered a useful means of assisting a creditor when an absconding defendant to pending legal proceedings threatens to dispose of assets in this country so as to make unenforceable an order of the court. It is known as a Mareva *injunction after the case in which it was first used.*[113] *The limits of these injunctions were tested in the case of* The Siskina.[114]

It concerned a dispute between the owners of a ship of that name and the cargo owners, which the latter wanted litigated in the United Kingdom. Neither party had any connection with this country but the vessel was insured at Lloyd's. The Court of Appeal had to decide whether the courts had jurisdiction to grant a Mareva *injunction restraining removal from the jurisdiction of the insurance moneys. The point turned upon the interpretation of the Rules of the Supreme Court, which are made by a body known as the Rule Committee. Allowing an appeal against the order of a single judge who had refused jurisdiction, the Master of the Rolls, Lord Denning, said:*

It was suggested that this course is not open to us because it would be legislation; and that we should leave the law to be amended by the Rule Committee. But see what this would mean: the shipowning company would be

---

[113] *Mareva Compania Naviera SA* v *International Bulkcarriers SA* [1975] 2 Lloyd's Rep 509.
[114] *Owners of cargo lately laden on board the vessel Siskina* v *Distos Compania Naviera SA* [1977] 3 All ER 803, 815.

able to decamp with the insurance moneys and the cargo owners would have to whistle for any redress. To wait for the Rule Committee would be to shut the stable door after the steed had been stolen. And who knows that there will ever again be another horse in the stable? Or another ship sunk and insurance moneys here? I ask: why should the judges wait for the Rule Committee? The judges have an inherent jurisdiction to lay down the practice and procedure of the courts; and we can invoke it now to restrain the removal of these insurance moneys. To the timorous souls I would say in the words of William Cowper:

> Ye fearful saints fresh courage take,
> The clouds ye so much dread
> Are big with mercy, and shall break
> In blessings on your head.

Instead of 'saints', read 'judges'. Instead of 'mercy', read 'justice'. And you will find a good way to law reform!

> *Lord Denning's view carried the day in the Court of Appeal, but was overturned unanimously in the House of Lords, in which tribunal the Lord Chancellor, Lord Hailsham of St Marylebone, rebuked Lord Denning with the following comments, with which two of his colleagues agreed:*

The second point on which I wish to comment is the argument of the Master of the Rolls, Lord Denning, fortified by the authority of a quotation from *Hymns Ancient and Modern*, that the judges need not wait for the authority of the Rules Committee in order to sanction a change in practice, indeed an extension of jurisdiction, in matters of this kind. The jurisdiction of the Rules Committee is statutory, and for judges of first instance or on appeal to pre-empt its functions is, at least in my opinion, for the courts to usurp the function of the legislature. Quite apart from this and from technical arguments of any kind, I should point out that the Rules Committee is a far more suitable vehicle for discharging the function than a panel of three judges, however eminent, deciding an individual case after hearing arguments from advocates representing the interests of opposing litigants, however ably.

> *Of course, he had a point, but it was a pity that the House could not have found a way to achieve the result that Denning (and justice) had called for.*

The length of the Chancellor's foot

The most potent constraint upon judicial law-making is the constitutional relationship between the courts and the legislature. It is illustrated by a case concerning a strike that threatened to bring the nation to its knees.[115]

In the late 1970s the nationalised British Steel Corporation was locked in industrial conflict with a trade union known as the Iron and Steel Trades Confederation over a matter of pay. The union decided to extend the strike to the private sector (which was not in any way involved) in such a way as would bring to a halt all movement of steel throughout the United Kingdom. Fifteen private steel companies sought injunctions to prevent the union from doing so.

At that time trade unions had statutory immunity from an action for damages when acting 'in furtherance ... of a trade dispute'. The companies contended that an act was not done in furtherance of a trade dispute unless it was intended to have an immediate adverse trade or industrial effect on the other party to the dispute. The judge at first instance rejected that argument and the companies appealed to the Court of Appeal. The court, presided over by Lord Denning, granted the injunctions on a ground which had not been advanced on behalf of the companies, namely that the extension of the strike constituted a second dispute between the union and the government which was not a trade dispute because the government was not an employer. The union then appealed to the House of Lords, which took the view that the Court of Appeal's reasoning was 'not tenable' and that an act was in furtherance of a trade dispute if the person doing the act honestly believed that it might further the cause of those taking part.

Two distinguished members of the House cautioned against any interpretation of the statute which would fail to give effect to the will of Parliament. Lord Scarman observed:

My Lords, this appeal raises two specific questions as to the interpretation of a statute, the Trade Union and Labour Relations Act 1974, as amended. But

---

[115] *Duport Steels Ltd* v *Sirs* [1980] 1 All ER 529, 534.

below the surface of the legal argument lurk some profound questions as to the proper relationship in our society between the courts, the government and Parliament. The technical questions of law pose (or should pose) no problems. The more fundamental questions are, however, very disturbing; nevertheless it is on my answer to them that I would allow the appeal. My basic criticism of all three judgments in the Court of Appeal is that in their desire to do justice the court failed to do justice according to law. When one is considering law in the hands of the judges, law means the body of rules and guidelines within which society requires its judges to administer justice. Legal systems differ in the width of the discretionary power granted to judges: but in developed societies limits are invariably set, beyond which the judges may not go. Justice in such societies is not left to the unguided, even if experienced, sage sitting under the spreading oak tree.

In our society the judges have in some aspects of their work a discretionary power to do justice so wide that they may be regarded as lawmakers. The common law and equity, both of them in essence systems of private law, are fields where, subject to the increasing intrusion of statute law, society has been content to allow the judges to formulate and develop the law. The judges, even in this, their very own field of creative endeavour, have accepted, in the interests of certainty, the self-denying ordinance of *stare decisis*, the doctrine of binding precedent; and no doubt this judicially imposed limitation on judicial law-making has helped to maintain confidence in the certainty and even-handedness of the law.

But in the field of statute law the judge must be obedient to the will of Parliament as expressed in its enactments. In this field Parliament makes and unmakes the law. The judge's duty is to interpret and to apply the law not to change it to meet the judge's idea of what justice requires. Interpretation does, of course, imply in the interpreter a power of choice where differing constructions are possible. But our law requires the judge to choose the construction which in his judgment best meets the legislative purpose of the enactment. If the result be unjust but inevitable, the judge may say so and invite Parliament to reconsider its provision. But he must not deny the statute. Unpalatable statute law may not be disregarded or rejected, merely because it is unpalatable. Only if a just result can be achieved without violating the legislative purpose of the statute may the judge select the construction which best suits his idea of what justice requires. Further, in our system the *stare decisis* rule applies as firmly to statute law as it does to the formulation of common law and equitable principles. And the keystone of *stare decisis* is loyalty throughout the system to the decisions of the Court of Appeal and this House. The Court of Appeal may not overrule a House of Lords decision; and only in the exceptional circumstances set out in the practice statement of 26 July 1966 will this House refuse to follow its own previous decisions.

Within these limits, which cannot be said in a free society possessing elective legislative institutions to be narrow or constrained, judges, as the remarkable judicial career of the Master of the Rolls, Lord Denning, himself shows, have a genuine creative role. Great judges are in their different ways judicial activists. But the constitution's separation of powers, or more accurately functions, must be observed if judicial independence is not to be put at risk. For, if people and Parliament come to think that the judicial power is to be confined by nothing other than the judge's sense of what is right (or, as Selden put it, by the length of the Chancellor's foot), confidence in the judicial system will be replaced by fear of it becoming uncertain and arbitrary in its application. Society will then be ready for Parliament to cut the power of the judges. Their power to do justice will become more restricted by law than it need be, or is today.

Lord Diplock added:

My Lords, at a time when more and more cases involve the application of legislation which gives effect to policies that are the subject of bitter public and Parliamentary controversy, it cannot be too strongly emphasised that the British constitution, though largely unwritten, is firmly based on the separation of powers: Parliament makes the laws, the judiciary interpret them. When Parliament legislates to remedy what the majority of its members at the time perceive to be a defect or a lacuna in the existing law (whether it be the written law enacted by existing statutes or the unwritten common law as it has been expounded by the judges in decided cases), the role of the judiciary is confined to ascertaining from the words that Parliament has approved as expressing its intention what that intention was, and to giving effect to it. Where the meaning of the statutory words is plain and unambiguous it is not for the judges to invent fancied ambiguities as an excuse for failing to give effect to its plain meaning because they themselves consider that the consequences of doing so would be inexpedient, or even unjust or immoral. In controversial matters such as are involved in industrial relations there is room for differences of opinion as to what is expedient, what is just and what is morally justifiable. Under our constitution it is Parliament's opinion on these matters that is paramount....

It endangers continued public confidence in the political impartiality of the judiciary, which is essential to the continuance of the rule of law, if judges, under the guise of interpretation, provide their own preferred amendments to statutes which experience of their operation has shown to have had consequences that members of the court before whom the matter comes consider to be injurious to the public interest. The frequency with which controversial legislation is amended by Parliament itself (as witness the 1974 Act, which was amended in 1975 as well as in 1976) indicates that legislation, after it has come into operation, may fail to have the beneficial effects which Parliament expected or may produce injurious results that Parliament did not anticipate. But, except by private or hybrid Bills, Parliament does not legislate for individual cases.

Public Acts of Parliament are general in their application; they govern all cases falling within categories of which the definitions are to be found in the wording of the statute. So in relation to section 13(1) of the 1974 Act, for a judge (who is always dealing with an individual case) to pose himself the question, 'Can Parliament really have intended that the acts that were done in this particular case should have the benefit of the immunity?' is to risk straying beyond his constitutional role as interpreter of the enacted law and assume a power to decide at his own discretion whether or not to apply the general law to a particular case. The legitimate questions for a judge in his role as interpreter of the enacted law are, 'How has Parliament, by the words that it has used in the statute to express its intentions, defined the category of acts that are entitled to the immunity? Do the acts done in this particular case fall within that description?'

> *The decision of the five-man House of Lords was unanimous — as had been, in the opposite sense, the decision of the three-man Court of Appeal.*

The delicate balance

The subordinate role of the judges in law-making was also acknowledged in the Appellate Committee of the House of Lords by Lord Mustill (himself no timid spirit) when he said:[116]

It is a feature of the peculiarly British conception of the separation of powers that Parliament, the executive and the courts have each their distinct and largely exclusive domain. Parliament has a legally unchallengeable right to make whatever laws it thinks right. The executive carries on the administration of the country in accordance with the powers conferred on it by law. The courts interpret the laws, and see that they are obeyed. This requires the courts on occasion to step into the territory which belongs to the executive, not only to

---

[116] *R* v *Secretary of State for the Home Department, ex parte Fire Brigades Union* [1995] 2 All ER 244, 267.

verify that the powers asserted accord with the substantive law created by Parliament, but also, that the manner in which they are exercised conforms with the standards of fairness which Parliament must have intended. Concurrently with this judicial function Parliament has its own special means of ensuring that the executive, in the exercise of delegated functions, performs in a way which Parliament finds appropriate.

Ideally, it is these latter methods which should be used to check executive errors and excesses; for it is the task of Parliament and the executive in tandem, not of the courts, to govern the country. In recent years, however, the employment in practice of these specifically Parliamentary remedies has on occasion been perceived as falling short, and sometimes well short, of what was needed to bring the performance of the executive into line with the law and with the minimum standards of fairness implicit in every Parliamentary delegation of a decision-making function. To avoid a vacuum in which the citizen would be left without protection against a misuse of executive powers the courts have had no option but to occupy the dead ground in a manner, and in areas of public life, which could not have been foreseen 30 years ago. For myself I am quite satisfied that this unprecedented judicial role has been greatly to the public benefit. Nevertheless, it has its risks, of which the courts are well aware. As the judges themselves constantly remark, it is not they who are appointed to administer the country. Absent a written constitution much sensitivity is required of the Parliamentarian, administrator and judge if the delicate balance of the unwritten rules evolved (I believe successfully) in recent years is not to be disturbed, and all the recent advances undone.

I do not for a moment suggest that the judges of the Court of Appeal in the present case overlooked this need. The judgments show clearly that they did not. Nevertheless some of the arguments addressed would have the court push to the very boundaries of the distinction between court and Parliament established in, and recognised ever since, the Bill of Rights 1688. Three hundred years have passed since then, and the political and social landscape has changed beyond recognition. But the boundaries remain; they are of crucial significance to our private and public lives; and the courts should, I believe, make sure that they are not overstepped.

Over the particular issue in this case Lord Mustill found himself in the minority. See Flying in the face of common sense *in chapter 1.*

Griffin

9. SCANDALISING THE COURT

or

The Law of Contempt

The dependence of society upon an unswerved judiciary is such a commonplace in the history of freedom that the means by which it is maintained are too frequently taken for granted without heed to the conditions which alone make it possible.

Mr Justice Frankfurter in *Bridges* v *California*.[117]

**Laughing gas
A quaint old-fashioned ring
Silence is not an option
The experience of history
No cloistered virtue**

---

[117] See under *The experience of history*.

Every law student knows the report that speaks in delightful law French of the prisoner who:

> *ject un Brickbat a le dit Justice que narrowly mist, & pur ceo immediately fuit Indictment drawn per Noy envers le prisoner, & son dexter manus ampute & fix al Gibbet sur que luy mesme immediatement hange in presence de Court.*[118]

While the modern punishments for contempt are not as draconian as they were in the seventeenth century, courts — in this country at least — still feel the need for some means of controlling obstructions to the administration of justice.

The case of the rowdy students disrupting the work of a court in order to give publicity to the cause of the Welsh language is fairly mundane stuff, though the way with which Lord Denning dealt with the appeal is a delight (see under A quaint old fashioned ring*). Potentially more serious was the attempt by a bored solicitor's clerk to inject gas into one of the Crown Courts at St Albans. The overturning of his sentence on appeal may seem to some surprising, but in the end justice was probably done (*Laughing gas*).*

An allegation of contempt against a member of the Bar (and a future Lord Chancellor) is not something that occurs every day, but it did give Lord Denning the opportunity to offer some wise words on the liability of judges to criticism (Silence is not an option*).*

The United States Supreme Court has been reluctant to extend the power to punish for contempt. Not all members of the Court agreed. Among the dissenters was the redoubtable Felix Frankfurter, part of whose opinion is reproduced below (The experience of history*).*

Laughing gas

Physical attacks on judges and their courts were not confined to the seventeenth century but continue to this day, although the chosen

---

[118] (1631) Dy (1688 ed.) 188b.

instrument in the following case was decidedly twentieth-century.
Let Lord Denning tell the story in characteristic style.[119]

There is a new courthouse at St Albans. It is air-conditioned. In May of this year the Crown Court was sitting there. A case was being tried about pornographic films and books. Stephen Balogh was there each day. He was a casual hand employed by solicitors for the defence. Just as a clerk at £5 a day, knowing no law. The case dragged on and on. He got exceedingly bored. He made a plan to liven it up. He knew something about a gas called nitrous oxide, N_2O. It gives an exhilarating effect when inhaled. It is called 'laughing gas'. He had learned all about it at Oxford.

During the trial he took a half-cylinder of it from the hospital car park. He carried it about with him in his briefcase. His plan was to put the cylinder at the inlet to the ventilating system and to release the gas into the court. It would emerge from the outlets which were just in front of counsel's row. So the gas, he thought, would enliven their speeches. It would be diverting for the others. A relief from the tedium of pornography. So one night when it was dark he got on to the roof of the court house. He did it by going up from the public gallery. He found the ventilating ducts and decided where to put the cylinder. Next morning, soon after the court sat, at 11.15 a.m., he took his briefcase, with the cylinder in it, into court 1. That was not the pornography court. It was the next-door court. It was the only court which had a door leading up to the roof. He put the briefcase on a seat at the back of the public gallery. Then he left for a little while. He was waiting for a moment when he could slip up to the roof without anyone seeing him. But the moment never came. He had been seen on the night before.

The officers of the court had watched him go up to the roof. So in the morning they kept an eye on him. They saw him put down his briefcase. When he left for a moment, they took it up. They were careful. There might be a bomb in it. They opened it. They took out the cylinder. They examined it and found out what it was. They got hold of Balogh. They cautioned him. He told them frankly just what he had done. They charged him with stealing a bottle of nitrous oxide. He admitted it. They kept him in custody and reported the matter to Mr Justice Melford Stevenson, who was presiding in court 1 (not the pornography court).

At the end of the day's hearing, at 4.15 p.m., the judge had Balogh brought before him. The police inspector gave evidence. Balogh admitted it was all true. He meant it as a joke. A practical joke. But the judge thought differently. He was not amused. To him it was no laughing matter. It was a very serious contempt of court.

---

[119] *Balogh v Crown Court at St Albans* [1974] 3 All ER 283, 285.

Balogh was committed to prison for six months. He left court with 'an uncouth insult' to the judge. More practically, he sought the assistance of the Official Solicitor who instructed counsel to lodge an appeal in the Court of Appeal.

The Court, presided over by the Master of the Rolls, took the view that, while Mr Balogh may have been guilty of stealing the bottle of gas, his acts were merely preparatory to a contempt and did not amount to the completed offence. They quashed the committal. On the wider issue, Lord Denning observed:

This power of summary punishment is a great power, but it is a necessary power. It is given so as to maintain the dignity and authority of the judge and to ensure a fair trial. It is to be exercised by the judge of his own motion only when it is urgent and imperative to act immediately so as to maintain the authority of the court — to prevent disorder — to enable witnesses to be free from fear — and jurors from being improperly influenced and the like. It is, of course, to be exercised with scrupulous care, and only when the case is clear and beyond reasonable doubt: ... But properly exercised, it is a power of the utmost value and importance which should not be curtailed.

A quaint old-fashioned ring

A judge can be faced with a difficult decision when a contempt is committed in his (judicial) presence. This happened before Mr Justice Lawton when his court was disturbed by a group of boisterous Welsh students demonstrating in support of the Welsh language. They were arrested and committed to prison. Despite the judge's subsequent clemency some of the contemners appealed to the Court of Appeal, presided over by the Master of the Rolls, Lord Denning. This is how he described what happened.[120]

Last Wednesday, just a week ago, Mr Justice Lawton, a judge of the High Court here in London, was sitting to hear a case. It was a libel case between a naval officer and some publishers. He was trying it with a jury. It was no doubt an important case, but for the purposes of today it could have been the least important. It matters not. For what happened was serious indeed. A group of

---

[120] *Morris v Crown Office* [1970] 1 All ER 1079, 1080.

students, young men and young women, invaded the court. It was clearly prearranged. They had come all the way from the University of Aberystwyth. They strode into the well of the court. They flocked into the public gallery. They shouted slogans. They scattered pamphlets. They sang songs. They broke up the hearing. The judge had to adjourn. They were removed. Order was restored.

When the judge returned to the court, three of them were brought before him. He sentenced each of them to three months' imprisonment for contempt of court. The others were kept in custody until the rising of the court. Nineteen were then brought before him. The judge asked each of them whether he or she was prepared to apologise. Eight of them did so. The judge imposed a fine of £50 on each of them and required them to enter into recognisances to keep the peace. Fourteen of them did not apologise. They did it, they said, as a matter of principle and so did not feel able to apologise. The judge sentenced each of them to imprisonment for three months for contempt of court.

> **Lord Denning (b. 1899) was the son of a Hampshire draper. Of his four brothers, two died in the Great War ('They were the best of us'), one was an Admiral and the other a General. He liked to tell students: 'When I was a judge of first instance, sitting alone, I could and did do justice. But when I went to the Court of Appeal of three I found that the chances of doing justice were two to one against'. A lawlord for five years, he stood down to become Master of the Rolls (or head of the Court of Appeal) retiring in 1982.**

In sentencing them in this way the judge was exercising a jurisdiction which goes back for centuries. It was well described over 200 years ago by Chief Justice Wilmot in an opinion which he prepared but never delivered. He said:

> it is a necessary incident to every Court of Justice ... to fine and imprison for a contempt to the Court, acted in the face of it.

The phrase 'contempt in the face of the court' has a quaint old-fashioned ring about it; but the importance of it is this: of all the places where law and order must be maintained, it is here in these courts. The course of justice must not be deflected or interfered with. Those who strike at it strike at the very foundations of our society. To maintain law and order, the judges have, and must have, power at once to deal with those who offend against it. It is a great power — a power instantly to imprison a person without trial — but it is a necessary power. So necessary indeed that until recently the judges exercised it without any appeal. There were previously no safeguards against a judge exercising his jurisdiction wrongly or unwisely. This was remedied in 1960. An appeal now lies to this court; and, in a suitable case, from this court to the House of Lords. With these safeguards this jurisdiction can and should be maintained. Eleven of the appellants have exercised this right to appeal; and we have put all other cases aside to hear it. For we are here concerned with their liberty; and our law puts the liberty of the subject before all else.

After reviewing the law Lord Denning held that the judge had not exceeded his powers. He went on:

[*Counsel for the appellant*] says that the sentences were excessive. I do not think that they were excessive, at the time they were given and in the circumstances then existing. Here was a deliberate interference with the course of justice in a case which was no concern of theirs. It was necessary for the judge to show — and to show to all students everywhere — that this kind of thing cannot be tolerated. Let students demonstrate, if they please, for the causes in which they believe. Let them make their protests as they will. But they must do it by lawful means and not by unlawful. If they strike at the course of justice in this land — and I speak both for England and Wales — they strike at the roots of society itself, and they bring down that which protects them. It is only by the maintenance of law and order that they are privileged to be students and to study and live in peace. So let them support the law and not strike it down.

But now what is to be done? The law has been vindicated by the sentences which the judge passed on Wednesday of last week. He has shown that law and order must be maintained, and will be maintained. But on this appeal, things are changed. The appellants here no longer defy the law. They have appealed to this court and shown respect for it. They have already served a week in prison. I do not think it necessary to keep them inside it any longer. The appellants are no ordinary criminals. There is no violence, dishonesty or vice in them. On the contrary, there is much that we should applaud. They wish to do all they can to preserve the Welsh language. Well may they be proud of it. It is the language of the bards, of the poets and the singer — more melodious by far than our rough English tongue. On high authority, it should be equal in Wales with English. They have done wrong — very wrong — in going to the extreme they did. But, that having been shown, I think we can, and should, show mercy on them. We should permit them to go back to their studies, to their parents and continue the good course which they have so wrongly disturbed.

There must be security for the future. They must be of good behaviour. They must keep the peace. I would add, finally, that there is power in this court, in case of need, to recall them. If it should become necessary, this court would not hesitate to call them back and commit them to prison for the rest of the sentence which Mr Justice Lawton passed on them.

Subject to what my brethren will say in a few moments, I would propose that they be released from prison today, but that they be bound over to be of good behaviour, to keep the peace and to come up for judgment if called on within the next 12 months.

The fact that Lord Denning had once worn the shoulder flash of a Welsh regiment could, of course, have played no part in his merciful judgment.

Silence is not an option

Even the Court of Appeal is not immune from criticism, in the following instance by a future Lord Chancellor, no less.

The Rt Hon. Quintin Hogg PC, QC, MP (as he then was) wrote an article in Punch *magazine criticising the 'unrealistic, contradictory and, in the leading case, erroneous' decisions of the Court of Appeal in the field of gaming law. Mr Blackburn, a sturdy defender of the underdog, moved the court to declare Mr Hogg guilty of contempt. Rejecting the application, the Master of the Rolls, Lord Denning, said:*[121]

This is the first case, so far as I know, where this court has been called on to consider an allegation of contempt against itself. It is a jurisdiction which undoubtedly belongs to us, but which we will most sparingly exercise: more particularly as we ourselves have an interest in the matter. Let me say at once that we will never use this jurisdiction as a means to uphold our own dignity. That must rest on surer foundations. Nor will we use it to suppress those who speak against us. We do not fear criticism, nor do we resent it. For there is something far more important at stake. It is no less than freedom of speech itself. It is the right of every man, in Parliament or out of it, in the press or over the broadcast [*sic*], to make fair comment, even outspoken comment, on matters of public interest. Those who comment can deal faithfully with all that is done in a court of justice. They can say that we are mistaken, and our decisions erroneous, whether they are subject to appeal or not. All we would

---

[121] *R* v *Metropolitan Police Commissioner, ex parte Blackburn (No. 2)* [1968] 2 All ER 319, 320.

ask is that those who criticise us will remember that, from the nature of our office, we cannot reply to their criticisms. We cannot enter into public controversy. Still less into political controversy. We must rely on our conduct itself to be its own vindication. Exposed as we are to the winds of criticism, nothing which is said by this person or that, nothing which is written by this pen or that, will deter us from doing what we believe is right; nor, I would add, from saying what the occasion requires, provided that it is pertinent to the matter in hand. Silence is not an option when things are ill done.

Mr Blackburn's application was dismissed. Mr Hogg, as Lord Hailsham of St Marylebone, subsequently became Lord Chancellor.

The experience of history

The United States Supreme Court has by a majority rejected extension of the power to punish for contempt where it conflicted with the right of free speech.

Harry Bridges was president of the International Longshoremen's and Warehousemen's Union (ILWU). In the autumn of 1937 the ILWU was in rivalry with the International Longshoremen's Association (ILA) for control of a local (or branch) in San Pedro Harbor. Longshoremen belonging to ILA obtained a court injunction preventing the officers of ILWU from transferring allegiance to that union. The defendants moved for a new trial and for vacation of the judgment. There was great public interest in the case.

Mr Bridges sent a telegram to the Secretary of Labor which found its way into the press. It was expressed in terms described by the court as implying that if an attempt were made to enforce the decision 'the ports of the entire Pacific Coast would be tied up' and 'a direct challenge to the court that 11,000 longshoremen on the Pacific Coast would not abide by its decision'. For this contempt he was fined $125 under a California statute, whereupon he challenged the constitutional propriety of the legislation.

When the case came before the Supreme Court the majority view was that the California legislation was contrary to the due process clause of the Fourteenth Amendment to the Constitution. Among the dissenters was Mr Justice Frankfurter who in the course of his opinion said:[122]

Our whole history repels the view that it is an exercise of one of the civil liberties secured by the Bill of Rights for a leader of a large following or for a powerful metropolitan newspaper, to attempt to overawe a judge in a matter immediately pending before him. The view of the majority deprives California of means for securing to its citizens justice according to law — means which, since the Union was founded have been the possession hitherto unchallenged of all the states. This sudden break with the uninterrupted course of constitutional history has no constitutional warrant. To find justification for such deprivation of the historic powers of the states is to misconceive the idea of freedom of thought and speech as guaranteed by the Constitution.

Deeming it more important than ever before to enforce civil liberties with a generous outlook but deeming it no less essential for the assurance of civil liberties that the federal system founded upon the Constitution be maintained, we believe that the careful ambiguities and silences of the majority opinion call for a full exposition of the issues in these cases. . . .

A trial is not a 'free trade in ideas', nor is the best test of truth in a courtroom 'the power of the thought to get itself accepted in the competition of the market'. A court is a forum with strictly defined limits for discussion. It is circumscribed in the range of its inquiry and in its methods by the Constitution, by laws, and by age-old traditions. Its judges are restrained in their freedom of expression by historic compulsions resting on no other officials of government. They are so circumscribed precisely because judges have in their keeping the enforcement of rights and the protection of liberties which, according to the wisdom of the ages, can only be enforced and protected by observing such methods and traditions.

The dependence of society upon an unswerved judiciary is such a commonplace in the history of freedom that the means by which it is maintained are too frequently taken for granted without heed to the conditions which alone make it possible. . . .

Of course, freedom of speech and of the press are essential to the enlightenment of a free people and in restraining those who wield power. Particularly should this freedom be employed in comment upon the work of

---

[122] In a judgment jointly with the Chief Justice, Mr Justice Roberts and Mr Justice Byrnes in *Bridges* v *California*, 314 US 252 (1941).

courts who are without many influences ordinarily making for humor and humility, twin antidotes to the corrosion of power. But the Bill of Rights is not self-destructive. Freedom of expression can hardly carry implications that nullify the guarantees of impartial trials. And since courts are the ultimate resorts for vindicating the Bill of Rights, a state may surely authorize appropriate means to ensure that the process for such vindication be not wrenched from its rational tracks into the more primitive melee of passion and pressure. The need is great that courts be criticized but just as great that they be allowed to do their duty.

The common law tradition
The 'liberty' secured by the Fourteenth Amendment summarizes the experience of history. And the power exerted by the courts of California is deeply rooted in the system of administering justice evolved by liberty-loving English-speaking peoples. From the earliest days of the English courts they have encountered obstructions to doing that for which they exist, namely to administer justice impartially and solely with reference to what comes before them. These interferences were of diverse kinds. But they were all covered by the infelicitous phrase 'contempt of court', and the means for dealing with them is historically known as the power of courts to punish for contempt. As is true of many aspects of our legal institutions, the settled doctrines concerning the mode of procedure for exercising the power of contempt became established on dubious historical authority. Exact legal scholarship has controverted much pertaining to the origin of summary proceedings for contempt.... But there is no doubt that since the early eighteenth century, the power to punish for contempt, for intrusions into the living process of adjudication, has been an unquestioned characteristic of English courts and of the courts of this country.

The judicatures of the English-speaking world, including the courts of the United States and of the 48 states, have from time to time recognized and exercised the power now challenged.

A declaratory formulation of the common law was written into the Judiciary Act of 1789 by Oliver Ellsworth, one of the framers of the Constitution, later to become Chief Justice; the power was early recognized as incidental to the very existence of courts in a succession of opinions of this Court; it was expounded and supported by the great Commentaries that so largely influenced the shaping of our law in the late eighteenth and early nineteenth centuries, those of Blackstone, Kent and Story; its historic continuity withstood attack against state action under the Due Process Clause, now again invoked.

As in the exercise of all power, it was abused. Some English judges extended their authority for checking interferences with judicial business actually in hand to 'lay by the heel' those responsible for 'scandalizing the court', that is, bringing it into general disrepute. Such foolishness has long since been disavowed in England and has never found lodgment here. . . .

It is trifling with great issues to suggest the question before us is whether eighteenth-century restraints upon the freedom of the press should now be revived. The question is rather whether nineteenth and twentieth-century American institutions should be abrogated by judicial fiat.

That a state may under appropriate circumstances prevent interference with specific exercises of the process of impartial adjudication does not mean that its people lose the right to condemn decisions or the judges who render them. Judges as persons or courts as institutions are entitled to no greater immunity from criticism than other persons or institutions. Just because the holders of judicial office are identified with the interests of justice they may forget their common human frailties and fallibilities. There have sometimes been martinets upon the bench as there have also been pompous wielders of authority who have used the paraphernalia of power in support of what they called their dignity. Therefore judges must be kept mindful of their limitations and of their ultimate public responsibility by a vigorous stream of criticism expressed with candor however blunt. 'A man cannot summarily be laid by his heels because his words may make public feeling more unfavourable in case the judge should be asked to act at some later date, any more than he can for exciting public feeling against a judge for what he already has done.'

But the Constitution does not bar a state from acting on the theory of our system of justice, that the 'conclusions to be reached in a case will be induced only by evidence and argument in open court, and not by any outside influence, whether of private talk or public print'. . . .

'The right to sue and defend in the courts is the alternative of force. In an organized society it is the right conservative of all other rights and lies at the foundation of orderly government.' This has nothing to do with curtailing expression of opinion, be it political, economic or religious, that may be offensive to orthodox views. It has to do with the power of the state to discharge an indispensable function of civilized society, that of adjudicating controversies between its citizens and between citizens and the state through legal tribunals in accordance with their historic procedures. Courts and judges must take their share of the gains and pains of discussion which is unfettered except by laws of libel, by self-restraint, and by good taste. Winds of doctrine should freely blow for the promotion of good and the correction of evil. Nor should restrictions be permitted that cramp the feeling of freedom in the use of a tongue or pen, regardless of the temper or the truth of what may be uttered.

Comment however forthright is one thing. Identification with respect to specific matters still in judicial suspense, quite another. A publication intended to teach the judge a lesson, or to vent spleen, or to discredit him or to influence him in his future conduct, would not justify exercise of the contempt power....

The purpose, it will do no harm to repeat, is not to protect the court as a mystical entity or the judges as individuals or as anointed priests set apart from the community and spared the criticism to which in a democracy other public servants are exposed. The purpose is to protect immediate litigants and the public from the mischievous danger of an unfree or coerced tribunal. The power should be invoked only where the adjudicatory process may be hampered or hindered in its calm, detached and fearless discharge of its duty on the basis of what has been submitted in court. The belief that decisions are so reached is the source of the confidence on which law ultimately rests.

It will not do to argue that a state cannot permit its judges to resist coercive interference with their work in hand because other officials of government must endure such obstructions. In such matters 'a page of history is worth a volume of logic'. Presidents and governors and legislators are political officials traditionally subject to political influence and the rough and tumble of the hustings, who have open to them traditional means of self-defense. In a very immediate sense, legislators and executives express the popular will. But judges do not express the popular will in any ordinary meaning of the term. The limited power to punish for contempt which is here involved wholly rejects any assumption that judges are superior to other officials. Because the function of judges and that of other officials in special situations may approach similarity hard cases can be put which logically may contradict the special quality of the judicial process. 'But the provisions of the Constitution are not mathematical formulas having their essence in their form; they are organic living institutions transplanted from English soil. Their significance is vital not formal; it is to be gathered not simply by taking the words and a dictionary but by considering their origin and the line of growth.'

Sitting in judgment on state power
We are charged here with the duty, always delicate, of sitting in judgment on state power. We must be fastidiously careful not to make our private views the measure of constitutional authority. To be sure, we are here concerned with an appeal to the great liberties which the Constitution assures to all our people, even against state denial. When a substantial claim of an abridgment of these liberties is advanced, the presumption of validity that belongs to an exercise of state power must not be allowed to impair such a liberty or to check our close examination of the merits of the controversy. But the utmost protection to be accorded to freedom of speech and of the press cannot displace our duty to give due regard also to the state's power to deal with what may essentially be local situations.

Because freedom of public expression alone assures the unfolding of truth it is indispensable to the democratic process. But even that freedom is not absolute and is not predetermined. . . .

How are we to say that California has no right to model its judiciary upon the qualities and standards attained by the English administration of justice, and to use means deemed appropriate to that end by English courts? It is surely an arbitrary judgment to say that the 'Due Process' Clause denies California that right. For respect for 'the liberty of the subject' though not explicitly written into a constitution is so deeply embedded in the very texture of English feeling and conscience that it survives, as the pages of Hansard abundantly prove, the exigencies of the life and death struggle of the British people.

No cloistered virtue

Let the great Lord Atkin have the last word.[123]

The path of criticism is a public way: the wrong-headed are permitted to err therein: provided that members of the public abstain from imputing improper motives to those taking part in the administration of justice, and are genuinely exercising a right of criticism, and not acting in malice or attempting to impair the administration of justice, they are immune. Justice is not a cloistered virtue: she must be allowed ·to suffer the scrutiny and respectful, even though outspoken, comments of ordinary men.

---

[123] Delivering the judgment of the House of Lords in *Ambard v Attorney-General for Trinidad and Tobago* [1936] AC 322, 335.

Field Court, Gray's Inn

10. HOMER NODDING

or

Judicial Infirmities

In the very pursuit of justice, our keenness may outrun our
sureness, and we may trip and fall.

Lord Denning in *Jones v National Coal Board*.[124]

Injudicious
The Great Architect
The sanctimonious judge
No well-tuned cymbal
The Judge Who Closed His Eyes
To judge the judges
Humility

---

[124] See *No well-tuned cymbal*.

Few can resist a frisson of ignoble pleasure at the shortcomings of those in authority. How much more so when the authority figure is supposed to be the embodiment of fairness and probity. As a counterweight to the judicial wisdom, courage and eloquence which fills the rest of this book this chapter contains examples of judicial shortfallings — together with other embarrassments of a less ignoble nature.

There is, for example, the judge whose unwise remarks were the subject of perhaps the most famous put-down in English legal history (see under The sanctimonious judge*), the gentle chiding by Lord Denning of the judge who spoke too much (* No well-tuned cymbal*) and the embarrassment of the judge who, when condemning a prisoner to death, discovered to his horror that he was bound to him by ties of honour (* The Great Architect*).*

The tart comments of an American judge concerning those sat in judgment over him will ring a bell with many lawyers (To judge the judges*). And it is a pleasure to read the gracious acknowledgement of error on the part of a member of the highest court in this country (* Humility*).*

We begin with a salutary example of the nemesis that ultimately visits all who come to believe that they enjoy a unique knowledge of human behaviour.

Injudicious

Rayner Goddard was the firmest (or, if you prefer, most reactionary) Lord Chief Justice of the twentieth century — and, incidentally, the first non-political holder of that office. Widely admired in the profession, he stood four-square against the violence that seemed to be sweeping post-war England. Yet on one notable occasion he overstepped the bounds with a comment more suited to the bar room than the bar. In sentencing two young thugs, brothers aged 17 and 14, at an Old Bailey trial on 3 December 1952, he said:

Nowadays, the cane is never used at school. It would have done them good if they had had a good larruping. What they want is to have someone who would give them a thundering good beating and then perhaps they would not do it again. I suppose they were brought up to be treated like little darlings and tucked up in beds at night.

As Anthony Mockler observed:[125]

These were doubly unfortunate comments, and by them Goddard effectively scuppered his own cause, firstly because by the use of such an outmoded word as 'larruping' and by the whole tone of his remarks he gave journalists and commentators a field-day: here was an eminently Victorian judge acting more like a propagandist, as Michael Foot put it, than a professional arbiter. Secondly because, as it happened, the two brothers came from a broken home and had been beaten almost every night — the precise remedy which, the Lord Chief Justice alleged, ought to have stopped their crime.

The Great Architect

Care is taken to ensure that a judge is not called upon to try anyone he has any association with, but it is not always possible to rule out this possibility, as the trial of Frederick Henry Seddon in 1912 demonstrates.

Seddon was an insurance agent who owned and lived in a house in north London in which he had a number of lodgers. One of these, a middle-aged spinster named Miss Barrow, was described as unattractive of character but possessed of inherited capital of £3,000. Miss Barrow was persuaded to make over her fortune to Seddon in return for an annuity of £150 per year. She was later taken ill and died. Her cousin became suspicious when she discovered the arrangement concerning the annuity and the body

---

[125] *Lions under the Throne* (Frederick Muller Ltd, 1983), p. 282.

was exhumed. An autopsy revealed two and a half grains of arsenic in the body and Seddon and his wife were put on trial for murder. The Attorney-General, Sir Rufus Isaacs, led for the Crown. Sir Edward Marshall Hall KC was retained for the defence. At 10 days' duration it became the longest capital trial in which the latter was to be involved. (O tempora! O mores!)

To understand the following account[126] of the denouement it is necessary to know that Seddon was described as having been 'quite a light in the Masonic world'. The Great Architect is the term used by Masons to describe the Supreme Being.

The jury retired at 8.58, and returned into court exactly an hour later. They found Seddon guilty. His face flushed, but otherwise he maintained his composure. Immediately afterwards they pronounced his wife not guilty. Seddon went across, embraced her, and kissed her on the lips. So silent was the court that every one present must have heard the sound of that tragic gesture of farewell. Immediately afterwards she was taken away to be discharged. Much of the prejudice that had gathered round the prisoner was dissipated by this one incident. Many were moved to tears by it. Then the formal question was asked, by the officer of the court, to which very seldom is an answer given by the prisoner, at any rate in capital cases, where no words of his can affect his sentence. 'Frederick Henry Seddon, you stand convicted of wilful murder. Have you anything to say for yourself why the court should not give you judgment of death according to law?'

Then a surprising thing happened. 'I have, sir', replied the prisoner. He cleared his throat, took out some notes, and made a calm and admirable little speech in his own defence. He declared his innocence of the murder and denied any knowledge of it. Finally, knowing the judge to be a zealous Freemason, he made it clear to the judge that they belonged to the same brotherhood, whose members bind themselves solemnly to help each other through life, and especially in extremity. 'I declare', he concluded, 'before the Great Architect of the Universe, I am not guilty, my Lord.'

This appeal utterly unnerved the judge. His clerk arranged the black square of cloth upon his head, which seemed to overshadow and darken his whole face. The chaplain was summoned, and the usher called out, 'Oyez ! Oyez! Oyez!

---

[126] From Edward Marjoribanks MP, *The Life of Sir Edward Marshall Hall KC* (Victor Gollancz, 1929).

My Lords the King's justices do strictly charge and command all persons to keep silence while sentence of death is passing upon the prisoner at the bar, upon pain of imprisonment. God save the King!'

But no words came from the judge: in a silence that could be felt there were only two sounds to be heard — ticking of the court clock and the loud sobs of the judge about to speak the words of condemnation. It seemed a long time before be could pull himself together, yet it could not have been more than a minute in all. Then, in a voice broken with emotion, the judge admonished the prisoner for his barbarous crime. 'It is not for me to harrow your feelings', he said.

'It does not affect me,' said the prisoner; 'I have a clear conscience.'

'Try to make peace with your Maker', the judge continued.

'I am at peace', said the prisoner.

'You and I know we both belong to the same brotherhood, and it is all the more painful to me to have to say what I am saying. But our brotherhood does not encourage crime; on the contrary it condemns it. I pray you again to make your peace with the Great Architect of the Universe. Mercy — pray for it, ask for it.... And now I have to pass sentence. The sentence of the court is that you be taken from hence to a lawful prison, and from thence to a place of execution, and that you be there hanged by the neck until you are dead; and that your body be buried within the precincts of the prison in which you shall have been confined after your conviction; and may the Lord have mercy on your soul.'

The sanctimonious judge

A brilliant barrister with a cruel wit can sometimes strip bare the pretensions of a weak judge. And few barristers were more brilliant than Frederick Edwin Smith KC, 1st Earl of Birkenhead. The following story is told by his son.[127]

His worst insults were reserved for Judge Willis, a worthy, sanctimonious county court judge, full of kindness expressed in a patronising manner. FE had been briefed for a tramway company which had been sued for damages for injuries to a boy who had been run over.

The plaintiff's case was that blindness had set in as a result of the accident.

---

[127] *The Life of F. E. Smith, First Lord Birkenhead by his Son* (Eyre and Spottiswoode, 1959), p. 98.

The judge was deeply moved. 'Poor boy, poor boy', he said. 'Blind. Put him on a chair so that the jury can see him.'

FE said coldly: 'Perhaps your honour would like to have the boy passed round the jury box.'

'That is a most improper remark', said Judge Willis angrily.

'It was provoked', said FE, 'by a most improper suggestion.' There was a heavy pause, and the judge continued, 'Mr Smith, have you ever heard of a saying by Bacon — the great Bacon — that youth and discretion are ill-wed companions?'

'Indeed I have, your Honour; and has your Honour ever heard of a saying by Bacon — the great Bacon — that a much talking judge is like an ill-tuned cymbal?'

The judge replied furiously, 'You are extremely offensive, young man'; and FE added to his previous lapses by saying: 'As a matter of fact we both are; the only difference between us is that I'm trying to be and you can't help it.'

FE, as he was widely known, had a glittering career at the Bar which was recognised by his appointment as Lord Chancellor at the age of 47.

No well-tuned cymbal

The same phrase of Bacon was once quoted, more accurately, by Lord Denning in the Court of Appeal.

The case concerned a judge who had taken a substantial part of the examination of the defendant's witnesses out of the hands of his counsel. He had also hampered by undue interventions the cross-examination of the plaintiff's witnesses.

Allowing the appeal Denning said:[128]

In the system of trial which we have evolved in this country the judge sits to hear and determine the issues raised by the parties, not to conduct an investigation or examination on behalf of society at large, as happens, we

---

[128] *Jones v National Coal Board* [1957] 2 All ER 155, 159.

believe, in some foreign countries. Even in England, however, a judge is not a mere umpire to answer the question, 'How's that?' His object above all is to find out the truth and to do justice according to law; and in the daily pursuit of it the advocate plays an honourable and necessary role.

Was it not Lord Chancellor Eldon who said in a notable passage that 'truth is best discovered by powerful statements on both sides of the question' ... and the Master of the Rolls, Lord Greene, who explained that justice is best done by a judge who holds the balance between the contending parties without himself taking part in their disputations? If a judge, said Lord Greene, should himself conduct the examination of witnesses, he, so to speak, descends into the arena and is liable to have this vision clouded by the dust of the conflict. . . .

Yes, he must keep his vision unclouded. It is all very well to paint justice blind but she does better without a bandage around her eyes. She should be blind indeed to favour or prejudice, but clear to see which way lies the truth; and the less dust there is about the better. Let the advocates one after the other put the weights into the scales — the 'nicely calculated less or more' — but the judge at the end decides which way the balance tilts, be it ever so slightly. So firmly is all this established in our law that the judge is not allowed in a civil dispute to call a witness whom he thinks might throw some light on the facts. He must rest content with the witnesses called by the parties. . . . So also it is for the advocates, each in his turn, to examine the witnesses, and not for the judge to take it on himself lest by so doing he appears to favour one side or the other; . . . And it is for the advocate to state his case as fairly and strongly as he can, without undue interruption, lest the sequence of his argument be lost. . . .

The judge's part in all this is to hearken to the evidence, only himself asking questions of witnesses when it is necessary to clear up any point that has been overlooked or left obscure; to see that the advocates behave themselves seemly and keep to the rules laid down by law; to exclude irrelevancies and discourage repetition; to make sure by wise intervention that he follows the points that the advocates are making and can assess their worth; and at the end to make up his mind where the truth lies. If he goes beyond this, he drops the mantle of a judge and assumes the robe of an advocate; and the change does not become him well. Lord Bacon spoke right when he said that:

Patience and gravity of hearing is an essential part of justice; and an over-speaking judge is no well-tuned cymbal.

Such are our standards. They are set so high that we cannot hope to attain them all the time. In the very pursuit of justice, our keenness may outrun our sureness, and we may trip and fall. That is what has happened here. A judge of acute perception, acknowledged learning, and actuated by the best of motives, has nevertheless himself intervened so much in the conduct of the case that one of the parties — nay, each of them, has come away complaining.

The Judge Who Closed His Eyes

Judges, like lorry drivers, are prone to let their attention wander, though, fortunately, not with the same disastrous consequences, as the following 'fable' demonstrates.

A JUDGE of Considerable Experience was Trying on a Summer's Day a Case of Un-exampled Dullness. Counsel for the Plaintiff was Opening. He Continued to Cite to the Judge a Multitude of Authorities, including the Well-known Decision of the House of Lords in *The Overseers of the Parish of Criggleswick* v *The Mudbank-super-Mare Dock and Harbour Board Trustees and Others*, and the Judge was Satisfied that he had Never been So Bored in the Whole Course of his Professional Life. At about Three-Thirty P.M. the Judge Allowed his Attention to Wander Slightly, as he Felt Sure that Counsel for the Plaintiff would not have Finished his Opening at the Rising of the Court. Five Minutes Later he Fell into a Gentle Doze Which Soon Developed into a Profound Sleep. He was Aroused at Four O'clock by the Sudden Cessation of Counsel's Droning and the Cries of 'Silence' with which the Usher Preluded the Coming Judgment. The Case was Over, and the Judge had no Notion what Counsel for the Defendants had been Talking about. Was the Judge Dismayed? Not at all. He Assumed a Look of Lively Intelligence and Said that, as he had Formed a Clear Opinion, no Useful Purpose would be Served by his Reserving his Judgment. He Admitted that During the Course of the Excellent Arguments which had been Addressed to him his Opinion had Wavered. But, After All, the Broad Question was whether the Principle so Clearly Stated in the House of Lords in *The Overseers of the Parish of Criggleswick* v *The Mudbank-super-Mare Docks and Harbour Board Trustees and Others* Applied to the Facts of the Present Case. On the Whole; despite the Forceful Observations Made on Behalf of the Defendants, to which he had Paid the Closest Attention, he Thought it Did. It was Therefore Unnecessary that he should Discuss a Variety of Topics which, in the View he Took, Became Irrelevant. There would, accordingly, be Judgment for the Plaintiffs, with Costs; but, as the Matter was One of Great Public Interest, there would be a Stay of Execution on the Usual

Terms. The Judgment, which was Appealed Against in Due Course, was Affirmed both in the Court of Appeal and the House of Lords; the Lord Chancellor Commenting, in the Latter Tribunal, on the Admirably Succinct Manner in which the Experienced Judge had Dealt with a Complicated and Difficult Problem.

Moral. — *Stick to the Point.*[129]

To judge the judges

Judges, whatever litigants may sometimes think, are only human and do not always appreciate being overruled. The following comments[130] come from Chief Justice Bleckley of Georgia.

Some courts live by correcting the errors of others and adhering to their own. On these terms courts of final review hold their existence, or those of them which are strictly and exclusively courts of review, without any original jurisdiction, and with no direct function but to find fault, or see that none can be found. With these exalted tribunals who live only to judge the judges, the rule of *stare decisis* is not only a canon of the public good, but a law of self-preservation. At the peril of their lives they must discover error abroad, and be discreetly blind to its commission at home. Were they as ready to correct themselves as others, they could no longer speak as absolute oracles of legal truth; the reason for their existence would disappear, and their destruction would speedily supervene.

Nevertheless, without serious detriment to the public or peril to themselves, they can and do admit now and then, with cautious reserve, that they have made a mistake. Their rigid dogma of infallibility allows of this much relaxation in favor of truth unwittingly forsaken. Indeed, reversion to truth, in some rare instances, is highly necessary to their permanent well-being. Though it is a temporary degradation from the type of judicial perfection, it has to be endured, to keep the type itself respectable. Minor errors, even if quite obvious, or important errors, if their existence be fairly doubtful, may be adhered to, and repeated indefinitely; but the only treatment for a great and glaring error affecting the current administration of justice in all courts of original jurisdiction is to correct it.

---

[129] *Forensic Fables by O* (Butterworth & Co., 1926).
[130] *Ellison v Georgia Railroad and Banking Co.*, 13 SE 809 (Ga 1891).

When an error of this magnitude, and which moves in so wide an orbit, competes with truth in the struggle for existence, the maxim for a supreme court — supreme in the majesty of duty as well as in the majesty of power — is not *stare decisis*, but *fiat justitia ruat coelum*.[131]

Humility

Judges are usually careful to avoid (at least in their judgments) explicit criticism of their brethren, often preferring to describe a bad decision not as 'wrong', but as having been 'decided on its special facts'. Academics do not feel the same constraint. A notable exercise in judicial self-abasement was the comment of Lord Bridge of Harwich in the House of Lords,[132] where he said:

I cannot conclude this opinion without disclosing that I have had the advantage, since the conclusion of the argument in this appeal, of reading an article by Professor Glanville Williams entitled 'The Lords and impossible attempts, or *quis custodiet ipsos custodies?*'[133] The language in which he criticises the decision in *Anderton v Ryan* is not conspicuous for its moderation, but it would be foolish, on that account, not to recognise the force of the criticism and churlish not to acknowledge the assistance I have derived from it.

The article referred to began:

The tale I have to tell is unflattering of the higher judiciary. It is an account of how the judges invented a rule based upon conceptual misunderstanding; of their determination to use the English language so strangely that they spoke what by normal criteria would be termed untruths; of their invincible ignorance of the mess they had made of the law; and of their immobility on the subject, carried to the extent of subverting an Act of Parliament designed to put them straight.

---

[131] *Stare decisis* is lawyers' Latin for the doctrine of precedent. *Fiat justitia ruat coelum* means let justice be done though the heavens fall.
[132] *R v Shivpuri* [1986] 2 All ER 334, 335.
[133] [1986] CLJ 33.

What had happened was that Parliament had amended the law of attempt and the amended law had fallen to be interpreted by the House of Lords.[134] *Lord Bridge's unexampled* amende honorable *is all the more to be admired when it is realised that he was not only a party to the decision in the earlier case but also the author of one of the two opinions approved by the majority which must, in his words, be taken to have expressed the House's* ratio *(or reasoning).*

---

[134] *Anderton* v *Ryan* [1985] 2 All ER 355.

New Court, Lincoln's Inn

11.   WITH RESPECT

or

The Art of the Advocate

... he did not care to speak ill of any man behind his back, but
he believed the gentleman was an attorney.

James Boswell, *The Life of Samuel Johnson* (1791).

Captain-general of iniquity
Bardell* v *Pickwick
Marshall Hall's scales of justice act.
The loose union nut
Attorney for the damned
Never such slaughter

In classical times the study of rhetoric, or the rules of oral persuasion, was obligatory for most educated men, whether for use in the council chamber or the halls of justice. By the eighteenth century those rules had fallen into disuse, but the style of advocacy was still in the classical mould, as exemplified by the extract reproduced below from the speech of Edmund Burke at the trial of Warren Hastings (see under Captain-general of iniquity*). To the modern ear his address sounds overblown and orotund, but no doubt it had a powerful effect on those present.*

Probably the greatest influence on English advocacy has been the jury. No one knew the ways of an advocate better than Charles Dickens and his description of Serjeant Buzfuz's address to the jury in an action for breach of promise of marriage cannot have been far from the truth. The subsequent short exchange between disappointed client and his solicitors is a gem of its kind. (Bardell v Pickwick.)

The cult of the advocate was at its height at the end of the nineteenth century, particularly in jury trials — by then rapidly being reduced to criminal cases. Edward Marshall Hall KC was the foremost advocate of his generation. He defended the Seddons in the famous poisoning case (1912) and George Smith, the 'brides in the bath' murderer (1915). He also acted in the scandalous Russell divorce (1923). Personally self-effacing, in court he could dominate the proceedings with art and artifice, as an extract from his most well-known biography demonstrates (Marshall Hall's scales of justice act*).*

After his death the mantle of Marshall Hall fell on Sir Norman Birkett KC, an example of whose devastating cross-examination of an 'expert' witness is set out below (The loose union nut*).*

The charismatic orator is by no means rare on the other side of the Atlantic. The most outstanding was Clarence Darrow, part of whose speech in one of his lesser known, but quite extraordinary, cases is reproduced here (Attorney for the damned*). Contemporary advocacy, at least in this country, is bland by comparison.*

A burden of exceptional responsibility fell on the advocates at the Nuremberg trials at the end of the Second World War. Given the circumstances, the proceedings were conducted with a surprising degree of fairness. Responsibility for this rested in no small measure on the qualities of the judges, but the example set by the advocates contributed greatly. Extracts from the addresses of the principal English and American prosecutors are set out below (Never such slaughter.)

Captain-general of iniquity

Westminster Hall has seen many curious sights, but few as strange as the proceedings for the impeachment of a Governor-General of India which began at the bar of the House of Lords on 13 February 1788 and lasted more than seven years (although the total number of hours sat was only 149).

In 1750 at the age of 26 Warren Hastings had gone to Calcutta as a writer in the service of the East India Company. His abilities had caused him to rise rapidly to British Resident, member of the Council and Governor of Bengal. He became Governor-General in 1773. His achievements were great and he acquired a large, but for his day and circumstances not immense, fortune.

Unfortunately for Hastings, he incurred the wrath of Edmund Burke, one of the ablest lawyers and politicians of his day, who suspected him of corruption, or worse. Burke opened the trial with a speech[135] which has long been regarded as a cynosure of its type. Hilary St George Saunders, a former Librarian of the House of Commons, described his performance as follows:[136]

Burke required four days to open the case for the prosecution. The efforts he made were prodigious and did full justice to his reputation; but he preferred declamation to argument, and his speech throughout was that of a parliamentary orator, not of an advocate. It abounded in violent contrasts and flaming metaphor, in wide generalities and harrowing details, some of which caused sensitive ladies such as Mrs Sheridan to swoon. Every word of abuse which the orator could call to mind was made to serve, and

---

[135] *Burke's Speeches* (Bohn's British Classics), vol. 1.
[136] *Westminster Hall* (Michael Joseph, 1951), p. 274.

the accused was deluged with a roaring stream of vituperation which at first disconcerted him until he became used to it. No trick of the theatre, no device of oratory was disdained by Burke. He shouted, he whispered, he 'dropped his head in his hands a few minutes and towards the end was seized with a cramp in his stomach and was disabled from going on'. But not before he had delivered himself of a peroration which sent his audience, accustomed as they were to the set speech, the classical harangue, into ecstasies of admiration.

The following extracts give a fair impression of the whole:

... the crimes which we charge in these articles, are not lapses, defects, errors, of common human frailty, which, as we know and feel, we can allow for. We charge this offender with no crimes, that have not arisen from passions, which it is criminal to harbour; with no offences, that have not their root in avarice, rapacity, pride, insolence, ferocity, treachery, cruelty, malignity of temper; in short, in nothing, that does not argue a total extinction of all moral principle; that does not manifest an inveterate blackness of heart, died in grain with malice, vitiated, corrupted, gangrened to the very core. If we do not plant his crimes in those vices, which the breast of man is made to abhor, and the spirit of all laws, human and divine, to interdict, we desire no longer to be heard upon this occasion. Let everything that can be pleaded on the ground of surprise or error, upon those grounds be pleaded with success: we give up the whole of those predicaments. We urge no crimes, that were not crimes of forethought. We charge him with nothing that he did not commit upon deliberation; that he did not commit against advice, supplication, and remonstrance; that he did not commit against the direct command of lawful authority; that he did not commit after reproof and reprimand, the reproof and reprimand of those, who are authorised by the laws to reprove and reprimand him. The crimes of Mr Hastings are crimes not only in themselves, but aggravated by being crimes of contumacy. They were crimes not against forms, but against those eternal laws of justice, which are our rule and our birthright. His offences are not, in formal, technical language, but in reality, in substance, and effect, high crimes and high misdemeanours.

So far as to the crimes. As to the criminal, we have chosen him on the same principle, on which we selected the crimes. We have not chosen to bring before you a poor, puny, trembling delinquent, misled, perhaps, by those, who ought to have taught him better, but who have afterwards oppressed him by their power, as they had first corrupted him by their example. Instances there have been many, wherein the punishment of minor offences, in inferior persons, has been made the means of screening crimes of a high order, and in men of high description. Our course is different. We have not brought before you an obscure offender, who, when his insignificance and weakness are weighed against the power of the prosecution, gives even to public justice something of the appearance of oppression; no, my lords, we have brought before you the first man of India in rank, authority, and station. We have brought before you the chief of the tribe, the head of the whole body of eastern offenders; a captain-general of iniquity, under whom all the fraud, all the peculation, all the tyranny, in India, are embodied, disciplined, arrayed, and paid. This is the person, my lords, that we bring before you. We have brought before you such a person, that, if you strike at him with the firm and decided arm of justice, you will not have need of a great many more examples. You strike at the whole corps, if you strike at the head. . . .

Four days later Burke concluded with this peroration:

I, therefore, charge Mr Hastings with having destroyed, for private purposes, the whole system of government by the six provincial councils, which he had no right to destroy.

I charge him with having delegated to others that power which the act of Parliament had directed him to preserve unalienably in himself.

I charge him with having formed a committee to be mere instruments and tools, at the enormous expense of £62,000 per annum.

I charge him with having appointed a person their dewan,[137] to whom these Englishmen were to be subservient tools; whose name to his own knowledge, was by the general voice of India, by the general recorded voice of the Company, by recorded official transactions, by everything that can make a man known, abhorred, and detested, stamped with infamy; and with giving him the whole power which he had thus separated from the council-general, and from the provincial councils.

I charge him with taking bribes of Gunga Govin Sing.

I charge him with not having done that bribe service, which fidelity even iniquity requires at the hands of the worst of men.

I charge him with having robbed those people, of whom he took the bribes.

I charge him with having fraudulently alienated the fortunes of widows.

I charge him with having, without right, title, or purchase, taken the lands of orphans, and given them to wicked persons under him.

---

[137] The collector of revenues of an Indian state.

I charge him with having removed the natural guardians of a minor rajah, and with having given that trust to a stranger, Debi Sing, whose wickedness was known to himself and all the world; and by whom the Rajah, his family and dependants were cruelly oppressed.

I charge him with having committed to the management of Debi Sing three great provinces; and thereby, with having wasted the country, ruined the landed interest, cruelly harassed the peasants, burnt their houses, seized their crops, tortured and degraded their persons, and destroyed the honour of the whole female race of that country.

In the name of the Commons of England, I charge all this villainy upon Warren Hastings, in this last moment of my application to you.

My lords, what is it, that we want here to a great act of national justice? Do we want a cause, my lords? You have the cause of oppressed princes, of undone women of the first rank, of desolated provinces, and of wasted kingdoms.

Do you want a criminal, my lords? When was there so much iniquity ever laid to the charge of any one? No, my lords, you must not look to punish any other such delinquent from India. Warren Hastings has not left substance enough in India to nourish such another delinquent.

My lords, is it a prosecutor you want? You have before you the Commons of Great Britain as prosecutors; and, I believe, my lords, that the sun, in his beneficent progress round the world, does not behold a more glorious sight than that of men, separated from a remote people by the material bounds and barriers of nature, united by the bond of a social and moral community; all the Commons of England resenting, as their own, the indignities and cruelties that are offered to all the people of India.

Do we want a tribunal? My lords, no example of antiquity, nothing in the modern world, nothing in the range of human imagination, can supply us with a tribunal like this. My lords, here we see virtually in the mind's eye that sacred majesty of the Crown, under whose authority you sit, and whose power you exercise. We see in that invisible authority, what we all feel in reality and life, the beneficent powers and protecting justice of his Majesty. We have here the heir apparent to the Crown, such as the fond wishes of the people of England wish an heir apparent of the Crown to be. We have here all the branches of the royal family in a situation between majesty and subjection, between the sovereign and the subject, — offering a pledge in that situation for the support of the rights of the Crown and the liberties of the people, both which extremities they touch. My lords, we have a great hereditary peerage here; those, who have their own honour, the honour of their ancestors, and of their posterity, to guard; and who will justify, as they have always justified, that provision in the constitution, by which justice is made an hereditary office.

My lords, we have here a new nobility, who have arisen and exalted themselves by various merits, by great military services, which have extended the fame of this country from the rising to the setting sun: we have those, who by various civil merits and various civil talents have been exalted to a situation, which they well deserve, and in which they will justify the favour of their sovereign, and the good opinion of their fellow subjects; and make them rejoice to see those virtuous characters, that were the other day upon a level with them, now exalted above them in rank, but feeling with them in sympathy what they felt in common with them before. We have persons exalted from the practice of the law, from the place in which they administered high though subordinate justice, to a seat here, to enlighten with their knowledge, and to strengthen with their votes those principles which have distinguished the courts in which they have presided.

My lords, you have here also the lights of our religion; you have the bishops of England. My lords, you have that true image of the primitive Church in its ancient form, in its ancient ordinances, purified from the superstitions and the vices which a long succession of ages will bring upon the best institutions. You have the representatives of that religion, which says that their God is love, that the very vital spirit of their institution is charity; a religion, which so much hates oppression, that, when the God whom we adore appeared in human form, he did not appear in a form of greatness and majesty, but in sympathy with the lowest of the people, — and thereby made it a firm and ruling principle, that their welfare was the object of all government; since the person, who was the Master of Nature, chose to appear himself in a subordinate situation. These are the considerations, which influence them, which animate them, and will animate them, against all oppression; knowing that He, who is called first among them, and first among us all, both of the flock that is fed, and of those who feed it, made Himself 'the servant of all'.

My lords, these are the securities which we have in all the constituent parts of the body of this House. We know them, we reckon, we rest upon them, and commit safely the interests of India and of humanity into your hands. Therefore, it is with confidence, that, ordered by the Commons — I impeach Warren Hastings, Esq., of high crimes and misdemeanours.

I impeach him in the name of the Commons of Great Britain in Parliament assembled, whose Parliamentary trust he has betrayed.

I impeach him in the name of all the Commons of Great Britain, whose national character he has dishonoured.

I impeach him in the name of the people of India, whose laws, rights, and liberties he has subverted; whose properties he has destroyed, whose country he has laid waste and desolate.

I impeach him in the name, and by virtue of those eternal laws of justice, which he has violated.

I impeach him in the name of human nature itself, which he has cruelly outraged, injured, and oppressed in both sexes, in every age, rank, situation, and condition of life.

At the end Hastings was acquitted but was ordered to pay a substantial sum in costs. The East India Company provided him with a pension for his declining years. Perhaps the most balanced judgment is that of Lord Macaulay who wrote:

His principles were somewhat lax. His heart was somewhat hard. But though we cannot with truth describe him either as a righteous or as a merciful ruler, we cannot regard without admiration the amplitude and fertility of his intellect, his rare talents for command, for administration, and for controversy, his dauntless courage, his honourable poverty, his fervent zeal for the interests of State, his noble equanimity, tried by both extremes of fortune and never disturbed by either.[138]

Burke too in later years fell on hard times. As Thomas Paine famously observed of his performance in a Parliamentary debate, 'As he rose like a rocket, he fell like a stick'.[139]

Bardell v Pickwick

The style that would move a nineteenth-century jury would seem out of place today, as the following extract from that most famous of all literary trials illustrates.[140] Mr Pickwick is being sued for breach of promise of marriage.

The ushers again called silence, and Mr Skimpin proceeded to 'open the case'; and the case appeared to have very little inside it when he had opened it, for he

---

[138] 'Warren Hastings', in *Essays*.
[139] *Letter to the Addressors on the Late Proclamation*.
[140] Charles Dickens, *The Posthumous Papers of the Pickwick Club* (1836–7, revised 1867), ch. 34.

kept such particulars as he knew, completely to himself, and sat down, after a lapse of three minutes, leaving the jury in precisely the same advanced stage of wisdom as they were in before.

Serjeant Buzfuz then rose with all the majesty and dignity which the grave nature of the proceedings demanded, and having whispered to Dodson, and conferred briefly with Fogg, pulled his gown over his shoulders, settled his wig, and addressed the jury.

Serjeant Buzfuz began by saying, that never, in the whole course of his professional experience — never, from the very first moment of his applying himself to the study and practice of the law — had he approached a case with feelings of such deep emotion, or with such a heavy sense of the responsibility imposed upon him — a responsibility, he would say, which he could never have supported, were he not buoyed up and sustained by a conviction so strong, that it amounted to positive certainty that the cause of truth and justice, or, in other words, the cause of his much-injured and most oppressed client, must prevail with the high-minded and intelligent dozen of men whom he now saw in that box before him.

Counsel usually begin in this way, because it puts the jury on the very best terms with themselves, and makes them think what sharp fellows they must be. A visible effect was produced immediately; several jurymen beginning to take voluminous notes with the utmost eagerness.

The jury found for the plaintiff and awarded her £750 damages. The following exchange then took place between the disappointed defendant, Mr Pickwick, and his solicitors. Similar exchanges must have taken place on many occasions.

'Well, gentlemen', said Mr Pickwick.

'Well, sir', said Dodson; for self and partner.

'You imagine you'll get your costs, don't you, gentlemen?' said Mr Pickwick.

Fogg said they thought it rather probable. Dodson smiled, and said they'd try.

The office of Serjeant was intermediate in rank between King's Counsel and the outer (or utter) Bar. Serjeants had an exclusive right of audience in the Court of Common Pleas. This right was abolished in 1846 and the requirement that judges be appointed from among their number in 1875. In that year Mr Justice Lindley was the last English Serjeant to be appointed to the Bench. He died in 1921. The office lingered on in the person of the notable Irish Serjeant, A. M. Sullivan QC, who died in 1959.

Marshall Hall's scales of justice act

It is sometimes said that it is better to have a strong case than a clever lawyer. Nevertheless, a skilled advocate can ensure that even the weakest case is presented to its best advantage. The theatrical courtroom style of Sir Edward Marshall Hall KC snatched victory from disaster on many an occasion. A characteristic example was the trial of Edward Lawrence, a brewer and well-known local character.

Lawrence had left his wife to live with a beautiful barmaid. The police were called to the house and found her lying on the floor with a bullet wound in her right temple and a slight wound in her right arm. At one stage Lawrence said: 'I'm glad I did it. She is best dead: she drove me to it. You don't know what a wicked woman she has been.' Later he said: 'She shot herself'. The barmaid subsequently died and Marshall Hall was instructed to represent Lawrence at his trial for murder. The case against his client was not made any the easier in light of the fact that the revolver found on the defendant appeared to have been reloaded in order to conceal its having been fired twice. In the words[141] of Edward Marjoribanks, Marshall Hall's most celebrated biographer:

Marshall Hall made one of the most dramatic and masterly orations of his life, and for the first time performed the dramatic exhibition which came to be known as 'Hall's scales of justice act'. He began by admitting, and almost making capital out of, Lawrence's previous bad character. 'We are not trying this man for drink. We are not trying this man for immorality. We are not trying this man for error of judgment or human frailty. We are not trying him because, like a fool, he has left his wife and children for other women. One thing stands out in this case, and that is that his wife, in spite of the provocation, has not deserted him. When this awful trial is over, I hope there will be one verdict which you will see your way to find, a verdict of ''not guilty'' and thereby

---

[141] Edwards Marjoribanks MP, *The Life of Sir Edward Marshall Hall KC* (Victor Gollancz, 1929).

restore this man to his freedom. I trust he will make use of that freedom, and repay with that freedom the devotion of his wife and endeavour to devote the rest of his life to making her happy, and to making amends for the misery he has caused her in the past.'

He drew the portrait of the drunken, jealous woman in broad, eloquent phrases. Always jealous and violent, from the moment Lawrence had turned to other women she had become mad, and when, a few days after her last return, Lawrence ordered her out of the house, she was in a frenzy. 'She had taken that revolver down, knowing that her life with Lawrence was finished, and intending to finish Lawrence too. She was desperate, defiant, dangerous.' Then, dealing with the final tragedy, Marshall, seeking as he always did to make each juryman put himself into the place of the prisoner, took up the revolver. 'When he entered the room,' he said, 'he saw her pointing the revolver like this.' As he spoke, he pointed the revolver straight at the jury. 'He saw the hammer rising, as you may see it rising now as I pull the trigger. It was hard to pull, and it might have been that her arm was weakened by the injury of the first shot. It might have been that she was feeling the sting of that injury, and that it aroused all the worst passions in her beyond her control, and that she was then in the act of shooting him.'

Finally came the peroration in which he made the comparison of a trial of a man for his life with the weighing of a substance in a pair of scales. But the time-honoured simile became original and compelling with his dramatic treatment. With outstretched arms he illustrated his words by the swaying of his body and the gestures of his hands. 'It may appear that the scales of justice are first weighed on one side in favour of the prisoner, and then on the other against the prisoner. As counsel on either side puts the evidence in these two scales I can call to my fancy a great statue of justice holding those two scales with equally honest hands. As the jury watch the scales, they think for a moment that one scale, and then that the other, has fallen and then again that they are so level that they cannot make up their minds which was lower or higher. Then in the one scale, in the prisoner's scale, unseen by human eye, is placed that overbalancing weight, the weight of the presumption of innocence. When the balance is so struck that you cannot tell which pan is nearest the ground, then it is your duty to remember the invisible weight of that invisible substance — the right of every man to demand the acceptance of his innocence until he is proved guilty.... I will leave it in your hands. Try this case upon the evidence, and upon the evidence with the help of God.'

Mr Sherwood in his reply, constantly interrupted as he was by the judge, who was now obviously in favour of an acquittal, threw over his original demand for a verdict of 'murder' or nothing, and asked the jury for a verdict of 'manslaughter' if they were not satisfied as to murder.

The judge summed up in favour of the prisoner, being obviously impressed by his evidence. He had been more than doubtful as to the wisdom of the Criminal Evidence Act,[142] but in his summing up he boldly stated his conversion. 'If this was the only case I had ever tried,' he said, 'I would be thankful because of this change in the law. Had it been that this man's mouth had been shut, I do not think he could possibly have escaped at least a verdict of manslaughter.'

The jury retired and returned after 20 minutes. 'We have carefully gone through the evidence with honest sincerity,' the foreman said, 'and our verdict is one of "not guilty"'. Addressing the prisoner, Mr Justice Jelf said, 'Before I discharge you, I have to add a few words of advice to those which your brilliant counsel, I have no doubt, has already given you. You have had a most terrible lesson.... You have seen that your wife is ready to forgive you.... If you will turn over a new page in your life, you may yet have a happy time with your lawful wife and children, and then, perhaps, God will forgive you for the life you have led.... I earnestly trust that what I have said to you will bear fruit in your heart and in your life.'

It is sad to know that Lawrence learnt very little from his troubles, and paid no heed to the kindly judge's warning. For, only three days afterwards, he was charged with a violent assault on a man in an inn at Wolverhampton. However, his acquittal was received with wild enthusiasm in the town, for Marshall Hall had not merely convinced the judge and jury, but turned the tide of public opinion, which at first had been running strongly against the drunken and immoral brewer. Thus ended, according to Marshall Hall's expressed opinion, his greatest victory in a murder trial.

Marshall Hall was knighted in 1917 and died 10 years later.

The loose union nut

Outside fiction, witnesses are seldom 'destroyed' by a single question from a brilliant cross-examiner. However, a carefully thought-out question can sometimes cause irretrievable damage to a witness's credibility. So it was in the trial for murder of Alfred Arthur Rouse, in which Norman Birkett KC was instructed for the Crown.

---

[142] An Act of 1898 which permitted the accused to give evidence in his own defence. Before that it had been assumed that such an opportunity would merely be an invitation to perjury.

Two young men were walking back home from a dance in the early hours of Bonfire Night, 1930, when they turned a corner of a Northamptonshire lane to see a bright red glow in the distance and a hatless man climbing out of a ditch. After commenting that 'It looks as if someone has had a bonfire', the man went on his way, apparently uncertain in which direction to go.

The blaze turned out to be a Morris Minor car on fire. The car was owned by a 36-year-old commercial traveller. A police constable was called and the fire put out. At this point the body of a man was discovered in the driving seat. The car was traced to Rouse who was later identified as the hatless man. Rouse was an ex-soldier who had been badly wounded in France. He lived with his wife but had had numerous affairs with other women. After the fire Rouse had gone to his wife's home in London and then fled to Monmouthshire where he lived bigamously with a young woman who was pregnant by him. When he read about the fire in the papers Rouse realised that he would be identified and took a coach to London where he was arrested.

Rouse's story was that he had given a hitch-hiker a lift. Stopping the car to relieve himself he suggested to his passenger that he should meanwhile fill the petrol tank from a can. The man asked for a smoke. When Rouse next looked back the car was on fire. He left the scene in panic.

At the trial expert evidence was called by the prosecution to the effect that the petrol union nut had been loosened one turn. The defence countered by arguing that the fire might have started accidentally in any one of a number of ways. They called evidence from two 'expert' witnesses, one of whom had volunteered to give evidence. He was Arthur Isaacs, who described himself as an engineer and fire assessor. Birkett's first question[143] to Isaacs was the beginning of the end.

What is the coefficient of the expansion of brass?[144] — I am afraid I cannot answer that question off-hand.

---

[143] H. Normanton (ed.), *Trial of A. A. Rouse* (Notable British Trials series) (William Hodge & Co.).
[144] The coefficient of expansion of brass is 0.00001 075.

If you do not know, say so. What do I mean by the term? — You want to know what is the expansion of the metal under heat?

I asked you what is the coefficient of the expansion of brass? Do you know what it means? — Put that way, probably I do not.

You are an engineer? — I dare say I am. I am not a doctor, nor a crime investigator, nor an amateur detective. I am an engineer.

What is the coefficient of the expansion of brass? You do not know? — No, not put that way.

After some further questions about the effect of heat on metal and the loosening of nuts, Birkett turned to the witness's theory that the fire might have been started by the passenger's cigar while he was picking up the petrol tank at the front of the car.

Does it destroy your theory to hear that the can was at the back of the car? — I do not think so.

Would anything destroy your theory? Birkett retorted, as he resumed his seat.

After a retirement of only a quarter of an hour the jury returned a verdict of guilty. Shortly before being hanged Rouse confessed that he had throttled and then burnt the hitch-hiker, seemingly in order to fake his own death. To this end he admitted loosening the union joint. The identity of the victim was never established.

Birkett was appointed a judge of the King's Bench Division of the High Court in 1940 and, later, alternate to Lord Justice Lawrence, as a judge at the Nuremberg tribunal. He became a Lord Justice of Appeal in 1950 and was raised to the peerage in 1958, dying in 1962.

Attorney for the damned

The American attorney, Clarence Darrow, was not born to controversy. He made his name as a successful corporation lawyer and only later turned to the defence of workers in labour relations cases and thence to the criminal bar. Among his more famous cases was the Chicago trial of the Communists charged with conspiring to overthrow the American government by force, the 'monkey trial' in Dayton, Tennessee, when he defended the right of teachers to teach the theory of evolution, and the defence of the two young murderers, Leopold and Loeb.

Less well known, this side of the Atlantic at least, is the Sweet *case in Detroit in 1926.*

Dr Ossian H. Sweet was a gynaecologist who had worked under Madame Curie on the effects of radium. He was also black. Returning from Europe, he moved into a house in a predominantly white area along with his wife and two-year-old daughter. No doubt anticipating trouble, he brought with him 10 guns and a supply of ammunition. Trouble was not long in coming.

A white crowd gathered outside the house the first night but without disorder. The following night a larger crowd, estimated at several hundred, appeared and the police had to be called. In the house with Dr Sweet were his two brothers, Otis, a dentist, and Henry, a student. Shots were fired from the window of the Sweet house killing one white man and injuring another. The Sweets were arrested and charged with first-degree murder. For the defence, it was contended that the shots had been fired in self-defence. The prosecution relied on police evidence that there was no mob around the house at the time, but Darrow was able to cast doubt on this. The result was a direction for a mistrial.

At the retrial of Henry Sweet alone Darrow changed his tactics; he charged the jury with prejudice![145]

My friend [*the prosecutor*] says, gentlemen, that this isn't a race question. This is a murder case. We don't want any prejudice; we don't want the other side to have any. Race and color have nothing to do with this case. This is a case of murder.

I insist that there is nothing but prejudice in this case; that if it was reversed and 11 white men had shot and killed a black while protecting their home and their lives against a mob of blacks, nobody would have dreamed of having them indicted. I know what I am talking about, and so do you. They would have been given medals instead. Ten colored men and one woman are in this indictment, tried by 12 jurors, gentlemen. Every one of you are white, aren't you? At least you all think so. We haven't one colored man on this jury. We couldn't get one.

[145] Arthur Weinberg (ed.), *Attorney for the Damned* (Macdonald, 1957).

One was called and he was disqualified. You 12 white men are trying a colored man on race prejudice.

Now, let me ask you whether you are not prejudiced. I want to put this square to you, gentlemen. I haven't any doubt but that every one of you is prejudiced against colored people. I want you to guard against it. I want you to do all you can to be fair in this case, and I believe you will. A number of you have answered the question that you are acquainted with colored people. One juror I have in mind, who is sitting here, said there were two or three families living on the street in the block where he lives, and he had lived there for a year or more, but he didn't know their names and had never met them. Some of the rest of you said that you had employed colored people to work for you, are even employing them now. All right. You have seen some colored people in this case. They have been so far above the white people that live at the corner of Garland and Charlvoix that they can't be compared, intellectually, morally and physically, and you know it. How many of you jurors, gentlemen, have ever had a colored person visit you in your home? How many of you have ever visited in their homes? How many of you have invited them to dinner at your house? Probably not one of you. Now, why, gentlemen? There isn't one of you men but what knows just from the witnesses you have seen in this case that there are colored people who are intellectually the equal of all of you. Am I right? Colored people living right here in the city of Detroit are intellectually the equals and some of them superior to most of us. Is that true? Some of them are people of more character and learning than most of us. . . .

Now, why don't you individually, and why don't I, and why doesn't every white person whose chances have been greater and whose wealth is larger, associate with them? There is only one reason, and that is prejudice. Can you give any other reason for it? They would be intellectual companions. They have good manners. They are clean. They are all of them clean enough to wait on us, but not clean enough to associate with. Is there any reason in the world why we don't associate with them excepting prejudice? I think not one man of this jury wants to be prejudiced. It is forced into us almost from our youth, until somehow or other we feel we are superior to these people who have black faces.

Now, gentlemen, I say you are prejudiced. I fancy everyone of you is, otherwise you would have some companions amongst these colored people. You will overcome it, I believe, in the trial of this case. But they tell me there is no race prejudice, and it is plain nonsense, and nothing else.

Who are we, anyway? A child is born into this world without any knowledge of any sort. He has a brain which is a piece of putty; he inherits nothing in the way of knowledge or of ideas. If he is white, he knows nothing about color. He has no antipathy to the black. The black and the white both will live together and play together, but as soon as the baby is born we begin giving him ideas.

We begin planting seeds in his mind. We begin telling him he must do this and he must not do that We tell him about race and social equality and the thousands of things that men talk about until he grows up. It has been trained into us, and you, gentlemen, bring that feeling into this jury box.

You need not tell me you are not prejudiced. I know better. We are not very much but a bundle of prejudices anyhow. We are prejudiced against other people's color. Prejudiced against other men's religions; prejudiced against other people's politics. Prejudiced against people's looks. Prejudiced about the way they dress. We are full of prejudices. You can teach a man anything beginning with the child; you can make anything out of him, and we are not responsible for it. Here and there some of us haven't any prejudices on some questions, but if you look deep enough you will find them; and we all know it.

All I hope for, gentlemen of the jury, is this: that you are strong enough, and honest enough, and decent enough to lay it aside in this case and decide it as you ought to.

The jury returned a verdict of not guilty.

Darrow was as much reviled as admired and it is easy to pick out qualities and actions that might with hindsight have been amended, but his integrity, ability and reforming zeal cannot be doubted. The Supreme Court Justice, William O. Douglas, described him posthumously as follows:

Darrow was widely read and well versed in the humanities. His addresses sparkle with analogies, with historic examples, with figures of speech taken from the masters.

But his intellectual achievements were not the secret of his success. Darrow knew people. He ran the gamut of emotions in his jury speeches. His arguments are a full orchestration, carrying great power even in cold print. They must have been overwhelming as they came from his tongue. Yet he was not the flamboyant type. His words were the simple discourse of ordinary conversation. They had the power of deep conviction, the strength of any plea for fair play, the pull of every protest against grinding down the faces of the poor, the appeal of humanity against forces of greed and exploitation.

Darrow used the law to promote social justice as he saw it. Yet the law and the lawyers were to him reactionary forces. Their faces were usually turned backward. Great reforms came not from within the law but from without. It was not the judges and barristers who made the significant advances toward social justice. They were made in conventions of the people and in legislative halls. Yet Darrow, working through the law, brought prestige and honor to it during a long era of intolerance.[146]

Never such slaughter

But how is the advocate to conduct himself when the crimes he is charged to prosecute are of such enormity as to beggar the imagination?

When the victorious Allied armies swept into Germany in 1945 one of their first acts was to round up the defeated Nazi leaders responsible for the war and for the holocaust to which it gave rise. Winston Churchill, fearful of the charge of a 'show trial', would rather have seen them executed summarily on capture.[147] America, the dominant partner, thought otherwise and its view prevailed. There followed an unprecedented experiment in law making, the setting up of the International Military Tribunal at Nuremberg. The legality of the London Charter, upon which the Tribunal rested, did not go unchallenged. With hindsight, however, the trials probably did more good than harm and similar tribunals are in session even as this book is being prepared. Much of the credit for this must go to the outstanding lawyers involved as judges and advocates at Nuremberg.

Sir Hartley Shawcross, the Attorney-General of the Attlee Government, was Chief British Prosecutor. Robert H. Jackson, an Assistant Justice of the United States Supreme Court was Chief Counsel of the American team. Shawcross was an experienced criminal lawyer. Jackson, perhaps the lesser advocate, has been described[148] as 'a brilliant legal stylist and orator'.

---

[146] Foreword to Arthur Weinberg (ed.), *Attorney for the Damned* (Macdonald, 1957).

[147] See Ann and John Tusa, *The Nuremberg Trials* (Macmillan, 1983).

[148] H. Shawcross, *Life Sentence, The Memoirs of Hartley Shawcross* (Constable, 1995).

Jackson spoke first. He began his opening speech for the prosecution as follows:[149]

In the prisoners' dock sit 20-odd broken men. Reproached by the humiliation of those they have led, almost as bitterly as by the desolation of those they have attacked, their personal capacity for evil is forever past. It is hard now to perceive in these miserable men as captives the power by which as Nazi leaders they once dominated much of the world and terrified most of it. Merely as individuals their fate is of little consequence to the world.

What makes this inquest significant is that these prisoners represent sinister influences that will lurk in the world long after their bodies have returned to dust. We will show them to be living symbols of racial hatreds, of terrorism and violence, and of the arrogance and cruelty of power.... They have so identified themselves with the philosophies they conceived, and with the forces they have directed, that any tenderness to them is a victory and an encouragement to all the evils which are attached to their names. Civilization can afford no compromise with the social forces which would gain renewed strength if we deal ambiguously or indecisively with the men in whom those forces now precariously survive.

What these men stand for we will patiently and temperately disclose.... The catalog of crimes will omit nothing that could be conceived by a pathological pride, cruelty, and lust for power. These men created in Germany, under the *Führerprinzip*, a National Socialist despotism equalled only by the dynasties of the ancient East. They took from the German people all those dignities and freedoms that we hold natural and inalienable rights in every human being. The people were compensated by inflaming and gratifying hatreds towards those who were marked as scapegoats. Against their opponents, including Jews, Catholics, and free labor the Nazis directed such a campaign of arrogance, brutality, and annihilation as the world has not witnessed since the pre-Christian ages. They excited the German ambition to be a master race, which of course implies serfdom for others. They led their people on a mad gamble for domination. They diverted social energies and resources to the creation of what they thought to be an invincible war machine. They overran their neighbors. To sustain the master race in its war-making, they enslaved millions of human beings and brought them into Germany, where these hapless creatures now wander as displaced persons. At length, bestiality and bad faith reached such excess that they aroused the sleeping strength of imperilled Civilization. Its united efforts have ground the German war machine to

---

[149] This and all other extracts from the Nuremberg trial are taken from the *Trial of the Major War Criminals before the International Military Tribunal* (Nuremberg, 1947).

fragments. But the struggle has left Europe a liberated yet prostrate land where a demoralized society struggles to survive. These are the fruits of the sinister forces that sit with these defendants in the prisoners' dock....

Never before in legal history has an effort been made to bring within the scope of a single litigation the developments of a decade, covering a whole continent, and involving a score of nations, countless individuals, and innumerable events....

Before I discuss particulars of evidence, some general considerations which may affect the credit of this trial in the eyes of the world should be candidly faced. There is a dramatic disparity between the circumstances of the accusers and of the accused that might discredit our work if we should falter, in even minor matters, in being fair and temperate.

Unfortunately, the nature of these crimes is such that both prosecution and judgment must be by victor nations over vanquished foes. The worldwide scope of the aggressions carried out by these men has left but few real neutrals. Either the victors must judge the vanquished or we must leave the defeated to judge themselves. After the First World War we learned the futility of the latter course. The former high station of these defendants, the notoriety of their acts, and the adaptability of their conduct to provoke retaliation make it hard to distinguish between the demand for a just and measured retribution, and the unthinking cry for vengeance which arises from the anguish of war. It is our task, so far as is humanly possible, to draw the line between the two. We must never forget that the record on which we judge these defendants today is the record on which history will judge us tomorrow. To pass these defendants a poisoned chalice is to put it to our lips as well. We must summon such detachment and intellectual integrity to our task that this trial will commend itself to posterity as fulfilling humanity's aspirations to do justice....

If these men are the first war leaders of a defeated nation to be prosecuted in the name of the law, they are also the first to be given a chance to plead for their lives in the name of the law. Realistically, the Charter of this Tribunal, which gives them a hearing, is also the source of their only hope. It may be that these men of troubled conscience, whose only wish is that the world forget them, do not regard a trial as a favor. But they do have a fair opportunity to defend themselves — a favor which, when in power, they rarely extended even to their fellow countrymen. Despite the fact that public opinion already condemns their acts, we agree that here they must be given a presumption of innocence, and we accept the burden of proving criminal acts and the responsibility of these defendants for their commission.

When I say that we do not ask for convictions unless we prove crime, I do not mean mere technical or incidental transgression of international conventions. We charge guilt on planned and intended conduct that involves moral as well as legal wrong. And we do not mean conduct that is a natural and human, even if illegal, cutting of corners, such as many of us might well have committed had we been in the defendants' positions. It is not because they yielded to the normal frailties of human beings that we accuse them. It is their abnormal and inhuman conduct which brings them to this bar. . . .

We would also make clear that we have no purpose to incriminate the whole German people. We know that the Nazi Party was not put in power by a majority of the German vote. We know it came to power by an evil alliance between the most extreme of the Nazi revolutionists, the most unrestrained of the German reactionaries, and the most aggressive of the German militarists. If the German populace had willingly accepted the Nazi programme, no storm troopers would have been needed in the early days of the Party, and there would have been no need for concentration camps or the Gestapo, both of which institutions were inaugurated as soon as the Nazis gained control of the German State. Only after these lawless innovations proved successful at home were they taken abroad.

The German people should know by now that the people of the United States hold them in no fear, and in no hate. It is true that the Germans have taught us the horrors of modern warfare, but the ruin that lies from the Rhine to the Danube shows that we, like our Allies, have not been dull pupils. If we are not awed by German fortitude and proficiency in war, and if we are not persuaded of their political maturity, we do respect their skill in the arts of peace, their technical competence, and the sober, industrious and self-disciplined character of the masses of the German people. In 1933, we saw the German people recovering prestige in the commercial, industrial and artistic world after the setback of the last war. We beheld their progress neither with envy nor malice. The Nazi regime interrupted this advance. The recoil of the Nazi aggression has left Germany in ruins. The Nazi readiness to pledge the German word without hesitation and to break it without shame has fastened upon German diplomacy a reputation for duplicity that will handicap it for years. Nazi arrogance has made the boast of the master race a taunt that will be thrown at Germans the world over for generations. The Nazi nightmare has given the German name a new and sinister significance throughout the world, which will retard Germany a century. The German, no less than the non-German world, has accounts to settle with these defendants.

And he ended:

I am too well aware of the weakness of juridical action alone to contend that in itself your decision under this Charter can prevent future wars. Judicial action always comes after the event. Wars are started only on the theory and in the confidence that they can be won. Personal punishment to be suffered only in the event the war is lost will probably not be a sufficient deterrent to prevent a war while the war-makers feel the chances of defeat to be negligible. But the ultimate step in avoiding periodic wars which are inevitable in a system of international lawlessness, is to make statesmen responsible to law. And let me make clear that while this law is first applied against German aggressors, the law includes, and if it is to serve a useful purpose, it must condemn aggression by any other nations including those which sit here now in judgment. We are able to do away with domestic tyranny and violence and aggression by those in power against the rights of their own people only when we make all men answerable to the law. This trial represents mankind's desperate effort to apply the discipline of the law to statesmen who have used their powers of State to attack the foundations of the world's peace, and to commit aggression against the rights of their neighbours....

Civilization asks whether law is so laggard as to be utterly helpless to deal with crimes of this magnitude by criminals of this order of importance. It does not expect that you can make war impossible. It does expect that your juridical action will put the forces of international law, its precepts, its prohibitions and, most of all, its sanctions, on the side of peace, so that men and women of good will, in all countries, may have 'leave to live by no man's leave, underneath the law'.[150]

The evidence of the horrors of the Nazi regime adduced before the Tribunal was overwhelming; sometimes, as in the showing of the British film of the concentration camp at Buchenwald, intolerably so. In the course of his closing speech for the prosecution, Shawcross said of the defendants:

The total sum of the crime these men have committed — so awful in its comprehension — has many aspects. Their lust and sadism, their deliberate slaughter and degradation of so many millions of their fellow creatures that the imagination reels, are but one side of this matter. Now that an end has been put to this nightmare, and we come to consider how the future is to be lived, perhaps their guilt as murderers and robbers is of less importance and of less effect to future generations of mankind than their crime of fraud — the fraud by which they placed themselves in a position to do their murder and their robbery. That

---

[150] All we have of freedom, all we use or know —
   This our father bought for us long and long ago.
   Ancient right unnoticed as the breath we draw —
   Leave to live by no man's leave underneath the law.
('The Old Issue'). Kipling was quoted twice by Jackson in his statement.

is the other aspect of their guilt. The story of their 'diplomacy', founded upon cunning, hypocrisy and bad faith, is a story less gruesome but no less evil and deliberate. And should it be taken as a precedent of behaviour in the conduct of international relations, its consequences to mankind will no less certainly lead to the end of civilised society. Without trust and confidence between nations, without the faith that what is said is meant and what is undertaken will be observed, all hope of peace and security is dead. The Governments of the United Kingdom and the British Commonwealth, of the United States of America, of the Union of Soviet Socialist Republics and of France, backed by and on behalf of every other peace-loving nation of the world, have therefore joined to bring the inventors and perpetrators of this Nazi conception of international relations before the bar of this Tribunal. They do so, that these defendants may be punished for their crimes. They do so also, that their conduct may be exposed in all its naked wickedness, and they do so in the hope that the conscience and good sense of all the world will see the consequences of such conduct and the end to which inevitably it must always lead. Let us once again restore sanity and with it also the sanctity of our obligations towards each other.

And he ended:

Some, it may be, are more guilty than others; some played a more direct and active part than others in those frightful crimes. But when those crimes are such as you have to deal with here — slavery, mass murder and world war — when the consequences of the crimes are the deaths of over 20 million of our fellow men, the devastation of a continent, the spread of untold tragedy and suffering throughout the world, what mitigation is there that some took less part than others, that some were principals and others mere accessories? What matters it if some forfeited their lives only a thousand times whilst others deserved a million deaths?

In one way the fate of these men means little; their personal power for evil lies for ever broken; they have convicted and discredited each other and finally destroyed the legend they created round the figure of their leader. But on their fate great issues must still depend, for the ways of truth and righteousness between the nations of the world, the hope of future international cooperation in the administration of law and justice, are in your hands. This trial must form a milestone in the history of civilisation, not only bringing retribution to these guilty men, not only marking that right shall in the end triumph over evil, but also that the ordinary people of the world (and I make no distinction now between friend or foe) are now determined that the individual must transcend the State.

The State and the law are made for man, that through them he may achieve a fuller life, a higher purpose and a greater dignity. States may be great and powerful. Ultimately the rights of men, made as all men are made in the image of God, are fundamental. When the State, either because as here its leaders have lusted for power and place, or under some specious pretext that the end may justify the means, affronts these things, they may for a time become obscured and submerged. But they are immanent and ultimately will assert themselves more strongly still, their immanence more manifest. And so, after this ordeal to which mankind has been submitted, mankind itself — struggling now to re-establish in all the countries of the world the common, simple things — liberty, love, understanding — comes to this court and cries 'These are our laws — let them prevail'.

Jackson began his closing speech as follows:

It is impossible in summation to do more than outline with bold strokes the vitals of this trial's mad and melancholy record, which will live as the historical text of the twentieth century's shame and depravity.

It is common to think of our own time as standing at the apex of civilization, from which the deficiencies of preceding ages may patronizingly be viewed in the light of what is assumed to be 'progress'. The reality is that in the long perspective of history the present century will not hold an admirable position, unless its second half is to redeem its first. These two-score years in this twentieth century will be recorded in the book of years as some of the most bloody of all annals. Two world wars have left a legacy of dead which number more than all the armies engaged in any war that made ancient or medieval history. No half-century ever witnessed slaughter on such a scale, such cruelties and inhumanities, such wholesale deportations of peoples into slavery, such annihilations of minorities. The Terror of Torquemada pales before the Nazi Inquisition. These deeds are the overshadowing historical facts by which generations to come will remember the decade. If we cannot eliminate the causes and prevent the repetition of these barbaric events, it is not an irresponsible prophecy to say that this twentieth century may yet succeed in bringing the doom of civilization.

He concluded:

It is against such a background that these defendants now ask this Tribunal to say that they are not guilty of planning, executing, or conspiring to commit this long list of crimes and wrongs. They stand before the record of this trial as bloodstained Gloucester stood by the body of his slain King. He begged of the widow, as they beg of you: 'Say I slew them not.' And the Queen replied, 'Then say they were not slain. But dead they are.'

If you were to say of these men that they are not guilty, it would be as true to say there has been no war, there are no slain, there has been no crime.[151]

Of the 22 accused three (Schacht, Von Papen and Fritsche) were acquitted of all charges. Of the remainder, 13 were sentenced to death by hanging, one of whom, Hermann Goering, cheated the executioner by committing suicide.

Few advocates, we must hope, will have the opportunity to address a court on crimes of such magnitude again.

---

[151] Shawcross was later to comment of this peroration, 'None of the arts of the actor was on view. This was no dramatic declamation, but uttered calmly, in words of dignity and authority, the demand of a lawyer and statesman that law and justice should in the end prevail.' Op. cit. (note 142).

The Ostler's Hut, Lincoln's Inn

12. THE HIGH PROFESSION

or

The Life of a Lawyer

I will for ever at all hazards, assert the dignity, independence
and integrity of the English Bar without which impartial justice,
the most valuable part of the English constitution, can have no
existence. From the moment that any advocate can be permitted
to say that he will or will not stand between the Crown and the
subject arraigned in the court where he daily sits to practise,
from that moment the liberties of England are at an end.

Thomas Erskine in *R* v *Paine*.[152]

The choicest fruit
The privilege of an advocate
The less attractive task
No mere mouthpiece
Not entirely fiction
The country attorney ...
... and the City Silk

---

[152] See under *The choicest fruit*.

Judges in this country are drawn from the profession of advocate, formerly the bar alone but increasingly from the solicitors' branch also. It is as advocates that English judges learn their trade. This chapter looks at the life of the lawyer, its admirable as well as its less creditable faces.

Since the earliest days the barrister has had a vigorous appreciation of the need for independence in defence of his client's interests. It is difficult to attend a Bar mess dinner without hearing of an incident in which someone had to stand up to an overbearing judge. Since overbearingness is not the most obvious characteristic of the modern judge one suspects that many of the stories derive as much from folk memory as historical record; but the attitude is a healthy one.

The need for independence was very real in the eighteenth century when Thomas Erskine, under pressure from the mob, felt forced to assert in imperishable language 'the dignity, independence and integrity of the English bar' *(see under* The choicest fruit*). In a subsequent, associated trial Stewart Kyd expressed himself in equally forceful terms* (The privilege of an advocate*).*

Almost as important as his independence is the duty of the barrister to accept — subject only to availability and the absence of conflict — a brief from whosoever may wish to instruct him, as Lord Pearce noted only recently (The less attractive task*).*

*The flip side of a proper concern for his client is the temptation — particularly to the politically committed lawyer — to identify the client's interests too closely with his own. The dangers of this attitude were made clear by Mr Justice Crampton over a century and a half ago (*The temple of justice*), but it persists to this day.*

For centuries the life of a lawyer changed little. The result has been delay and cost to the client, perhaps most vividly depicted in fiction, as for example in Blackmore's Lorna Doone *(set in the seventeenth century) and Dickens's* Bleak House *(in the nineteenth). How glacially slow change can be in the law may be seen by comparing Dickens's account of an early nineteenth-century solicitor's office*

*(*Not entirely fiction*) with Reginald Hine's exquisite exercise in nostalgia for the firm with which he was given articles at the beginning of the twentieth century (*The country attorney . . .*). The chapter ends with a vignette of the appearance of a Queen's Counsel in a magistrates' court in the 1950s (. . . and the city Silk).*

A contemporary barrister's chambers may be bristling with fax machines and word processors, but his way of life, like that of the attorney, has changed in substance hardly at all. There is still little logic in the division between the two branches of the profession and, apart from a nod in the direction of conditional fees, almost nothing has been done in the past half century to improve access to the law for most people. Instead of reform the public has been offered a sterile debate about the wearing of wigs.

The choicest fruit

In England a defending barrister stands at the bar of the court, literally and metaphorically between his client and the tribunal. On occasion he has to assert his independence, even from the court itself.

The classic statement of the advocate's duty of independence is to be found in the remarks of one of the greatest of barristers, Thomas Erskine, at the trial of one of the greatest of libertarians, Thomas Paine.

Few individuals have had as much influence on the affairs of nations as Tom Paine. Variously a stay maker, mariner, schoolmaster, exciseman and tobacconist, he went to America where his widely read pamphlet, Common Sense, *was a match to the independence movement. After a patchy public career there he returned to England where he published another book,* The Rights of Man, *defending the French revolution.*

Arraigned for seditious libel, Paine prudently fled the country. Then at the height of his powers as an advocate, Erskine accepted the defence against the advice of his friends. During the course of a four-hour address[153] he offered this stirring defence of the role of the advocate.

... my name and character have been the topics of injurious reflection. And for what — only for not having shrunk from the discharge of a duty, which no personal advantage recommended, and which a thousand difficulties repelled. But, gentlemen, I have no complaint to make, either against the printers of those libels, nor even against their authors: the greater part of them, hurried perhaps away by honest prejudices, may have believed they were serving their country by rendering me the object of its suspicion and contempt and if there have been amongst them others who have mixed in it from personal malice and unkindness, I thank God I can forgive them also.

Little indeed did they know me, who thought that such calumnies would influence my conduct: I will for ever at all hazards, assert the dignity, independence and integrity of the English Bar without which impartial justice, the most valuable part of the English constitution, can have no existence. From the moment that any advocate can be permitted to say that he will or will not stand between the Crown and the subject arraigned in the court where he daily sits to practise, from that moment the liberties of England are at an end. If the advocate refuses to defend, from what he may think of the charge or of the defence, he assumes the character of the judge; nay, he assumes it before the hour of judgment; and in proportion to his rank and reputation, puts the heavy influence of perhaps a mistaken opinion into the scale against the accused, in whose favour the benevolent principle of English law makes all presumptions, and which commands the very judge to be his counsel. ...

If I were to ask you, gentlemen of the jury, what is the choicest fruit that grows upon the tree of English liberty, you would answer: security under the law. If I were to ask the whole people of England the return they looked for at the hands of government, for the burdens under which they bend to support it, I should still be answered: security under the law; or, in other words, an impartial administration of justice. So sacred, therefore, has the freedom of trial been ever held in England — so anxiously does Justice guard against every possible bias in her path — that if the public mind has been locally agitated upon any subject in judgment, the forum has either been

---

[153] *R* v *Paine* (1792) 22 St Tr 357, 412

changed or the trial postponed. The circulation of any paper that brings, or can be supposed to bring, prejudice, or even well-founded knowledge, within the reach of a British tribunal, on the spur of an occasion, is not only highly criminal, but defeats itself, by leading to put off the trial which its object was to pervert. . . .

Milton wisely says, that a disposition in a nation to this species of controversy, is no proof of sedition or degeneracy, but quite the reverse. . . . In speaking of this subject, he rises into that inexpressibly sublime style of writing, wholly peculiar to himself. He was, indeed, no plagiary from anything human; he looked up for light and expression, as he himself wonderfully describes it, by devout prayer to that great Being, who is the source of all utterance and knowledge; and who sendeth out His seraphim with the hallowed fire of His altar to touch and purify the lips of whom He pleases. 'When the cheerfulness of the people', says this mighty poet, 'is so sprightly up, as that it has not only wherewith to guard well its own freedom and safety, but to spare, and to bestow upon the solidest and sublimest points of controversy and new invention, it betokens us not degenerated nor drooping to a fatal decay, but casting off the old and wrinkled skin of corruption, to outlive these pangs and wax young again, entering the glorious ways of truth and prosperous virtue, destined to become great and honourable in these latter ages. Methinks I see in my mind a noble and puissant nation rousing herself, like a strong man after sleep, and shaking her invincible locks; methinks I see her as an eagle mewing her mighty youth, and kindling her undazzled eyes at the full midday beam; purging and unscaling her long-abused sight at the fountain itself of heavenly radiance; while the whole noise of timorous and flocking birds, with those also that love the twilight, flutter about, amazed at what she means, and in their envious gabble would prognosticate a year of sects and schisms'.

Gentlemen, what Milton only saw in his mighty imagination, I see in fact; what he expected, but which never came to pass, I see now fulfilling: methinks I see this noble and puissant nation, not degenerated and drooping to a fatal decay, but casting off the wrinkled skin of corruption to put on again the vigour of her youth. And it is, because others as well as myself see this, that we have all this uproar: France and its constitution are the mere pretences. It is because Britons begin to recollect the inheritance of their own constitution, left them by their ancestors: it is because they are awakened to the corruptions which have fallen upon its most valuable parts, that forsooth the nation is in danger of being destroyed by a single pamphlet.

Erskine concluded:

Gentlemen, I have but a few more words to trouble you with: I take my leave of you with declaring, that all this freedom which I have been endeavouring to assert, is no more than the ancient freedom which belongs to our own inbred constitution: I have not asked you to acquit Thomas Paine upon any new lights, or upon any principle but that of the law, which you are sworn to administer: — my great object has been to inculcate, that wisdom and policy, which are the parents of the government of Great Britain, forbid this jealous eye over her subjects; and that, on the contrary, they cry aloud in the language of the poet, adverted to by Lord Chatham on the memorable subject of America, unfortunately without effect,

Be to their faults a little blind,
Be to their virtues very kind;
Let all their thoughts be unconfin'd,
And clap your padlock on the mind.

Engage the people by their affections, — convince their reason — and they will be loyal from the only principle that can make loyalty sincere, vigorous, or rational, — a conviction that it is their truest interest, and that their government is for their good. — Constraint is the natural parent of resistance, and a pregnant proof, that reason is not on the side of those who use it. You must all remember Lucian's pleasant story: Jupiter and a countryman were walking together, conversing with great freedom and familiarity upon the subject of heaven and earth. — The countryman listened with attention and acquiescence, while Jupiter strove only to convince him; — but happening to hint a doubt, Jupiter turned hastily around and threatened him with his thunder. 'Ah! ah!' says the countryman, 'now, Jupiter, I know that you are wrong; you are always wrong when you appeal to your thunder.'

This is the case with me — I can reason with the people of England, but I cannot fight against the thunder of authority.

Gentlemen, this is my defence for free opinions. With regard to myself, I am, and always have been, obedient and affectionate to the law: — to that rule of action, as long as I exist, I shall ever give my voice and my conduct; but I shall ever, as I have done today, maintain the dignity of my high profession, and perform as I understand them, all its important duties.

Erskine's eloquence counted for nothing. Even before the Attorney-General could rise to respond the foreman of the jury announced

that no reply was necessary: the verdict was one of guilty. Paine was sentenced (ineffectively) to be outlawed.

Despite being carried shoulder high from the Guildhall to Saint Paul's Cathedral Erskine's defence of Paine cost him the post of Attorney-General to the Prince of Wales. Eventually, however, he rose to become Lord Chancellor, a position he filled with not half as much distinction as he had displayed as a barrister.

In revolutionary France Paine was elected as a deputy to the National Convention, where he incurred the wrath of Robespierre by voting with the Girondists for the King to be treated mercifully. He was imprisoned for 11 months before being released and restored to his seat. Paine died in squalor in New York, his last book, The Age of Reason, *having displeased George Washington. William Cobbet stole his bones but they were lost on his death.*

The privilege of an advocate

Paine's book, The Age of Reason, *was also the subject of a prosecution, not by the government this time but by the Society for the Suppression of Vice and Immorality; and not for a seditious libel but for a blasphemous libel. The book's publisher, Thomas Williams, found himself in the dock prosecuted by — of all people — Erskine.*

Defending Williams was Stewart Kyd. In his early years a political radical, Kyd had once been committed to the Tower for high treason, from which indictment he had been discharged without trial. At the trial of Williams Kyd had to stand up to the judge, Lord Kenyon, who had also presided over Paine's case.

When Kyd turned his attention to some of the Bible stories in the book Kenyon said, 'I cannot sit in this place and hear this kind of discussion'. Kyd memorably retorted:[154]

---

[154] *R v Williams* (1797) 26 St Tr 653, 687–8.

My lord, I stand here on the privilege of an advocate in an English court of justice: this man has applied to me to defend him; I have undertaken his defence; and I have often heard your lordship declare that every man had a right to be defended; I know no other mode by which I can seriously defend him against this charge, than that which I am now pursuing; if your lordship wish to prevent me from pursuing it, you may as well tell me to abandon my duty to my client at once.

To which Lord Kenyon responded somewhat churlishly:

Go on, sir.

Williams was convicted and given a year's hard labour.

The less attractive task

One of the noblest traditions of the English Bar is the duty it takes upon itself to defend all who seek its services, whatever their reputation and whatever the opinion of the barrister himself.

Nearly 200 years after the trial of Tom Paine Lord Pearce quoted Erskine's words in that case and observed:[155]

It is easier, pleasanter and more advantageous professionally for barristers to advise, represent or defend those who are decent and reasonable and likely to succeed in their action or their defence than those who are unpleasant, unreasonable, disreputable, and have an apparently hopeless case. Yet it would be tragic if our legal system came to provide no reputable defenders, representatives or advisers for the latter; and that would be the inevitable result of allowing barristers to pick and choose their clients. It not infrequently happens that the unpleasant, the unreasonable, the disreputable and those who have apparently hopeless cases turn out after a full and fair hearing to be in the right. It is also a judge's (or jury's) solemn duty to find that out by a careful and unbiased investigation. This they simply cannot do, if counsel do not (as at

---

[155] *Rondel* v *Worsley* [1967] 3 All ER 993,1029.

present) take on the less attractive task of advising and representing such persons however small their apparent merits.

The decision of the House upheld the ancient immunity of a barrister from suit. How relevant that immunity is today is another matter.

No mere mouthpiece

Nearly as pernicious as the advocate who spurns the 'unworthy' defendant is the one who, for political or ideological reasons, too ardently identifies himself with his client's cause. He is not a new phenomenon.

Daniel O'Connell (known in Ireland as the Liberator) was a successful barrister and a fighter for Irish independence. He formed an association which was instrumental in obtaining Catholic emancipation. He became a Member of Parliament and founded the Repeal Association, which sought to end the Union with England. In 1844 he was sentenced, along with others, to 14 weeks' imprisonment for conspiracy to raise sedition. He appealed against this conviction on a variety of grounds (some of which, such as the incorrect naming of a juryman, being quite fanciful to modern eyes). His appeal was unsuccessful, but in the course of the hearing Mr Justice Crampton found it necessary to address these words to defence counsel.[156]

Now, as the learned counsel[157] has been so good as to remind the judges of their duties, I am sure he will not take it ill of me, if I remind him that he has taken rather a narrow view of the duties of counsel upon a criminal trial. The learned counsel said the advocate's first duty was to his client, the second to himself, and the third to the public. His client was entitled to all that the counsel's zeal and ability could effect. He was bound to maintain his own independence with

---

[156] *R v O'Connell* (1844) 7 ILR 261, 312.
[157] Mr Whiteside QC.

all due respect to the Bench, and he was bound to assert the rights and liberties of the public: and all these duties the counsel in this case has, no doubt, ably discharged. Now, I do not quarrel with the learned counsel that he casts all these duties upon the counsel; but I do say, that the British advocate has still higher duties to regard; his duties as a man and as a Christian are paramount to all other considerations.

This court in which we sit is a temple of justice; and the advocate at the Bar, as well as the judge upon the Bench, are equally ministers in that temple. The object of all equally should be the attainment of justice; now justice is only to be reached through the ascertainment of the truth, and the instrument which our law presents to us for the ascertainment of the truth or falsehood of a criminous charge is the trial by jury; the trial is the process by which we endeavour to find out the truth. Slow and laborious, and perplexed and doubtful in its issue that pursuit often proves; but we are all — judges, jurors, advocates and attorneys — together concerned in this search for truth: the pursuit is a noble one, and those are honoured who are the instruments engaged in it. The infirmity of human nature, and the strength of human passion, may lead us to take false views, and sometimes to embarrass and retard rather than to assist in attaining the great object; the temperament, the imagination and the feelings may all mislead us in the chase, — but let us never forget our high vocation as ministers of justice and interpreters of the law; let us never forget that the advancement of justice and the ascertainment of truth are higher objects and nobler results than any which in this place we can propose to ourselves. Let us never forget the Christian maxim, 'That we should not do evil that good may come of it'. I would say to the advocate upon this subject, — let your zeal be as warm as your heart's blood, but let it be tempered with discretion and with self-respect; let your independence be firm, uncompromising, but let it be chastened by personal humility; let your love of liberty amount to a passion, but let it not appear to be a cloak for maliciousness....

Another doctrine broached by another eminent counsel I cannot pass by without a comment. That learned counsel described the advocate as the mere mouthpiece of his client; he told us that the speech of the counsel was to be taken as that of the client; and thence seemed to conclude that the client only was answerable for its language and sentiments.

Such, I do conceive, is not the office of an advocate. His office is a higher one. To consider him in that light is to degrade him. I would say of him as I would say of a member of the House of Commons — he is a representative, but not a delegate. He gives to his client the benefit of his learning, his talents and his judgment; but all through he never forgets what he owes to himself and to others. He will not knowingly misstate the law — he will not wilfully misstate the facts, though it be to gain the cause for his client. He will ever bear in mind that if he be the advocate of an individual, and retained and remunerated (often inadequately) for his valuable services, yet he has a prior and perpetual retainer on behalf of truth and justice; and there is no Crown or other licence which in any case, or for any party or purpose, can discharge him from that primary and paramount retainer.

On release from prison O'Connell fell out with the Young Ireland movement. He died three years later in Genoa.

Not entirely fiction

This fictional description[158] of a nineteenth-century attorney's office needs no introduction. It probably came pretty close to the mark.

In the ground-floor front of a dingy house, at the very furthest end of Freeman's Court, Cornhill, sat the four clerks of Messrs Dodson and Fogg, two of his Majesty's Attorneys of the Courts of King's Bench and Common Pleas at Westminster, and solicitors of the High Court of Chancery: the aforesaid clerks catching as favourable glimpses of Heaven's light and Heaven's sun, in the course of their daily labours, as a man might hope to do, were he placed at the bottom of a reasonably deep well; and without the opportunity of perceiving the stars in the day-time, which the latter secluded situation affords.

The clerks' office of Messrs Dodson and Fogg was a dark, mouldy, earthy-smelling room, with a high wainscotted partition to screen the clerks from the vulgar gaze: a couple of old wooden chairs: a very loud-ticking clock: an almanack, an umbrella-stand, a row of hat-pegs, and a few shelves, on which were deposited several ticketed bundles of dirty papers, some old deal boxes with paper labels, and sundry decayed stone ink bottles of various shapes and sizes.

In 1827 Dickens himself became a clerk to the law firm of Edward Blackmore in South Square, Gray's Inn. The building stands there today.

---

[158] Charles Dickens, *The Posthumous Papers of the Pickwick Club* (1836–7, revised 1867), ch. 20.

The country attorney ...

The following extract is taken from that minor masterpiece of legal literature, Reginald Hine's Confessions of an Uncommon Attorney.[159] *Hine was articled in 1901 and the book illustrates how little things had changed in the course of half a century since Dickens's days. (It contains, incidentally, one of the longest sentences in modern literature.)*

My good fortune lay in the fact that, for 35 years, first under articles, then as assistant solicitor, I was attached to one of the oldest firms in the land, that of Messrs Hawkins & Co. of Hitchin. Some day my history of that firm, from 1591 onwards, will be published; and it would be a pity to quote at large from it now. But the best of my days were spent half doing my duty in a state of life into which it had not pleased God to call me, and by the good nature of my master and father-in-the-law, William Onslow Times, I devoting the other half to the discovery of manuscripts for the history of a royal and ancient manor.

For the sort of life I had in mind to follow, the conditions were ideal. The office in Portmill Lane (sometimes, in pleasant banter, styled Chancery Lane) was housed in a comely Jacobean building. It had two front doors, and several bolt-holes or back doors. A stranger, ringing the bell, would be puzzled by the lack of any apparent welcome. Somewhat mysteriously, the door would open, but only half an inch, the catch being released by a wired device, worked by a clerk far too busy and superior to descend from his high engrossing stool. If the stranger entered at his peril, and, in his ignorance, asked to see 'Mr Hawkins', he was once again abashed. 'Sorry you can't, he died in 1877.' But there was a deferred welcome within, and strangers became clients, and clients developed into friends.

It would not be correct to describe the interior as comely. Like most lawyers' offices (but why, why, why!) the rooms — littered with files, the dust of ages upon them — looked dishevelled and untidy. The wallpapers were of the mock varnished and grained pine in favour a century before, though if you explored with a penknife you might light upon five or six other specimens, each more attractive than the one above. The windows were made to open; but a ponderous legalistic atmosphere hung about the chambers: a curious conglomerate of

---

[159] (J. M. Dent and Sons Ltd, 1945).

parchment, sealing wax, corroding ink, calf bindings, stale tobacco, escaping gas, and myriad decaying matters. But very soon one became 'part and parcel' of all this; one accepted, one even liked one's surroundings; they were all of a piece with the antiquity of the firm; one was proud to be able to smell one's way back to Elizabethan times.

Then there were other attractions. One's fancy was caught by the double doors of some of the principal rooms, an inner door of baize, warranted to muffle the guiltiest of intimate confessions. The room I occupied possessed a secret chamber, opened by a hidden spring in the wall, large enough to conceal a confidential clerk if earshot evidence of a ticklish interview were needful. Everywhere one came upon cupboards, some of them undisturbed for centuries, filled with family skeletons and other surprising things. One of the first I opened contained the reports and the account books of the celebrated McAdam (1756–1836), whom the firm, as clerks to the local Turnpike Trusts, had called in to 'macadamise' and improve the Hitchin-to-Welwyn and Hitchin-to-Bedford roads.

In another cupboard I came upon a marked catalogue of the sale of Byron's furniture and books, and I remembered that on 13 July 1824 his funeral cortège passed through Hitchin, with a black slave and a Greek attendant, and that some of Hawkins & Co.'s clients had been privileged, for one memorable moment, to take up the precious casket enshrining the poet's heart, and hold it in their hands, and that one of the women friends was 'scandalously reported to have kissed it'. Tied up with a bundle of title-deeds in another cupboard I found two letters from the Cromwellian and Restoration poet Andrew Marvell, written when member for Hull in 1670, and complaining that no one could expect promotions, spiritual or temporal, unless he made his court to the King's mistress, the Duchess of Cleveland.

On a shelf in that same cupboard, deep in dust, reposed the draft of a Bill introduced into the House of Commons in 1770, forbidding any woman 'to impose upon, seduce, or betray into Matrimony any of His Majesty's subjects by means of scent, paints, cosmetic washes, artificial teeth, Spanish wool, iron stays, hoops, high-heeled shoes, or bolstered hips'. Any marriage so contrived was to be null and void. . . .

In two shelved recesses of my room, lingered the remains of the original library; and to a bibliophile like myself it gave perpetual pleasure to gaze upon its lordly folios — Star Chamber reports, High Commission Court reports, manuscript books of precedents compiled by dead-and-gone practitioners, and a hundred others. And how I loved to run my hands over their ribbed spines and calf and vellum bindings! But sometimes I would dislodge a huge tome, shake off the top inch of Jacobean and Georgian dust from the open window on to the surprised heads of those walking the street below, and settle down beside the fire to read. Most of all I liked to dip into Coke upon Littleton marvelling at the misguided talent of that young poet who, doomed to take up law, turned this very learned and laborious treatise into rhyming couplets. One marvelled, too, at the bastard Law-French, in which most of the early black-letter reports were written, and that it should have continued for so long. During the interregnum, Cromwell, that master of vernacular English, had his dictatorial way. But no sooner was he dead than the customary language was revived. 'The law', said Richard North, 'is scarce expressible in English.' With that acid comment the lawyers of England heaved a sigh of relief at the Restoration, and once again, in reporting, it was possible to concoct sentences like the famous one of 1631 so dearly beloved of our profession: *Il ject un brickbat a le dit Justice que narrowly mist.*[160]

A flight of stairs led from this room into two attics, where often in busy idleness I would apply a remedy 'aganis' my own ignorance, for the boxes and the shelves contained nearly all I needed to know of my adopted town and of those who, in their brief day and generation, had sojourned in it. In summer it was stifling under the roof, for the windows refused to open, and at each movement, however stealthy, clouds of dust would arise. But like Sir Henry Chauncy, the first historian of my county, I could always spend fascinated hours in 'the study of old ledger-books, the ransacking of mouldy parchments, and examining over-worn and blind records', and I never tired of spying into the history of the foremost Hertfordshire families.

Once you were able to prise open the narrow wooden boxes — so reminiscent of coffins — there, when the dust had died away, there it all was, from the cradle to the grave; extracts of baptism from the parish register, pedigree notes and achievements of arms on vellum, the first stilted essays 'much after' Cicero and Addison submitted to the family tutor and preserved by doting parents, college reports of a later date, bills 'for sumptuose clothing and banquettings' incurred at Oxford or Cambridge, the resettlement of the estate at 21, batches of love letters, letters of a more scandalous character from the black sheep of the family, which 'family skeletons', if brought to the light of day, had to be tactfully reinterred, myself retaining a funny-bone just for remembrance, settlements upon mistresses, maintenance of natural children, abductions, seductions, blackmailings, breaches of promise, letters in dishonourable exile from the uttermost parts of the earth, first at frequent, then at infrequent, intervals, fading at last into silence; records of the more reputable members of the family; their pre-arranged matches with heiresses of estates that marched with their own; the begetting of sons and heirs; household account

---

[160] For the full report see chapter 9.

books vividly reflecting their style and manner of life; farming accounts accompanied in many a box by advisory letters or the essays on the *Management of Hogs* (1769), or the *Essay on Manures* (1804), or the *General View of the Agriculture of Hertfordshire* (1804), by Arthur Young who, despite his experimental knowledge, and with the authority of the Board of Agriculture behind him, farmed at a heavy loss nearby at North Mimms; notes of evidence taken in the squire's private 'justice room'; calendars and notes of cases heard at Quarter Sessions; voluminous accounts of expenditure over the honourable but much-to-be-avoided office of High Sheriff, with hundreds of pounds to pay for hogsheads of port for the gentry and barrels of strong beer for the javelin-men, the ringers and the link-men, tobacco and snuff for the prisoners, sirloins of beef, capons, sack, and music for the judge's lodgings, and five guineas for printing the Assize sermon; still more voluminous accounts of those aspiring landowners who ventured to stand for the county, with not hundreds but thousands of pounds to fork out in alehouses and market ordinaries on the Tom, Dick, and Harry 40-shilling freeholders (two guineas for a plumper) for the securing of their votes; records of a more retired, country-house character in the squire's mature and later years the catalogue of his growing library, correspondence with Kent or Capability Brown in home-made attempts at landscape gardening, game, archery, and pigeon-shooting books, hunting diaries, the making or enlargement of parks, the marrying off of daughters, and at the latter end the solemn last will and testament not only signed but sealed, the last Polonius-like instructions to the son and heir, the last bedside words of farewell to the family retainers, the ejaculation *in articulo mortis* of those pious sentiments which the family chaplain would quote and enlarge upon in the funeral sermon, to be printed in due time with double lines of mourning on each tearful, laudatory page.

And so, with the hatchment of arms by ancient custom suspended from the window of the death-chamber, and subsequently borne aloft in the carefully marshalled procession to the church, and the family coach and the deceased's charger draped in black, another Hertfordshire squire would be gathered to his fathers, proclamation would be made for his heirs, and another wooden box of muniments would be opened for the next 'estate-holder' by the solicitors in Portmill Lane.

Reginald Hine FSA, FRHistS (1883–1949) was born in Baldock, Hertfordshire, the third son of a farmer. An antiquarian and local historian of note, his Confessions *were published in 1945.*

... and the City Silk

The highest rank of barrister is that of Queen's Counsel, or Silk (after the material of his or her gown). A QC has the right to sit 'within the bar' of the court, unlike an 'utter barrister', so called because he sits outside the bar of the court. Francis Bacon was the first QC, receiving his patent in 1596.

This mid-twentieth century description[161] of the entry of leading counsel into the court of a Metropolitan Stipendiary Magistrate comes from the pen of one of the more colourful Metropolitan magistrates' clerks, with whom the editor once had the privilege of working.

When the King's Counsel stalked into court with his junior his nod to anyone whose face seemed familiar was meant to be friendly but appeared condescending. As he took his seat his hands would make a movement behind him as though involuntarily adjusting the gown he was accustomed to wear in more exalted courts. He addressed the magistrate in a confidential way. Leaning forward and speaking in a quiet tone which said very plainly, 'Well, here we are, old chap. You and I know each other very well. We speak the same language. We can soon get the little matter cleared up satisfactorily between us.'

His affability extended to the witnesses, whether they were for him or against him. He coaxed them into saying what he wanted them to say, stroking them along and purring happily as he got the desired answers. He didn't lose his equanimity when he came up against a blank wall or received the lie direct, although a tiny grimace or a slight gesture might express his regret for the unreasonableness of human beings.

When it became apparent that he was fighting a lost cause he might, if he thought his image would suffer from association with defeat, decide to give his junior an opportunity to justify his fee and hurry off to keep another appointment, but he might admit with the frankness a great man should be capable of when circumstances are adverse, that his cause was indeed lost, and then wax eloquent with a masterly plea in mitigation of the offence. Before leaving he would often look into the gaoler's office for a few words and a cup of tea with the sergeant gaoler and the matron, both of whom knew him when

---

[161] Stanley French, *Crime Every Day* (Barry Rose Law Publishers, 1976).

he was trying his prentice hand on behalf of petty thieves and common assaulters with a legal aid certificate issued to a solicitor who was too busy to appear for them himself.

There were exceptions, but generally speaking the 'Silks' who came so impressively to my courts were models of good manners, bonhomie, tact and competence and their visits were stimulating and enjoyable.

The Middle Temple Gardens

13.   THE LIFE OF THE LAW

or

The Law And Justice

... the path of the law is strewn with examples of open and shut
cases which, somehow, were not; of unanswerable charges
which, in the event, were completely answered; of inexplicable
conduct which was fully explained; of fixed and unalterable
determinations that, by discussion, suffered a change.

Mr Justice Megarry in *John* v *Rees*.[162]

The Bashi-Bazouks, the SS and the NKVD

---

[162] See under The Fount Of Justice.

The judicial oath requires judges to dispense, not justice, but 'justice according to law'. But what is justice and whence comes the law?

THE FOUNT OF JUSTICE

We like to call the buildings in which judges sit courts of justice. Some States even boast of having ministers of justice (although experience suggests that this title affords no guarantee of superior performance). The Concise Oxford Dictionary *defines 'just' as 'acting or done in accordance with what is morally right or fair', yet no two people will necessarily agree on what is morally right or fair in any given situation. Justice, like mercy, is what might be called an irreducible concept: it cannot be helpfully defined further.*

As Baron Rolfe reminded us in the early nineteenth century:

> ... if we lived for a thousand years instead of about sixty or seventy, and every case was of sufficient importance, it might be possible, and perhaps proper ... to raise every possible inquiry as to the truth of statements made.... In fact mankind finds it to be impossible.[163]

A similar point was made in a characteristically forthright way by the American advocate, Clarence Darrow, when he said to a judge:

> If there is such a thing as justice it could only be administered by one who knew the inmost thoughts of the man to whom he was meting it out. Aye, who knew the father and mother and the grandparents and the infinite number of people back of him. Who knew the origin of every cell that went into the body, who could understand the structure and how it acted. Who could tell how the emotions that sway the human being affected that particular frail piece of clay. It means more than that. It means that you must appraise every influence that moves men, the civilization where they live, and all society which enters into the making of the child or the man! If your Honor can do it — if you can do it you are wise, and with wisdom goes mercy.[164]

---

[163] (1810) 2 Camp 391.
[164] Closing argument in the Leopold and Loeb trial, 1924. Arthur Weinberg, *Attorney for the Damned* (Macdonald, 1957).

Mr Justice Megarry, as he then was, questioned the term 'natural justice':

... among most savages there is no such thing as justice in the modern sense. In a state of nature, self-interest prevails over any type of justice known to civilisation; the law of the jungle is power, not justice. Nor am I clear what the word 'natural' adds to the word 'justice'. It cannot be intended to indicate the antithesis of 'unnatural justice', which would indeed be an odd concept; I imagine that it is intended to suggest justice that is simple or elementary, as distinct from justice that is complex, sophisticated and technical.

The term 'natural justice' has often been used by eminent judges, and although Mr Justice Maugham said that it 'is, of course, used only in a popular sense', I would prefer to regard it as having become something of a term of art. To extract the quintessence of the process of justice is, indeed, notoriously difficult. 'The ideas of natural justice', said Mr Justice Iredell, 'are regulated by no fixed standard; the ablest and the purest men have differed on the subject.'

But, as Sir Robert Megarry also made clear, there are recognised minimum standards of fairness in the conduct of litigation and the courts will resist any attempts at limiting them. When a member of a university was deprived of his degrees without being given an opportunity to defend himself Mr Justice Fortescue said:[165]

The laws of God and man both give the party an opportunity to make his defence, if he has any. I remember to have heard it observed by a very learned man upon such an occasion, that even God himself did not pass sentence upon Adam, before he was called upon to make his defence. 'Adam (says God) where art thou? Hast thou eaten of the tree, whereof I commanded thee that thou shouldest not eat?' And the same question was put to Eve also.... Even if the law permits the principles of natural justice to be effectually excluded by suitable drafting, I would not readily construe the rules as having achieved this result unless they left me in no doubt that this was the plain and manifest intention.

---

[165] *Fountaine* v *Chesterton* (1968) 112 SJ 690, *The Times*, 20 August 1968.

Put a little differently, I would say that if there is any doubt the applicability of the principles of natural justice will be given the benefit of that doubt. The cry, 'That isn't fair' is to be found from earliest days, in nursery, street and school alike; and those who wish to confer on the committee or other governing body of a club or association a power to act unfairly or arbitrarily in a derogation of a common and universal expectation must make it plain beyond a peradventure that this has been done.

Litigants and even lawyers have been known to bridle at observing the rules designed to assure a fair trial. Megarry dealt with such objections as follows:[166]

It may be that there are some who would decry the importance which the courts attach to the observance of the rules of natural justice. 'When something is obvious,' they may say, 'why force everybody to go through the tiresome waste of time involved in framing charges and giving an opportunity to be heard? The result is obvious from the start.'

Those who take this view do not, I think, do themselves justice. As everybody who has anything to do with the law well knows, the path of the law is strewn with examples of open and shut cases which, somehow, were not; of unanswerable charges which, in the event, were completely answered; of inexplicable conduct which was fully explained; of fixed and unalterable determinations that, by discussion, suffered a change. Nor are those with any knowledge of human nature who pause to think for a moment likely to underestimate the feeling of resentment of those who find that a decision against them has been made without their being afforded any opportunity to influence the course of events.

If pure justice, then, is the preserve of the angels mere mortals must content themselves with their rights at law.

WHAT IS LAW?

That great defender of the common law, Sir Edward Coke, proudly claimed that:[167]

---

[166] *John v Rees* [1969] 2 All ER 274, 309.
[167] *The First Part of the Institutes of the Laws of England* (1628).

Reason is the life of the law, nay the common law itself is nothing else but reason.

The American judge, Oliver Wendell Holmes, writing three centuries later, countered more realistically:[168]

The life of the law has not been logic: it has been experience. The felt necessities of the time, the prevalent moral and political theories, intuitions of public policy, avowed or unconscious, even the prejudices which judges share with their fellow-men, have had a good deal more to do than the syllogism in determining the rules by which men should be governed.

This was echoed by Lord Justice Du Parcq when he observed:

The common law of this country has been built up, not by the writings of logicians or learned jurists, but by the summings-up of judges of experience to juries consisting of plain men, not usually students of logic, not accustomed to subtle reasoning, but endowed, so far as my experience goes, as a general rule, with great common sense, and if an argument has to be put in terms which only a schoolman could understand, then I am always very doubtful whether it can possibly be expressing the common law.[169]

For his part Lord Scarman put in a bid for principle:[170]

It is, of course, a judicial commonplace to proclaim the adaptability and flexibility of the judge-made common law. But this is more frequently proclaimed than acted on. The mark of the great judge from Coke through Mansfield to our day has been the capacity and the will to search out principle, to discard the detail appropriate (perhaps) to earlier times and to apply principle in such a way as to satisfy the needs of his own time. If judge-made law is to survive as a living and relevant body of law, we must make the effort, however inadequately, to follow the lead of the great masters of the judicial art.

---

[168] *The Common Law* (1881).

[169] *Smith* v *Harris* [1939] 3 All ER 960, 967. Schoolmen were theologians renowned for the subtlety of their reasoning.

[170] *Gillick* v *West Norfolk and Wisbech Area Health Authority*. See *A view so much out of date* in chapter 7.

But it is perhaps too much to elevate principle as the main arbiter of judicial decision-making. Elsewhere in this volume we find Oliver Wendell Holmes admitting:[171]

General propositions do not decide concrete cases. The decision will depend on a judgment or intuition more subtle than any articulate major premise.

And Lord Halsbury added:[172]

A case is only authority for what it actually decides. I entirely deny that it can be quoted for a proposition that may seem to follow logically from it. Such a mode of reasoning assumes that the law is necessarily a logical code, whereas every lawyer must acknowledge that the law is not always logical at all.

That the law is not an exact science was judicially acknowledged some two centuries ago. A party to litigation had successfully placed a bet of £50 on whether a decree of the Court of Chancery would be reversed on appeal to the House of Lords. When the gambler went to court to recover his winnings Lord Mansfield had to rule on whether the wager was a contract void for illegality. His judgment was candid. It began:[173]

... the law of England would be a strange science indeed if it were decided upon precedents only. Precedents serve to illustrate principles, and to give them a fixed certainty. But the law of England, which is exclusive of positive law, enacted by statute, depends upon principles; and these principles run through all the cases according as the particular circumstances of each have been found to fall within the one or other of them.

... it would be very hard upon the profession, if the law was so certain, that everybody knew it: the misfortune is that it is so uncertain, that it costs much money to know what it is, even in the last resort. ... From my own memory of this cause, if there ever was uncertainty in any case it was in this.

When a nice question therefore is depending, it may be a point upon which even persons in the profession may differ; and if

---

[171] *Lochner* v *New York*, 198 US 45 (1906). See *Liberty perverted* in chapter 6.
[172] *Quinn* v *Leatham* [1901] AC 495.
[173] *Jones* v *Randall* (1774) 1 Cowp 37.

either they or any two other persons bet about the decision, provided there be no fraud or colour in the case, I see no reason why they should not do so. The present case being of that sort, and not being prohibited by any positive law nor contrary to any principle of sound policy or morality, I do not think we are at liberty to prevent the plaintiff from bringing his action to recover the money he has won.

We must assume that at least some of these remarks were made tongue in cheek.

The greater part of the law is now in the form of Acts of Parliament, but much of it remains uncodified. This is not necessarily a drawback, as Lord Chief Justice Cockburn once pointed out:[174]

Whatever disadvantages attach to a system of unwritten law, and of these we are fully sensible, it has at least this advantage, that its elasticity enables those who administer it to adapt it to the varying conditions of society, and to the requirements and habits of the age in which we live, so as to avoid the inconsistencies and injustice which arise when the law is no longer in harmony with the wants and usages and interests of the generation to which it is immediately applied.

THE PROBLEM OF INTERPRETATION

If the common law had in truth been as flexible as Cockburn claimed it would not have been necessary for Parliament to produce an abundance of legislation to correct its faults and remedy its deficiencies. Why, then, if so much care has been spent in carefully formulating the law should it sometimes be so difficult to fathom?

At the heart of statute law lies the question of how the courts should interpret the legislator's wishes as recorded in an Act of Parliament. The problem is illuminated by the following speech of Lord Simon in a case concerning the right to political asylum.

---

[174] *Wason* v *Salter* (1868) LR 4 QB 73, 93.

The Bashi-Bazouks, the SS and the NKVD

A Taiwanese citizen was detained under the aliens legislation pending extradition to the United States of America. He sought his release by seeking a writ of habeas corpus, which was refused. He appealed unsuccessfully to the Court of Appeal and then to the House of Lords. The House held by a majority that the appeal should be dismissed: Lord Simon of Glaisdale thought otherwise.[175] Although obviously concerned at the implications of his decision, he believed that the issue of substance should be resolved by politicians and not judges. Simon's speech illustrates graphically the problems involved in the interpretation of statutes.

Taiwan (formerly called by its Portuguese name of Formosa) is a large island off the mainland of China. Its population is of mixed origin; but it was principally settled from mainland China after the Ming Empire was overrun by the Manchus in the seventeenth century. In 1683 the island fell to the Ch'ing (Manchu) Empire and became part of Fukien Province; in 1886 it became a separate province of China. In 1895 China ceded Taiwan to Japan; but after the Japanese defeat in 1945 Taiwan was handed over to the Chinese Nationalist government (under generalissimo Chiang Kai-Shek), pursuant to the Cairo Agreement of 1943. The Nationalist government thereafter suffered a succession of defeats by Chinese Communist armies on the mainland; and during 1949–50 a stream of Nationalist troops, government officials and other refugees, numbering some 2 million persons, poured into Taiwan, which, indeed, became thereafter the main effective territory of the Nationalist government; though, according to the evidence filed in this case, that government claims to be the rightful government of all China and to be perpetually at war with the Communist government on the mainland. It has maintained martial law in Taiwan continuously since 1949.

Today Taiwan contains two major populations — 12 million of native Taiwanese origin and about 2 million of recent mainland origin. An independence movement arose during the 1960s claiming to represent the native Taiwanese majority; it is now called the World United for Formosan Independence ('WUFI'). This resistance movement does not apparently have a common political ideology but it is united in asserting that the Nationalist government is unrepresentative of its sole authentic body of subjects (the Taiwanese) and that it is oppressive and corrupt. The independence movement

---

[175] *Tzu-tsai Cheng* v *Governor of Pentonville Prison* [1973] 2 All ER 204, 210.

is at one in seeking the overthrow of the Nationalist government. The evidence contains allegations of a massacre of about 20,000 Taiwanese in 1947, and of continuing summary imprisonments and suppression of civil liberties.

Your Lordships have no means of knowing how far such allegations are justified, nor is such knowledge necessary for the decision of this appeal; the mere fact that there is a large organised party making such allegations and agitating against a hated regime constitutes the classic situation in which offences of a political character are committed. It appears that resistance to the regime takes the form of a partisan movement in Taiwan itself and of organised groups of exiles. They claim that the detested government is only able to maintain itself in power owing to the political, military, diplomatic and economic support of the government of the United States. By 1970 Chiang Kai-Shek's son, Chiang Ching Kuo, was 'Vice-Premier' of the Nationalist government in Taiwan, and was regarded as his aged father's 'heir apparent'. In his evidence before the chief metropolitan stipendiary magistrate the appellant described Chiang Ching-Kuo as, in addition, 'head of the secret police and also responsible for the execution of about 200 political prisoners each year in Taiwan'. He added: 'I regarded him as the symbol of the regime oppressive to the Taiwanese'. In 1970 Chiang Ching-Kuo visited the United States: his opponents regarded this visit as being for the purpose of strengthening United States support for his regime.

The appellant was born in Taiwan in about 1937. It appears that during his teens he became opposed to the Chiang Kai-Shek regime. After some military incident which is left obscure he decided to go into exile. He went to the United States, where he had a distinguished academic career, culminating in his qualification and practice as an architect. There are about 10,000 Taiwanese in the United States; and, from his arrival, the appellant became politically active in the United States branch of WUFI; by 1970 he had become its executive secretary. In evidence before the chief metropolitan stipendiary magistrate the appellant described the organisation's long-term objective as 'to overthrow Chiang Kai-Shek's regime and to establish a free and democratic Republic of Taiwan'. A secondary, short-term, immediate, objective was to try to change the American government's policy towards Taiwan.

On 24 April 1970 the appellant took part in a demonstration outside the hotel where Chiang Ching-Kuo was staying during his visit to the United States. The appellant had leaflets for distribution. These denounced both the Nationalist government and Chiang Ching-Kuo personally; but they also included passages protesting against United States support for the Taiwan regime — for example:

It is our urgent plea that the United States discontinue its support of the Chiang regime and refrain from providing the Chinese Nationalists with weapons of terror. . . . These weapons are ultimately aimed at suppressing the legitimate aspirations of the people of Taiwan.

The question of attempting to assassinate Chiang Ching-Kuo during his visit had been discussed in the executive committee of the United States branch of WUFI, but rejected. However, during the demonstration the appellant's brother-in-law, Peter Huang, drew a pistol and fired, though without causing injury. The appellant was observed to be conducting a diversionary campaign: and it was later given in evidence in the United States that he was implicated in procuring the pistol which Peter Huang had used. Both the appellant and Peter Huang were indicted for attempted murder. Peter Huang pleaded 'Guilty'. The appellant pleaded 'Not guilty', but was convicted.

He was remanded for sentence on bail, but failed to appear, having fled the country. He was extradited from Sweden in the summer of 1972 but, having fallen ill during the journey to the United States, he was landed in this country, where he was ultimately detained pursuant to the Aliens Order 1953. The United States requested his extradition, and on 30 November 1972 the chief metropolitan stipendiary magistrate ordered him to be detained pending extradition. The appellant then applied in the Queen's Bench Division for a writ of habeas corpus, which was refused. The Divisional Court gave leave to appeal to your Lordships' House, the question of law being whether the appellant's extradition crime was an offence of a political character within the meaning of section 3(1) of the Extradition Act 1870. Counsel for the respondent contends that it was not — on the grounds that the appellant's offence was against the criminal code of the United States, whereas his political dispute was not with the United States but with Chiang Kai-Shek's government. The appeal therefore depends on the meaning of the words 'offence . . . of a political character' in section 3 (1) of the Extradition Act 1870. . . .

It is significant that the phrase 'of a political character', which recurs almost obsessively through the Act, is not defined. 'Fugitive criminal' is defined to mean 'any person accused or convicted of an extradition crime committed within the jurisdiction of any foreign state who is in or is suspected of being in some part of Her Majesty's dominions'. Parliament has therefore contemplated the escape of a person who, like the appellant, had been actually convicted of an extradition crime; though providing that he should not be extradited if the offence in respect of which of his surrender is demanded was one of a political character. 'Extradition crime' is defined as 'a crime which, if committed in England or within English jurisdiction would be one of the crimes described in the first schedule to the Act'. Schedule 1 sets out the list of extradition crimes. They include attempt to murder and other serious crimes. They do not include such crimes as treason, sedition or lèse-majesté; this indicates that 'offence . . .

of a political character' does not mean merely the type of political offence which is necessarily committed against the State seeking extradition, since such offences are in any event unscheduled crimes. Here is an important internal linguistic guide to interpretation.

THE FIRST OR 'GOLDEN' RULE OF CONSTRUCTION

English law provides a number of guides to statutory interpretation, or 'canons of construction'. A difficulty arises that various canons could return conflicting answers; since English law has not yet authoritatively established any complete hierarchy among the canons. Fortunately, this presents no difficulty in the instant case; because all the many relevant canons of statutory construction in question here return the same answer — in favour of the appellant's construction.

What Maxwell calls 'the first and most elementary rule of construction' is that (except in technical legislation) it is to be assumed the words and phrases are used in their ordinary and natural meaning. Moreover:

> It is a corollary to the general rule of literal construction that nothing is to be added to ... a statute unless there are adequate grounds to justify the inference that the legislature intended something which it omitted to express.

'It is a strong thing [*said Lord Mersey*] to read into an Act of Parliament words which are not there and, in the absence of clear necessity, it is a wrong thing to do.' If Parliament had intended to say 'offence ... of a political character against (or in respect of) the foreign State demanding such surrender' nothing would have been easier than to have inserted such words. Since they are not there it is not for the courts to supply them.

This primary rule of construction is so fundamental that it is sometimes called the golden rule. It was so stated by Baron Parke:

> It is a very useful rule, in the construction of a statute, to adhere to the ordinary meaning of the words used ... unless that is at variance with the intention of the legislature, to be collected from the statute itself, or tends to any manifest absurdity or repugnance, in which case the language may be varied or modified, so as to avoid such inconvenience, but no further.

The primary or golden canon of construction, always potent, is particularly so in two sets of circumstances. First, if Parliament is likely to have envisaged the actual forensic situation, she will use plain words in the expectation that the courts will, in pursuance of the primary canon of construction, apply them to that situation in the way that Parliament intended. Secondly, if Parliament considers that it is difficult to frame a definition which may not either go too far or fall too short in various situations (whether envisaged or merely hypothetical), Parliament will use plain words in the expectation that the courts will apply them in their natural sense (without omissions or additions) to various forensic situations as they occur.

Did Parliament in 1870 envisage the situation that, say, an attempt on the life of a ruling figure of State A might be made in the territory of State B? It seems highly likely. In the third quarter of the last century various movements liable to use violent methods to overturn established authority were notoriously operating internationally — from Mazzini's republican nationalists to the anarchists. There had been a number of recent attempts to assassinate heads of State, members of their families or prominent ministers, many successful. Such persons were frequently at risk abroad, either on business in diplomatic congress, or on holiday at the watering places which they frequented.

It is not to be thought that the British Parliament in 1870 approved political violence, whether committed in the assassin's home country or abroad. Nevertheless, the privilege of asylum for offences, however atrocious, of a political character was paramount; and this country never included in any extradition treaty the *attentat* clause pioneered by Belgium in 1856.

But, even if Parliament or her draftsman did not have the instant forensic situation in contemplation, the primary rule of construction that plain words should be given their ordinary, literal and natural meaning, without addition or omission, is still of even more than ordinary potency. In advisedly refraining from defining a crucial phrase in the statute Parliament left it to the courts to apply the statutory words to forensic situations as they arose, in the expectation that they would be so applied in their ordinary, natural and literal sense without addition or omission. The difficulty of providing a definition of crimes which were to be non-extraditable because they were of a political character was already notorious. By 1870 France had entered into 53 extradition treaties, as compared with this country's three. All the French treaties (including those entered into during the dictatorship of Napoleon III, against whose life several attempts had been made) contained an exception for political offences (*'crimes ou délits politiques'*); and in none was the concept defined, France leaving it entirely to the State to whom the extradition request was made to decide whether the offence was of a political character: such evidence is available to show the facts which must be assumed to have been within the contemplation of the legislature when the statute was passed. . . .

By reason of this primary and golden rule, therefore, the words 'offence . . . of a political character' must be read in their natural ordinary and literal sense, without the addition of the words 'against (or in respect of) the foreign State demanding such surrender', which are not in the Act. Asked whether the appellant's crime was an 'offence ... of a political character', even the most harassed commuter from Clapham would, I think undoubtedly answer, 'Of course'. Indeed, I cannot conceive that it would occur to anyone except a lawyer that the appellant's offence could possibly be described as other than of a political character.

But this is too harsh a reflection on the law. Legal analysis, in fact, returns the same answer as common sense. Oppenheim's *International Law* has a chapter significantly entitled 'Principle of 'non-extradition of political criminals'. Oppenheim wrote:

> Although the principle became, and is generally recognised that political criminals should not be extradited, serious difficulties exist concerning the conception of 'political crime' ... many writers consider a crime 'political' (i) if committed from a political motive, others call 'political' (ii) any crime committed for a political purpose; again, others recognise such a crime only as 'political' (iii) as was committed both from a political motive and at the same time for a political purpose; and, thirdly, some writers confine the term 'political crime' to (iv) certain offences against the State only, such as high treason, lèse-majesté and the like.
>
> So far as the 1870 Act is concerned, (iv) cannot be the meaning, since these are not scheduled extradition crimes at all. Such crimes may be included in 'offence ... of a political character', especially for the purpose of the second limb of section 3(1) of the 1870 Act. But 'offence ... of a political character' cannot be confined to such crimes. Therefore, except for those who favour this fourth (excluded) category, no jurist stipulates that the political character of the crime must be judged vis-à-vis the State seeking extradition. The appellant satisfies the most exacting relevant test, namely (iii) his crime was committed both from a political motive and for a political purpose. So the leading jurists in this field would concur with the man in the street that the appellant's crime was 'an offence ... of a political character'.

CONSTRUCTION ACCORDING TO HISTORICAL SETTING AND THE MISCHIEF RULE

A second leading canon of statutory construction reinforces here the primary or golden rule that words of a statute are to be read in their natural and ordinary sense, without omission or addition, unless some secondary meaning must be preferred, or some omission or addition must be made, in order to make sense of the provision. This second canon of construction consists in ascertaining, first, the general situation in which Parliament was legislating and, secondly, the particular situation for which Parliament was providing a remedy. These are really different aspects of the same canon of construction; though the former is sometimes called construction according to 'historical setting', the latter 'the mischief rule'.

Historical examination can leave no doubt what was Parliament's object and attitude in enacting section 3(1). In other than exceptional cases, criminal law operates territorially only. A foreigner who commits an extradition crime abroad does not infringe the English criminal code. Nevertheless, the 1870 Act conferred on the Crown the right to implement by Order in Council treaties stipulating that persons who had committed crimes abroad and taken refuge here might be handed over to the State where the crime was committed, in return for that State reciprocally engaging to hand over to Her Majesty's government persons who had committed crimes in this country and taken refuge in the territory of that other power. The general purpose of the Act is therefore not difficult to discern: as it was to enable States to cooperate in the suppression of crime. But from the general power of extradition and in derogation from this purpose of international cooperation in the suppression of crime, Parliament, in conformity with general international law, made an exception. Perpetrators of extradition crimes were nevertheless not to be extradited if their offence was of a political character. Why should Parliament have made such an exception? The explanation was given by my noble and learned friend, Lord Reid:

> In reading the Act of 1870 one is entitled to look through mid-Victorian spectacles. Many people then regarded insurgents against Continental governments as heroes intolerably provoked by tyranny, who ought to have asylum here, although they might have destroyed life and property in the course of their struggles. But, although such views may have given rise to section 3(1) of the Act of 1870, I do not think that its scope can be limited to such cases. We cannot inquire whether a fugitive criminal was engaged in a good or a bad cause. A fugitive member of a gang who committed an offence in the course of an unsuccessful putsch is as much within the Act as the follower of a Garibaldi; but not every person who commits an offence in the course of a political struggle is entitled to protection. If a person takes advantage of his position as an insurgent to murder a man against whom he has a grudge, I would not think that that could be called a political offence. So it appears to me that the motive and purpose of the accused in committing the offence must be relevant, and may be decisive. It is one thing to commit an offence for the purpose of promoting a political cause, and quite a different thing to commit the same offence for an ordinary criminal purpose.

If, as Lord Reid says, the motive and purpose of the offence is relevant and may be decisive, the appellant's was certainly an offence of a political character.

The insight of my noble and learned friend is fully borne out by an examination of the preceding history. Even Lord Castlereagh, no friend of subversives, denounced in 1816 the practice of handing over political refugees. Garibaldi and Kossuth, criminals in the eyes of the absolute governments of Europe, had been subjects of wild enthusiasm on their visits to London; and it is inconceivable that this country would have handed the former over to King Bomba on the ground that he had been responsible for the death, not of a Neapolitan, but of an Austrian, soldier or official in the Kingdom of the two Sicilies. Only a few years before the 1870 Act there had occurred the Orsini affair. Orsini was an Italian republican follower of Mazzini who had thrown a bomb at Napoleon III. He was discovered to have had links with some Italian refugees in London and the explosives had been made in England. In response to French protests Palmerston proposed to introduce a Conspiracy to Murder Bill to make it a felony, instead of merely a misdemeanour, to plot in England to murder someone abroad. This aroused such indignation that Palmerston, normally a highly popular and powerful minister, suffered Parliamentary defeat, and his government fell.

Then again, the reason why Great Britain had only three extradition treaties by 1870, as against France's 53, was because of the difficulty of getting the necessary enabling Bill through Parliament, in view of that body's jealousy of any infringement of this country's traditional freedom of political asylum. None of the three treaties or enabling Acts contained any express reservation relating to political crimes. This was because Parliament took it for granted that the government would not hand over criminals whose offence was of a political character or who were liable to be tried or punished for such an offence if handed over for some other extradition crime; and that was the way the treaties were in fact operated. . . .

Against such an historical background it is impossible to suppose that Parliament intended section 3(1) to be construed other than as benevolently in favour of the fugitive offender: certainly an artificially narrow construction is quite inadmissible.

It was suggested on behalf of the respondent, that the intention behind section 3(1) was the fear that a fugitive offender might not get a fair trial if he were handed over to the very government against whom he had offended politically. I cannot accept this. First, 'the intention of Parliament must be deduced from the language used'. Secondly, by international law a fugitive offender was not to be handed over if he would not get a fair trial in the country seeking extradition, whether his offence was political or not. Thirdly, it is absurd to suppose the legislature contemplated that, though someone in the position of the appellant would get a fair trial in the United States, President Lincoln's assassin, say, would not.

329

PRESUMPTION AGAINST CHANGES IN THE COMMON LAW

International lawyers were not unanimous whether comity required a State to extradite offenders against the criminal law of a foreign State; but the overwhelming modern view is that any international obligation to extradite is imperfect, needing treaty to perfect it. There can be no question, though, what answer the English common law returned: no English authority had the right to extradite. This was indeed the inevitable result of the following fundamental principles of English common law: (1) no one can be deprived of his liberty except for an offence against English law; (2) this liberty is vindicated by the writ of habeas corpus, statute in this respect merely embodying the common law; (3) criminal law being (other than exceptionally) territorial, an offence against a foreign criminal code is no offence against English law; (4) therefore anyone taken into custody for the purpose of delivery to a foreign State in respect of an offence against the criminal code of that foreign State could secure his release by habeas corpus proceedings.

A fugitive offender against the criminal law of a foreign State being thus protected by the common law from arrest for the purpose of extradition, the Extradition Act 1870 and the Orders in Council implementing it were necessarily in derogation from the common law. It follows that the positive powers under the Act should be given a restrictive construction and the exceptions from those positive powers a liberal construction. Even if it were otherwise permissible to read section 3(1) as allowing the implication that 'offence ... of a political character' refers only to an offence which is of a political character as regards the State seeking extradition, the presumption against changes in the common law would preclude such an implication and demand the construction proposed by the appellant. The construction proposed by the respondent cannot possibly be said to be a 'necessary' implication from the language of the statute, nor can it possibly be said that Parliament has expressed 'with irresistible clearness' the intention that the political character of the offence should be limited to the politics of the State seeking extradition.

Since the common law, as so often, favours the freedom of the individual, the rules enjoining 'strict construction of a penal statute' or of a provision in derogation of liberty merely reinforce the presumption against change in the common law.

PRESUMPTION IN FAVOUR OF CONFORMITY WITH INTERNATIONAL LAW

... A case has occurred which is indistinguishable from the instant. In 1934 two Croatians named Pavelic and Kwaternik were alleged to be implicated in the murder of King Alexander of Yugoslavia and M. Barthou, the French Foreign

Minister, in Marseilles while the King was on a State visit to France. There were other, incidental victims. The alleged assailants fled to Italy, and the French government requested their extradition. The extradition treaty between France and Italy of 1870 excluded political crimes from the category of extraditable offences; and the accused pleaded before the Court of Appeal of Turin that the alleged crimes were of a political nature. This plea was upheld.

The report of the case to which your Lordships were referred might be susceptible of the suggestion that the case depended purely on the provision in the Italian Criminal Code defining 'political crime'. But the original report makes it clear that this was not so.... If the respondent were right in his construction of the English Act, Pavelic's alleged complicity in the murder of M. Barthou was an 'offence of a political character', but not his alleged complicity in the murder of King Alexander. Yet extradition was refused unconditionally by the Italian court and not conceded on condition that proceedings should only be taken in respect of King Alexander's death....

Just as international law precluded Pavelic's extradition for the alleged murder of King Alexander in France, so it also precludes the appellant's extradition for the attempted murder of Chiang Ching-Kuo in the United States; and the 1870 Act should be construed accordingly, in the absence of contrary indication.

PRESUMPTION AGAINST ANOMALY OR ABSURDITY

This presumption is an application of the canon of statutory construction enjoining an interpretation most agreeable to justice and reason. 'An intention to produce an unreasonable result is not to be imputed to a statute if there is some other construction available'. This is, it is true, a secondary canon of construction, subordinate to the 'golden' rule that the words of a statute should prima facie be read in their ordinary, natural and literal sense, without addition or omission; but in the instant case the presumption against anomaly and absurdity reinforces the 'golden' rule, and precludes the interpretation advocated by the respondent, whereby the political character of the offence must be as regards the State seeking extradition.

Take the Pavelic case, and suppose the suspects had fled to England and not Italy. On the respondent's construction of the 1870 Act King Alexander's murder would have been an extraditable offence, but not that of M. Barthou; though the acts were virtually simultaneous, their common motives and purposes were political, and their political character was only distinguishable in that Barthou symbolised French support for the Yugoslav regime whereas King Alexander symbolised that regime itself. If it could be ascertained which assassin killed which victim, one would be extradited and the other not.

Then take the hypothetical case of an attempted assassination, not of the Vice-Premier of Nationalist China, but of the Vice-President of the United States. Counsel for the respondent accepted that this would be 'an offence ... of a political character' if committed solely in protest against United States support of Chiang Kai-Shek's government and if perpetrated on United States territory — say, at the United States end of the Niagara Bridge. But if the purporting assailant followed the Vice-President across the bridge, and made the attempt at the Canadian end of the bridge, it would in some extraordinary way cease to be 'an offence ... of a political character'. Its correct characterisation if the attempt were made laterally as the Vice-President was actually crossing the frontier would, I think, strain the subtlety even of a scholastic metaphysician.

Take, finally, two other actual assassinations, and apply the respondent's argument. In 1898 an Italian anarchist, Lucheni, murdered the Empress Elizabeth of Austria at Geneva. Asked why, he replied, 'As part of the war on the rich and great. . . . It will be Humbert's turn next.' In 1900 another Italian anarchist, Bresci, duly murdered King Humbert of Italy near Milan. Between these two events, at an international conference in Rome, Great Britain (together with Belgium and Switzerland) refused to give up her traditional privilege of asylum or to agree to surrender suspected anarchists on demand of their native countries. Yet, if both assassins had taken refuge in England, on the respondent's argument Bresci's crime would have been an offence of a political character under section 3(1) and non-extraditable, while Lucheni's, similar in all respects except the fortuitous and temporary location of the victim, was not an offence of a political character and was therefore extraditable. . . .

Such anomalies and absurdities would pose a serious problem of interpretation even if the phrase 'in respect of the State seeking extradition' were actually found in the statute following the words 'offence ... of a political character'. Certainly they preclude such a phrase being merely implied, even if other canons of construction did not do so. . . .

CONCLUSION

My Lords, it must be rare for so many canons of statutory construction and an authoritative treatise, forensically approved in this regard, to concur in pointing to a particular interpretation.

It is unlikely that the world will ever be free of political crime: subjects will always tend to feel grievance against their governors, there will always be conflicts of ideology and some people seem to have a natural propensity to express themselves in violence. But there is the less excuse for, and therefore will be the less public condonation of, political violence if there is institutional power to influence the decisions of government and if substantial freedom of expression is safeguarded by the law. This country prides itself on its tradition of constitutional government and freedom under the law. Our tradition of asylum for political criminals is closely associated with our cherishing of our own rights.

I am, my Lords, naturally conscious that this instant appeal takes place at a time when horrifying acts of political terrorism are much in the public mind. Although it is perhaps more acute today, the problem how to reconcile a policy of asylum for political criminals with the curbing of terrorism is not new, and it has so far defied a generally acceptable solution. Oppenheim himself proposed a way of dealing with the matter. Although these paragraphs have been omitted from recent editions, Oppenheim's distinguished editor has this to say of the proposed Convention against Terrorism consequent on the assassination of King Alexander of Yugoslavia:

> It is doubtful whether States wedded by their law and tradition to the principle of non-extradition of political offenders will acquiesce in any conventional regulation impairing the asylum hitherto granted to political offenders. Such acquiescence on their part is unlikely at a time when the suppression of individual freedom and the ruthless persecution of opponents in many countries tend to provoke violent reactions of a treasonable character against the governments concerned.

Bashi-Bazouks[176] had nothing to teach the SS or the NKVD, nor is the world yet emancipated from tyranny. In view of the increase in power of weapons of destruction and the greater likelihood of innocent persons suffering, it may well be that the time has come to seek once again a solution to the problem. But this will be for governments in international conclave: there is no advantage in marginal and anomalous judicial erosion of traditional immunities.

Notwithstanding this eloquent speech, the appellant's claim was denied by the decision of a majority of the court. A message had, however, been sent to Parliament concerning the need for reform of the law.

---

[176] Bashi-Bazouks were mercenary soldiers of the Ottoman Empire in the nineteenth century notorious for their indiscipline and barbarity.

Middle Temple Gardens

14. WHEN THE WIND BLOWS

or

The Rule of Law

More than any other characteristic perhaps, a civilised society is distinguished by the willingness of the majority to refer their grievances to the arbitration of an impartial body according to an agreed set of rules. The case for the rule of law has never been better put than by the character of Sir Thomas More in Robert Bolt's play, A Man for All Seasons.

Henry VIII wanted to put aside his marriage to his wife, Catherine of Aragon (which he claimed to regard as void) in order to marry Anne Boleyn. In this he flew in the face of objections from many of the clergy, including his Chancellor, Sir Thomas More, who was eventually moved to resign office over the issue pleading ill health. A few years later the Act of Settlement required More, like everyone else, to swear an oath of allegiance to the issue of the King's marriage to Anne, 'renouncing all obedience to the bishop of Rome' and acknowledging Henry as head of the Church of England. More refused to take the oath but declined to give his reasons for so doing. He was tried for treason at the instigation of Thomas Cromwell, Henry's great minister.

Richard Rich, once befriended by More, gave fatal — and probably perjured — evidence against him. In the play Rich's treachery is forecast in a powerful exchange between More, his daughter,

Margaret, and Roper, her husband-to-be. Rich has just left the room.

MARGARET: Father, that man's bad.

MORE: There is no law against that.

ROPER: There is! God's law!

MORE: Then God can arrest him.

ROPER: Sophistication upon sophistication!

MORE: No, sheer simplicity. The law, Roper, the law. I know what's legal not what's right. And I'll stick to what's legal.

ROPER: Then you set Man's law above God's!

MORE: No, far below; but let me draw your attention to a fact — I'm not God. The currents and eddies of right and wrong, which you find such plain-sailing, I can't navigate, I'm no voyager. But in the thickets of the law, oh there I'm a forester. I doubt if there's a man alive who could follow me there, thank God.... (*He says this to himself.*)

ALICE: (*exasperated, pointing after RICH*): While you talk, he's gone!

MORE: And go he should if he was the Devil himself until he broke the law!

ROPER: So now you'd give the Devil benefit of law!

MORE: Yes. What would you do? Cut a great road through the law to get after the Devil?

ROPER: I'd cut down every law in England to do that!

MORE (*roused and excited*): Oh? (*Advances on Roper.*) And when the last law was down, and the Devil turned round on you — where would you hide, Roper, the laws all being flat? (*Leaves him.*) This country's planted thick with laws from coast to coast — Man's laws, not God's — and if you cut them down — and you're just the man to do it — d'you really think you could stand upright in the winds that would blow then? (*Quietly.*) Yes, I'd give the Devil benefit of law, for my own safety's sake.

Ironically, More's faith in the law proved to be misplaced. He was condemned to a traitor's death, a sentence 'mercifully' commuted to execution. Ultimately, as Learned Hand observes in the Epilogue to this book, law is merely the instrument of a free people. Take away the freedom and the law goes too.

Cromwell fell out of favour and went himself to the block some five years after More. The vile Rich went on to become Lord Chancellor

— some say, not a bad one — and died in his bed. More was beatified in 1886 and canonised in 1935, the only common lawyer to be so sanctified.

WILDY & SONS

Specialists in LAW BOOKS
ANCIENT & MODERN
BOOK BINDING
IN ALL ITS BRANCHES
Established 1830

EPILOGUE:
THE SPIRIT WHICH IS NOT TOO SURE THAT IT IS RIGHT

In 1944, two weeks before the Allied landings in Normandy, 150,000 newly naturalised citizens of the United States of America were assembled in Central Park, New York, to swear the oath of allegiance to their adopted country. Before leading them in this ceremony Billings Learned Hand, Chief Judge of the United States Circuit Court of Appeals for the Second Circuit, made a brief speech.

Like Lincoln's address at Gettysberg (to which it may legitimately be compared), Hand's speech[177] was the shortest of the day and little noted at the time. It is now recognised as one of the most potent reminders of the purpose and limitations of man's laws.

We have gathered here to affirm a faith, a faith in a common purpose, a common conviction, a common devotion. Some of us have chosen America as the land of our adoption; the rest have come from those who did the same. For this reason we have some right to consider ourselves a picked group, a group of those who had the courage to break from the past and brave the dangers and the loneliness of a strange land.

What was the object that nerved us, or those who went before us, to this choice? We sought liberty; freedom from oppression, freedom from want, freedom to be ourselves. This we then sought. This we now believe that we are by way of winning.

What do we mean when we say that first of all we seek liberty? I often wonder whether we do not rest our hopes too much upon constitutions, upon laws and upon courts. These are false hopes; believe me, these are false hopes. Liberty lies in the hearts of men and women. When it dies there, no constitution, no law, no court can save it. No constitution, no law, no court can even do much to help it. While it lies there, it needs no constitution, no law, no court to save it.

And what is this liberty which must lie in the hearts of men and women? It is not the ruthless, the unbridled will. It is not freedom to do as one likes. That is the denial of liberty, and leads straight to its overthrow. A society in which men recognize no check upon their freedom soon becomes a society where freedom is the possession of only a savage few; as we have learned to our sorrow.

What then is the spirit of liberty? I cannot define it; I can only tell you my own faith. The spirit of liberty is the spirit which is not too sure that it is right. The spirit of liberty is the spirit which seeks to understand the minds of other men and women. The spirit of liberty is the spirit which weighs their interests alongside its own without bias. The spirit of liberty remembers that not even a sparrow falls to earth unheeded. The spirit of liberty is the spirit of Him who, near two thousand years ago, taught mankind that lesson it has never learned, but has never quite forgotten: that there may be a kingdom where the least shall be heard and considered side by side with the greatest.

And now in that spirit, that spirit of an America which has never been, and which may never be; nay, which never will be, except as the conscience and the courage of Americans create it; yet in the spirit of that America which lies hidden in some form in the aspirations of us all; in the spirit of that America for which our young men are at this moment fighting and dying; in that spirit of liberty and of America I ask you to rise and with me to pledge our faith in the glorious destiny of our beloved country — with liberty and justice for all.

---

[177] Reproduced in *The Reader's Digest*, September 1944, at pp. 57, 58.